The Rural Face of White Supremacy

The Rural Face of White Supremacy

Beyond Jim Crow

MARK SCHULTZ

UNIVERSITY OF ILLINOIS PRESS

Urbana and Chicago

Library of Congress Cataloging-in-Publication Data
Schultz, Mark, 1964–
The rural face of White supremacy : beyond Jim Crow /
Mark Schultz.
p. cm.
Includes bibliographical references and index.
ISBN 0-252-02960-7 (alk. paper)
1. Hancock County (Ga.)—Race relations. 2. Hancock County
(Ga.)—Rural conditions. 3. Racism—Georgia—Hancock County—
History—20th century. 4. African Americans—Georgia—Hancock
County—Social conditions—20th century. 5. Whites—Georgia—
Hancock County—Social conditions—20th century. 6. African Ameri-
cans—Georgia—Hancock County—Interviews. 7. Whites—Georgia—
Hancock County—Interviews. 8. Hancock County (Ga.)—Biography.
I. Title.
F292.H3S385   2004
305.8'96073'0758623—dc22   2004006944

For my wife,
Cathleen Mary McDonnell Schultz,

and for my parents,
Don and Luann Schultz

Ad Maioram Dei Gloriam

The expression "Solid South" . . . is of
questionable value to the historian. . . .
The solidarity of the region has long been
exaggerated. . . . Boasts of white solidarity that
impressed outsiders were often loudest in the
presence of division.

—C. Vann Woodward, *Origins of the New South*

Contents

List of Figures

Preface

HISTORY LIES CLOSE to the surface in Hancock. Tom Harrison, formerly of Linton, owns a rifle once used by his revolutionary ancestors. The lock and hammer are missing, removed by cautious but not malicious Union soldiers as they passed through on their way to Savannah. A more earthy relic is the outdoor "house of necessity," owned by Dave Dyer, that once seated the most influential Georgians of the Civil War era. African Americans, enslaved and then impoverished, have fewer physical souvenirs of the past, yet theirs may be the more vibrant oral tradition. Some remember stories passed on from their African ancestors, tales of life, love, repression, and resistance under slavery. Some elderly men and women preserve the memories and genealogies of whole communities. They remember who married whom, where long departed neighbors buried their otherwise forgotten children, where they moved, and where their now-demolished homes once stood. When the descendants of Hancock's many migrants return, as those both white and black often do, they frequently seek out these modern American griots to learn about their ancestors and hence themselves.

I entered Hancock County, Georgia, in the fall of 1988 to collect data for a research paper I was writing during my second year of graduate school. I anticipated that the evidence would confirm my expectations of race relations in the rural South: frequent lynching, systematic segregation, and universal black poverty and disfranchisement. My guide, William Bryant, a black educator who had formerly lived in the county, directed me on the ninety-mile drive southwest from Atlanta. He then took me on a series of visits with elderly Hancock African Americans that confounded my expectations and piqued my curiosity. He started by introducing me to Frank Guill Jr., a gregarious man with olive skin and straight hair. Guill enthusiastically described his racially ambiguous life and his kinship ties to Hancock's racial communities, both black and white. His parents had openly maintained a lifelong interracial relationship, something I had thought impossible given the strident antimiscegenation laws and culture of the Jim Crow era. Perhaps to drive home the point, Bryant later took me by a little country store owned by an interracial couple, Billy and Mildred Boyer. I next encountered some old men who gathered at a black barbershop, where I heard snippets of conversations that added humanizing texture to the simple generalizations I had held about the rural South. Then we talked with Samuel Williams, who modestly but matter-of-factly told me about growing up on a portion of his black grandfather's two-thousand-acre estate in the middle of a black land-owning community. We finished the tour with James MacMullen, an elderly black educator. In a couple of uncomfortable hours, he dryly undermined much of what remained of my sweeping assumptions concerning the "Solid South."

I have spent the past sixteen years trying both to make sense of the divergent worlds I encountered on that first day in Hancock County and to reconcile them with my understanding of the general historical literature. I spent much of this time interviewing people from rural Hancock, asking them about the primary ways that white and black lives intersected in their personal experiences. I tape-recorded interviews with over 180 people and interviewed dozens more informally. I spoke with people from as many groups as I could: black and white; landowners, tenants, lumber workers, tradespeople, soldiers, teachers, and preachers; men and women; migrants from Hancock to northern cities and lifelong residents of the county. All personally remembered at least a portion of the years from 1900 to 1950. A few remembered all these years. Most began their first-person stories in the 1920s. All remembered the 1930s. My interpretations of these stories have continued to evolve since I began, and I'm sure that I don't yet have it right. I hope that by publishing this study, I might join the conversation of the larger community of scholars, where better answers might be found.[1]

Acknowledgments

I AM DEEPLY CONSCIOUS that I am a hopeless debtor. This study would not have been possible without the support of more people than I have space to name. Although all responsibility for errors lies wholly with me, I wish to thank some of those who have contributed to the completion of this project.

I wish to thank the University of Georgia, the University of Chicago, the Lilly Foundation, and the National Academy of Education/Spencer Foundation for financial support at different stages in the development of this study. The education chapters, which attracted the attention of the National Academy of Education, grew until they required separate treatment in a forthcoming volume of their own. Those interested in a preliminary treatment of the rise of a modern education system in Hancock are invited to see my dissertation, "The Unsolid South: Race, Class, and Geography in Hancock County, Georgia, 1910–1950" (University of Chicago, 1999), 307–91. I am grateful to Lewis University, and particularly to the College of Arts and Sciences, for its consistent support of my research. I also owe thanks to the helpful and skilled reference librarians at the Georgia State Archives in Atlanta, who directed me to materials that became essential to my understanding of Hancock County. I thank Rick Kloser, who saved me from graphing purgatory; Br. Rob Wilsbach, a Lewis University research librarian; and particularly Ben Feicht, Laurie Markatos, and James Mattera, who as students helped me sift through country store ledgers and newspaper microfilm.

My sincere thanks go to William Leary of the University of Georgia for enduring my purple prose as he taught me the craft of writing. I still reread his detailed corrections on old papers. I owe him my thanks also for introducing me to the method and value of publishing. I thank Bill McFeely for encouraging my initial explorations into Hancock. He, Numan Bartley, Peter Hoffer, Bob Pratt, and Ben Wall gave me a first-rate introduction to the challenges and rewards of doing southern history and made the process exciting.

I am grateful to my advisor at the University of Chicago, Thomas Holt, for the painfully difficult questions he asks in seminars. This study did not begin with a clear thesis. It originated in my attempt to resolve my confusion about the great gap I noted between the stories that older Hancock people told me and the histories I read. I sensed that the diverse topics I take up in the different chapters of this study were not mutually independent phenomena but rather parallel manifestations of a common culture. Professor Holt's probing questions helped me discover the themes that unify this study. I thank Kathleen Conzen, Barry Karl, and Martin Marty, my other committee members, for the challenging ideas they raised as they mentored me. I am aware that my intellectual direction has been shaped by their incisive and humane approach to doing history.

I would also like to thank E. M. "Woody" Beck, Jacquelyn Dowd Hall, Will Holmes, John Inscoe, William Link, Al Moss, Joel Williamson, and Bertram Wyatt-Brown for helping me think through especially difficult problems that lay in their areas of expertise. I will not forget their generosity in taking time with me when I, as a graduate student, called them out of the blue. I am deeply grateful to Ewa Bacon, Marshall Boyer, Fitz Brundage, Vernon Burton, Mark Cooney, Eugene Genovese, Steven Hahn, Katie Hunt, Lu Ann Jones, Carlton Morse, John Rozier, Cathleen Schultz, Melissa Walker, Mae Warren, and particularly J. Morgan Kousser and Robert McMath for reading through part or all of this manuscript at one of its many stages. My special thanks go to James Anderson and Pete Daniels, who besides reading my manuscript repeatedly shared their broad knowledge with me, encouraged my ideas, and greatly improved the work as a whole. My editor at the University of Illinois Press, Laurie Matheson, offered regular and invaluable assistance as I turned a dissertation into a book. The sharp eyes and open ears of Bruce Bethell turned the copyediting process into a stimulating conversation.

My colleagues in the graduate program at the University of Georgia set a high standard for research and historical thinking and infused in me their excitement about sharing ideas in scholarly forums. I'll never forget the tipsy poetry readings at Glenn Eskew's house that turned into debates about E. P. Thompson, Antonio Gramsci, and competing regional variations of barbecue. Glenn, Jonathan Bryant, Beth Hale, Mary Lynn Peterson-Cluff, Mary Gambrell Rolinson, Jenny Lund-Smith, and many others made Georgia an exciting and safe place to think creatively about southern history.

My friends at the University of Chicago also helped carry me through my education. Jill Nicholas's assistance and good cheer pulled me through the most difficult challenge in my educational career. Fred Beuttler, Betsy Braun, Lendol Caldor, Melinda Campbell, Jill DuPont, Anne Kauth, Jennifer Utrata, Jeff Webb, and Stewart Winger all contributed in many ways to stretching my mind and keeping me sane. Tim Gaudin, my old and dear friend, accompanied me on my trip from Athens, Georgia, to Chicago; I thank him for the judiciously savage fouls on the basketball court that pulled my mind out of the ether and reattached it to the concreteness of life. My further thanks go to him and his wife, Sue, for introducing me to the offbeat thinking and merrymaking that goes on at the U.C. Department of Anatomy and Organismal Biology. And my special thanks go to them for making their home in Hyde Park an oasis of southern hospitality.

My colleagues at Lewis University and my wife's at the University of St. Francis have been delightful in conversation and generous in support. Ewa Bacon, Fr. Leo Gleuckert, Sr. Mary Lauranne Lifka, Eileen McMahon, Br. Bob Murphy, and Br. John Vietoris have all stimulated my mind with their wide-ranging scholarly interests. Pat Brannon, Jeff Chamberlain, and Aurelie Hagstrom challenged me to keep pace with their ambitious scholarly commitments, while they have blessed Cathy and me with their convivial friendship, adventurousness, and good humor.

I owe many thanks also to my supportive family, especially my parents, Don and Luann Schultz, for all the years of love, support, and encouragement. Thanks also for caring about my writing enough to give me feedback on it and for braving Atlanta traffic to bail me out with missing tax digest and draft card data. My wife and intimate friend, Cathy, has encouraged and assisted me in countless ways. She has been my companion-in-arms throughout the writing of our dissertations. She has made my writing and my life richer and better. My debt to her exceeds words. Thanks also to our children, Annie, Brennan, and Nate, chiefly for the many wonderful distractions.

Finally, this study would not have been remotely possible without the generous assistance of hundreds of people from Hancock. I have come to believe that the history of the rural South from 1900 to 1950 cannot be told without the oral assistance of rural southerners. Black and white, the people of Hancock County have been, almost without exception, generous, engaging guides and neighbors during my years in their county. I am lucky to have been able to have spent the past dozen years among such decent folk. I hope that they will recognize their stories in this study. I hope they will find in the examination of their past a clearer sense of the roots of the problems of racism, poverty, and social alienation that confront all Americans equally—not just rural southerners. I also hope that, as they hear each other's recollections of interracial intimacy—often privately held—they will find the stories to be the source of hope I find them to be. I cannot begin to list all the people who assisted me with stories of their personal experiences of life in Hancock. Even the list of interviewees at the back of this book is partial, including only those who were directly cited in the text. I do wish to thank William Bryant for introducing me to the county. I am grateful for the generosity of Billy and Mildred Boyer and Willis Hubert, who gave me places to stay during long periods when I was conducting interviews in Hancock. Finally, I cannot bear not to express my gratitude to Billy Boyer, Marshall Boyer, Kenneth Coleman, Solomon Harper, Willis Hubert, Charity Hunt, Katie Bell Hunt, Mary Hunt, J. E. Johnson, James McMullen, Carlton Morse, A. J. Parker, Alma Dixon Smith, Sid and Trudy Trawick, Lizzie Mae Warren, Leroy Wiley, Samuel and Julia Williams, and James Wilson for repeated and valued friendly guidance and hospitality. In particular, I am grateful for the opportunity to have gotten to know Katie Hunt and Dave Dyer, who I came to admire for who they had been in their youth and who they had become in their senior years.

The Rural Face of White Supremacy

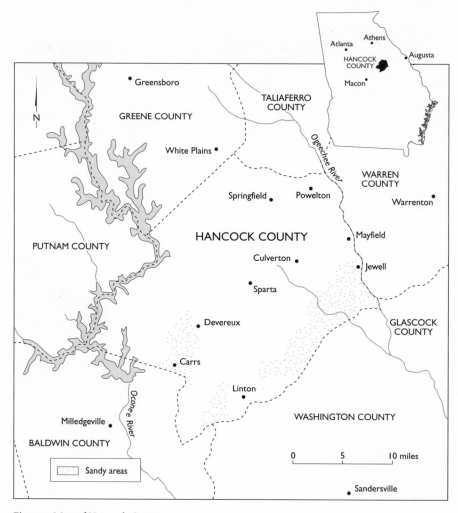

Figure 1. Map of Hancock County

Introduction:
A Place in Time

WE LEARN BEST about history through an ongoing dialogue between two approaches: on the one hand, overarching regional and national studies drawn from generalized sources, such as census reports and major newspapers; on the other, narrow, local, more highly textured studies. Unlike historians of the rural West and North and even the urban South, who have produced large numbers of local studies, historians of the rural South have undervalued local history—especially that of the first half of the twentieth century.[1] This study employs oral history to examine regional patterns of race relations as they took shape in one county.

It may fairly be asked whether Hancock County represents anything beyond itself. The same question could be asked about any other county in the United States, however—or more to the point, about the Mississippi Delta, which has drawn more studies than any other part of the South. As it turns out, the delta is not the boiled-down essence of the American South but rather a truly unique region, making it no more appropriate a premise for generalizations about the entire South than are the Appalachians, the wire-grass sections, or the lower piedmont.[2] Ultimately, there is no "most representative" state in a region or county in a state.

What Hancock represents, therefore, is the lower piedmont of Georgia, a band that overlaps the uppermost portion of the black belt. It speaks also for the old planter-dominated region of the South Atlantic, with its high black population (about 73 percent in Hancock over the course of this study), aristocratic leadership, and cotton monoculture. Although the lower and eastern portions of Hancock rest on the infertile sandy fall line, most of the county was rich enough to withstand decades of abusive farming practices until it was exhausted and gullied by the end of the nineteenth century.

Hancock County was established in middle Georgia in 1793 between the Ogeechee River to the east and the Oconee River to the west. The county's original Virginian and North Carolinian settlers may have been of lowly estate and limited educations, but cotton soon changed that. Shortly after 1810 county planters had purchased Hancock's permanent black majority. By 1820 the planters were replacing their primitive dwellings with the classic symbols of their economic, political, and social arrival. By the old statistical method that counted African American slaves as property and nothing else, antebellum Hancock County became one of the nation's wealthiest counties per capita. In 1840, when southerners called cotton "white gold," Hancock led the state in cotton production, raising almost twice as much as Morgan County, the second richest. In 1860, 430 Hancock County residents collectively owned 8,137 slaves, and 6 of them owned more than 100 each. Just 65 planters owned more than half the land in the county. Of course, hidden within such a picture of wealth lay the impoverished producers of that wealth. African American slaves accounted for 68 percent of the population that year; poor white laborers, about 8 percent.[3]

With wealth came political power and social leadership. In the antebellum period Hancock citizens shaped the course of Georgia politics. When the state capital reflected the power of the plantation belt, it was located in Milledgeville, a few miles west of Hancock in neighboring Baldwin County. As long as cotton was king, Hancock sent more than its share of men to occupy the governor's mansion and to hold other prominent positions. White Hancock citizens also assumed educational and ecclesiastical leadership in the state and contributed in other ways to the creation of genteel aristocratic southern culture.[4]

Comfortable and confident in their security, Hancock County voters usually leaned toward the Whig Party. In the contentious election of 1860 they looked for a compromise by supporting John Bell and the Constitutional Union Party. They then chose the Democratic ticket in presidential elections for the next hundred years. During Reconstruction black voters turned Hancock Republican at the state level and sent two black men, Eli Barnes and William Henry Harrison, to the Georgia legislature. By combining violence with a legal ploy, the Democrats reasserted political white supremacy in the county in 1870. When the Populist movement of the 1890s threatened the rule of white elites, Georgia Democrats gerrymandered Hancock onto the Populist congressman Tom Watson's district. As planned, the county's Democratic leaders controlled the election in a corrupt and rancorous contest. This seizure of power ended all meaningful political debate in the county until the civil rights movement came to Hancock in 1966.

Although the southern part of the county had lain in Sherman's path, most of Hancock's buildings survived the Civil War. After reasserting control over their labor force, therefore, Hancock planters returned to respectable wealth. Hancock whites continued to maintain the county as a cotton center and even made a little room for industrious and well-connected African American farmers to claim a share through the acquisition of farmland. Then the boll weevil arrived in 1921, and the total wealth in the county dropped by half in one year, never to recover. Other areas with richer soil were able to bounce back from the weevil, but Hancock's long legacy of soil erosion finally caught up with it, holding down yields. The Great Depression further undermined the economy. Finally, World War II defense plants in nearby Milledgeville inched the local wage scale toward national standards, thus ending the profitability of labor-intensive cotton cultivation.

Over the following decades Hancock's farmers migrated, took jobs in neighboring cities, or went on welfare. Those who owned land planted pine trees for paper pulp. The county is now deeply impoverished. Most of Hancock's current income derives from social security, welfare, and a state-supported education payroll. Driving through many parts of the county, one finds few signs that the area had been inhabited, much less a center of importance. There are only the rows of pines that replaced the precolonial oaks and hickory and the occasional decaying mansion or shack, remains of a cotton kingdom.

In the years between the Civil War and the civil rights movement, as the county's white citizens gradually lost prominence in the state, its black communities nurtured a surprisingly large number of talented state and national leaders. Many of Georgia's black leaders in education and religion came from Hancock, among them the Colored Methodist Episcopal bishop Lucius Henry Holsey, Georgia State Industrial College's president Benjamin Hubert, and Fort Valley State College president Henry Hunt. A number of Hancock's black economic and social elites worked closely with their white counterparts, finding backdoor routes to power and influence within Hancock's paternalistic framework.

Then, decades after its devastating economic revolution, the county underwent a turbulent political one. With minimal fanfare hundreds of blacks returned to the polls beginning in 1946. For the following twenty years they played an important role in county elections, although they could not hold office themselves. In 1966, a year after the Voting Rights Act was passed, Hancock's African Americans registered in truly large numbers and began voting for black candidates. By 1968 they had redeemed their three-to-one electoral majority and assumed political control of the county, sweeping white politicians from office. Whites would have had a difficult time accepting this transition in power in any event, but the self-consciously confrontational style of some new black leaders exacerbated tensions. Hancock's central political figure during the civil rights movement, John McCown, rejected interracialism in favor of "black-power" rhetoric. Unfortunately McCown also seems to have become an opportunist who used the movement to embezzle government and philanthropic funds. He later escaped near-certain federal indictments for misuse of funds only by dying when his private plane crashed. He is still a highly controversial figure in Hancock, with the division falling mainly but not exclusively along race lines.[5]

McCown has become the symbol of the county's polarization. But interracial tensions obviously did not begin with him. Instead, it seems that McCown scraped away the paternalistic padding that had previously cushioned race relations in Hancock. Tensions are still palpable, and a battle for control of the county continues to be waged. The few white landowners and businesspeople who control any real wealth in the county feel alienated and resist using their funds to create new jobs. Many have relocated, along with their checkbooks. Conversely, the black politicians have raised property taxes in this impoverished county until they have become the highest in the state. Although Hancock's black and white citizens remain publicly civil toward one another—often even friendly—everyone feels the tension, and many remark on it. Some report greater distance and coolness as a result of these recent events. The current atmosphere doubtlessly influenced what my interviewees told me. The openness of the current conflict may make race relations in the distant past appear more congenial. Yet clearly almost all black interviewees feel better about present race relations—however tense—than about past patterns. Current tensions have not grown so great as to obscure their memories of what they described as the great personal affronts and exploitations of the past. For a further discussion of my oral history methods, see appendix A.

* * *

The hundreds of stories told me by elderly Hancock citizens portray a kind of Deep South society that conflicts with our conventional view of the region. Although clearly dominated by a white supremacist ideology, this black majority county was not characterized by many of the phenomena we associate with the "solid" Jim Crow South. Notable in their absence were systematic segregation, universal black disfranchisement, and ritualized public lynching. Instead, a wholly different mode of race relations operated in rural Hancock, one marked by personal intimacy, personal violence, and ritual displays of deference. Additionally, although some African Americans in the area knew grinding hunger and humiliation, others experienced greater personal empowerment than is usually assumed to have been possible in a rural southern context.

The term "Solid South" evokes a powerful image, one that has shaped how the region was perceived from the end of the Reconstruction until the civil rights movement. It suggests unanimity of belief and action at the points where white southerners dealt with African Americans. In many way this perception was accurate, for a widespread white commitment to white supremacy did characterize the period. Politically, the Democratic Party controlled southern elections. Whites denied blacks all formal expressions of racial equality. Public dissent from Jim Crow in print or speech seems to have been rare by the beginning of the twentieth century and was usually subject to harsh social sanction. The term certainly expresses something that was very real.

In other ways, however, this term obscures the many obvious fracture points of the Solid South. African Americans were, after all, southerners. Poor, middle-class, and elite white southerners had different interests and competed frequently—and sometimes sharply—with one another. And southern subregions vary widely in their cultures. Ultimately, the Solid South was not a permanent feature of southern life. It was built. The elites constructed it politically through the disfranchisement of most black and white voters. The urban middle class constructed it socially, by passing a series of segregation laws to criminalize public interracial mixing. Furthermore, it was most obvious and most effective in shaping people's behavior in formal, public spaces. The official symbols of the South were indeed solid by the turn of the twentieth century, but public symbols reflect hopes and fears as much as they do experienced reality. Instead of exploring the Solid South as an abstraction, we might do better to examine it in local places, such as Hancock County, to detail how it was observed and suspended in actual experience.

Hancock was characterized by a stable, conservative, and wholly self-assured merchant-planter class that dominated the county from the antebellum period until World War II. These wealthy white men controlled some of the richest cotton estates in Georgia—and thousands of the poor, mostly black dependent farmers who tended them. The planters maintained attenuated paternalistic ties with these laborers. They also controlled the political and law-enforcement apparatus of the county and set the tone for social relations, between classes as well as between races. Their confidence in their control led them both to suppress mob violence—an unpredictable force and, from their perspective, redundant at best—and to allow some African American individuals relatively wide social, economic, and political latitude.

In rural Hancock power usually meant personal power, whether it took the form of wealth, political connections, or the capacity for violence. Before World War II few institutions mediated interpersonal relationships. Low taxes kept local government small and weak. The largely private and under-funded schools provided few students with a means for upward mobility. Most people who needed a loan visited a planter or merchant, not a bank. The county's "big men" jealously guarded the prerogatives that their positions gave them. This culture of personalism allowed planters to brutally exploit or even kill dependent African American farmers. It also allowed them to assist in the economic rise of a favorite tenant or to live openly with a black wife, all without meaningful legal or social penalties. Ultimately, this culture of personalism allowed for the toleration of widely varying modes of race relations among different individuals across the county.[6]

Geography also played a role in developing Hancock's culture. The broken terrain and poor transportation and communications networks of rural Hancock encouraged the development of distinctive traditions in race relations—a culture of localism. In the cities individuals were anonymous, but the standardized racial codes were enforced by all whites. In rural Hancock the opposite was true: all individuals were known within their communities, and each person and neighborhood personalized the unwritten racial customs.[7]

Barbara Fields's revolutionary essay in 1982 freed historians from the assumption that race and racism are given biological forces at work in history.[8] They are, rather, social constructs shaped by other forces (in her essay, by class; in more recent literature, by gender). We must be willing to see how racial identity and racialized behavior differed from one historical context to another. In Hancock rural localism created a number of distinctive contexts for constructing racial meanings. Although this study will not explore the ways that black and white people understood racialized identities, it will examine the ways in which class and gender shaped interracial interaction. For example, poor black farmers living among poor white sharecroppers had experiences of race very different from those of domestic servants working in the homes of wealthy planters or of black landowners living in communities of black yeomen.

As I use the term here, *personalism* has two overlapping meanings. In one sense, it refers to the personal nature of power in rural Hancock. In another, it points to the face-to-face nature of rural communities, which allowed greater flexibility than was found in areas where black and white people related to one another primarily as impersonal abstractions. Despite the ways that "blackness" or "whiteness" were constructed in the larger culture, rural people regularly encountered them in their nonstereotyped, personalized, corporeal forms. Both meanings of personalism are facets of premodern society, as described earlier by historians and sociologists.[9]

The security of the planters, localism, and the culture of personalism all help explain why powerful whites sometimes tolerated a surprising degree of interracial intimacy and black assertiveness. Some blacks remained unmolested as they built sizable plantations of their own. Furthermore, although this varied widely across the county, many rural people participated socially in an interracial culture—a culture marked by intimacy as well as white supremacy. Sometimes African Americans were allowed to use retaliatory violence (or the threat thereof) against whites as long as they did not threaten white supremacy generally. Finally, Hancock whites tolerated the participation of a favored few African Americans in the political process long after official disfranchisement.

In each of these patterns of white acceptance of black empowerment, the "transgression" in question was personal and individualistic. The whites who held the reins in Hancock repeatedly showed that they would not tolerate any classwide challenge to their power specifically or to white supremacy generally. When seriously threatened during Reconstruction and the Populist movement, they united and crushed their opponents decisively.

Nonetheless, it is also clear that their methods for defending white supremacy differed greatly from those used by their white urban contemporaries: segregation and race riots. Segregation is simply an inadequate model for understanding race relations in rural Hancock County during the first half of the twentieth century. The laws and customs of systematic segregation penetrated the rural South far less than they did the urban centers—at least until the end of World War II. Until then intimacy, including both ritualized deference and highly personal violence, largely characterized race relations in rural Hancock.

Some readers may find it odd to speak of interracial intimacy in the period that witnessed such a brutal and systematic rejection of African American claims to equality. We have been conditioned by our national narrative to think of intimacy and hierarchy as opposites, unlikely to coexist. Yet it is our own nation's segregated story that constitutes the real historical anomaly. In cultures around the world and through millennia, elites have mixed intimately with their subordinates. Indeed, the ritualized submission of social inferiors seems often to have been one of the most prized benefits of elite status. Anyone requiring further proof that hierarchy is in no way antithetical to intimacy is invited to consider the history of marriage. The segregation of races, like the segregation of classes, is a modern, Western innovation, and we should not expect to discover it everywhere, as if it emerged spontaneously out of human nature.

In many ways the rural South of the early twentieth century had not yet been penetrated by the modernist impulse. The South's premodern, personal system rested ultimately on the region's labor-intensive agricultural system and its separation from the higher wage scale of the rest of the country. It persisted until a series of new forces originating outside the region diminished cotton's value to the planters and opened new options for poor dependent farmers. The profitable cotton kingdom was devastated as the boll weevil and international competition arose in the 1920s. Additionally, World War I opened new northern employment opportunities for southern sharecroppers stuck in cycles of dependency. This new opportunity closed quickly with the coming of the Great Depression, but the new wage scales hinted at by the New Deal and more fully imported with World War II defense plants finally broke open the separate, closed economy of the South. The decline of rural Hancock's separate economy roughly paralleled a diminishing of the distinctive forms of race relations that had prevailed in the area through the first half of the century.

This book does not repudiate studies of race relations in other southern communities. In particular, it does not contradict the recollections of individuals who had other southern experiences during the period under study. Indeed, I am arguing precisely that different southern contexts gave rise to many different experiences and hence different memories of the "true" South. Although I have found some areas of Georgia's lower piedmont that were relatively more accommodating to African Americans, I see little reason to doubt the reality of the unremittingly harsh rural worlds of the Mississippi Delta as remembered by the author Richard Wright and the bluesman Robert Johnson. The complicated stories I have heard in some two hundred different experiences within one southern county have impressed on me the need to frame all accounts of the South both geographically and chronologically.

The rising wave of historians clearly recognize southern variation over time and space.[10] Postemancipation studies of black resistance and white disunity are stretching forward in time toward the backward reach of similar themes in pre–civil rights studies. These projects have added dynamism and texture to the long Jim Crow period, which had previously seemed a dismal lull between revolutions. Nevertheless, these movements have not yet fully joined. There is still a broad consensus for a "Solid South" period of black docility and white solidarity in the first decades of the twentieth century. As this study will argue, however, the clear public white unity against black claims to citizenship rights did not translate into private white unanimity against other claims by African Americans. In many ways the public nineteenth-century struggles—for economic independence, security, and dignity—continued, translated into private conflicts in the rural South. We need to carefully redefine the meaning of the "Solid South."

Unfortunately, some contemporary scholars still display a marked tendency to flatten and homogenize the southern experience, an attitude most recently exemplified by Leon Litwack.[11] He still speaks for the revisionist historians of the 1960s, who heroically helped make the case for federal intervention in the South by describing it as a region that has run out of options, where African Americans had for centuries been victims and rarely agents. Theirs was, to my mind, the most socially responsible historical school of the twentieth century. Because systems that disempower African Americans relative to European Americans remain in place, this project is still important. In calling forth the necessary crusade, however, these historians inevitably cast their story in the starkest manner possible. Litwack is still fighting this fight. In *Trouble in Mind* he assembled an encyclopedia of systematic, horrifying acts of brutality that white southerners perpetrated against their helpless black neighbors. His text is a visceral, heart-rending indictment of our long, racist American heritage. Litwack is striving not for historical nuance but rather for a sense of moral outrage at the long delay of justice, especially in the context of America's current conservative retreat from civil rights. As I am sure Litwack hopes, many will be moved by this text to attempt to build a more just society.

Like Litwack, I desire justice and truly equal opportunity for all, and what is more, I desire Martin Luther King Jr.'s "beloved community." But whereas Litwack's fire-and-damnation message calls only for whites to repent their evil deeds and break utterly with the past, I doubt that history can be so simply disposed of. I believe that whites need to hear these stories, a history that can empower them to act justly and build interracial community. As C.

Vann Woodward argued nearly fifty years ago, they need to see that they have multiple historical traditions from which to draw, some soaked in innocent blood and some open to more hopeful possibilities. Would anyone, black or white, attempt to work for King's expanded vision of community if she believes that universal, violent racism and perpetual, despairing victimhood sum up the American experience?

Unfortunately, Litwack's interpretation leaves African Americans essentially where Stanley Elkins's *Slavery* left them, as the descendants of a long line of pawns and impotent victims, which evokes not fellow feeling but pity and condescension.[12] Interestingly, a series of authors quickly corrected the revisionist excesses in the historiography of slavery, drawing attention to slave insurrections, personal violence, religious faith, and other means of physical and psychic resistance to the slave regime. A strong literature has accumulated to detail the ways that slaves contested with their masters for a limited degree of control over their lives. Yet as the literature on slavery has increasingly emphasized the variation of experience and the capacity for resistance, the literature describing the African American experience after slavery—and especially after Reconstruction—has until recently continued to stress the homogeneity of the southern landscape and the fruitlessness of struggle. As historian Glenda Gilmore recently wrote, "What is most important about white supremacy remains least documented: African American resistance."[13] Neither the story of flight, in terms of the Great Migration, nor that of the urban, middle-class reform societies seems to fill this void satisfactorily. Instead, particularly in works on the period after Populism's failure, the emphasis seems to have fallen on the futility of resistance in the face of lynching, disfranchisement, segregation, and systematic pauperization through tenancy.[14] Oddly, this scholarly blind spot has made African Americans appear more empowered during the decades before Reconstruction than during those after it.

The black men and women I interviewed in Hancock recognized and spoke of the burdensome weight of white supremacy—a weight they themselves had borne most of their lives. Yet they also spoke of their challenges to white oppression: victories won that to them seemed quite significant. A number took obvious pride in these acts of resistance and self-direction. They spoke of having had resources to carve out lives with a measure of dignity: religious faith, the love of family, the support of community, retaliatory physical violence, reputations as valued workers, force of character, or even ties to local whites who some named as personal allies. Many recognized the threats of white supremacy but refused to surrender to it. Katie Hunt, for one, was never anybody's fool or helpless victim throughout her long life. Obviously this realization should in no way suggest that African Americans have enjoyed an equal share of power in Hancock—each chapter of this study offers clear evidence to the contrary. Yet I can see no purpose served in arguing that African Americans were helpless pawns, unable or unwilling to act in defense of their interests, their lives, and their dignity.

Finally, and not least important, I believe that my interpretation is not merely the more "usable" past but also the more historically accurate account. It reinforces the complex worlds described in the growing number of black southern autobiographies as well as in the classic studies of the South's rural sociologists. I have passed versions of this study, (including the completed manuscript) among a number of elderly people in Hancock, black and white. Although a few offered corrections—which I was glad to make—they agreed that I had gotten the story right.

Thus scholarly, political, and personal reasons have led me to this examination of race relations in rural Hancock County. Most centrally I am disturbed by Americans' apparently increasing acceptance of a racially balkanized society as inevitable and even—according to some authors, both black and white—desirable. We are coming to accept separate cultures, separate societies, separate opportunities, and separate lives rather than pursue the dream of the beloved community. Because our sense of possible futures draws from our sense of our past, historians have a role in helping to construct a national sense of the possible. Clearly it would be foolish to seek an interracial "golden age" in the white-supremacist culture of early twentieth-century rural Hancock. Nonetheless, recognizing that interracial intimacy is as much a part of our national heritage as are segregation and exclusion might strengthen our resolve to find new ways to reawaken that tradition within a new, egalitarian context. And recognizing the continuity of black resilience and strength seems a better way to honor African Americans than does focusing solely on their dehumanization. Whereas white scholars have often celebrated the low-down isolation and resignation of the blues tradition, they have tended to ignore the equally vibrant spiritual and gospel traditions, which celebrate community, hope, and healing.[15] The human condition under Jim Crow is honestly told only when both traditions are taken into account.

1

"Friendship Was Better than Money"

ONE DAY IN 1936 thirteen-year-old Carlton Morse was at school with his brothers and sisters. His family—black—worked on shares for a white Hancock planter. Midway through the schoolday a brother who had stayed home sick arrived with a note for Carleton to give his teacher. Before he delivered it, curiosity nudged him to open the note. It said simply that the Morse children needed to be excused from class. At home he learned why: the landlord had told his father that "the children didn't have time to go to school. The bushes needed cutting. Take them out." That day he had believed that his education had come to an end. Sixty years later he still became angry recalling the incident.[1]

Fourteen years earlier and a few miles north of the Bennett family, a white farmer, Dick Sykes, rode a horse to the farm of Katie Hunt, a black woman in her early thirties. Hunt and her husband, Wilkins, were relatively independent, renting land from a nearby white planter. Wilkins had gone to work in New York for the summer and was sending money to help his family through the first boll weevil year, while Katie and her children were taking care of their cotton acreage and substantial garden. Hunt was sitting on her porch when Sykes approached. The white man made small talk for a while and then hinted that the planter from whom she rented would like her to take her children out of summer school and set them to work poisoning the boll weevils. She answered: "He can't tell me to tell my children what to do, 'cause he isn't the daddy of nary a one of them. Every one of them is mine and Wilkins Hunt's—their daddy." The planter, she continued, "hain't got but one child that I know of—is Sarah—and that's the onliest person he can tell to go on out there and go—is his own daughter." Sykes laughed and said that he was going on to the next farm. "I just told them plain out," remembered Katie Hunt; "I didn't never bite my tongue." She laughs every time she relates the story.[2]

These stories illustrate that far from being "solid," the South provided for diverse experiences and widely differing self-direction among rural African Americans. The highly personal nature of the postbellum southern economy created many different economic platforms on which black and white southerners worked out their relationships. This rural southern diversity persisted until the region's distinctive agricultural system was subsumed into the national economy by forces unleashed in World War II. Yet our historical literature has not fully come to reflect this diversity. Where, for example, are the Katie Hunts in our histories of the rural South? Where, indeed, are any rural African Americans who achieved more than marginal economic or personal independence? Until recently much of the historical literature describing race relations in the postbellum rural South has taken for granted that the structure of the agricultural economy homogenized the region's African Americans into general poverty, dependence, and relative defenselessness. A number of writers have commented that their position was little removed from slavery.[3] This is ironic, for dozens of recent studies have commented on the diversity of experiences collected under the title of "the" slave experience.[4]

Beyond question, the experience of "freedom" offered much less than the freedmen had hoped for, beset as they were by white violence and largely denied the franchise, education, and land. Their freedom was further circumscribed by the limitations of the pre–World War II cotton culture—a culture that stifled urban growth, inhibited the development of a diversified economy, and held down southern wages generally.

The experience of African American southerners in the century after the Civil War has to be understood in the economic context of the region as a whole. While the rest of the country moved increasingly toward either industrialization or agricultural mechanization, southerners held fast to traditional farming technologies and labor-intensive farming strategies. As the rest of the country became accustomed to the cash-driven consumer economy and adapted to the bureaucratic, impersonal, modern culture it produced, many rural southerners remained in a distinctive semisubsistence cultural backwater: cash poor, local, personal, and in many regards, premodern. In the twentieth century as in the antebellum period, the cotton culture of Georgia's piedmont meshed "rationally" with the national economy while preserving a distinctive, "less rationalized" set of relationships within the South. In the decades after the Civil War, however, King Cotton became a petty, decrepit baron as worldwide cotton production rose and the price of cotton sank. A series of forces—some intentional and personal, others diffuse and impersonal—trapped African American farmers within this decaying industry and somewhat isolated world. Sometimes for better but more often for worse, they remained thralls to a diminished, increasingly miserly lord, until forces set into motion by the world wars opened a means of escape and integrated the South, economically, socially, and culturally, into the main currents of the nation.[5]

From the end of Reconstruction until World War II, Hancock's planters and merchants exerted local control over the internal structure of this impoverished, insular culture. Although they lacked either the funds or the inclination to mechanize, the planters did control a large labor force, which they consciously kept unskilled through their manipulation of the education system. Whenever dependent agricultural laborers challenged their control, either politically or economically, they closed ranks to destroy the threat through legal means or violence. Yet, while they united to defend their system against organized attack, they separated to administer it. Throughout this period powerful white southerners enhanced their own personal power by upholding a decentralized authority structure and a culture of personalism. Individual planters therefore held direct and personal control over a majority of Hancock's black laborers and answered to no one for their manner of administration. This system gave the planters a sense of confidence in their control—a confidence that fostered their tolerance of a rural culture marked by interracial intimacy and by autonomy and even resistance on the part of individual African Americans.

In rural Hancock the African American experience of earning a living was far from homogeneous. Although most black farmers were never able to buy land, a surprising number successfully navigated all impediments to become farm owners. Many others, such as the Hunts, used the tenant system in ways that gave them a level of security that they themselves described as meaningful. Others carved independent, nonagricultural niches for themselves in the rural economy. Simultaneously, many families found nothing but an inescapable cycle of poverty, with many losing control over important aspects of their lives. Yet the story of black farmers in the South must include the many who continued to make meaningful choices about their own lives. W. E. B. Du Bois, commenting on the situation from Atlanta in 1908, wrote: "Few among modern groups show a greater internal differentiation of social conditions than the Negro American, and the failure to realize this is the cause of much confusion. ... The forward movement of a social group is not the compact march of an army, where the distance covered is practically the same for all, but is rather the straggling of a crowd, where some of whom hasten, some linger, some turn back, some reach far-off goals before others even start, and yet the crowd moves on." Du Bois's assessment applied even among the farms of Georgia's piedmont.[6]

It is tempting to search for black economic progress to which Du Bois referred only in terms of success in the traditional capitalist economy. Until World War II, however, southern farmers sometimes engaged the market in ways that offered greater personal autonomy instead of the hope of higher cash income. Local economies in at least some parts of the rural South were somewhat removed from the homogenizing logic of the market economy.[7] These rural economies could vary a great deal within themselves. Some Hancock farms were fully "rationalized" and driven by dependence on northern credit and the impersonal laws of supply and demand.[8] Other Hancock farms, through neighborhood exchanges of food and labor and the persistence of semisubsistence strategies, maintained alternative ways to engage the market and hence somewhat expanded autonomy. These non-market-oriented approaches broke down, along with the entire cotton culture, when the national economy made deep inroads into the southern economy during World War II and created high-wage jobs in the region. The economic modernization of the 1940s and 1950s transformed the material basis of race relations in rural Hancock, modernizing and systematizing it. Until then, poverty, rural isolation, and the embedded traditions of personalism and paternalism kept Hancock County—and places like it—in an eddy apart from the "main" currents of U.S. society.

The Context of Southern Poverty

After emancipation freedmen attempted to fashion for themselves a meaningful autonomy. They envisioned themselves as yeomen farmers, as participants in government, as heirs to the social respect due citizens, as people free to worship in a manner of their own choosing, and—through their children—as literate people. Taken together, their goals spoke primarily of their desires to make meaningful choices and to enjoy autonomy from external coercion, a desire surely forged by their experience of slavery.[9] Arguably, chief among their claims on freedom was the desire for land—for "forty acres and a mule," as the popular saying proclaimed. Instead of finding autonomy, however, most freedmen became landless, dependent farmers, working as wage laborers, sharecroppers, share tenants, or cash renters. These forms of land tenure were not systematically administered across the South, and tenants and landlords often renegotiated terms at the start of each growing season, but the planters held most of the cards in these negotiations: ownership of the land, the threat of violence, and the right to write and interpret the law.[10]

For three generations following emancipation, white planters and black farmers struggled over the direction of labor and the division of steadily shrinking cotton profits. The ex-slaves had the misfortune of emerging into the free market just as the country entered three decades of economic turbulence. Although the value of all goods declined during this period, the prices of agricultural products fell even more precipitously. Cotton farmers in the South doubled their production between 1870 and 1890, thereby glutting the market. During these years the price of cotton fell from eighteen cents per pound to only seven. With expanded wartime demand and a restriction on worldwide trade, the price soared for a short, delirious period around World War I. Then it plummeted again, eventually hitting bottom at five cents per pound. Southern cotton growers also came to face competition from cotton plantations in Egypt and India and, early in the twentieth century, from huge, mechanized, state-subsidized cotton plantations in California and the Southwest. The South—unmechanized, beset by the boll weevil, and broken into small, overworked farms—ultimately could not compete and lost cotton supremacy to California by the end of the 1950s. Despite the plant's decreasing value, southern farmers continued to plant cotton as their primary market crop in the first half of the twentieth century. This decision left few profits to divide between landowners and laborers in places such as Hancock.[11]

The profits of southern cotton farmers were further reduced by region-wide rural overpopulation. Until World War II, too many people attempted to wring their livelihoods from an industry that simply could not decently support them all. The abundance of labor in the South suppressed competition among employers and lowered the wages of dependent farmers. As the rural population grew, these farmers worked on smaller and smaller plots of land. They plowed with mules, thinned the crop with hoes, and picked the cotton by hand, employing essentially the same methods and equipment used by farmers centuries earlier.[12] Meanwhile, California's agribusinesses, using subsidies from the U.S. Department of Agriculture, built complex irrigation systems and invested in enormous tractors that could do the work of a dozen manual workers. The unmechanized, labor-intensive cotton culture survived as long as it did in the South only because the extremely meager wages paid to dependent farmers kept labor costs low. In essence, the high profits of the modern agribusinesses were subsidized by the federal government, while the marginal earnings of landowners in the Georgia piedmont were subsidized by their own impoverished tenants.[13]

According to the economist Gavin Wright, the South became an isolated regional labor market, an insular low-wage economy within a national high-wage one.[14] But why did cotton farmers choose to remain within this impoverished economy? One group of historians has argued that poor farmers—especially poor black farmers—literally had no choice. They were trapped on southern farms by white planters who recognized them as a valuable and exploitable resource. In many parts of the South, planters and merchants consciously offered credit at high interest to ensnare dependent farmers in cycles of debt. According to this interpretive model, planters used debt to extend their control: farmers who could not repay their furnish at the end of a bad year were legally barred from leaving the plantation until they had cleared their debt. Once ensnared, they were trapped for life. The planter or merchant to whom the farmer owed money often insisted that cotton—the only reliable cash crop—be planted instead of food crops. This drew the farmer out of a semisubsistence economy and more fully into the market, which in turn necessitated a larger furnish and more debt.

Literal peonage did exist across the South. In many places sharecroppers who owed a landlord at the end of the year were compelled to remain with that landlord until they paid off their debts. None of the people I interviewed mentioned this kind of peonage in Hancock, but another kind of coerced labor did exist. Those who were jailed and allowed planters to pay their fines were bound over by the courts to work off their debts in the cotton fields. If they attempted to escape or committed some other infraction, the courts extended their terms of servitude. This system obviously created opportunities for gross exploitation. Sometimes men convicted of petty crimes had their terms of service extended for years. In some counties local law-enforcement officers cooperated with planters by trumping up false charges against black men to secure their labor.

These abuses led to legislation designed to protect workers' freedom of movement. Congress made peonage illegal in 1867, and the U.S. Supreme Court upheld the law in 1905. Furthermore, the Georgia state legislature outlawed convict leasing in 1908. Nevertheless, the state winked at loopholes that allowed planters to continue these practices for decades. Some judges and county leaders simply defied the law, a reality that highlights legal history's need for a social history context.[15] As one Hancock planter, J. E. Johnson, said, "If you needed a hand, you went to the chain gang to get a worker.

When a man was on the chain gang for a year, he was cleaned out. You knew he was in good health, well fed, has worked, and is hardened to it. And he's accustomed to taking orders, is disciplined. You didn't want a thief around your place, though." Johnson maintained that "you could pay people out of jail past World War II." For men who were convicted of serious crimes, "you could send a lawyer to the state parole board, and they'd parole them to you." Moreover, Hancock planters enjoyed political connections that helped them solve any difficulties. Two Hancock men served at different times as speaker of the house in Atlanta. "A word from them," Johnson remembered, "would get a man paroled to you." If that wasn't enough, Johnson could walk into the offices of Congressman Carl Vinson or Governor Eugene Talmadge and seal a deal with a handshake.[16]

Yet these systems of coerced labor apparently failed to hold down a large percentage of African American farmers. Black interviewees believed that few tenants fell subject to any kind of legal restrictions on their movement. In fact, planters throughout most of the region complained frequently about sharecroppers' tendencies to move annually. The 1930 Agricultural Census shows that one-third of Hancock's tenant farmers had been on their current farms for less than one year. Another third were evenly spread between one and four years of stability. A final third reported staying five or more years on the same place, but these records fail to indicate whether their stability was due to satisfaction, resignation, or entrapment (see figure 2). Most sharecroppers interviewed for this study confirmed the census data, saying they had

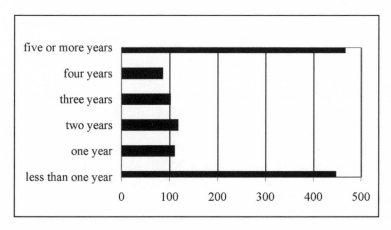

Figure 2. Duration of Tenancy on Present Farm, 1930 (*source:* 1930 Agricultural Census).

moved several times during their work lives. Some moved almost every year, whereas others stayed in one place for fifty years or more. Not one person, however, stated that he or she had been forced by a planter to remain on a farm after the expiration of a one-year contract. Given that southern planters failed to restrict the mobility of their laborers, peonage cannot explain why most southern farmers stayed on the farms until the middle of the twentieth century.

Instead, as Gavin Wright has argued, the bonds of family, culture, and ignorance of the larger world tied poor farmers to the southern soil.[17] But the most important factor took another form: black southern farmers were hemmed in by a lack of opportunities elsewhere. Africa offered little prospect of hope, although a few desperate souls (including some from Hancock) sailed there in the late nineteenth century.[18] In addition, tens of thousands of immigrants from Tennessee, Mississippi, and Louisiana flowed west to Oklahoma and Kansas during that period, but making a start in cereal crops or cattle on the plains required an outlay of capital—precisely what most black southern farmers lacked.[19] The northern cities, too, offered little escape from the cotton culture. African Americans were excluded from most occupations, especially well-paying ones. Labor unions barred them from a number of skilled trades. Ultimately the great majority of black cotton growers found no realistic possibilities for escape until World War I. They were effectively imprisoned within an impoverished economic system. As long as large numbers of them remained in the rural South, moreover, they gave planters the leverage with which to dominate the region and their lives. The persistence of Hancock County's distinctive culture hinged entirely on the maintenance of this abundant supply of cheap labor.

The impoverished conditions in Hancock improved in the first two decades of the twentieth century, particularly from 1917 to 1920 as World War I pushed up the international demand for cotton. Over these three years the total wealth in the county nearly doubled, although wartime inflation diminished buying power somewhat. African Americans shared in this bounty, with their share of the county's total reported wealth rising from 11.5 percent to 18.7 percent. Even tenants bought cars. To the very oldest interviewees, this last, brief spike of prosperity seemed to have become the "normal times" against which they measured their ensuing decades of hardship. They remembered most vividly the calamitous fall in 1921 and spoke of it bitterly, not as a resumption of the long decline of southern agriculture, but as the beginning of something new and awful.[20]

Shortly after the war, and nearly a decade before the Depression hit the rest of the country, the rural South began its own, much longer depression. For many in Hancock, especially small farm owners and tenants, the stock market crash of 1929 had little significance. Their struggle flowed seamlessly from the early 1920s to the end of the 1930s. When asked how the Great Depression had affected their lives, many Hancock farmers laughed and said that they had not known much about it, for times had always been hard.[21] The tale of the tax digest confirms their story, as figure 3 indicates.

When asked when the hard times started, those who were old enough to remember it invariably pointed to the year when the boll weevil invaded their farms in force. Over several decades the weevil rolled like a wave across the South, inundating the farmland of Georgia's piedmont between 1919 and 1923. While other areas recovered somewhat, this soil-depleted region, which had dominated cotton growing in the nineteenth century, sank to marginal productivity. Few cotton fortunes would ever again be made there. Production of cotton in Hancock collapsed from 20,000 bales in 1919 to 12,000 in 1920 and an abysmal 710 bales in 1922. From 1920 to 1922 the number of active cotton gins in the county fell from twenty-three to six. As he surveyed the wreckage in 1921, Hancock's agricultural extension agent declared the year's cotton yield to be about one-eighteenth its normal amount. He added: "The cotton crop which has been depended on for so long seems to be a source of little income now." Cotton yields increased slightly later in the 1920s, yet in every meaningful sense, Hancock's long depression began in 1921.[22]

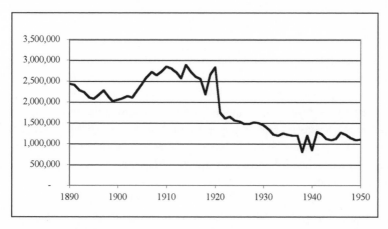

Figure 3. Total Wealth in Hancock County, 1874–1960, adjusted for inflation (*source:* Hancock County Tax Digests, 1874–1960, Georgia State Archives, Atlanta).

For many rural people, the post–World War I crash intensified the pressure to move from the farm to the city and the North. Mary Hunt, born to black renters in 1907, remembered that her family could not survive by farming after the weevil came, so her father went off to work digging the New York subways and supported them with money sent home to Georgia.[23] Marshall Boyer, the son of black landowners, remembered a similar tale: "The boll weevil sent my [sharecropping] uncles and aunts to Detroit." Quite a few of Hancock's dependent farmers joined them. Between 1920 and 1930 the number of tenants in Hancock diminished nearly by half, from 2,171 to 1,136. In all, fully one-third of Hancock's people, black as well as white, left during this first Great Migration.[24]

According to a New Deal study of the Georgia piedmont, after people fled the weevil's devastation, "an enormous acreage of abandoned crop land lay idle." The lower piedmont in particular lost population and active farms. In Hancock the agricultural extension agent reported that one-third of the county's farms were abandoned and "left to be grown up as forest."[25]

The weevil tightened the bonds of debt on most of those who chose not to leave. Dependent farmers saw their livestock, personal possessions, and even food confiscated to satisfy debts they could no longer raise money to pay.[26] Small landowners lost their farms to banks and planters. And because the rural southern economy was constructed on a pyramid of indebtedness, planters and merchants themselves had to struggle with outstanding debts and constricted capital. According to Jewell Thompson, the weevil closed her father's general store when he could not collect outstanding debts. "His shirt-tail," she quipped, "wasn't long enough to cover the whole load."[27] Scores of other Hancock country store owners were overexposed to debt or could not bring themselves to foreclose on the property of impoverished neighbors and so lost their businesses. At least one merchant-planter made heroic efforts to help his neighbors through the crisis. The Trawick general store is missing the 1921 ledger. According to Sid Trawick, his grandfather burned that year's book when he realized the financial condition of his debtors. He took out a loan from a western bank and spent the rest of his life clearing that debt.[28] Some creditors collected only part of their debts by seizing nonessential assets. As a boy J. E. Johnson accompanied his grandfather, a wealthy white merchant-planter, on rounds to renegotiate debts after the first boll weevil year. They forgave $80,000 in debts that year and the next, collecting what they could. The grandfather explained that by taking only the offspring of debtors' livestock and leaving draft animals, he could maintain the debtor in a position to continue making payments—and thus recoup more than he would have by confiscating all the debtors' meager property.[29] Still others found that they could quickly settle their own debts by gouging their creditors and cheating their tenants.

As landlords balanced on the edge of bankruptcy in the next few years, they were hard pressed to furnish their sharecroppers with food, fertilizer, and other store-bought goods. Arthur Raper, in his sociological study of Greene County, found that the traditional paternalism of "normal" cotton prices was broken by the new economic realities. Perhaps Hancock residents' commonly remembered reliance on subsistence gardening emerged only after 1921, as older patterns of market dependency were abandoned. In 1936 a grant writer describing Georgia's lower piedmont for the Farm Security Administration noted that "until the boll weevil, it paid to farm cotton exclusively and simply buy food and feed from merchants." After the weevil came, planters apparently cut back on wage labor, reduced the furnish, and threw the tenants more fully on their own resources. If so, the severing of traditional ties must have been shocking. In 1922 one black Hancock County man testified in court that a planter had given him grim news: "He didn't have any work then and you would have to sorter look out for yourself. The boll weevil was in the country." No interviewees, however, recalled this restructuring of Hancock's personal and economic relationships.[30]

Enduring the Great Depression: The Rural Culture of Semisubsistence and Barter

It is difficult to judge the degree to which southern farmers engaged the market as consumers and producers and to what degree they stood apart from it. The evidence is fragmented and contradictory, with variations over time and between classes. Antebellum planters and small landowners in the Georgia piedmont had achieved a high degree of self-sufficiency, raising food as well as cotton. In the decades following the Civil War, farmers expanded their cotton acreage and reduced corn and livestock. In doing so, they seem to have been seduced by the expanding national consumer culture. Advertisements in the local newspapers and Sears catalogues hawked a growing list of glittering products. In the pages of the *Sparta Ishmaelite*, clothing store owners promised the most up-to-date fashions, which they had personally selected on trips to New York. New cooking, sewing, and cleaning machines offered efficiency and modern sophistication to women. Miracle drugs promised vitality, confidence, and well-being. Telephone ads purred about freedom from day-to-day loneliness and from isolation in times of emergency. Eventually, phonographs, automobiles, and radios emerged as objects of desire and badges of personal success. Only cotton profits could allow piedmont farmers to share in this modern bounty of comfort and expansive self-image.[31]

By the twentieth century, country stores had proliferated, widening southern farmers' access to this brave new world of ready-made goods. Some leaped right in. Planters, of course, had long been able to use their purchasing power to separate their peronal appearances and home interiors from those of humbler rural folk. Indeed, during these years many of them had physically separated themselves from other farmers by becoming town folk. By the late nineteenth century, however, smaller landowners and substantial renters had begun to join them in making regular and substantial purchases at the stores. Their young people in particular pointedly exchanged their rural clothes for modern attire. As historian Ted Ownby discovered in Mississippi, even poor black sharecroppers took on attributes of modern consumers, walking into stores and flipping through Sears catalogues. During the 1930s, in an area just across Hancock's northern border, sociologist Arthur Raper found that one-half of white sharecroppers and one-third of black ones had purchased used cars, even though, Raper suggested, the money "might better have gone into food, or clothing, or education, or doctors' bills."[32] And yet contradictions remained.

Even as they bought cars and other consumer goods, farmers held onto strands of homemade culture. They continued to live on the corn they grew. Whether the cotton crop boomed during World War I or busted in the 1920s, the country store ledgers indicate little change in their habits of purchasing food. In the good years tenant families might have bought delicacies such as a few tins of sardines or oranges to celebrate in the fall or at Christmas. Ready-made clothes and new shoes might have been more widely worn during good spells, whereas more folks made do with purchases of cloth, leather patches, and tacks during poor years. All in all, however, they seemed to put extra money into cars or land and held onto semisubsistence traditions in daily consumption.[33]

Farm Security Administration photographs showing the homes of poor southern farmers in the 1930s indicate that many families owned few consumer goods. Eva Reese spoke for many of Hancock's poorer farmers when she described the home into which she was born in 1908 and the one in which she began her marriage in the 1920s and 1930s. Except for one wardrobe, all the furniture was made by her father or husband throughout all these years.

Until the World War I boom, her family cooked on the fireplace, not on a stove. They used iron pots, ceramic plates, and steel utensils. An oilcloth covered the table. The thin board walls were insulated with sheets of papier-mâché from newspaper. In the early 1940s Reese joined 1,600 other Hancock women in making her family's first real cotton-filled mattresses through a program funded by the Federal Surplus Commodity Corporation and promoted by home demonstration agents. Before this, she, like many Hancock people, had slept on a rough mattress stuffed with corn shucks, pine needles, or straw. She couldn't recall having had other significant possessions before her husband got a factory job in World War II. Henrietta Glover told a similar story. In her childhood her family illuminated their home with a rag stuffed into a jar of kerosene. They kept warm under blankets pieced together first by her mother and then by herself. They used spoons they had carved from cedar branches, and they kept water in a tin bucket, using a guard dipper for drinking it. A bucket they had cut from a cedar tree stored the extra water they had carried from their well.[34]

Like Reese and Glover, most rural people in Hancock and the surrounding piedmont region operated close to the edge of the market in a cash-poor, semisubsistence economy. A descendant of African American Hancock farmers, Willie Butts, observed, "Nobody had no money. But then, you didn't need a whole lot of money."[35] Marvin Turner, a white man who ran a small family farm, concurred, saying simply, "Wasn't no money."[36] Subsistence farming as a supplement to a plot of cotton supplied this region's poor farmers with basic necessities. By working in the cotton culture, most people obtained a place to live. By working as domestics or lumber workers, they brought in a little cash for clothes and other store-bought items. Most of the food rural people ate, however, came from subsistence agriculture and barter. Katie Hunt, an African American renter born in 1891, remembered: "We lived on a farm, and in Depression time we always had something to eat. We didn't have money, really much. But food . . . we never went hungry."[37]

Most interviewees from all social classes echoed Hunt's statement in affirming that they never went hungry. Poor as they were by today's standards, Hancock farmers—including most sharecroppers—drew from a culture of self-sufficiency and subsistence agriculture that generally protected them from hunger, a resource less available to city dwellers. Most rural women planted substantial gardens, growing peas, okra, collard greens, turnips, tomatoes, and sweet and white potatoes, usually with help from their children. Although some sharecroppers were not reticent about accusing landlords of serious crimes (including murder), not one stated that the landlords had limited the size of her garden to make more room for cotton cultivation. In other parts of the South the cotton still "grew up to the doorstep," but by the twentieth century the depleted soil of the piedmont did not repay landlords for such tactics. As a result, instead of feeding tenants at their own commissaries, as planters did in South Georgia and Mississippi, piedmont planters furnished paltry support for their tenants but did not so narrowly restrict their use of the land. From the time when the first greens sprouted in the spring until the time when the peas were picked in the fall, the garden provided the only vegetables that most farm families would eat.[38]

The ledgers of several country stores show that most farmers bought no vegetables, poultry, or eggs. During the boom years of 1919 and 1920, fewer than half the customers at the Lowe store bought any meat at all, and only 30–35 percent of these made more than one meat purchase. Some bought sugar, lard, cornmeal, and flour, but others bought little food of any kind, although they did purchase coffee and tobacco. In winter, diets often comprised only the canned goods that women had put up and foodstuffs that preserved well: cured pork, potatoes, dried peas, molasses, and of course, corn.[39]

All small landowners and tenants with whom I spoke grew corn as their primary means of sustenance. Although cotton acreage eclipsed acreage for food crops in the years after the Civil War, the boll weevil reversed these priorities. By 1925 cotton acreage in Hancock had fallen to 17,000 acres, a third of the acreage in 1920, and it continued to diminish. Total corn acreage, on the other hand, held steady at around 33,000 acres throughout the first half of the twentieth century, despite a steady exodus of the county's farmers. In other words, in the 1920s and 1930s fewer farmers were growing more corn. After harvest they stored it in the ear and took it to mills to be ground as needed. Many of these farmers also grew wheat, sugarcane, or sorghum for private use. Usually the grower contracted with specialists who owned harvesters or mills to process the crop in return for a portion of the yield. Only rarely did cash enter into transactions.[40]

Most farmers also supplied themselves with meat without recourse to the market. Poorer rural families hunted and fished to supplement their diet. Additionally, almost all rural families raised chickens for eggs and meat. Most farmers, including the poorest sharecroppers, had at least one or two hogs, which made up their primary meat supply. Cows were more expensive and required silage or grazing space and so were less common. In 1938 the county agent reported that over five hundred farms in the county did not have a cow.[41] Yet many poor families circumvented their lack of grazing land by taking advantage of a tradition of open range that persisted in abbreviated form in some sections of Hancock into the 1940s, well after state fencing laws were thought to have completely abolished the system. After crops were gathered in the fall, farmers, by mutual agreement, cut holes in fence lines to let their livestock graze wherever they wished.[42] At slaughtering time as well, farmers often fell back on traditional ways of neighborhood cooperation. Sometimes families would take turns butchering at one another's farms, or they would exchange poorer cuts of meat for the labor of neighbors who did not raise hogs.

Networks of exchange operated freely in the rural South's cash-poor economy. Ralph Walker, a white small landowner, remembered farmers swapping chickens or hogs for wheat in the 1930s.[43] Many others described similar barterings of vegetables, fish, wild berries, fruit, and labor among members of extended families, churches, and neighborhoods. Personal ties had great economic significance in rural Hancock.

The barter-oriented system of exchange that characterized neighborhood interaction extended into transactions at country stores as well. From an early age children learned the exchange value of eggs relative to candy. Farmers could easily calculate the number of eggs or the amount of butter they would need to obtain a certain quantity of flour, lard, or cloth. Particularly in the disastrous years of the early 1920s, country store registers recorded payments in eggs, produce, and labor as well as in cash.[44] It is no wonder that older rural folk still speak of "trading at" a particular store rather than "shopping" there.

Beyond barter, a culture of gift giving distributed "excess" goods, especially perishables, within a local community. One white yeoman farmer, Francis Frazier, reported that neighbors would share milk with someone whose cow had gone dry, knowing they too might soon be dependent on community assistance.[45] "Folks just helped each other out" is a regularly repeated refrain. One white sharecropper, A. J. Parker, stated that "friendship was better than money." The interviewees generally agreed that race did not present a barrier to gift giving. When Earnest and Annie Macklin farmed a small plot in southern Hancock, they regularly shared their garden produce with white neighbors, the Hoods and the Harrisons. "We didn't sell to each other," Earnest Macklin said; "We gave back and forth." In return, the Hoods shared from their apple and peach orchards, and according to the Macklins, "Tom Harrison wouldn't never sell us nothing. Just let us have." Black and white neighbors of similar economic status regularly assisted one another with work or food through sickness, injury, and hardship. Hungry families asked others for food in both directions across the race line. Although these exchanges often took place between economic equals, other forms of gift giving symbolically reinforced the social hierarchy and the culture of paternalism.[46]

Some sharecroppers offered their landlords what black sharecropper James Wilson remembers calling a "taste out of their garden."[47] Some planters reciprocated by giving tenants dairy products, fruit, meat scraps, and even secondhand furniture, rugs, and wedding dresses. Sometimes these "gifts" were in fact the only wages paid domestic servants.[48] Black landowners also took part in exchanges between unequals. Mary Hunt, the granddaughter of a wealthy black landowner, declared that her grandfather "never charged cash money for anything." If people could not afford to buy or barter for his produce, he would let them sweep a floor and then give it to them.[49]

Most farm folk spoke of keeping fed during the Depression and otherwise just getting by, but others experienced awful deprivation. For them, barter, exchange, and gift giving drew the line between hardship and starvation. Josie Mae Ingram, an African American whose mother sharecropped on poor, sandy soil, said, "We had to share to survive."[50] Those who had nothing material to barter offered their labor, chopping wood or doing household chores in return for food. Such exchanges were the primary form of welfare available to rural people during the Depression years. Although the Red Cross distributed some flour in Sparta in the early 1930s, and some rural people found jobs with the Works Progress Administration (WPA), no one interviewed for this study remembered receiving any government or charitable rations during the Depression. For the most part, it was personal exchanges, not institutional support, that carried Hancock's rural people through hard times.

Usually Hancock families that were reduced to hunger had been undermined by a complex of problems that dragged them under despite the traditional support networks. Severe deprivation could result when death, abandonment, alcoholism, or prolonged injury or illness left a family dependent on the labor of a single adult. To make ends meet, farm families needed at least two contributing adults (sometimes drawn from the extended family), as well as a supplement of child labor. When Newton Boyer, a white tenant farmer, died in 1926, his wife, Carrie, and their five young children were unable to secure a plot on which to sharecrop. The family sheltered in the poorest shacks but was repeatedly evicted when the rent came due.[51] Poor soil, too, could undercut a family's ability to provide for itself. Some land simply would not grow crops sufficient to feed a family through the year. Mamie Washington, an African American sharecropper from the infertile sandy-soil belt at the southern part of the county, remembered that her family was reduced to one and a half meager meals a day for long stretches during the South's Depression.[52] As I will discuss later, exploitation by ruthless landlords could also push poor families over the edge.[53]

The evidence does not clearly show how commonly hunger and malnutrition afflicted Hancock County farmers. Two studies of black piedmont sharecroppers in the 1920s found that, on average, they grew only one-half as much food as black landowners did over the course of a year and ate only one-third the meat that black landowners consumed. Instead, their diet consisted mainly of cornmeal and flour, supplemented by fatty cuts of meat, molasses, and some sweet potatoes. Malnutrition was exacerbated from December to May, when farmers could not "eat out of their gardens." This lack of protein and vitamins led to high rates of rickets, pellagra, tuberculosis, and anemia across the region.[54] Of course, landowners and renters fared much better, and in Hancock the majority of tenants rented their farms. Another study indicates that pellagra actually declined as the cotton market hit bottom, for farmers were forced to raise more food to diminish their dependence on the shrinking furnish of cornmeal.[55]

During World War II Sparta's Dr. R. C. Jernigan wrote a letter to the *Sparta Ishmaelite* to testify that after examining one hundred of Hancock's draft rejections, he had decided that malnutrition ranked only fourth among factors determining their unfitness to serve. However, another letter chided, "White landowners can no longer be indifferent to poverty, malnutrition, and ill health among negroes, or among white tenants. . . . Many tenant families never had enough milk, meat, eggs, and vegetables, or proper medical care, and the sons are not fit to fight and more landowners' sons must take their places in the armies."[56]

Hancock people tell many stories of life reduced to the impoverished basics through the Depression but relatively few stories of actual hunger. This might result in part from the interviewing process. Some evidence suggests that hunger did weigh on more homes during the worst boll weevil years, from 1922 to 1925, than at any other time. Perhaps those who lived through these years have let their memories of this period blur. Nevertheless, evidence from other sources, the general store ledgers, and anecdotes told by Hancock's home demonstration and agricultural extension agents also suggest that the culture of subsistence cushioned the impact of the long agricultural depression for most poor farmers. Even if many farmers had abandoned aspects of the subsistence culture long before, it remained a cultural resource, a viable option into which farmers could retreat (at least partially) to escape the vicissitudes of the market. On a farm most families could at least feed themselves. Willie Butts, an African American born to Hancock farmers in

1921, sometimes went to a nearby town to see movies. He remembered that the 1930s newsreels preceding the main feature sometimes showed clips of city folks lined up with cups in their hands waiting for doughnuts and coffee. Years later he recollected, "I thought we were rich."[57]

The Work

Those who worked in the cotton culture retained vivid memories of the experience decades later. Some remembered the cool, clingy dampness of newly turned dirt as they plowed behind straining mules. Many, in contrast, carry intense, painful memories of sun-seared, hard-packed red clay beneath their bare feet as they chopped with hoes to thin the crop. Scents fill people's recollections: the smell of the earth, the sweat of mules and men, the acrid tang of arsenic dust shaken through a burlap bag to kill the weevils, or the sweet stickiness of molasses and arsenic carried in buckets and brushed indiscriminately onto cotton bolls, overalls, and skin. Some spoke of their tactile memories, the bites of insects, the weight of the Georgia sun, the heavy stillness of humid air, or the growing weight of burlap bags as men, women, and children worked their way up and down the rows in the fall. Others recollected the ache of their stooped backs as they walked or crawled, picking from first light to last. Many noted the corrosive work of the spiny cotton bolls as pickers stabbed in their fingers to pluck out their soft tufts. David Harper, the son of a black landowner, seemed struck by the sounds of life on a cotton farm. Most people imagine farm life to have been quiet, but Harper knew otherwise: "It was noisy! If chickens weren't crowing, dogs were barking, or cows and pigs were making noise."[58]

Some interviewees described working in isolation, focusing all day on the task just ahead. Others worked side by side with friends or family members, talking as they moved up the rows together. Some sang to pass the time. Julia Hillman and her father used to make up songs to narrate the day's events or to tease each other. Many years later she could still improvise a song on the spot. Narrating their stories, some elderly people spoke with nostalgia as they remembered the simple pleasures of outdoor work and the vigor of their younger selves. Yet others spoke only of their gratitude that those experiences were far behind them.[59]

The interviewees who spoke at length about their work also make it clear that farming—even sharecropping—was skilled labor. Only wage laborers made no meaningful agricultural choices. Many tenants took considerable pride in explaining their ability to understand the numerous tasks involved in successful farming. Cotton, the primary commercial product, required care and a good sense of timing at critical points in its cultivation. Everyone also grew corn, which had its own requirements. Many farmers also had plots of other field crops, such as sugarcane, field peas, and sweet potatoes, as well as the family garden. Additionally, farmers had to know how to care for livestock and work with the famously cantankerous mule. Besides raising their food, farmers had to know how to preserve it by canning, salting, or other methods. Finally, they had to be able to repair most of their equipment. After talking at length about the various tasks that commercial and subsistence agriculture required sharecroppers to perform over the course of the year, James Wilson raised his eyebrows and shook his head. "If you didn't know what you were doing," he summarized, "you were a lost ball in the weeds."[60]

Tenancy: The Struggle for Control

Throughout the Depression, Hancock remained a planter-dominated county. Whereas black and white yeoman farmers comprised the majority in the county's northern part, its central section and most southern parts were firmly controlled by the planters. Militia district 116, which lies in the west-central part and surrounds Devereux, is representative of this area.[61] In 1910, 43 percent of the land in this large district was owned by ten men who held from five hundred to several thousand acres each. As smaller farmers lost land to weevils and low cotton prices, the big planters increasingly dominated this section. By 1930 this elite class owned 54 percent of all land in the district.[62]

Between 1910 and 1940 the majority of these large estates were worked by tenant farmers, nearly 90 percent of whom were African American. In 1910, 88 percent of the county's 2,032 black farmers and 48 percent of the county's 807 white farmers worked as tenants.[63]

These tenant farmers were not evenly distributed across the county. The largest planters, in the best land across the central and western parts of the county, seem to have preferred black labor. In contrast, the poor, sandy pine barrens of the southern and eastern sections of the county supported a relatively large number of white tenant farmers. Even in these areas, however, white tenants did not predominate but composed a significant minority among the black tenants.

Prospective sharecroppers began their work year by approaching a landowner in the spring to see whether a tract of land was open. The position was not available to all. Sharecropping was family work, and a family had to have sufficient labor to be acceptable—usually children old enough for fieldwork. Sometimes a husband, a wife, and one or two young children worked together throughout the growing season. Sometimes a husband would work the fields with an older child while the other children attended school and the wife tended to the garden, the chickens, and the house, until labor-intensive periods in the growing season brought them all into the fields together. Leslie Barksdale, a black woman who worked on shares in the northern part of the county, believes that men took the primary role in the fieldwork, probably because of the heavy upper-body work that plowing required. Still, a number of black Hancock women spent periods of their lives wrestling with plows and coaxing mules. The interviews suggest that as the twentieth century progressed, women became increasingly less likely to work the plow. Roberta Andrews remembered being impressed when her mother told her she had plowed. At least one Hancock woman performed an even greater feat of strength. When she was a child in the 1920s, Creasy Walker knew an old woman named Sally Green whose shoulders bore scars that Green said she had gotten from pulling a plow herself.[64]

When the family spokesperson (usually the father) approached the land-owner to set up a sharecropping contract, he had to negotiate the details. The number of acres to be used by a sharecropper family depended on the number of hands they could put in the field and the landowner's estimation of the family's capacity for hard work. A good reputation was essential. In rural communities everyone knew everyone else's personal work record. Although there was a high rate of turnover among tenant farmers from year to year, most of them remained in the same area, where they were known and where they could use their personal ties with planters. The World War I draft cards from Hancock County show that of all draft-age black men born in the Devereux area and still living in Hancock, 88 percent remained in the Devereux district.[65] If a young couple was starting out for the first time as croppers, the planter would go by their reputations as wage laborers. The planter would also consider the family history of a potential sharecropper, "the apple doesn't fall far from the tree" being an often-repeated saying in the conservative and personal South.[66]

Tenancy followed several distinct patterns. The more resources a dependent farmer brought to the negotiation, the greater his share of the profits. Landless farmers who possessed some capital as well as tools, draft animals, and supplies could become tenants by cash renting. More commonly, however, renters in twentieth-century Hancock County agreed to pay the landlord a single bale of cotton at the end of the year for the use of a one-mule farm. These farmers made up 60 percent of all Hancock tenants in 1910 and 50 percent in 1920. Traditionally they exercised full control over the use of the land, their labor, and the crop.

Many other landless farmers had less control. One-third of Hancock's tenants worked under crop-sharing agreements in 1910, and half did so in 1920.[67] Farmers who owned a mule could work as share tenants by agreeing to pay the landlord one-third of the corn crop and one-fourth of the cotton at the end of the year. Those who brought only their own labor to the negotiations usually worked "on halves" as sharecroppers. The landlord gave them a furnish, which included the use of a mule, plow, seed, fertilizer, and credit to purchase food through the growing season. Because of postbellum alterations of the legal code, sharecroppers were legally viewed as the landlord's employees, not partners. Accordingly, at year's end the landlord paid the sharecroppers half the crop instead of the croppers' paying the landlord. This arrangement, the most common in the more fertile parts of the postbellum South, gave the landlord much legal power to swindle the sharecropper out of his rightful share.[68]

Although the previously described labor agreements fairly well cover the types of arrangements employed, they must be seen only as models. Never fully standardized, they varied somewhat, both over time and across the region. Local customs set the parameters of contracts, but the arrangements had to be renegotiated regularly, with each battle refought. Accordingly, these rough categories allowed for a diverse mix of human experiences. A few contracts were truly unconventional. Mary Lattimore and her husband annually worked with a white man who brought them dairy calves and dry milk. For bottle-feeding the calves, they got to keep half of them. They also worked halves for him raising peas and corn to be used as animal feed. The three of them invented this unusual arrangement after the boll weevil began ravaging Hancock in 1921, thus demonstrating the flexibility of the sharecropping system.[69]

Croppers made their profits solely from the proceeds from their halves of the crop. Planters, however, had access to a second revenue source that tradition embedded into the sharecropping relationship. They received interest on the loans for furnish—frequently at steep rates. Early in the twentieth century bigger planters sometimes had a commissary or country store as well, which they might require their croppers to patronize. Goods there were usually offered at higher prices than found in town, especially if the purchases were made on credit, as the purchases of sharecroppers almost always were. Sometimes sharecroppers bypassed the planter and purchased supplies on credit directly from a country store. If so, the results were essentially the same: a growing bill with interest rapidly accruing from spring to picking time. Some lenders obviously gouged their debtors with outlandish interest, ranging, as one Mississippi critic of the system put it, "from 25 percent to grand larceny." As economists have discovered, however, these rates were universally high because the merchants themselves paid high interest rates to southern bankers, who in turn paid high rates to northern lenders. The fragility and uncertainty of the southern economy—and the high risk investing in it entailed—was ultimately to blame for the rates. Country store owners suffered a high bankruptcy rate in the rural South, and they did their best to hedge their bets on chancy loans.[70]

If a sharecropper came out behind at the settlement, a planter could take out a lien against the next year's crop—usually the cropper's only collateral. The planter would then have first claim on the as-yet-ungrown crop. This method was used to bind sharecroppers to one farm through cycles of debt. The lien also gave the planter the explicit legal right to require that the cropper plant enough cotton to satisfy the debt, even to the exclusion of the food crops that the family needed for personal use. The planter's order to emphasize cotton thus effected the last turn of a tight spiral of indebtedness. Not raising their own food would force the family to get more food supplies on credit through the market. By the 1920s, however (thus within living memory), the crop lien was not being used in Hancock to stabilize labor. No interviewee claimed to have been forced to remain on a plantation because of debts or to have known anyone who was constrained in this way. Perhaps the persistent mobility of sharecroppers finally wore down the system. In Hancock the planters used another vehicle for recouping their losses.

"If you didn't make nothin'," said Mary Lattimore, a Hancock sharecropper, "if you didn't pay back [to the planter] what little you made, they'd take it." The landlords or merchants would come and "they'd say they had the law." Sometimes they would take food out of the mouths of a poor family. "If you make any corn, peas, if you had any hogs, chickens—anything that would get their pay"—they would take it. White folks, Lattimore summarized, "were death on colored folks." About one-fourth of the black sharecroppers interviewed for this study stated that planters had at least once declared them still in debt after the settle and had confiscated some or all of their food crops as payment. Most of the confiscations reported involved corn only, which was the primary component of poor southerners' diets. Without actually confiscating it, one planter nevertheless used food as a lever to exact payment from his croppers. As a child Annie Macklin endured a period of hunger when the landowner for whom her sharecropping family worked nailed boards across the barn door to keep them from the corn they had raised. He told them they could have access to it when they repaid all they owed him. Sometimes, as happened to Josie Ingram, mules could be confiscated, which dealt a severe blow to the family's earning potential the next year. Sometimes the payment exacted seemed out of proportion to the debt incurred. Hyndenberg Dixon remembered when all his cattle were confiscated to settle an outstanding debt on a single mule.[71]

The previously described means constituted the legal ways that a landlord could profit from the sharecropping system. As Dixon's testimony suggests, however, some planters employed other methods as well to tap into their tenants' shares of the crop. Landlords could insist on driving their croppers' cotton to be ginned and marketed. On returning, they would report how much was made and give the sharecropper his half, minus deductions. Some sharecroppers reported that landlords took advantage of this obvious opportunity to cheat.

But in the end, planters intent on defrauding their croppers needed to go no further than the desk in which they stored their account ledgers. At the year-end settle they announced the bill owed them for the furnish. This bill, calculated in their own handwriting and in their own books, was not subject to debate. Usually, Hyndenberg Dixon remembered, the planter would announce, "You just come out. You did pretty good!" He would then give the sharecropping family "a little for a dress." Many sharecroppers found an alarming correlation between the amount they had produced that year and the debt that the planters claimed they owed at the settle. Mary Worthening, the daughter of black sharecroppers, said that after one successful season of farming in the 1930s, when her family had raised corn, peas, and potatoes in addition to eleven bales of cotton, the landlord "took it all." They "were too scared to argue" but knew that they had been treated unfairly. "Every time we made a big crop," she said, "whites took it all." The political, legal, and economic power of the planters allowed them to cheat flagrantly at the settle. The event was usually masked in cordial speech, but that fooled no one involved. One white man recalled sitting on his uncle's porch at the settle. As black tenants would come up, one by one, the merchant-planter, with his book in his lap, would say, "'You owe me such and so at the store out of your share. But you did alright. You cleared $150 this year.' And he and I and the tenant all knew that he should have gotten more than that." It wasn't hard to calculate whether a man was being cheated, he explained: "They'd have made so many bales at so much a pound. You'd know they were being robbed. It was just sorry." The frequency with which landlords shaved off pieces of their tenants' shares led W. E. B. Du Bois to estimate in 1912 that white landlords had withheld about three-fourths of the profits due their tenants since the end of slavery.[72]

Besides contracting with an honest landowner, there were few ways to avoid being defrauded through the planter's arbitrary power at the settle. James McMullen, a black educator, related the story of a black sharecropper he knew who carried only a portion of his cotton to market. He reported the amount and price of the cotton he had ginned and sold, at which point the planter informed him that, according to his calculations, he had come out dead even that year. When the sharecropper then confessed that he had more cotton left over—with which he now expected to make some money—the planter exclaimed, "Dang it! Now I have to work out these figures again!" Variations on this anecdote floated around the South for years.[73] Apocryphal or not, this story held power because it matched the experiences and expectations of so many poor men and women. McMullen also stated that some black landowners used their privileged, independent position to assist nearby black sharecroppers. If they were fairly certain that a man was going to be cheated at the settle, some black landowners would secretly carry some of his cotton to market, claiming it as their own crop, and then deliver the profit to the sharecropper. Only one man described such interactions, so it is not possible to guess at their frequency.

It must be clearly stated that planters were far from uniform in their treatment of dependent farmers. Some African American interviewees generalized without distinction that planters "would cheat you if they could." Of her father's experience as a sharecropper, Mary Worthening stated, "Everyone he farmed with, they took his crop away from him." But others said that they had never been cheated at the settle, and still others spoke favorably of the way that specific planters treated them but criticized others. There seems to have been no clear pattern of cheating. Leslie Barksdale, who worked shares for a small farmer, and Mamie Washington, who did so for a large planter, both claimed to have been treated fairly by the landowners with whom they worked. The written memoirs of other sharecroppers in the South also testify to the uneven patterns of honesty among landlords. Ed Brown, who worked on shares in the 1920s and 1930s about sixty miles south of Hancock, farmed for one planter who manipulated the books to confiscate all his crops, his firewood, his garden produce, and most of his livestock. He also worked for landlords whom he remembered as fair men and women and one woman who actively helped him purchase a tract of land. Others fell somewhere between these poles: "I also got my share of white people that was not too good or too bad either. Just ordinary. Them I cheated, but not too bad, every once in a while when I got the chance, just like they did me." As Hancock's Clinton Pearson said, "Being cheated depended on who you worked for." Some planters stated that by treating their sharecroppers fairly, they developed a reputation that stabilized their own workforce or made it easier for them to procure reliable families in the spring. But others clearly did not see the situation this way. The uncertain consciences and varying economic strategies of planters thus heightened the innate unpredictability of farming generally. When surveying the cotton opening in their fields in the fall, a sharecropper could not yet assume that she would make money that year. She could only hope.[74]

Ultimately, a poor African American farmer who knew that he had been cheated of his share had few options. He could not sue or protest through any formal channels. That the government did not represent African Americans had been ensured by the violent destruction of Reconstruction, and that the government did not represent landless farmers of any color had been decided by the fraudulent destruction of Populism. After Populism the primary function of southern state and local governments was to place poor people—especially African American laborers—at the mercy of white employers and landlords. Whites could decide whether to fully exploit that legally granted right; the decision was purely personal. Bound only by the private dictates of conscience or a sense of noblesse oblige, some landlords treated their dependent farmers equitably. Others cheated them ruthlessly. Whether honest individuals or cheats, however, they responded to political crises by acting nearly in unison to ensure that they retained economic justice as a privately determined option for their class. In rural Hancock personalism and paternalism were not merely idiosyncratic appendages to the economic structure. Because of disfranchisement and the blatant injustice of the courts, these personal ties composed the day-to-day structure of Hancock's economy. Within the traditional political economy of Hancock, defrauded sharecroppers had nowhere to turn for redress of grievances. They could protest legally only by moving to another farm for the next season.

Some sharecroppers, however, pursued extralegal measures to even the score. Evidence indicates that some cases of arson in the rural South were acts of sabotage by dependent farmers who felt that they had been ill-used by landlords. More often sharecroppers simply tried to steal back a portion of what they thought was rightfully theirs. The year a white landlord confiscated all her family's cotton and food crops, Mary Worthening's father "had to steal some bushels of corn and take them to grind to feed his family."[75]

As they had in the antebellum period, most whites apparently attributed black theft to their "naturally thievish" nature. Such an interpretation reinforced whites' sense of the social order's "natural" rightness. Small personal losses could be borne with paternalistic condescension. Yet other whites recognized petty theft as a response to real deprivation and hunger. One black woman who had separated from her husband said that a white landowner refused her bid to sharecrop on account of her large family. "You're sure gonna steal with all those children," she remembered him saying. He knew that the sharecropping system could not guarantee a single mother enough food or income to feed her family, no matter how diligently she worked.[76]

Many white landlords seemed to expect black sharecroppers to steal some produce. Some seemed to take it in stride, unless too much of their food supplies disappeared too quickly. One white man who felt that his flour was being raided too brazenly rigged his flour barrel with a steel trap; the following morning he lectured the black sharecropper whom he found standing with his hand caught in the trap. Although stealing and other petty crimes were usually addressed privately by the landowner, on many occasions whites publicly charged blacks with theft and sent them to jail or the chain gangs. Once there, they often served their whole term. Although planters sometimes bought other convicts—including murderers—out of prison, they tended not to want men convicted of theft around their own property. The irony in the manner that public justice was meted out for theft was not lost on James Wilson, a black sharecropper. While telling of a black man who was imprisoned for theft, Wilson commented with a laugh: "It's the white man's job to steal. He didn't want no one else stealing." So whereas a number of relatively wealthy whites stole largely and openly, backed by the complicity of the legal and political system, a number of poor blacks stole in ways small and secret, in fear of legal repercussion. In a way, the piecemeal stealing of food was a miserable attempt by the most impoverished rural people to regain some control. But it made a poor substitute for the autonomy that African Americans had sought after emancipation.[77]

Within the narrow parameters established by the international cotton market, white planters had established the overall structure of the southern agricultural system through group action, primarily organized violence and control of the political and legal systems. Meanwhile, black dependent farmers contested this system individually by private negotiations and theft. During "normal" times, then, the planters embraced the culture of personalism to magnify their own individual power, but during times of crisis and challenge they molded themselves into a tightly knit group to defend their collective interests. Whenever poorer farmers united to threaten planter dominance, the planters employed the tactics they had learned during the overthrow of Reconstruction to reassert their control.

In the 1890s white yeoman farmers had attempted to break the planters' political dominance by building a class-based coalition with black yeomen and dependent farmers. Their united attack on the planter's political control in Hancock and throughout the South nearly succeeded; in the end, the planters defeated it only through transparent fraud and public violence. But defeat it they did, and decisively. No similarly regionwide, class-based movement ever emerged again in the South.

Beyond that, only rarely and subregionally did poor twentieth-century southern rural workers organize to challenge the planters' economic control. Twice in the mid-1930s southern dependent farmers organized unions. The Alabama Sharecroppers' Union, made famous by Ned Cobb's autobiography, tried to protect poor farmers from landlord creditors who sought to confiscate their property. It also sought to negotiate contracts for tenants collectively. The union was quickly crushed by legally sanctioned violence. The Southern Tenant Farmers' Union formed at the same time. At its height it was an interracial union comprising as many as twenty-five thousand members from six southern states. This union, too, met with violent resistance from white landlords and the law-enforcement officers who served their interests.[78]

Hancock and the rest of the eastern piedmont did not seem to have been touched by these labor movements. Evidence from the turn of the century shows, however, that whites in this area feared that black dependent farmers might organize to improve the condition of their class. In 1887, in the county abutting Hancock's northeast border, a white northerner was shot and seriously wounded for attempting to organize black wage laborers to strike for higher pay. In 1901 the editor of the *Sparta Ishmaelite* warned: "There is no question of the fact that the negro laborers of the South are rapidly enrolling themselves in secret organizations whose object is to insure bigger pay for less effective service." He closed by goading his readers: "And what are you going to do about it?" A few years later the white citizens of Hancock demonstrated their intentions. In 1909 the *Ishmaelite* reported that another white northerner suspected of organizing black laborers in Hancock had been confronted by a group of angry whites. They warned him to leave the county, which the *Ishmaelite* cheerfully reported he did "right speedily." Violence and the threat of violence remained the primary weapons whites used to defend the economic and political status quo from organized black resistance.[79]

By ensuring that neither government nor unions would represent the interests of laborers, the planters maintained a highly private and personal economic system in which economic power was mediated individually, not corporately or institutionally. This ensured that those individuals with the most personal power—not just economic, political, and social power but also the capacity for violence—remained securely in charge.[80]

Being unable to organize openly to pressure landlords, dependent black farmers were left to struggle individually as well as they could. In the spring their shrinking winter stores forced them to sign sharecropping contracts so that they could live on the furnish until their gardens began producing. They could not easily hold out for better contracts at such a time. When the September picking time arrived, however, and the cotton opened clean and vulnerable in the fields, the landlords became the desperate ones. Whereas the law held tenants to the contracts they had signed in the spring, wage laborers, who were free to contract anew each day, sometimes used the land-owners' dilemma to bargain for higher wages. The *Ishmaelite* periodically registered complaints over the "unreliability" and "shiftlessness" of black pickers as they held out for higher wages. By forcing planters to bid against one another for scarce labor, they were sometimes able to raise the general level of wages for picking.[81]

Interestingly, farmers were not the only ones attempting to hold out for more money. In 1906 the editor of the *Ishmaelite* complained about other workers, too: "The servant shortage in Sparta and the surrounding county continues to grow worse with time—washerwomen especially." He suggested that white Spartans respond to the increasing "unreasonableness" of "the demands of these tub tyrants" by organizing a cooperative laundry. Decades later, around 1932, a black man came to the county to organize black domestics. He lived at the home of young Walter Green Clayton, who remembered hearing him speak at the Macedonia Baptist Church, urging women to hold out for better wages and save their earnings. Afterward he was threatened and had to slip away one night. Clayton remembered that whites similarly resented less-militant attacks on the standard low wage paid to domestics. When a white preacher, new to Hancock, began paying his domestic help too much, he too had to leave the county.[82]

Outside the brief picking season, however, dependent farmers had little leverage in labor struggles. The poor returns of the dismal cotton market simply could not support good profits for laborers. Furthermore, the low wages of the cotton economy depressed area wages generally, so that the few alternative livelihoods in the region provided little economic leverage for dependent cotton farmers to use against landlords. Even if dependent piedmont farmers had been able to organize, they would likely not have been able to greatly improve the wages they received.

Again, the battle for control was generally a private, personal one. Land-owners and dependent farmers contested not only over wages but also over control of the crop, the daily work routine, and tenants' private lives. The sharecropper experience in the area varied widely during the first half of the twentieth century. Some planters came to exercise extraordinary control over their dependent farmers; others rarely saw them.

On some plantations, especially in the first decades of the twentieth century, planters minutely directed tenants' labor, both seasonally and daily. Planters could retain the right to tell croppers how much corn to grow relative to the cotton crop. They could ring bells to call all their tenants to the fields, to lunch, or to their homes at the end of the day. Some planters even demanded personal services from tenants. James Wilson remembered—and continued to resent—how his father was required to hitch horses to the planter's buggy on Sunday so the planter and his family could attend church. His father had to stay home from church to be ready to unhitch the team when the planter returned. Then, before retiring into the house for the day, the white man would sometimes organize the black men on the plantation to work. Wilson said that even the men "on the chain gang got to lay up in camp on Sunday." His family, he said, "was slaving for those white people." One elderly black woman remembered hearing her grandfather say that, as a boy late in the nineteenth century, he had been required to fan his landlord's family as they ate dinner.[83]

White farm owners exercised control over the children of black parents in other ways, too. They often required that sharecroppers' children work in the fields, sometimes even at very early ages. Carlton Morse, a student at black Hancock schools in the 1920s and 1930s and the principal of a black high school there in the 1940s, remembered that the white superintendent of education would allow black county schools to open for two or three weeks in August before closing them for cotton picking. The white schools, meanwhile, remained open—although many white interviewees reported that their parents had withdrawn them to help with fieldwork during this critical period. White child labor was a private, family decision, but the labor of black children clearly was viewed as a community resource by the white planters who stood behind the school board and superintendent. Morse remembered the trucks that the bigger planters sent to pick up black children and bring them to their fields as wage laborers. Compliance with these orders was not optional. Morse recalled that one black principal in another county lost his job for refusing to close his school. Some planters required their tenants' children to miss school, even when it was open, in order to work. Earnest Macklin remembered that his family was forced to move two times because white landlords resented his father's decision to keep some of his younger children in school. Macklin himself had been working full time since the age of nine.[84]

Marshall Boyer, from neighboring Baldwin County, described an even more intense level of control on some of the largest plantations, a control that seems to have bordered on a sense of ownership. In the 1920s one white planter in an adjacent county was well known for pushing his tenants hard during the day. Boyer remembered the man saying, "'If the mule dies, I'll buy a new one; if the nigger dies, I'll hire another one.' Those were Sam Innis's words." Although he controlled work life on his plantation, however, Innis allowed almost any kind of criminal activity after hours. Interposing his authority between his tenants and the law, Innis refused to allow the state to prosecute them as long as they worked on his plantation. He handled all conflicts personally and would not allow law-enforcement officers to come onto his property. According to Boyer, tenants on his land seemed invulnerable to arrest. Innis seems to have viewed them as his people, not citizens of the state. "If they had to put a name to you," explained Boyer, planters like Innis would say, "'That's my nigger.' No name, no nothing. That's all needed to be said." It was, Boyer continued, "a slaveryism. They had just got out of [slave times], but it was still in the minds of a lot of people." Some interviewees knew of landlords or overseers who beat tenants or wage laborers. One Hancock man noted that a plantation in Hancock still contained a jail that had been built by a slaveowner. He could not say whether it had been used after slavery, but he did not think the possibility improbable. At its extreme, individual planter control could be thoroughgoing.[85]

Nonetheless, most ex-sharecroppers from Hancock stated that from the 1920s on their landlords had rarely or never directed them closely. Although Mamie Washington's father was told how much cotton and corn to plant each year, the family decided how to care for and manage the crop. Her father also drove the cotton to market. The planter did not direct their labor and did not employ an overseer to do so. Washington's family and the other five sharecroppers on their plantation controlled the work routine of their own family members as well, assigning tasks to each. The adults also decided when to pull their children from school and set them to work, although economic necessity forced most of them to do so early. These were the meaningful choices that, in limited but concrete form, gave shape and substance to the abstraction called freedom.

Even the plantation bell, that potent symbol of slavery, had its own varied history in twentieth-century Hancock. Some tenant families acquired their own bells, perhaps in part to appropriate the symbolic control of their own work routines. In some neighborhoods a chorus of bells—from planters, yeomen, and tenants—sounded the significant hours, diluting the central power of the planters' own bells and attesting to a communal agreement as to proper times to work and to rest.[86]

* * *

The testimony of ex-sharecroppers reveals a continuum of autonomy. Sometimes dependent farmers sought to increase their freedom actively by negotiating and playing planters against one another. At other times they did so passively, accepting expanded responsibility as planters increasingly moved to town and became somewhat detached absentee landlords. Words such as *tenant* and *sharecropper* may evoke stereotypes, but in Hancock they hid within them a wide range of meanings.

This theme of diversity emerges when oral testimonies from Hancock are compared with one another. Other motifs leap from almost all stories. Most people spoke of the difficult struggle to make a living out of the weevil-ridden red clay of the piedmont. Although most people in this cash-poor economy raised cotton for the market, they also remembered the importance of subsistence strategies in providing the basic necessities of life. Contestation and personalism also constitute central themes by which these elderly ex-farmers from Hancock structured the narratives of their working lives before World War II. Working as families and supported by neighborly assistance, most farmers struggled not with institutions but with other men and women to eke out a simple living.

Some African Americans found positions of surprising strength in this contest for self-direction. In the decades surrounding the turn of the twentieth century, black landowners established themselves all over the South, including Hancock. Although forgotten by modern historians, their stories—as well as their contributions to their communities—were considerable.

2

The Other Rural Workers: Landowning and Working for Cash

MANY SHARECROPPERS HOPED that sharecropping would be a transitional stage—a rung on a ladder that would eventually lead to greater economic independence and possibly landownership. It usually didn't work out that way. Mary Worthening's father, a black Hancock County farmer, worked hard his entire life and never progressed beyond sharecropping. According to Worthening, whenever he made a good crop and his prospects rose, a planter would confiscate his crop, leaving him back at the bottom. He moved regularly, hoping to improve his condition, but the rungs kept breaking under his feet. For most, according to rural sociologist Anthony Tang, southern agriculture was a treadmill, not a ladder. Sometimes the agricultural ladder even worked in reverse. Leslie Barksdale's father had to give up working on shares when his wife died. Without enough workers in the family, her father could not secure a contract and was forced to return to wage labor. Nonetheless, by 1910 over two hundred thousand southern African American landowners testified to the real possibility of success. For Calvin Travis's father, the ladder held securely as he climbed it. After renting for a while (the rung next to the top), one good cotton crop put a fair bit of money in his hands, and he purchased a plot of land.[1]

Economic diversity in Hancock meant more than variation in land tenure, significant though that was. Farming brought most Hancock people a place to live and raise their food, but most black and white families made their spending money largely through rural alternatives to farming. Either for a season or a lifetime, women engaged in domestic work and laundering; men, in the lumber and pulpwood industries, moonshining, and artisan trades. By providing cash, these occupations gave many poorer farmers a taste of the consumer culture and prepared them for the time when they would migrate to meet the national market or the market would break into Hancock, as it finally did during World War II.

Landowning: The Independent Farmers

Although most African Americans in the postbellum South remained life-long dependent agricultural laborers, a significant minority successfully navigated the obstacles and rose to landowner status. Historians still do not know much about their origins, how they fared after the decline of southern agriculture, or how effectively their deeds to property helped realize their dreams of freedom.

Independent black farmers have become largely invisible when we imagine the landscape of the American South. If we think of rural African Americans, we usually think only of sharecroppers and wage laborers. If we think of the black middle class, our minds typically turn automatically to the urban centers. To the extent that we indulge these stereotypes, however, our imaginations are overruling our statistics.[2]

Indeed, the statistics are clear. In his groundbreaking book *Black Property Owners in the South*, Loren Schweninger demonstrated that black farmers made impressive gains toward landownership after the Civil War. By 1880 one out of five black southern farmers was a landowner. By 1910 one out of every four black southern farm families owned the land they tilled; in the Upper South an amazing one-half of black farmers owned their land. Given the absence of federally mandated land reform and the resistance of white southerners, their progress forty-five years after emancipation was startling. They made most of this headway into the teeth of the same long agricultural depression that reduced a large portion of the white yeomanry to tenancy. One expects land to concentrate into the hands of the wealthiest when money is scarce. In Hancock, however, the poorest somehow made their most rapid advances during this period. Even though they are now largely forgotten, they were once a significant part of the southern landscape.[3]

But not all regions of the South were equally hospitable to black landowning aspirations. The rise of the rural black middle class progressed much more slowly in the Deep South than it did in the Upper South. Whites in the southernmost curve of the traditional plantation belt seem generally to have been less willing to sell land to African Americans and more willing to do anything necessary to maintain them as dependent agricultural labor. Georgia consistently had the lowest levels of black landholding in the entire

South. In 1910 only 13 percent of the state's black farmers owned land—well below the regional average.[4]

Variation continued within states as well. Black landowners were not evenly distributed across Georgia. Although relatively few African Americans farmed the rolling hills of the state's northern third, many of those who did were able to buy land. They generally prospered there unless molested by jealous white neighbors, who grew increasingly hostile to black landowners as the twentieth century progressed. Black landowners were most densely concentrated in the poor, sandy soil of southern and particularly coastal Georgia. The percentage of black landowners could be quite high in these areas—for example, in the early twentieth century 87 percent of black farmers in coastal McIntosh County owned their own land. The farms tended to be small, however—in McIntosh black-owned farms averaged only forty acres. Furthermore, crops in this area were generally sparse, and the land was not highly valued. Between these two zones lay the once-rich plantation belt. There, as across the South, where the soil offered either wealth or at least the recent memory of wealth, white landowners proved least willing to sell land to black farmers. But there again, a number of African American farming families found a way to landowning status.[5]

Demographically and geographically Hancock is the quintessential plantation-belt county. Whereas Hancock's African Americans made up 70 percent of the county's total population in 1910, tax digests reveal that the 9 percent of Hancock's black farmers who owned land had amassed only 8 percent of the total acreage of Hancock. Nevertheless, those digests also demonstrate great variation among different regions within the county. Militia districts divide Georgia counties into smaller units to facilitate taxation, voting, and census gathering. In one such district in the northern portion of Hancock County, African American farmers owned 26 percent of the farmland. In a nearby district they owned 27 percent. In two districts in the county's center, however, black farmers owned only 3 percent of the total acreage. In another district to the west they came to own only 2 percent of the land. So even within a single county, local rural communities could be more open—or more closed—to black landholding than the county average seems to indicate. In some areas Hancock's black farm owners were isolated and anomalous. In others they formed nearly all-black, self-contained communities of black yeomen. Their personal experiences and their impacts on the surrounding areas differed accordingly.[6]

Independent black southern farmers may well have been the largest group of African Americans to achieve economic security before the Great Migration created a large black middle class in the North. They were certainly the first African Americans to gain middle-class status in Hancock County. As figure 4 shows, the overwhelming majority of households that held assets worth at least six hundred dollars between 1880 and 1900 also owned one hundred or more acres of farmland; their city property, if they had any, was worth less than one hundred dollars. Few of them lived in Sparta, which was the county seat and the only town in Hancock. As indicated by figure 5, the same pattern holds for those who, from 1900 to 1930, owned property valued at three thousand or more dollars. For African Americans living in Hancock County during the late nineteenth and early twentieth centuries, farming provided the most reliable means to achieve economic success.

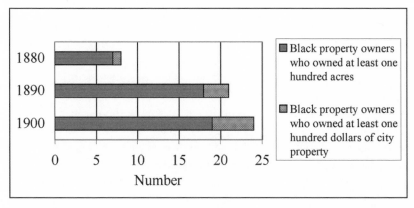

Figure 4. Blacks in Hancock Owning Property Worth over $600 (*source:* Hancock County Tax Digests, Georgia State Archives, Atlanta).

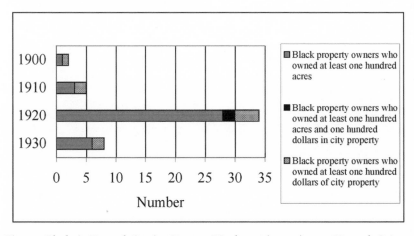

Figure 5. Blacks in Hancock Owning Property Worth over $3,000 (*source:* Hancock County Tax Digests, Georgia State Archives, Atlanta).

Through the nineteenth century the number of Hancock's African American landowners slowly grew. By 1900, 102 families owned more than 7 acres, space for a garden and a small cotton plot. Then, as figure 6 demonstrates, the number leaped to 200 by 1910 and reached 296 in 1920. By 1916 the value of farm acreage owned by African Americans made up more than half of all black wealth in the county. Notably, the families that would reach an elite status of three hundred acres did so by 1920. Although the number of African Americans who owned one hundred acres or less continued to creep upward after the arrival of the boll weevil in 1921, agriculture no longer provided a ladder to more significant wealth. One black landowner born in 1919 said that she believed that most black farmers who owned large estates during her lifetime had come into possession of them through inheritance.[7]

Figure 7 demonstrates that in 1920, at the peak of black landownership in the United States, African Americans owned nearly 34,700 acres of Hancock farmland. This included 212 families who held forty or more acres, 111 of which owned one hundred acres or more. A few owned over a thousand acres. The number owning small holdings of 7 acres or less grew by about 85 per year from 1900 to 1920, after which it continued to grow by about 43 per year until 1950. Most of these were homeowners with one- or two-acre yards.[8]

Statistics can show that black landowners were present even in Georgia's plantation belt, but one must turn to other sources to examine the human experience of landowning. We have come to know a great deal about the forces that kept most black families from purchasing land, yet we know relatively

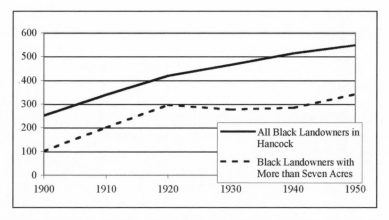

Figure 6. Number of Black Landowners in Hancock, 1900–1950 (*source:* Hancock County Tax Digests, Georgia Historical Archive, Atlanta).

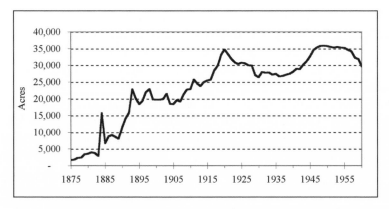

Figure 7. Black-Owned Farm Acreage in Hancock, 1875–1960 (*source:* Hancock County Tax Digests, Georgia State Archives, Atlanta).

little about the means by which some black families successfully navigated the many obstacles to landownership. Although no single story is representative of the whole, the family history of the Huberts from Hancock suggests some of the ways that one family successfully met these challenges.

Three brothers—Zach, Floyd, and David Hubert—were among the first African Americans to purchase sizable tracts of farmland in the county. Their family had entered freedom with a parting gift from the white Warren County family who had owned them but still recognized them as cousins. A bale of cotton allowed the Huberts to begin as well-supplied renters. Soon they prepared to reach for full agricultural autonomy. In 1871 they approached a white lawyer named Burke who had recently moved to Hancock and had purchased a plantation for speculative purposes. He agreed to sell the Huberts an undeveloped, rocky, and forested section in the northern part of the county. Without better options, the brothers agreed to a high price on a short (three-year) payment schedule and went to work. After putting up a simple log cabin, the Huberts began clearing the land. According to the family story, they worked ceaselessly from sunup to sundown. Additionally, they made themselves as self-sufficient as they could to avoid further debt and to direct all income toward the debt. Together, they raised the agreed upon sum within the time required. But sweat brought no equity. When they asked for the deed, the lawyer refused to sign it over, stating that the contract had been signed without witnesses and that he would not honor it. For two years the brothers then rented the land they had already purchased until they located another white lawyer in an adjoining county who agreed to try to compel Burke to honor the contract. The threat of legal action induced Burke to sign over the deed. Afterward the brothers split up the acreage they had earned together and succeeded separately as landowners. One, Zach, eventually acquired over a thousand acres of land.[9]

The Hubert story includes a few themes that recur in the stories that other black landowning families told about their means of ascent. First, individuals stood a better chance of success if they banded together to pool resources. In other parts of Hancock, too, adult brothers joined forces to purchase land together.[10]

Second, white landowners often sold only marginal or undeveloped land to African Americans. Mary Hunt's grandfather was Steve Warren, one of the most successful black landowners in the county. His holdings were scattered about because, according to Hunt, he could only buy and rent "bad land that no one wanted and wasn't going to use." Many of these tracts were irregularly sized and needed to be cleared of trees. She remembers that her grandfather and father "had to go far from home" to work these plots. Hancock's Emmie Mae Harper remembered her father saying that he had approached two white landowners about pieces of land for sale along roads, but "the whites wouldn't let him have them." Instead he found an isolated, unwanted piece of land in the southern part of the county and purchased it. Harper added that her father built a road to his land, using a spade to do so, after which he began to farm it. These isolated 107 acres turned out to be so sandy that Harper's mother was unable to grow a flower garden until her father carried in loads of dirt from elsewhere. Yet somehow that sorry soil nurtured the Harper family's independence. Many other black farmers also started the race for meaningful agricultural independence with this handicap, hobbled by unproductive hardscrabble.[11]

The northern fourth of Hancock County is hilly land, with rocks scattered about: neither hardscrabble nor prime farmland.[12] In this area—around Springfield, Powelton, and Mt. Zion—black farmers had the greatest success in obtaining titles to land. A few large planters lived in this area, but mostly the planters had settled on the richer, less rocky soil that spread through the center of the county. This northern section was farmed mainly by white yeomen, people who turned out a strong Populist vote in the 1890s. Side by side these black and white middling farmers derived a decent living from land that the big planters had passed by.[13]

The third recurring theme in the stories of black landowners in Hancock County is that of working extraordinarily hard to become economically self-sufficient and free from the danger of debt. In his classic study of adjacent

Greene County, Arthur Raper concurred that "the Negro owner is as near a live-at-home farmer as one finds in the Black Belt." All the black landowners I interviewed in Hancock mentioned self-sufficiency. Emmie Mae Harper remembered that her black landowning father had to plow with oxen, but still the Harpers raised enough food on the farm to provide, in her father's words, "all they needed and some of what they wanted." An extensive garden, corn, cattle, hogs, chickens, wheat, rye, potatoes, and even sorghum cane for tea cakes and ginger cakes kept the family well fed: "We didn't know nothing in the world about the grocery store." Harper's mother cared for the garden and made all the family clothing by hand—including undergarments. But their success in keeping the market at arm's length may have taken a toll on her, and she died in her forties. As Harper observed, "She was too busy to live."[14]

Fourth, this culture of personalism required prospective black landowners to have some support from white patrons. African Americans needed white assistance to navigate a system that was intentionally studded with legal and illegal barriers to black landownership. In 1927 Arthur Raper began his sociological study of Greene County. He found that "a most exacting and highly selective procedure" barred most black farmers from landownership. Raper wrote that black would-be landowners needed "a white sponsor" who would take their part before the white community. Usually these sponsors were men who had long experience with the would-be buyer, so the business transaction was "based on a personal equation." Among blacks who had purchased plots in Greene County, 90 percent had done so from white men. Of these, Raper found, 60 percent had bought their land from former landlords. Most of the remaining 40 percent bought their land from white merchants or money lenders with whom they had done business. In many of these cases, the sale of land appears to have been a reward for years of steady, productive labor. Furthermore, at least in Greene County, Raper found that the parcels purchased through these somewhat paternalistic ties were in fertile land, although they were usually not very large.[15]

Sometimes highly personal relationships—interracial kinship ties— smoothed an African American family's path to landownership. In 1885 one of the wealthiest white men in Hancock County, David Dickson, willed his entire estate (worth between half a million and one million dollars) to his interracial daughter, Amanda America Dixon. Although several other white fathers in the area willed large properties to "nonwhite" descendants, such aid was usually not made so publicly. Yet even small gifts from white family members could prove significant. Gordon Dixon, the "mulatto" son of a white planter, received only a little seed money and the use of a small plot of land and a house shortly after the Civil War. With herculean efforts Dixon and his wife made that small gift the first rung of a ladder that eventually reached a 2,000-acre estate. Six of the nine largest black landowners in Hancock County in 1910, including the five wealthiest, had made their start with assistance from white kin. The mulatto elite was not, after all, named for nothing.[16]

The other requirement for potential black landowners—and according to Arthur Raper, the most important one—was that they "be acceptable to the white community." Raper found that Greene County in the 1920s and 1930s was somewhat removed from the abstract logic of the market, which dictates that a person who wishes to sell something will sell to anyone who meets his price. Raper found that "just because a white man has land for sale does not mean that a Negro, even the one most liked and respected by him, can buy it even if he has the money." In the personal culture of the South, a white landowner had to be mindful of possible community sanctions that he might face if he sold land to a black farmer whom his white neighbors viewed as lazy, improvident, or unmindful of "his place."

Accordingly, black landowners had to constantly guard against appearing to transgress the boundaries that local whites constructed around the "proper place" for blacks. But displaying one's acceptability was no easy task. Many economically privileged African Americans hoped to gain white acceptance by showing that they could maintain the strictest standards of the Victorian ideal. They carefully cultivated the middle-class image of formal neatness in dress and home, self-discipline, education, unemotional religiosity, and a public display of commercial consumption.[17]

Some of these symbols of middle-class acceptability, however, could themselves draw resentment from some whites, who viewed them as marks of "uppitiness." Possibly fearful that whites would resent him for displaying these symbols, one of Hancock's wealthiest black men of the 1920s and 1930s, Sherman Ingram, regularly went to town wearing tattered and patched clothing and riding in a cart humbly pulled by oxen. Although he did not assume such exaggerated deference, Zach Hubert, too, appears to have been painfully aware that his "independent" position constantly rested on his willingness to humble himself before white neighbors. On several occasions late in the nineteenth century and early in the twentieth, he accepted verbal abuse from whites without responding in kind. He took care not to undercut white competitors at his grocery store. He did not demand payment from a white neighbor when the neighbor's mule trampled his corn, although that same neighbor had earlier demanded and received payment when Hubert's hogs got into his sweet potatoes. Once, when his sons sat down to dinner at the family picnic table beside a white crew that Hubert had hired to thresh his wheat, the white men left enraged. As soon as he heard of the event, Hubert immediately tracked them down to apologize and pay them extra to return. Later Hubert learned that the crew foreman was a Klan leader from Greene County and thought it likely that his house would have been burned had he not quickly assumed a submissive position. Although his lengthy obituary in the *Sparta Ishmaelite* suggested that he was well respected by Hancock whites, Zach Hubert's actions imply that he understood his economic security ultimately rested on his ability to reassure surrounding whites that he did not pose a challenge to their supremacy.[18]

Sometimes black landowners could be pinned between competing social demands: the demand to behave in a way appropriate to "their place" and the demand to be neighborly. This negotiation was especially complicated given that local geography created various configurations of dependent and independent whites and dependent and independent blacks. Local experience could shatter the "normative" stereotypes of race and class identity. In areas where poor whites and blacks lived near one another, it was understood that whiteness did not guarantee social or economic success. Conversely, those who lived near black landowners or well-off renters understood that blackness did not guarantee degradation. The realities of interpersonal exchanges within the rural culture of neighborly assistance gave the Hunt family a memorable experience of contradictory rural social expectations.

In the 1920s a very poor white family from Winder, in north Georgia, came to Hancock to sharecrop, hoping to improve their condition. They began working on a farm adjacent to the fairly prosperous farm that the Hunts rented. When an elderly member of the white family died, they were embarrassed to host their own family for the funeral, ashamed that their miserable furnishings would reveal their lack of success. Their black neighbors heard of their plight and decided to help. Katie Hunt recalled: "We moved our furniture in their house, took the rugs off our floor, put our stove in there, along with our dining room table. Then we furnished them food for the funeral." The white family was literally borrowing symbols of economic status from their black neighbors. Although it did not protect them from all the humiliations visited on African Americans living in the plantation belt under white supremacy, their economic status certainly gave the Hunt family an unconventional experience of the white supremacist South.[19]

The Hunts' story underscores the complexity of race and class relations in rural Hancock, but the majority of black landowners apparently did not display their wealth so openly. Most of them watched carefully lest they irritate white neighbors by appearing to step out of their "place."

Thus, through continual watchfulness, great sacrifice, hard work, connections, and a bit of luck, a number of black farmers raised themselves to the position of independent farmers. But how meaningful was their independence? Certainly African American landowning families enjoyed distinct advantages over dependent farmers. In 1915 Roy Roberts was born into a black family that owned thirty acres—and rented more—just beyond the northern boundary of Hancock. He recognized that a position of economic power supported his family in their relationships with whites. "Most black people hired themselves out to whites," remembered Roberts. "If they said, 'Get up at six o'clock and go to work,' they had to get up. If they said, 'Fifty cents a day,' that's all they got. But we didn't have to get up for nobody, because we were home. We had our own land—our own everything—and it made a difference. It made a difference."[20]

As the story of Katie Hunt's refusal to withdraw her children from summer school indicates (see pp. 13–14), black renters shared with landowners a considerable degree of independence from white control. The independent black farmers whom I interviewed spoke often and casually of the importance of choice in their lives. They determined the crops to be planted and the amounts, and they often devoted larger portions of their land to food crops than did sharecroppers. Although they worked quite hard, they had unquestioned control over their own work rhythms. Whereas sharecroppers were sometimes required to patronize commissaries operated by their landlords—and to accept the inflated prices and high interest rates they sometimes charged—black landowners decided where to buy supplies. They also decided where to sell their farm products and took their crops to market themselves, relieved of the need to trust a landlord's honesty at the settle. All in all, they managed their own finances and so enjoyed the fruits of their labor. Finally—a matter of no small importance—they decided when their children should work and when they should attend school.[21]

In fact, the children of Hancock's black landowners generally attended school longer than did the children of sharecroppers, black or white. Until the late 1930s African American students generally progressed no further than fourth grade, but the landowners' children usually received six years, the average for white children in the county. Often they received more. This state of affairs derived not only from the black landowners' relative independence from white control but also from a purely economic consideration. The state rarely subsidized the costs of education until the late nineteenth century, and it only gradually assumed the burden of cost through the first half of the twentieth century, first for whites and later for blacks. Until around 1930 "public" black schools were more or less privately supported. Accordingly, few rural African American southerners could afford to educate their children. Landowners could better afford to bear the costs of education, which included not only tuition and book expenses but also the cost of forgoing the student's labor, so essential to the survival of poor families.

Because of this, landowners were more likely than other African Americans to encourage their children's attendance all the way through high school. This was no easy commitment. Because no bus system for blacks operated in rural Georgia before the 1940s, and few families could afford to use a draft animal to transport their children to school, rural high-school students were usually sent to board in town or at rural Rosenwald schools. Again, access to education depended on a degree of financial independence.[22]

There were other benefits attendant on landowning status. Independent rural African Americans—a status landowners shared with renters, tradespeople, self-employed lumber workers, and even professional moonshiners—escaped many of the dangers and humiliations experienced by dependent laborers. The women of these families less frequently sought work as domestics, removing them from a sexually dangerous position in which many black women were exploited. They could sometimes afford cars and with them the expanding semiegalitarian rights and courtesies of the road. Furthermore, although independent black men across the South sometimes faced harassment, arson, and even lynching specifically because whites envied their privileged position, lynching victims were disproportionately poorer men.[23]

Black landowners also had a distinctive experience of Jim Crow segregation. When they rode to town, they may have felt the sting of segregation more sharply than did black sharecroppers. They possessed the funds but not the skin color that would admit them to restaurants, theaters, motels, and the better seats on trains. Additionally, when encountering whites they were subject to the same ritualized disrespect—in such things as terms of address and expected posture—as were all other African Americans. Because of this, some black landowners spoke of having limited their trips to town, going there only to purchase supplies they could not produce on their own. With pride as well as thrift to motivate them, many black landowning families became quite adept at supplying their own needs for both goods and recreation.

Self-sufficiency could emerge at the community level, too, with black

neighbors banding together to assist one another in attaining a more meaningful independence, one that undergirded a strong sense of pride. Samuel
Williams of Hancock said that the rural black community in which he grew
up during the 1930s contained everything he needed: a black-owned grocery
store, an excellent high school, a church with a dynamic preacher, and even
a community swimming pool. Because of this, Williams claimed, he was
sheltered from the scarring effects of the caste system.[24]

Sometimes black landowners testified that their wealth gave them power
and material comfort relative to their white neighbors. Zach Hubert loaned
money to his white neighbors. At least two Hancock landowning African
American families contracted with white agricultural wage laborers. These
landlords stated that they had no problems with the white workers themselves. Nonetheless, they did not contract with them often, lest their white
neighbors think they were forgetting their place. In terms of material wealth
and creature comfort, many of Hancock's black landowning families seem
to have realized their dreams.[25]

Nevertheless, although they could often gain economic security, offer
their children a chance at real educations, and (if they chose) retire into
their private worlds to reduce the public insult of Jim Crow, their privileged
economic status did not translate into political power. A small number of
black landowners continued voting through the twentieth century, but most
were disfranchised along with the poorest sharecroppers by the "progressive"
legislation passed at the turn of the century. Landed African Americans did
not always live in the world of white supremacy. Neither could they always
retire to the private enclaves they created. Like other African Americans in
Hancock, they lived within the limits set by their social context and their
own personal resources. Theirs, ultimately, was a compromised, although
privileged, position.

Wage Labor

Besides the landowners and the various kinds of tenants, a third group of
cotton farmers worked in Hancock. Wage laborers occupied a different kind
of ambiguous position. First of all, theirs was temporary work in two senses.
Most wage laborers were young people who had not yet built the social capital
or raised the family of children that would fit them to work on shares. Early in
their lives they would not yet have the labor available to run a forty-acre farm.
Until they did, most young people in Hancock worked for wages. Wage labor

was also temporary work in the seasonal sense. The demand for wage laborers exploded during the chopping and picking seasons and shrank during the winter. Some tenants worked part of the year as wage laborers. Sharecroppers, renters, and even landowners who had completed a phase of work on their own crop often contracted to work with farmers who had not yet done so. By chopping cotton by the hour or day and picking cotton at so much per hundred pounds, these farmers could supplement their incomes.[26]

Wage labor differed from other kinds of farmwork in another significant way as well. It was the only kind of agricultural work guaranteed to produce cash—albeit not much, for the wages were usually low. The pay for chopping cotton ranged from fifty cents per day during the Depression to one or even two dollars per day after World War II. Landowners, renters, and sharecroppers all gambled, with widely varying odds, on making good money when the cotton crop came in, but wage laborers knew that they could not possibly make much money. Nonetheless, these agricultural workers did carry home some cash each day or week. Some African American farmers saw this as a considerable advantage over other forms of agriculture. All other farmers, including landowners, saw cash only once a year, if at all. Because of this, Josie Mae Ingram stated that "working by the day . . . was better than shares."[27]

Yet working wages had drawbacks. Of all agricultural occupations, wage labor offered the least autonomy during the working day. Wage laborers reported to the planter or the overseer early in the morning and were given their daily assignments. They usually worked under the eye of a white person who set the pace of labor. They took their noon break together in response to the tolling of the bell. As they worked, they came in contact with whites much more frequently than did other kinds of farmers, and they were expected to display ritual deference to them. Although the regular money was no doubt attractive, the fact that so few African Americans made careers out of wage labor suggests how unpleasant they found these other aspects of the work.

Nonagricultural Labor

Cotton was the region's primary cash crop, but it was not always the means by which dependent farmers in Hancock earned money. Their contracts often gave them only houses in which to live and ground on which to grow food crops and raise livestock. Most of the slim profits from the cotton crop would not end up in their pockets. To bring in cash, most rural people in Hancock turned at some time to alternative rural industries.

Domestic Work

From week to week women provided the primary source of income for rural African American families. In the first decades of the twentieth century nearly one-third of black Georgians worked in domestic labor. Only farming provided more jobs.[28] Many women entered and left this work throughout life according to their needs for cash. Some girls began this work while they were still in school. For many, the work remained part-time, something fitted around the rest of their lives. Frequently women from sharecropping families earned extra money by performing domestic work in the landowner's house after they had finished working in the fields. For other women, this work established the primary shapes of their lives.

Domestic workers earned very low wages, probably the lowest in Hancock. So little was paid that all but the poorest white families could afford to employ a black domestic at least part-time. As a girl in the early 1930s, Oline Thomas earned $3.75 per week working after school for a white family. This was on the high end. Other women earned only around three dollars per week. Some domestics received leftover food, secondhand clothes and furniture, and other gifts. Sometimes these "gifts" substituted for pay.[29]

Some rural women specialized in laundry, work they could do in their own homes. During the Depression Josie Mae Ingram's mother used to boil clothes in lye, rinse them in bluing, hang them to dry, and fold and iron them—all for thirty cents per bundle. Ed Jones's mother earned only twenty-five cents per load during the same years.[30]

Women in the cities could make better wages than could those in the rural areas. In fact, they could often make better wages than their husbands could, for men had far fewer job opportunities in cities. During the 1930s Mary Hunt found domestic work in Milledgeville at four dollars per week. Later she moved to New York, where pay ranged from four to ten dollars per week. North or South, however, the wages for domestic work never supported more than a very simple living. Even after World War II defense plants raised wages generally in the South, work designated as "black women's work" remained grossly underpaid. Mary Wilson remembered that through the 1950s she still made only ten dollars per week working from seven in the morning until five at night at Sparta's white high school.[31]

Families often got by with the little extra money domestic workers earned, but the work required hard sacrifices from women, especially mothers. Mary Wilson got up at 4:30 A.M. on schooldays to cook breakfast for her family. Then she walked to school, arriving by seven. She lit five fireplaces and spent the day cleaning. In the evening she worked for a teacher, cleaning house and washing clothes. At ten the teacher drove her home, where she often found her children asleep. Older children often cared for younger siblings when mothers had to work such hours. When Mary Hunt found domestic work in Milledgeville, she had an elderly neighbor watch her children.[32]

Domestic work involved more intimate contact with whites than did any other form of black labor. In the worst settings it created situations personally abusive and fraught with the threat of rape. For this reason black landowners often did not allow their daughters to work as domestics. In the best settings black women and white families apparently arrived at cordial, mutually satisfactory, and sometimes lifelong relationships, although the unequal power within these relationships makes it difficult to assess them.[33]

Lumbering and Sawmilling

As domestic work did for women, lumber work followed farming as the second most common work for men. It was the most reliable way for a man to bring home cash. Like domestic work, lumbering and sawmilling were flexible jobs. A few men chose careers in migrating lumber camps, sometimes in or around Hancock, sometimes far away. Far more men, however, pursued it at some time in the off-season, as in the famous example of Alabama's Ned Cobb.[34]

The original old-growth oak and hickory forest of the piedmont belt had been logged out as cotton acreage expanded in the antebellum period. The first generation of cotton planters had worn down their soil's fertility and allowed the thin topsoil to wash away, leaving gullies and the exposed mineral subsoil for posterity. As fields became unprofitable, farmers abandoned them. Pine, it turned out, is the only crop ideally suited to grow in clay and sand, so periodically these fields filled in with voluntary second-growth pine, which was harvested as it matured. Though unsystematic, this approach gave regular work to a swarm of small, mobile "peckerwood" sawmills.[35]

This pattern of casual lumbering changed with the devastation wrought by the boll weevil. In neighboring Greene County sociologist Arthur Raper found that the weevil had forced many of that county's landowners to turn to their timber stands as a hedge against disaster.[36] A county study done by the Bureau of Agricultural Economics in 1935 reported that in Greene the lumber business had been the county's main support from 1919 until 1933, employing 1,300 men in one hundred small sawmills and six planing mills.

By 1935 the timber was "exhausted," and only ten mills were still in operation. Two 1935 studies on other nearby counties, Jones and Jenkins, found that the timber was "totally exhausted" in one and much reduced in the other.[37] Similar circumstances appear to have led to a razing of the woods in Hancock as well. Solomon Harper, from a black landowning family, remembered that his father began hauling lumber to Devereux to raise funds when the boll weevil came and reduced their usual eight to ten bales of cotton to only one-half a bale. In 1930 Hancock's black agricultural extension agent reported that little timber remained to be harvested, "as most of it has been used by the sawmills in the past five years."[38] A more foresighted approach, cultivating pine as a replenishable crop, would not arrive in the area for several years.

In a way the boll weevil caused the transition from the piedmont's traditional cotton economy to the managed forest economy that emerged after World War II. When the weevil cut Georgia's cotton production by 45 percent in 1921, tenants and owners alike abandoned the land.[39] Hancock suffered a 37 percent reduction in its number of farms during the 1920s. This trend continued into the early years of the Great Depression. In 1930 Georgia led the country in the number of abandoned farms: 65,000 in one year.[40] Although the onset of a national depression soon halted the mass emigration from rural areas, it did not repopulate abandoned farms. New Deal reports note that the soil, as well as the housing, on such tracts was too poor to attract tenant families.[41] So once more old cotton fields sprouted new pine forests. Forest planners would build on this haphazard beginning in the following decades. During the 1930s the Civilian Conservation Corps planted pine seedlings on public and private land across the South, including in Hancock. Then, when Georgia chemists learned how to manufacture southern pine into paper pulp in the late 1930s, huge new paper mills sprang up, creating a new rural industry and spreading a new creed of sustainable forest management. By 1960 almost every acre of Hancock bristled with pine. In the years since then a few highly mechanized professional lumber crews have replaced the thousands of traditional cotton farmers. Lumbering has become a full-time occupation for a few in contemporary Hancock, but it grew from much more democratic roots.

Before 1950 young men, who lacked the family they would need to work on shares, often spent time in the woods to pick up folding money. Carlton Morse remembered watching men riding on trucks piled high with lumber while he was working in a cotton field in the mid-1930s. "It looked cooler," he said, but he "found it was hard." Morse worked at a sawmill during his last two years of high school and used the money to pay for college. Besides giving them the chance to earn money, labor in the lumber industry offered young men admission to a masculine subculture. Benjamin Senior went to the sawmills in 1937, when he was seventeen years old. In the country, he said, "boys all got to brag about who's the best man. If you can't sawmill, well . . . you ain't no man." So young men, eager to prove their strength and manhood, often spent a "couple years" in the business. The camps involved hard work but could be an interesting break from the tedium of cotton cultivation on a family farm. According to Marshall Boyer, lumber and sawmill work was fun. He said you would "get with a bunch of fellas, laughing and talking and doing your work all day." Eugene Foster Jr. also remembered the camaraderie of living in abandoned houses with fifteen or twenty other men ranging in age from fifteen to fifty. "They didn't ask about age," he said, as long as you could do the work. Foster laughed, noting that the blues musician B. B. King had made the lumber camps' hard-living aspect famous. To Foster it was an adventure—better than farming and better paying.[42]

Mary Hunt remembered that her husband had made from eight to fourteen dollars per week working in sawmills in the late 1920s. She noted that $14 per week was "the same as wages in New York at that time" and that it would go a lot farther in the South. Sawmill wages seem to have held steady through the following decade. In 1935 a New Deal report stated that sawmill workers in Greene County earned around ten cents per hour for a fourteen-hour day, about three times what wage laborers earned on farms. Hancock's Benjamin Senior described a higher pay scale in place for pulpwood workers in the late 1930s and 1940s. On the crews with which he worked, sawyers and truck drivers made $2.25 per load; limbers, $2.00. They could haul four or five loads per day, using a four-man crew for small logs and a five-man crew for large ones. Working a six-day week under optimum conditions, then, skilled pulpwood workers could make from $54 to $67 per week; unskilled workers, from $48 to $60. Sharecroppers often didn't clear that much in a year. Years later Eugene Foster left Hancock to go to work at a sawmill in Athens, intending to get away for only a couple of weeks. He stayed on for two years. "You'd get home with twenty-five dollars," he said, "and thought you was rich."[43]

Although black men could earn more money by lumbering and sawmilling than by working in the cotton fields, they also seemed to spend the money they made there more quickly. This was partly because of their dependence on "store-bought" food, having no time and sometimes no land to devote to gardening. In the lumber camps the food that the lumber boss provided was deducted from their wages. In addition, the culture of the lumbercamps fostered spendthrift behavior, as do other work cultures created by young men toiling in exhausting and dangerous industries. Lumber workers lived in a masculine culture that glorified risk taking and the pleasures of Saturday night. Much of what they earned during the week was dissipated in liquor at blind tigers and at the gambling campfires. When Benjamin Senior lost all his week's wages in one night of gambling, he resolved simply to watch other lumber workers stake their earnings from then on. He remembered three different games played simultaneously at an isolated spot by the railroad tracks, with stakes ranging from cheap to truly expensive by Depression terms. "Gamblers would work the lower ones to get money to enter the big one." With the big game allowing bets of up to fifteen dollars on the first round, young men could lose their week's pay in a hurry. A parallel culture existed among Hancock's all-white quarrymen. Although they were the best-paid manual workers in the county at one dollar per hour, these white men also ran through their money as soon as they got it—in response to the high mortality rate caused by their dangerous work.[44]

Most Hancock men reported working only on racially homogeneous crews cutting lumber and hauling it to the mills. The lumber camps themselves were usually all white or all black, except for the sawyers, who were often white. One white sawmill operator reported: "Crews would fight and fuss if they were racially integrated. Crews would have to be all black or all white."[45]

Moonshining

Although official documents list farming, domestic work, and lumbering as the only substantial occupations in Hancock, there was a fourth. Moonshiners reported neither their occupation to the census taker nor their yearly earnings to the tax man. Their professional activities were chronicled only in court records and the newspaper. The *Sparta Ishmaelite* reported, sometimes at weekly intervals, the names of black and white men arrested as moonshiners. And no wonder. Selling bootleg whiskey, especially before the repeal of Prohibition in 1933, was the most lucrative profession a poor man could enter. In testimony in Sparta's court records, moonshine was valued at one dollar per quart in 1915. Some entrepreneurs tried to push the market's envelope; in Hancock's last flush year before the weevil, Bishop Reddock reportedly was asking $2.75 per pint at a juke joint. Bootlegging was also the easiest and least taxing work available.[46]

In the early 1940s, as a boy of fourteen, one white man asked one of the county's biggest black bootleggers, Laf Ingram, to set him up with a still.

"Does your daddy know?" Ingram asked.

"No."

"No."

The boy made himself a little still anyway, and when word got around, the black man made him a pure copper still, on credit, so that he would not poison anyone with bad moonshine. He hid it in the woods and carefully tended it. He regularly concealed his product in bushes by a dirt road, and a man in a car would stop, pick up the booze, and leave a fold of bills. Today the man can still rattle off the recipe he used as a boy: a peck of meal, a bale of sugar (equaling six gallons), and a double handful of Red Lion hog feed (for hops), all cooked in a 55-gallon drum. The recipe made six gallons of liquor, called a case. The sugar cost $12 per bale, and the rest of the ingredients cost $1.50. He could sell a case for $35, and he was turning out ten cases per week, so he was soon making real money. When his father found out what he was doing, he made the boy destroy the still. Nevertheless, the money he made paid off many family bills that year. Clearly, if a boy could earn that much money, the real professionals earned much more. To a degree, then, moonshine freed Hancock people from the constraints of their rural, low-wage economy. They sold some locally and in nearby cities such as Atlanta and Augusta, and shipped some to northern cities. It was the only finished product of consequence that Hancock ever produced.[47]

Some bootleggers operated on a massive scale. In 1921 John Simmons was caught with a two-hundred-gallon still and two or three thousand gallons of fermenting corn mash ready to run. One white man whose parents ran a rural general store remembered a black moonshiner named Harper, who would purchase sugar by the truckload. He recounted: "[I] saw Tit Harper count out Dad $2,000, $3,000 at a lick." But many worked stills on a temporary basis. One black man used moonshining to raise enough money to buy his first mule so that he could move from sharecropping to renting. Some quit after close brushes with the law. The county is full of hilarious anecdotes of how uncle so-and-so just barely escaped discovery by the sheriff. The manufacture and sale of alcohol were eventually legalized in 1933, yet to this day the taste for old-fashioned, untaxed corn liquor maintains a demand for moonshiners, who are still pursued by officers of the law.[48]

The moonshiners were a rough crowd. Beyond the protections and restraints of legal businesses, and hunted by law-enforcement officers, they lived lives that could be marked by violent encounters. Living outside conventional society seemed to loosen bootleggers' attachment to other customs as well. One black ex-farmer, Gaston Skrine, remembered two extended interracial families near Linton that ran large moonshine operations, branches of the Harpers and the Boyers. "If you bothered one Boyer," Skrine recalled, "you done bothered all the Boyers. They'd stick together, white and black." These interracial families were even known to take on the law in defense of their own. Once, when one was jailed, other family members reportedly broke him out. Booze and the money it brought did bring people together. In 1919 Hancock's grand jury expressed "amazement and shock" that "some who suppose themselves belonging to a higher social stratum allow themselves to be dragged down by thirst for strong drink into association" with lower-class black and white bootleggers. According to the grand jurors, some of Hancock's elites would "buy and drink" and even "transport their illicit product."[49]

Trades and Crafts

A number of men and women found smaller nonagricultural niches in the rural economy. Many of these were trades that African American slaves had dominated in the antebellum period: carpentry, masonry, and blacksmithing. Freedom did not deprive these men of their know-how, but it did sometimes remove their opportunities to apply it. In the recurring depressions of the late nineteenth century, many poor white men came to resent competition from black craftsmen. They appealed to racial solidarity and sometimes employed violence to push black men out of many of these positions. Although there is no positive evidence that this happened in Hancock, it may have, and it certainly did in many other places.[50]

Nonetheless, a number of black men continued to work as tradesmen in rural Hancock. Willie Butts, born in 1921, followed his father, grandfather, and great-grandfather into carpentry, and Solomon Harper learned carpentry, masonry, and blacksmithing from his father. But a few began new traditions. Asia Jackson, the son of renting farmers, literally taught himself carpentry by closely examining standing structures. At the age of seventeen he built his parents a barn.

Men could pursue carpentry throughout the year, but a number of seasonal trades existed as well. Benjamin Senior left school in the seventh grade to help his family by working for an independent rural black couple near Devereux. Under Mit and Rose Wallace, Senior learned to thresh peas and to butcher hogs and cattle for the couple's meat market. Mit Wallace also taught him how to make wooden shingles with a saw and a hammer and broad chisel. Besides observing Wallace run these businesses, Senior also watched him haul guano, soda, livestock, and wheat in his truck. A couple of rural black families even came to own country stores or cotton gins. One man, Pry Rainwater, made money trapping wild animals and selling the hides. Some black men, such as Solomon Harper, cooked sugarcane or sorghum for syrup. These men would usually have farmers carry the cane to their places, but for large canefields they would haul their equipment to the site.[51]

Although they served both black and white customers, black tradesmen faced special tensions when dealing with white purchasers. As Solomon Harper remembered, it could be difficult to collect from whites. A black man did not have much leverage—especially considering that he did not dare try to use the law to collect debts against whites. The conspicuous autonomy achieved by black store and gin owners could be especially precarious in a white supremacist world. One man had his gin burned by a white competitor. Another, Zach Hubert, the owner of a country store, feared that his place would be burned if white store owners found him too threatening. When his son, James, who was studying at Atlanta Baptist College, suggested that he lower prices and discontinue markups for goods bought on credit, he replied, "I don't want my place in ashes."[52] Hard-working and ambitious black families always had to consider the balance between security in a capitalist economy as defined by financial success and security in a white supremacist society as defined by "appropriate" deferential behavior.

These businesses and industries yielded Hancock's rural people the small amounts of cash they used to supplement the subsistence economy that supported their lives. According to Marshall Boyer, "You could live off five dollars per week and what you raised on the farm." These early experiences in earning cash eased rural Hancock people toward the future, because World War II brought an expansion of high-wage public work within the national commercial economy and a contraction of local subsistence economies—even in rural Hancock. As the traditional economy of rural Hancock crumbled under these new market forces, other unique cultural and social aspects of the county began to change as well, making Hancock increasingly similar to Atlanta or Chicago politically and educationally, as well as in its patterns of social race relations. Hancock became more democratic, more bureaucratic, more segregated, and less marked by interracial violence. The rest of this study will examine these cultural and social aspects of race relations in Hancock County from the early twentieth century through their transformation around World War II.[53]

3

Beyond Segregation: The Outlines of Interracial Social Relations in Rural Hancock

RACE RELATIONS IN rural Hancock County contrast sharply with our dominant image of a solidly segregated South. There, in the 1920s, it was possible to participate in an interracial social world. Children and adults could find interracial company in which to play sports, fish, hunt, or talk. On Sundays, and especially during week-long revivals in the late summer and fall, one could attend white churches with black visitors or black churches with white visitors. One might expect to participate in neighborly assistance networks irrespective of race in times of sickness, injury, or death.

How could this interracial social world exist in the Deep South at the height of Jim Crow segregation? The answer involves the area's rural nature, for segregation was a system of social control first developed in the cities to maintain white supremacy within the social structure particular to cities and towns. The physical separation of black from white bodies in all public spaces maintained caste divisions in an anonymous society. Backed by law-enforcement officers, segregation codes operated impersonally and uniformly to maintain African Americans in a conspicuous second-class status. But segregation was not designed with rural spaces in mind.

Modern people misplace their imaginings of the rural South by filling them with settings and spaces, such as restaurants and train stations, that are proper only to towns and cities. Neither they nor the segregation codes that applied to them existed in the rural areas. Segregation simply did not fit well with the economy, geography, and cultural traditions of the rural South. The plantation structure, growing out of slavery, brought black and white people into regular close contact with one another. From slavery the postbellum rural South also inherited a culture of personalism and localism, which continued to be reinforced by the broken geography and poor transportation that characterized these spaces well into the twentieth century. In isolated rural neighborhoods individuals and groups created many significantly differing patterns of race relations in the twentieth century. Finally, over the centuries black and white rural southerners constructed a shared culture that continued to draw them together for recreation and worship.

The absence of segregation, however, need not suggest the presence of integration. Black and white people did not interact as equals, however intimate their interactions. Indeed, a continuing clarity about racial subordination and asymmetry may have enabled the intimacy common to many rural areas to surpass that found in the more ambiguous space of the cities. The remembered experience of race relations in the rural South needs to be considered as a separate mode of interracial interaction, one for which there as yet seems to be no handy term. Without challenging white supremacy—indeed, while supporting it—rural race relations before World War II were marked not by physical distance but by physical proximity and intimacy.[1]

In rural Hancock the "traditional" social code for race relations was reshaped into many different permutations, some apparently purely personal and idiosyncratic but others generalized into patterns widely shared in specific social contexts. Sometimes the social rules were redefined to highlight the symbolic value of a particular space (inside a house or in a woods), a bodily posture (sitting or standing), or an age (childhood or young adulthood). Clearly, many unspoken rules and conventions shaped the behavior of rural Hancock people. Unlike the modern, systematic, and impersonal rules of segregation that regulated the racial order in towns, however, the rural codes reflected "premodern," personalized sensibilities. Where the urban racial boundaries were delineated by a tightly manicured hedge, boundaries in the rural context were marked by a sprawling thicket.

C. Vann Woodward, the founding voice of modern southern history, revealed in 1955 that this urban hedge was a recent planting, indisputably in the legal sense and to a still-debated degree in the cultural and social senses. Segregation has a history. It was a political response to changing social conditions, not an ahistorical natural reaction to immutable biology. Over the decades students and critics of Woodward have added nuance to this original vision. Leon Litwack demonstrated that segregation began in the antebellum North. Richard C. Wade found signs of it in antebellum southern cities, and Joel Williamson and Howard Rabinowitz dissected its dense penetration of the postbellum urban South. Recently John Cell, Charles Van Onselen, and

Grace Elizabeth Hale have identified this expanding segregationist movement as a quintessential child of modernity.[2]

The modern impulse, which may have peaked at the turn of the twentieth century, is to impose order first theoretically and then actually, to make the crooked straight and the rough places plane. Modernists relied on scientific rationalism to subdivide the world, to make it sensible and hence manageable. All was to be analyzed, compartmentalized, catalogued—and then manipulated for the service of humankind. Modern states sprouted rational bureaucracies and set about intensively managing their societies and their colonies. Modern industrialists examined and rationalized each step in production and merchandising. Medical researchers isolated newly discovered causes of disease; psychologists developed taxonomies of and treatments for mental illness; sociologists prescribed scientific solutions for social disorders. Few Americans dared publicly criticize these methods, which had brought such self-evident good to the world, building order, efficiency, and the expectation of unlimited Progress out of the disorder and confusion of the premodern, ignorant "traditional" world.[3]

Nineteenth-century racial theorists were also infected by the modern impulse to compartmentalize. By the late nineteenth century these scientific racists believed they had swept aside the antiquated protests of egalitarian creationists and sentimental romantics and had declared the scientifically "proven" inferiority of nonwhite peoples. They were buoyed in this belief by an overwhelming majority of the Western world's leading physical and social scientists—a consensus of modern learned people generally.

As scholars of race seemed to arrive at definitive proof of an immutable racial hierarchy, modern reformers—generally known as Progressives—moved to implement the implications of these findings as public policy. The Progressive reformers resolutely sought to use modern scientific methods to remedy social ills. They valued consistency, efficiency, and the voice of expert opinion. They reformed school systems, established sanitation departments, and fought inefficiency and corruption in government. They also devised clinical treatments for homosexuals, sterilized the insane, and in the South, segregated "inferior" races from contact with the "general public." In all things they sought out the scientifically approved solutions and applied them systematically. Segregation was to them a clean solution, a social order that neither required disturbing private violence to uphold it nor admitted exceptions for individuals. Best of all, it opened up sterile, impersonal space between black bodies and white bodies, eliminating both friction and troubling opportunities for "amalgamation." All in all, they did their best to construct a rational "Solid South." Segregation truly was the hobgoblin of modern minds.[4]

Yet segregation did not grow out of intellectual and cultural forces alone. Segregation clearly benefited whites economically, politically, and psychologically: it guaranteed them jobs in public spaces where blacks could not enter; it imposed constantly intimidating physical reminders of the reality of white supremacy in all public and hence potentially political contexts; and it gave to even the poorest whites a sense of personal superiority stemming from their possession of at least the legal right to go places where wealthier and better-educated blacks were denied access. It is not clear, however, that southern urban white supremacy would have taken the form it did had it not germinated in modern soil. After all, white supremacy could be and had been maintained by other means.[5]

In contrast to the modernists' goals, the racialization of public space had previously been characterized by haphazard randomness—even, to a degree, in urban areas before the 1890s. Although schools and cemeteries were universally segregated, local and personal variation typified usage for many other southern public spaces. Standards were imposed by individual proprietors and local custom, not by state fiat. In some places blacks were excluded from public accommodations and restaurants. In others partitions were raised to create jerry-rigged segregation, and in yet others no barriers whatsoever existed to prevent the interracial sharing of space. Moreover, some conservative whites were willing to recognize the special claims of the black middle class and to share public space with them. In some settings, however, such as trolleys, physical intimacy occurred in the South irrespective of race or class. Many black and white northern travelers in the postbellum South commented on the surprisingly casual proximity of black and white bodies, an intimacy that the white commentators often found discomfiting.[6]

In 1891 Georgia's legislature enacted the state's first Jim Crow law to segregate railroads. After the U.S. Supreme Court officially blessed railcar segregation in *Plessy v. Ferguson* (1896), reformers elaborated the rationalized, all-encompassing program of southern racial segregation. Over the following two decades college-educated, middle-class, urban Progressives systematically worked through the points at which black and white bodies shared public space.[7] The Georgia state legislature segregated the state prison farm in 1897, railroad sleeping cars in 1899, parks in 1905, and coastal steamships in 1912. Local ordinances extended the philosophy of separation. By 1910 most Georgia cities enforced segregation or the complete exclusion of blacks in trolley lines, cemeteries, restaurants, theaters, athletic stadiums, concert halls, parks, and playgrounds. Blacks were barred from public swimming pools and libraries. By law they entered factories at separate Jim Crow doors, collected checks at Jim Crow pay windows, and cashed those checks at Jim Crow deposit windows. In courtrooms black and white witnesses even swore on separate Bibles. Additionally, local customs hardened and extended far beyond legal segregation, creating a dense web of prohibition. Law and custom alike were generally understood within each community, allowing enforcement not only by police officers but also by conductors, restaurant owners, and essentially all white people. Although white expectation differed somewhat from place to place, causing serious problems for black travelers, the effect was uniformly the same. Public space unequivocally demonstrated the racial order. Institutionally few points of interracial contact remained in the twentieth-century South.[8]

Residential segregation was much more difficult to implement. It meant a break with antebellum traditions and inconvenience to white elites who lost easy access to their domestic servants when racial zoning ordinances pushed them farther away. Nonetheless, at the insistence of the educated white middle class, Atlanta adopted the state's first residential segregation ordinance in 1913. It took years to sort out the neighborhoods to the satisfaction of the reformers, particularly in the older cities such as Savannah and Augusta, but they pressed on in the work with deliberate firmness.[9]

Like other older towns, Sparta trailed behind the general twentieth-century trend of dividing space into black and white zones. John Rozier, a white man who grew up in Sparta, remembered that residential segregation was not rigidly enforced there, as "servants always lived in the backyard in Sparta, just like Charleston and Savannah."[10] Much else was segregated, however. Summarizing his memories of urban segregation, A. J. Parker, a white sharecropper, said: "In Milledgeville [a medium-sized town just west of Hancock County] the restaurants had a side for the white and a side for the blacks. Now in Sparta, they had a place for the whites, and the only place the colored would get served was at the window. They had water fountains at the courthouse—one on one side for the whites, one on the other side for the blacks. The schools wasn't mixed. The whites went to their schools; the colored went to their schools. That was the law. Nobody said nothing about it. But they had it."[11]

Mae Warren remembered that in the 1920s and 1930s Sparta was more segregated than the countryside, but less so than were cities such as Atlanta. She avoided the theater and the humiliation of its separate door that led directly to the colored gallery. The Sparta train station, too, was segregated, but not as systematically as stations in other cities she had visited. The station in Atlanta had separate entrances and separate ticket counters. Early in the twentieth century Atlanta whites expressed dissatisfaction with the initial barrier dividing the black and white waiting rooms because it did not prevent the separated travelers from seeing each other. Nothing less than a wall would do, and so one was built. At the Sparta station patrons used common doors and bought tickets at a common counter. Only separate bathrooms and a low wooden partition dividing the waiting room preserved the physical symbolism of Jim Crow. Out in Hancock's rural villages, the train stations lacked even these segregationist gestures. John Rozier recalled that the country stations "were so simple and few in clientele that there wasn't any distinction at all." At places such as Carrs Station and Culverton, shopkeepers "sold tickets for trains at the country store. It wouldn't have been practical to have had physical segregation in the architecture of the buildings." After buying their tickets, the travelers would stand under the eaves or sit on benches. Seats on the benches were not reserved by race, and Rozier remembered that if black and white passengers "knew each other, they would sit and talk on the benches." Of course, these rustic anachronisms in the hinterland were one reason that contemporary Atlantans took pride in their own contrastingly modern achievements. When examined closely, the South shows itself to have comprised not just two worlds, rural and urban, but many. As historian Neil McMillen put it, "precisely because so much was left to custom, particularity seemed to be the only universal rule."[12]

Over the first half of the twentieth century, many patterns of race relations in rural Hancock fitfully converged toward those already established in these urban spaces, finally coming to approximate them in the years after World War II. Nevertheless, some neighborhoods there seem to have persisted in traditional modes of interaction far longer than others did, and racial separation there generally lagged far behind such developments in urban settings. Some aspects of this face-to-face culture never did change. It is interesting that race relations in these different spaces underwent the modern movement toward general conformity at markedly different rates. Yet we know that historical processes do not move at the same pace or in the same way in all social contexts. As the evolutionary biologist Stephen Jay Gould often repeated, in making a parallel argument in his own field, "stasis is data too." Ultimately, neither change nor persistence can be predicted. They must be explored, case by case, through the available evidence. In the messiness of human experience, the two trends often swirled and eddied around each other in unpredictable ways.[13]

Our recent history has conditioned us to conceptualize race relations dualistically, in terms of intentional integration or segregation. This study examines something prior to both. When we think about the social aspects of race relations in the South, our minds may immediately turn to the powerful images caught on film during the civil rights movement. We usually think of segregated public spaces: schools, churches, neighborhoods, busses, train stations, restaurants, and parks. We may immediately recall the contorted faces of white southerners as they furiously screamed and struck at black southerners who quietly but resolutely moved to desegregate these contested spaces with their bodies. We may remember the impassioned proclamations of white southern politicians declaring that segregation had always and everywhere been a central pillar of southern culture. When recalling these images, it is easy to find oneself agreeing with these demagogues that white southerners were unified and had always been unified in the maintenance of racial segregation in all social contexts. It is easy to forget that these politicians were attempting to marshal white southerners in a defense of segregation and that their appeals to history were very political indeed. In actuality, all the scenes that so easily rush to our minds were located in the urban South of the 1950s and 1960s. The degree to which that particular South can be projected as *the* South, the solid and unchanging Jim Crow South, can be determined only following research into the social context of other southern worlds. This chapter will explore one of these other worlds: the rural one of Hancock County between World War I and the civil rights movement.

Neighbors and Neighborhoods

The degree to which people experienced residential segregation varied greatly among different sections of Hancock. In some regions interviewees described lifetimes of virtual separation from people across the color line. Poor black sharecroppers on many large estates spent most of their time in a space entirely their own. They had occasional contacts with white store owners and the planters whose land they worked. The rest of the time they lived, prayed, worked, and rested in a completely segregated all-black world. W. E. B. Du Bois, on a tour of a south Georgia county, described just such a setting. He traveled ten miles past decaying antebellum mansions and saw "no white face" but only a vast and impoverished "black peasantry."[14] The western third of Hancock epitomizes this pattern, but the entire belt of large plantations running east to west across the middle of the county represents it well enough. Lewis Walls's community of black renters near Carrs Station experienced this residential segregation. Walls remembered only black neighbors throughout his life. "There wasn't no white people close around," he stated; "didn't know any whites one on one."[15]

In addition, Hancock was scattered with racially homogeneous pockets of white or black yeomen within which few other-raced people ventured. Samuel Williams grew up in Springfield, at the center of a strong black land-owning community in the northern part of the county. "When we grew up," said Williams, "we didn't think nothing about no segregation because out here [my wife's] parents had mules; my people had mules; the [neighbors] had horses and mules. We just had what we needed right here. So we had a good life." Some black Hancock families made a point of keeping their children close to home specifically so that they would not experience any dangerous or humiliating personal contacts with whites. Charles Johnson, the Fisk sociologist, believed that this kind of avoidance was "the most common type of response to the personal implications of the race system."[16]

Nonetheless, when faculty and graduate students at Atlanta University interviewed 118 Atlanta-area African Americans who had been born around 1900, only ten spoke of having been told by their parents to avoid white people.[17] For most people in rural Hancock, avoiding people across the race line was not simple, whatever their parents advised them to do. Most residents had a different-race family living close at hand. Oral interviews and the ordering of households in the census manuscripts both testify to the salt-and-pepper mingling of white and black homes that was the rule across the farm country.[18] Unlike many other parts of the South, Hancock had no sections where only white tenants lived. They were scattered and interspersed among black tenants in a sweeping curve through the sandy soil along the far eastern and southern part of the county. Small white and black landowners likewise bought land where they could, regardless of the color of their neighbors. Many of them worked fifty- or one-hundred-acre farms in the northern part of the county, but many other white yeomen and a handful of black yeomen appear elsewhere, interspersed among the large planters' holdings.

The white planters' rural homes, furthermore, were islands surrounded by a sea of black sharecroppers. Although some sharecroppers who lived at a distance from the "big house" experienced segregated worlds, the planters decidedly did not. Indeed, many white planters had no white neighbors nearby. Those who resisted the temptation to give up on cotton and relocate to town moved regularly in a black world. They believed that they needed to live near their tenants so that they could direct their wage laborers and look in on their sharecroppers. The labor demands of the southern economy discouraged systematic residential segregation.[19]

At the turn of the twentieth century, during the height of the segregationist frenzy, a proposal was made to segregate the southern countryside. Clarence Poe, the editor of the widely read *Progressive Farmer,* campaigned to have rural spaces segregated as urban spaces were. Historian Jack Temple Kirby wrote of the bewilderment this caused among whites generally. "Politicians with well earned reputations as white supremacists thought it bizarre." Planters feared the loss of control over their laborers. As one Mississippi planter informed Poe, "We cannot get along without the blacks. The day comes when they are segregated, I want to go with the negro."[20]

Interestingly, the white men who lived in the big house seem to have had many more intimate contacts with African Americans than did their wives. Many elite rural white women seem to have been confined to their houses and to the fairly narrow social life of family, church, and white neighbors. They did, however, have long-term, close contact with a few African American servants: maids, laundresses, cooks, gardeners, and sometimes handymen. The women of middle-class rural families, both black and white, also seem to have been shielded somewhat from interracial contacts and encouraged to spend their time in the company of other women of their own race and class. It seems that middle-class people, regardless of race, shared concerns about sexual predation by men across the race line. Poorer women, however, seem to have had a range of interracial interactions roughly equivalent to that of their men.[21]

There was yet another exception to rural residential interracialism. A fair number of rural white southerners seem to have experienced psychological residential segregation. When asked about their nearest neighbors, they gave the names and locations only of white families until asked specifically about black families.[22] Yet most Hancock families did not experience this. Even without prompting, a slight majority of white interviewees and a great majority of black interviewees listed both black and white neighbors.

The geography of Georgia's lower piedmont featured wide spaces and a diffuse, largely nonsegregated interracial population. In Hancock rural residences were separated from one another by fields of cotton, corn, and cane; cow meadows; and woods, creeks, and swamps. Meandering unpaved roads, clay red in the northern two-thirds of the county and sand blond in the southern third, made travel difficult in the best weather and impossible in the worst. According to the tax digests for the first decades of the twentieth century, most rural farmers did not own a horse and buggy or even a wagon. Fewer still had automobiles. Most walked. Thomas Sigman, a white farmer in the northern part of the county, remembered the crisscrossing network of wagon roads and paths that passed through woods and along fields to connect people to their neighbors. The paths were narrow. "You'd walk one behind the other," Sigman said. But they were well used. "You get out on the main road, you wouldn't meet nobody, but you get on those paths, you might meet a dozen people within a mile or two." "And," he said, smiling, "you knew them all, knew them well."[23]

The people Sigman described knew one another in part because in rural areas one's neighbors were not placed there accidentally. They usually had ties, whether economic, domestic, social, or familial. One did not simply move into a rural area and live apart from the community. With black and white people living in close proximity, moreover, daily experiences added texture to interracial relationships. "An understanding developed between people that is hard to say," says Beautine DeCosta-Lee, an African American woman who spent much time in Hancock in the 1920s and 1930s. "Situations would come along," she added; "Roads were muddy. Some whites would stop and pull you out, and from then on, you had a different relationship. You could relate because you had a common story." Rural Hancock, unlike the segregated towns, gave black and white people many opportunities to build common stories in a face-to-face culture.[24]

Although the "urban" cultures of Atlanta, Sparta, and Linton differed greatly one from another, this study will consider "urban" any village large enough to appear on maps. In 1910 only 12 percent of Hancock's residents lived in Sparta, a town of 2,306. Of the other communities, the largest—Jewell, Mayfield, Devereux, Linton, and Powelton—held at most a couple hundred people each; the smallest, only a handful. The population then shifted through the twentieth century. Sparta grew, although slowly; the villages shrank and many failed; and the rural areas slowly emptied into urban centers elsewhere. During the period under study, however, the great majority of Hancock's people were scattered across farm country.[25]

These conditions did not isolate farmers from knowledge of the outside world. Farmers went to town to gather news on the courthouse porch. Radios and newspapers brought the outside world to the farm. And as the twentieth century unfolded, a growing number of rural Hancock households were writing letters to family members living outside the region. Nonetheless, rural conditions did tend to insulate them socially within local communities.[26] As a small group of individuals and families, black and white, lived and worked in one another's company for years—often for generations—they tended to form patterns of race relations that were unique to their own neighborhoods. In each geographically defined community, varying combinations of race and class identity set the basic framework of race relations. Purely personal beliefs, commitments, and encounters gave each neighborhood its own flavor, however, and personal relations between individuals diverged widely within each neighborhood. Beginning in childhood, and building on the inheritance of a family name, each person worked out the varying distance or intimacy of his or her relationship with every other person in the community.

This unpredictable complexity could make travel through the South treacherous for black people, whose accidental transgressions of local customs were sure to be punished more harshly than were those of white people. What was taboo in one rural community could be common practice in another not far away, and what had been considered acceptable behavior in a neighborhood in one decade might be roundly condemned in the next. Neither stable nor "solid" during the first half of the twentieth century, rural Hancock was instead characterized by widely varying and constantly renegotiated patterns of race relations.

In this chapter the primary voice heard is that of rural Hancock people who spoke of their interactions across the race line. Although a large proportion of the population, possibly the majority, experienced some degree of interaction, there were clearly other experiences. Many rural people lived segregated lives. However, if a person simply did not experience interracial social contacts, there were few follow-up questions left for an interviewer to ask in exploring the details of that "something" which did not happen. Still, it is not necessary to prove that all rural people interacted across the race line during this period. It is necessary only to show that the option was not foreclosed in rural space. That a significant portion of the rural population crossed the line, either occasionally or regularly, indicates that the option did exist.

Childhood

The absence of systematic residential segregation in rural Hancock created numerous opportunities for intimate personal contacts. One type of interracial social relationship seemed to carry almost Edenic connotations among most rural white Hancock residents and elicited recognition, but understandably less enthusiasm, among African Americans. Nearly all white and most black interviewees spoke of having interracial playmates early in life.[27] Usually geography mandated the integrated society of children. Only so many potential playmates could be found in a given rural community. If one did not play with whoever lived nearby, one played alone. A white sharecropper, A. J. Parker, offered this frank if unenthusiastic assessment: "We had to have fun with those black children, 'cause we didn't know nothing about no white children." Mozelle Arnold, the daughter of white yeoman farmer, declared of a black girl in her neighborhood: "I would rather play with her than eat." In fact, if any social identity seemed to influence the choice of playmates, it was class. The children of black and white sharecroppers and wage laborers sometimes described playing together, as did the children of renters and landowners.[28]

Although class lines sometimes cut them off from the general tumble of children in an area, the children of large landowning white farmers generally had unsegregated childhoods as well. Nearly all those born to wealthy white families described the children of their black domestic servants as being among their first playmates. Of course, from an early age these wealthy white children and the black children within their sphere knew who controlled the toys and the rules of play. Moreover, merely playing together did not necessarily develop respect between individuals whose race or class projected them into very different adulthoods. After all, white children of slaveowners also played with slave children without later losing much sleep considering the possibilities of human equality. At the same time, however, the experience of interracial play did not flow directly into a later belief in the "naturalness" and "inevitability" of Jim Crow segregation.[29]

For the children of white or black tenants or small landowners, the balance of power was not so clear and could be influenced by an individual's imagination, daring, or strength. Rural children's games could be wild and dangerous. Kelly Brookins, a white sharecropper, remembers one of the favorite games of his neighborhood. The boys, black and white, would take turns sitting on the top of a young pine tree after the other boys had bent it close to the ground. On a signal all would let go, and the human projectile would be flung in the general direction of a haystack or a pile of leaves—as often missed as hit. For those with the courage to attempt the flight, democracy reigned. The black and white children in Billy Boyer's neighborhood collectively raided the nests of hornets and bumblebees, swatting at the insects with slabs of wood until they were outnumbered and forced into temporary retreat. In addition, most rural children could afford few toys, so that the possession of commercial toys did not clearly divide white "haves" from black "have-nots." Some children built their own wagons, improvising wheels by cutting sections of tree trunks. A few bicycles, however, did find their way into the countryside. A. J. Parker got his first bicycle in the 1930s. It was the gift of a neighboring black sharecropper's son who had acquired a better bicycle. "It had no chain and no tires on the wheels," Parker said, so he pushed it repeatedly to the top of a hill to experience the exhilaration of coasting down. Another boy—a white sharecropper—was more enterprising and less generous with his bike. He charged black boys in his community five cents each to ride it a half-mile or so. Usually, however, children played such inexpensive standbys as tag, catch, and cowboys and Indians—with the African Americans in one neighborhood playing the Indians, Parker, remembered, "because they were dark."[30]

In none of the contexts I investigated did one rule of behavior hold for all rural people. Not all rural children played with children of other races. The black children who grew up on the plantations around Devereux rarely saw a white child, much less played with one. This isolation also characterized the experiences of children in a couple of communities of black or white independent farmers. A few parents, white and black, discouraged their children from playing with others across the race lines. Francis Frazier, a white woman who raised her children in a nearly all-white neighborhood, was surprised by the mother of the neighborhood's only black family, for the woman seemed determined to keep her son from playing with Frazier's child. Twice when the black boy came over to play with her son, she heard his mother call him back and then beat him, saying "'I said don't play with him, and I mean don't play with him.' Beat him scandalous." Frazier then told her own son not to play with the boy. Although she herself had little to do with African Americans socially, she seemed to think her neighbor's behavior peculiar. Moreover, whatever the black woman's reasons for segregating her son's childhood, her decision to do so, in the context of the experience of most rural Hancock people, was indeed odd.[31]

The separate social codes that governed the interracial interaction of children reflected their particular positions in society.[32] Children held no political or economic power, regardless of race, so their identities were removed from that public zone in which the behavior of black and white adults was most closely circumscribed.[33] Additionally, they were generally viewed as presexual and so were removed from the most highly regulated "private" zone. Therefore, the exceptions granted them posed no challenge to white supremacy, either concretely or symbolically. As they approached adolescence and the threshold of public identities—including sexual maturity—they became subject to adult rules regarding interracial relationships. As with much else in rural Hancock, however, the rules were applied differently depending on race and gender. Children did not cross this boundary at the same age. Black boys grew prematurely into objects of white sexual fear and learned to avoid any potentially compromising situation with white girls. White girls, likewise, were early forbidden to play with black boys. Some black girls—especially those from middle-class homes—also were warned against playing with white boys. As a result, same-sex playmates usually played together longer before being separated.

The relationships of children grew into the relationships of adults, with increased distance being the usual result. Although many rural African Americans from Hancock had white playmates as children, they had less to say about the experience. Perhaps when viewed from their perspective, the rough comradeship of childhood games had never been as egalitarian as whites remembered. Or possibly they felt their childhood friendships betrayed them when games gave way to business. Still, most rural children, black and white, began their experience of race relations with highly personal relationships, which at least suggested to forming minds some of the complexity of the multilayered matrix that is individual identity.

Whatever the effect of lessons about human identity that individuals learned at play, the children were soon socialized within a larger, racially organized system. The schools may have been their most powerful early experience of their personal positions within a racially hierarchical society. The schools' concrete forms, shabby or sturdy, demonstrated to each child his or her place in a public, institutionalized society. The children were separated into racial groups. They observed the condition of each other's schools—and learned. School demonstrated to rural children that racial identity determined "us" and "them." Several interviewees stated that it was in racially segregated groups on the way to school that they first encountered each other as racialized enemies. Several black interviewees claimed that in some neighborhoods, white children would ambush them as they went to or from school. Epithets, insults, fists, and rocks were thrown. But the black children were allowed to use force against white antagonists—sometimes for the only time in their lives—and—if they could—they were allowed to win. Mae Warren remembered that in the 1920s a group of white children tried to prevent black children from walking on the public road on their way home from school. The white children joined hands in a chain across the road and told their black neighbors that they had to walk in the pasture. Warren and her siblings ended that bit of childish white supremacy by charging through the line. She said that the white children did not try it again, neither group of children spoke of it, and interracial afterschool play resumed afterward.[34] Grover Thomas, born in 1920, believed that the "respectable" white community didn't mind if he and his brothers beat up the young white truants who sometimes waylaid them on their way to school.[35]

The experience of segregated schooling may have influenced rural southern children throughout their lives, but the institution itself dominated their lives for only about five to eight months per year over a span of three to eight years. After they left school, their social worlds frequently became more complex, ambiguous, and personal. Rural Hancock had few public spaces like those that urban segregation codes targeted. The culture of rural Hancock allowed individuals, families, and local communities to determine the extent of their interracial interaction. Whereas some chose to segregate themselves socially, others chose interracial social interaction.

Rural Recreation

During the period in question, social activities in rural communities tended not to be institutionally bounded and so were not easily segregated. There were only a few professionally organized entertainments and a few spaces set aside for leisure, most of them centered on the county seat, Sparta, which had a movie theater and a cluster of restaurants. Now and then the circus or a professional troupe of actors or blackface entertainers came to town. Sparta also hosted the annual white county fair, with a day set aside for black patrons, and the colored county fair, with a day set aside for whites.[36]

When rural people went to town, they entered this segregated culture. Some people who lived near town or had ready transportation went weekly. Others went only about once a year—a few, even less. In his most famous study the great southern sociologist Charles Johnson discovered that "the usual frequency" of black farmers' visits to town was once a month. And only so often, then, were they touched by a thoroughly segregated culture.

Out in farm country, too, a few institutional centers provided entertainment for mostly segregated audiences. The strictly segregated schools held annual spelling bees and sometimes miniplays or oratorical contests, which could be widely attended. The churches, which will be discussed later, provided local centers for worship, artistic expression, and community interaction. Church-centered activities could be segregated, although the actual commitment to segregation varied widely.

Some rural men and women joined segregated fraternal and sororal societies. These organizations, especially the Masons for men and the Eastern Stars for women, offered companionship, an opportunity for civic service, organization benefits such as insurance, and pledges of mutual assistance. Masons, for example, swore solemn oaths to aid any fellow Mason who gave a secret distress signal. Although they operated completely separately, black and white Masons from Hancock claimed in interviews that they honored these pledges, regardless of race. White Masons decidedly did not do so in some parts of the South, and black Masons may be protecting their good name in Hancock in the interest of the honor of the organization. In any event, some African American Masons from Hancock stated that they could flag down white Masons for assistance if, for example, their cars broke down on the road. Non-Masons agreed that they had seen such things happen. Perhaps they did.[37]

Mostly, rural people whiling away their few leisure hours had little but their natural surroundings; a few implements, such as guns and fishing poles; a Bible; the neighbors; and their own bodies and creativity. One white planter remembered one of his great-aunts say, "The only fun I ever had was getting children and trying to get them." She had fourteen.[38]

Entertainment was also found at fishing holes, which were shared or used on a first-come-first-served basis, and daylong and overnight hunting expeditions, which were sometimes interracial affairs. Mary and Elizabeth Thornton remember their father hunting rabbits on his small farm with a black barber named Adam Davis in the 1910s.[39] Eddie Roberts, a white yeoman farmer in the Linton area, used to spend much of his free time with a nearby black landowning family, the Hunts. "One of them," said Roberts, "Oscar Hunt, learned me how to hunt birds." Roberts stated that "all the boys in that family were good hunters," fair praise in a culture where hunting skills were respected. Because his family had no hunting dogs and the Hunts did, Roberts would walk the trail to their house to suggest hunting expeditions; in addition, the Hunts would also sometimes come to his home to invite him to join them. When he finally got a dog, Oscar Hunt helped him train it. Besides hunting together, Roberts, the Hunts, and sometimes young men from other black or white families in the neighborhood fished together and practiced their baseball skills using a bat and a rubber ball wrapped in cotton and sewed up in a sock.[40]

Sparta also had a semiprofessional baseball team, first "Cuban" and then all white, which drew large biracial but segregated crowds to a stadium in town. A black Sparta team, which sometimes played there as well, also drew a segregated biracial audience, but as was the case across the nation, black teams never played white teams in town. In the rural communities, however, a different space allowed different rules. James Wilson, a black sharecropper, remembered going to a pasture north of Devereux to watch the local baseball teams play teams from other small communities. Although Devereux was only a village, it provided a home for two teams, one black and one white. The spectators, "just country farmers, white and black," had no bleachers or separate standing areas. Indiscriminately, they "stood out by the bushes beside the field." Sometimes they would all pitch in and buy lemons and sugar to mix up a barrel of lemonade. After he returned from World War II, Benjamin Senior, a black man, played for the Devereux Blues, which was organized by older men who had played in the 1930s. Senior said that although his team did not officially play white teams, the separate black and white Devereux teams would occasionally practice against each other. By Senior's recollection, the Blues never had a white man on it, and the white Devereux team never fielded a black man.

Nevertheless, Wilson, who was a few years older than Senior, spoke of standing interracial teams in the Devereux area. "All the black and white would be there," he recollected, "play with and against each other—all colors." Teams came from all around the area to play. Some, such as Linton's team, came from within the county; others, such as the Putnam County Lighted Splinters or the Oconee County Hard Hitters, came from farther away. In Wilson's opinion, racial separation was suspended because "there was no money in the deal. It was to see who was the best out of the deal—was for fun—wasn't about money." Segregation was thus less important. Other men, too, remembered interracial teams in the county. Billy Boyer, who grew up as a white sharecropper in Linton, played some semipro ball in Ludowici, Georgia, after he had cut his teeth playing pickup interracial baseball in rural Hancock. Boyer said: "We were just around each other out here. We lived together, worked together. We didn't think nothing of it." The rural population, he explained, did not provide a deep pool of ballplayers. If they wanted to play, they sometimes had to play together, although they all understood that segregated play was enforced in Sparta and among the professional ballplayers.[41]

Not all scenes of racial integration were pastoral. Other scenes were egalitarian in that anyone could get his throat cut. Rowdy gamblers congregated at isolated cabins in the woods or swamps and at campfires out by the railroad tracks to roll dice, play Georgia skin (a card game), and drink moonshine. These late-night sessions usually took place after paydays at the quarries and lumbercamps. Although these sites tended to be predominately black or white, they were not exclusively either. Ultimately, to join these companies one needed only nerve, although a bit of money—and the willingness to lose it—helped.[42]

It was sometimes noted that the rules of segregation seemed much more important to the most educated, urban, and "progressive" elements of white society. In 1903 W. E. B. Du Bois complained that the color bar cut him off from conversations with his few white intellectual equals in Georgia, while "at the bottom of the social group, in the saloon, the gambling-hell, and the brothel, that same line wavers and disappears." Will Alexander, the white director of the Commission on Interracial Cooperation, seconded Du Bois's complaint. After World War I Alexander tried to organize urban black and white civic leaders to get to know one another so that they might work together to promote racial harmony. "The contacts between the Negroes and the whites were closest at the bottom of the social and economic level," Alexander observed, "and as you moved up culturally and economically, the distance between the groups increased. The distance between intelligent and educated Negroes and educated white men was much wider than the difference between white bootleggers and Negro bootleggers. Your contacts were at the bottom, and your separation was at the top."[43]

The love of music also nudged black and white people together in the rural South. Much has been written of the tutelage that many white southern musicians received at the hands of black bluesmen. In addition, whereas some white women in Sparta organized clubs to cultivate their appreciation of classical music, other whites found their way to the creative wellspring of Hancock's African Americans. A few black participants in dances at a black community center in the northern part of the county remembered white couples coming occasionally in the 1930s and 1940s. That a number of Hancock's whites felt drawn to black music is evident in an outburst in the *Sparta Ishmaelite* written in 1901 by the editor's brother, George Lewis. Using crude but plain language, Lewis expressed his outrage over what he believed to be the loss of "Southern individuality." He warned against rising white appreciation for "the rag-time coon song stuff." Lewis railed that white southerners were trading their traditional fare for love songs describing the "lust affairs of some nigger buck and his wench." Apparently black music was making inroads into white leisure culture deep enough to discomfit at least one strident Hancock cultural segregationist.[44]

Most entertainment centered on the famous southern propensity for talk. Talk happened everywhere—in the roads, in the fields, and especially on the front porches of the scattered country general stores. White and black interviewees remembered these places as socially open spaces, with white and black people coming and going or waiting around, telling jokes or fish stories, and commiserating over the boll weevil.

Thus, many people seem to have enjoyed interracial recreation, yet not all rural Hancock people socialized across the race line. One white woman, a small landowner and the daughter of small landowners, stated that few African Americans lived in her community. When asked to describe her relationships with them, she replied that her mother would sometimes hire a black man to help around the house, but she added that blacks "didn't hang around when they got through helping you. They was ready to go, if you had nothing else for them to do." This arrangement seem to have been completely to her satisfaction. When she grew up, she did her own housework and entered almost complete racial isolation. She rarely interacted with black people, never attended a black church, and did not pursue recreation in their company. Summing up race relations over the first half of the twentieth century, most of which she remembered personally, she said that blacks "done alright and stayed in their place, but helped you if you asked them to." That was all. In her eyes, African Americans were there simply to make life easier for whites and were to remain invisible the rest of the time.[45]

The fact that some black or white rural people chose to interact solely with others of their race does not undermine the central point of this chapter. Some rural people lived and played in an interracial world. Others did not. The point is that the option of interracial social interaction was present to rural Hancock people through the first half of the twentieth century. Systemic, enforced segregation, the urban mechanism for maintaining white supremacy, did not penetrate far into rural spaces. Rural southerners used other methods to ensure that each person knew his or her place in the social hierarchy.

The Etiquette of Subordination

The antebellum rural South developed a complex system of racial etiquette to ritualize at least an outer show of black acceptance of white supremacy. This system of word and gesture was transferred in modified form to the postbellum era.[46] Naming and the use of titles formed a significant component of this etiquette. At a basic level the rules of naming involve the creation of order. The way we name something reveals and reinforces our relation to it. Unlike the rules governing segregation, which usually required people not to do something they might otherwise have done—barring them, for example, from eating together, sitting together at theaters, or interacting socially—the rules of etiquette required blacks to do things they doubtlessly would not have chosen to do whenever they spoke with a white person. Racial segregation placed African Americans in embarrassing positions, but racial social etiquette caused them even more humiliation. It required blacks to participate regularly in their own ritualized subordination, to symbolically assent, however reluctantly, to the caste system. These rules regularly pointed to the social hierarchy and underscored in every exchange symbolic black accommodation to that hierarchy. Segregation was an impersonal system, used to enforce white supremacy on black strangers by white strangers. Many aspects of racial etiquette, however, pivoted on the fact of mutual familiarity. Until their deaths, the "old slavery days men," as many elderly Hancock blacks refer to them now, were often called "Marse Jim," "Marse John," and so on by African Americans. Whites born after slavery were referred to as "Mister" or "Miz" together with their given name or entire name, but not last name alone, as that would have suggested social equality.[47]

Insulting to begin with, the etiquette of naming could be pushed to ludicrous limits. As white children approached adulthood, they began to demand that blacks "put a handle" on their names. Eager to assume the markings of adult status, white adolescents of sixteen or less came to expect this sign of respect even from much older black men and women. Additionally, according to a story often repeated among elderly African Americans in Hancock, there was a country store in poor-white-dominated Warren County, just north of Hancock, in which African Americans were ordered to ask for "Mr. Prince Albert" tobacco and "Mr. Coca Cola." Although it may be a local retelling of a widespread southern folk tale, the story makes its point.

Whites, in contrast, addressed African Americans by their given name alone or as "boy," "girl," or among coarser whites, "nigger." Sometimes they added vocational titles, as in "Preacher Jones," "Dr. Dixon," or even "Professor Morse," the last used in reference to a respected black teacher. Additionally, many white interviewees emphasized that they were taught from an early age to use *uncle* and *aunt* as a terms of respect for older black men and women. No black interviewees found these terms respectful, however. As poor replacements for the terms required of blacks in return, they expressed condescension quite clearly. These terms stamped nearly every interracial conversation with the clear markings of caste—but not quite every one.

Although these terms of address were expected, they were not always given. Some African Americans simply refused to cooperate in the language of accommodation. Mae Warren remembered a spirited old black woman who in the 1920s pointedly called whites by their first names and continued to do so even when corrected. Because of her age, whites laughed off her open transgressions of racial etiquette as the singular privilege of elderly idiosyncrasy. But others rebelled as well, especially those in the generation rising to adulthood after World War II. Eugene Foster, born in 1932, simply refused to "Mister" white boys his own age. When a white youth told him, "I'm Mister Joe," he would reply, "Well you're no Mister Joe to me. 'Cause I'm as old as you are. I'm a man just like you are." He remembers a white man his age who complained that he did not give him any respect. Foster recalls answering, "Well, you give me respect; I'll give you respect. You call me 'Gene,' why am I going to call you Mister?" Foster believed that by the late 1940s, when he had reached young adulthood, violence was no longer a real threat for assertive African Americans. When confronted by his refusal to act deferentially, a white man would "just walk away, because it would make him look bad in front of the other guys" to stand there and argue. Foster faced no repercussions for his boldness, but he did leave Hancock for the North in the early 1950s. Many other members of the rising generation of the 1940s and 1950s who declared themselves dissatisfied with social discourtesy in the South headed north as well.[48]

The inferior status of African Americans was expressed largely in the daily courtesies that white men and women withheld from them. Whether those involved were black or white, rich or poor, southern cultures laid great emphasis on the value of good manners, although the forms differed somewhat among the different social groups. In public or formal situations white men removed their hats in the presence of white women but not black women, although black men were expected to remove theirs in any interaction with a white adult, male or female. Additionally, white southerners expected African Americans to speak quietly and humbly in their presence. White southerners usually avoided shaking hands with African Americans, refusing them that symbol of egalitarian goodwill and trust. African Americans entered white homes through back doors; whites entered black homes through front ones.[49] Each of these ritual gestures clearly articulated and reinforced the relative social status of black and white people in rural Hancock.

When standing at a sales counter, African Americans were sometimes expected to allow white customers to walk directly to the front of the line. At many clothing stores black customers, unlike whites, were not allowed to try on articles before buying them. These petty displays of white supremacy were perpetrated only unsystematically around Hancock, depending on the proprietor's disposition. Mae Warren remembered that blacks could avoid this slight by patronizing, as her family did, only those stores that demonstrated equal treatment. Three Jewish-owned clothing stores in Sparta drew her loyalty for the courtesy they extended to African Americans. She remembers whites cutting ahead of her at the register of one pharmacy, but the rule at the county's gas stations and in the long line at the cotton gin was always first come, first served.[50]

The etiquette surrounding white women could be especially strict. As historians Joel Williamson and Glenda Gilmore have forcefully argued, white women became a powerful symbol of racial status for white southern men around the end of the nineteenth century, when racism escalated to hysterical new heights. According to Williamson, the southern economy descended in a tailspin in the 1880s and 1890s, bringing a widespread loss of security and sometimes material deprivation. As white men found it increasingly difficult to assure themselves of their traditional masculine role as providers of food, clothing, and shelter, they found psychic solace by unconsciously remaking their role. They consequently became defenders, safeguarding white womanhood against a largely imaginary threat from black rapists. Unable to bring real security to their families, white men across the South took up a vicious-spirited and sometimes bloody crusade against their black neighbors to restore their own lost sense of manhood.[51]

Thus, although white men sometimes waived racial etiquette in private dealings with black men, the presence of white women often led them to insist that the rules be followed to the letter. As a result, black men had to be especially careful in their deportment around white women. As Eugene Foster, an African American, said, "You could play with them till you get fourteen years old. After fourteen, you couldn't play with them no more. They was 'Missey' to you. It was 'Yes, Ma'am; no, Ma'am.'" Whereas African Americans had to give right-of-way to all white pedestrians on the sidewalks of Sparta, black men had to be especially careful to step to the side—sometimes completely off the sidewalk—when passing a white woman. When in the presence of white women, black men generally had to avoid appearing to stare at them. James Wilson, a black sharecropper, remembered that "if you looked at a white woman in Sparta," someone would shout, "'What you looking at, nigger?'"[52]

There were additional indignities. African Americans were not supposed to argue with whites directly. They were expected to maintain an obliging and humble demeanor in the presence of whites. They were expected to avoid controversial topics within the hearing of white ears. One black Hancock man said, "Back then, you had to be careful what you said. There were some things you just couldn't talk about." And these restrictions all applied to dealings with whites who were acquainted with and sympathetic toward a black person. When dealing with a white person who did not know or like them, blacks could be subject to a myriad of additional insults and snubs.[53]

An important point needs to be reemphasized: the enforcement of these social rituals of subordination and dominance was considered a personal affair, to be left completely to private white citizens. Although these codes were often the primary manifestation of white supremacy—as it was experienced daily—they were not and never became matters of law. An individual or group of white individuals could suspend any part of the code privately and much of it publicly. At the same time, whites could, within limits, add additional demands to this code. Historian William McFeely has written that slavery was homemade; so too were rural southern race relations.[54] Nevertheless, no one I interviewed reported that the general code was ever entirely waived.

Planters, Paternalism, and Rural Interracial Intimacy

Because individual white men and women established the demands of white supremacy, the full range of individual variations defy any attempt to categorize them fully and systematically. Nonetheless, some general patterns can be discerned. One fruitful attempt to simplify the chaos into general currents, Joel Williamson's *Crucible of Race,* approaches the problem using intellectual history. In this seminal work Williamson divided white thought on race relations in the fin-de-siècle South into three general groups: liberals, who displayed an egalitarian impulse; conservatives, who, in the fashion of paternalistic elites, looked on blacks as children to be controlled and cared for; and radicals, who perceived blacks as dangerous beasts to be held down by indiscriminate violence. The liberals were never a forceful presence. The conservatives held power until racial radicalism swept up a majority of white southerners at the turn of the twentieth century, after which, following a brief and resigned sortie, the conservatives retired from the field. The great exception in Williamson's opinion was Hancock County's conservative leader, Governor William J. Northen. Against a growing crescendo of racist criticism, Northen campaigned for years across Georgia pleading for the return to a policy of responsible consideration for African Americans.

His solitary crusade left him emotionally and financially crushed and nearly alone. When he passed through Sparta during this period, the *Ishmaelite's* editor noted that many of Northen's friends showed up to greet him, but the paper summarized the purpose of his visit in a single sentence. The silence seems deafening.[55]

I did not use the kinds of manuscript sources that might have allowed me to extend Williamson's study of white racial attitudes as they were articulated and debated as public policy. Instead of examining the public rhetoric—which clearly set the tone of race relations in public areas controlled by popular sentiment, such as in urban spaces—I explored private behavior as it was enacted in rural spaces. Although the evidence does not allow an examination of divisions within rural Hancock based on formally articulated ideology, it does permit an exploration of the general patterns of interracial contact as lived by members of different classes.

The planter class of Hancock—those who inherited stately antebellum plantations and sometimes, to a lesser degree, the newcomers who bought them out—seemed to have had long-term, physically close relationships with a number of African Americans living near "the big house." These wealthy whites always had servants: cooks, maids, handymen, and sometimes gardeners and chauffeurs. Sometimes, too, they dealt regularly with the tenants who lived nearest their house and with the oldest African Americans on the place, but it is hard to determine whether this stemmed from noblesse oblige, a sentimental attachment to their symbolism of a romanticized past, or even personal affection.[56] It must be noted that the white planters gradually diminished as a presence in the countryside. Beginning with the decline of cotton prices in the 1880s and continuing through the twentieth century, many rural elites packed up and moved to town. There, as absentee landlords, they found greater conveniences, wider access to elite white companionship, and reduced contact with African Americans. They also ceased to be rural people, however, and so moved beyond the scope of this study.

The wealthiest planters held tremendous social, economic, and political power in the rural South. Under slavery they had been virtually a law unto themselves, particularly on their own land. Many did not see any reason to change after emancipation, especially because a few of them seemed to loan more money annually than did the county banks. Often they controlled credit for all families in an area. Some of these people—the men especially—were wildly eccentric characters about whom many stories still circulate in Hancock, although they are long dead. Their wealth, panache, and sometimes famous quirkiness gave them the prerogative to treat social convention as the dull background against which to paint their flamboyant self-portraits. If, like Lynn Rives, they chose to bring their black grandsons into restaurants to dine with them or, like Percy Moore, rode around in a limousine with their black mistresses, that was their business, and no one who might need a loan in the future dared say anything. Moreover, any would-be defenders of "propriety" who did not fear economic retribution for themselves still might not wish to expose their kinfolks to foreclosure at the hands of an outraged planter. Katie Hunt, a black woman born in Hancock in 1891, said of them, "If anyone had money, they'd do what they wanted." In Oglethorpe County, two counties north of Hancock, a black man explained why his grandfather, a wealthy white planter and banker, was not disturbed despite his public, lifelong, monogamous relationship with a black woman: "The white community was working for them, and those who were not wished to hell they were."[57]

A few of the oldest black interviewees told of relationships that were maintained between ex-slaves and ex-slaveowners of the planter class. Katie Bell Hunt said that an ex-slavemaster who lived near her "would not let me buy any fruit or vegetables" from his commissary. He insisted that she, like her mother and grandmother, take them for free because he recognized her as the granddaughter of one of his ex-slaves.[58] There are other, similar stories, mostly dating from the period before 1920. Some representatives of the older planter class seemed to value the continuity of paternalistic relationships begun in slavery. Additionally, throughout the plantation belt, many members of the planter elite who had owned slaves had relatives on the other side of the race line. Some planters and their families knew the black families that were kin to them. A few planters recognized their black kin by helping them directly or, more often, by attempting to indirectly influence the social setting for their benefit. When it came to public discussions of racial policy, these men were shouted down by (or converted to) a rising tide of radical racism in the 1890s, yet for years many quietly continued to act locally as conservative forces in the rural South.[59]

Not all freedmen and -women valued the antebellum relationships that they inherited. Some African Americans avoided contact with whites generally or with specific individuals, even when the white person in question seemed to be pursuing a greater intimacy. Katie Hunt remembered that every time her white grandfather came to visit for breakfast, his son—her father—would see him coming and abruptly leave the house to avoid talking with him. According to Hunt, he despised his father because his mother had related how the man had mistreated her under slavery. He had raped her, and the young black man would not forget it. Most of the painful relationships from slavery were probably simply broken off by the ex-slaves themselves, most of whom chose to relocate immediately following emancipation.[60]

Nonetheless, a number of interviewees spoke of continuing paternalistic relationships between wealthy planters and their black tenants. Some planters maintained highly personal relationships with African American laborers, a long-term hired workman, or domestic servants. Although close physically, these relationships could be marked by a great deal of psychic space between black and white individuals. Still, the main point is that segregation, the creation of physical distance between persons based on race, was not a significant aspect of race relations as experienced by the planters.[61]

As described in chapter 1, the absence of this distance sometimes led planters to rather high-handed intrusiveness in the lives of black men and women. They could demand extra services of tenants or their children. They could punish their tenants personally, and occasionally physically, or excuse them from legal punishment. James Wilson said, "If a black child was in court, all a white man had to do was speak a word for him . . . and that case is dismissed." No wonder that, according to sociologist Charles Johnson, many black sharecroppers actively sought the protection of white planters, despite the coercion that came with it. Some planters spoke furthermore of tenants who sought their advice on economic or personal matters. One white planter said that one of his newly married black tenant farmers once approached him and told him that had just discovered that his wife had tuberculosis. What should he do? The planter told him that he ought to "take the girl back to her father." He did so.[62]

Even black landowners sought the protection of influential white men. Black men who wished to buy land needed a white sponsor, whose continued patronage would be important in smoothing out any problems that might occur. Sanford Butts, one of the county's leading merchants, noted: "You had a wealthy white man behind every respectable black man." Marshall Boyer, a black man born in 1908 on the western boundary line of Hancock, said, "Every black person needed a white man to point at him and say: 'my nigger.'" The goodwill of an influential white man could keep a black man out of trouble with the law or with envious whites who might otherwise try to trap him in debt or even burn his property. Through the help of a white patron, a large merchant-planter, Boyer's father came to own a farm and a sawmill. The men spoke regularly and, to Boyer's young eyes, seemed to enjoy an openly warm relationship. Yet this patronage was not always what it appeared to be. When Boyer's father, on his own, constructed a cotton gin on his property, the same white man hired a black man to burn it down. It had been, the white man explained frankly and unapologetically, too close to the location of his own gin. He had ordered it burned to prevent competition. According to Boyer, the white planter seemed to continue to be helpful toward his father and assisted him out of other difficulties, and his father continued to describe their relationship as "good," as a "friendship."[63]

Katie Hunt, as usual, had her eyes wide open. After scornfully relating the story of a black woman she knew who went to pieces on hearing that her white patroness had died, Hunt declared that she had not relied on any white beneficiaries. "Sometimes," she explained, "your 'friend' was your worst enemy."[64]

Poor Whites and Rural Interracial Intimacy

If race and class identities overlapped neatly, as is often imagined of the rural South, paternalistic or frankly exploitative relationships between poor black sharecroppers and wealthy white planters might have exhausted the range of social relationships. They did not. As I discussed in the previous chapter, some black families in Hancock owned their own farms, and a few owned large plantations. A few black men and women worked as merchants or artisans. At the same time, even in planter-dominated Hancock, nearly half of all white farmers were tenants. Interracial relationships were influenced by the class as well as the race of the individuals concerned.[65]

A number of white and black sharecroppers explicitly recognized the similar position in which class had put them all, regardless of race. After speaking at length about the severe hardship that the Depression inflicted on her sharecropping family, exploited and disrespected by planters and surviving hand to mouth, Josie Mae Ingram observed, "Back in them days, poor white people had it just that rough too, I believe." Aware of the unbridgeable social gap between themselves and wealthier whites, poor whites seemed more willing than any other whites to accept interracial social intimacy. Several black sharecroppers stated that the poorer white folks were, the easier they were to get along with. In areas where they lived close together, many black and white sharecroppers would talk, eat, fish, hunt, worship, and engage in neighborly mutual assistance with one another.[66]

Mamie Washington worked as a black sharecropper in the far southern part of Hancock on the Louis Ray plantation. Three white and three black sharecropping families lived there in cabins scattered about the farm. They saw one another daily. According to Washington, they would "come to each other's houses, laugh and talk." She contrasted the attitude of the white sharecroppers with that of the white people she met when she went into the nearby village of Linton to buy supplies. "There," she said, "they'd speak to you when they took the notion. If they took the notion, they wouldn't speak to you at all." But the white sharecroppers could be different. "They were pretty good, some of them," Washington recalled. When asked why, she replied, "You were on the same level. They didn't have nothing and you didn't have nothing." Because of their poverty, "the white folks what had something wouldn't pay them no attention."[67]

Washington remembered black and white sharecroppers accompanying one another when fishing or going to church services, as well as visiting in one another's homes. She also recalls them going to Milledgeville in the same wagon during lay-by time or winter. The sharecroppers took turns transporting one another. "Sometimes their [own] wagon; sometimes others would borrow a wagon and go." On the way they would laugh, talk, and "have a heap of fun." You could, she said, "act like you were of the same family with close white sharecroppers." When they would reach town, with its unambiguous racial codes, the group would break up along racial lines: "They'd go attend to their business, and we'd attend to ours." Then the group would reunite at the wagon and talk their way home again. Clearly urban spaces had a different set of codes for interracial social etiquette than did the large plantation on which Washington and her black and white sharecropper neighbors lived. Apparently the sharecroppers moved easily between the two distinct spaces, aware of both systems. They accepted the dissonance or at least did not challenge the rules imposed by the white urban regime.[68]

A. J. Parker lived on the Ray place near Washington. He directly acknowledged the similarity in the condition of all poor rural farmers: "Back when I come up, the poor white people and the poor black people were in the same boat together." He added: "We was treated just alike. We didn't have nowhere to live mostly; didn't have no clothes to wear or nothing; didn't have no—the food we should have eaten." The families in Parker's neighborhood relied on a semisubsistence economy to survive. "The way we got what we had," said Parker, "was we raised it." Parker and his neighbors had little money with which to buy things at the stores, so "if they didn't make it [themselves], they didn't get it."[69] In his opinion, poor farmers "lived like chickens." During the summer, they "didn't know what a cool drink of water was." The walls of sharecroppers' cabins were constructed with only "one layer of lumber," roughly overlapping but leaving cracks through which the wind blew in winter. For them all, schooling was brief, food was simple, and the workday was long and hard. They would go to bed so tired that they could sleep "no matter how hot or cold."[70]

Among these sharecroppers, the two races lived side by side and under similar conditions. Parker bluntly equated their lives: "It wasn't no different. You take a poor white man and a poor black man—it was all equalized alike. There wasn't no highfalutin' going on." According to him, a false air of supremacy assumed by some whites "caused all the trouble between the black and the white."[71]

Despite his memories of the shared difficulty of life, Parker clearly enjoyed recalling other memories of interracial life on the Ray plantation, especially the end of the workday. In their adjacent fields, in the hour before the coming of dusk, Parker remembered, the older black women would begin "humming" together. "Damn!" he exclaimed, "that was something else to hear. . . . It was really worth listening at." Then, "late in the evening, as the sun was going down," everyone would quit work together and begin the day's last round of chores.

"They'd all come out of the field—the old lady, if she didn't have something already cooked, she would go on in there and be cooking supper. The old man would be feeding the stock—maybe water the pigs or feed the horses, the cows, whatever they had, if they was fortunate enough to have one. Then the children would be gathering up wood."

Parker recalled that "you could hear the black children and the white children . . . go on into the woods to pull the wood out to cook with. They was just singing and whooping and hollering and going on, just as happy as they could be—the white and the black." As Parker spoke, he remembered that the children's noise was not just the result of high spirits for the end of the workday. "Going down into the branch in the dark—what it was, they was scared and trying to make a fuss! They knowed that they had to go down," so they went down in a boisterous group to bolster one another's courage. "When they come out, they may have cornbread and butter beans for supper; they may have cornbread and peas for supper; or they may have . . . well, something to eat to fill, that's what it was." Parker remembered being able to smell the food cooking in each house—all good to his hungry nose. To him, and to other black and white sharecroppers, the tenants on interracial plantations were brought close together by a shared culture of poverty, hard work, and simple pleasures.[72]

Black sharecroppers also noted, however, that many of the poor whites with whom they had intimate relationships seemed reluctant to recognize their relationship in the presence of other whites. The planters seemed to have less difficulty exposing close interracial relationships to the view of white society. In part the difference may be attributed to different rhetorical resources available to rich and poor whites. The planters could wrap about themselves the old cloak of noblesse oblige. It was their duty, they could explain, to condescend to assist those who were not their social equals. They could maintain close relationships with African Americans without creating any sense of ambiguity in the vast caste difference between them. Poor whites could not adopt this posture and this language publicly, and they would not adopt the language that Tom Watson had urged them to accept in the early years of the Populist campaign, when he had proclaimed that the conditions of both black and white sharecroppers were equal, that they suffered under a common yoke, and that their only remedy lay in each group's openly embracing the other as an ally. Except for the planters who could translate private interracial relationships publicly as "my nigger," whites seem to have had no ways of publicly claiming relationships with black folks without risking being called "nigger lovers."

Separate from the white planters and sharecroppers were the members of the white middle class and lower middle class: merchants, clerks, and service professionals, largely clustered in Sparta. Because I focused exclusively on the rural areas of the county, this class surfaced only peripherally in interviews. Still, some African Americans discussed their relationships with them as a means of comparing their relationships with rural whites. Most of those who spoke of them stated that members of the white middle class seemed relatively more concerned about maintaining codes of interracial etiquette and seemed coldest and most distant in their relationships with blacks. Eugene Foster Jr. addressed these people and their concerns directly. "It was never the rich man [who insisted on segregation], because you couldn't afford to go and eat with him no way. So it didn't make no difference to him. It was always the middle-class person" who was concerned with segregating the "average restaurants" where blacks could afford to eat.[73]

According to a recent study of the Ku Klux Klan in Athens, Georgia, during the 1920s, it was exactly this class of people who made up the majority of Klan members. Although these people tended to have few personal relationships with African Americans, they were often concerned about policing other people's relationships across the race lines. In towns, where they made up a significant proportion of the population, they tended to homogenize urban race relations in accord with the segregation laws for which they fought and with their own private sense of the fitness of social distance between the races. They could make life very difficult for individuals, black or white, who disregarded racial convention.[74] Because they lived and worked in town, however, their influence did not extend far into the countryside. As you moved beyond the boundaries of towns, you moved beyond Jim Crow and entered a personal, face-to-face version of white supremacy. Out among the farms social integration continued where and to the degree that it was tolerated locally.

4

The Solid South and the
Permissive South

NONSEGREGATED RURAL RESIDENTIAL patterns in the age of Jim
Crow led to many forms of interracial intimacy. Some, such as the play of
children, are quite well known to historians, even if they have been less well
examined. The interracial recreation of rural adults has been occasionally
noted, although it has been even less well studied. There were, however, many
other points of social contact between black and white rural southerners
that seem more surprising inasmuch as the overwhelming majority of white
southerners were unquestionably invested in white supremacy. The deeply
personal experiences of birth, illness, and death brought black and white
neighbors into one another's homes as midwives, folk healers, and participants in the deathwatch. The search for meaning and beauty drew them into
one another's churches as visitors. The desire for human connection brought
them together for meals, sex, family, companionship, and even friendship.

The lives of many rural Hancock people were honeycombed with interracial social spaces. Nonetheless, as historian Neil McMillen put it when
writing of Mississippi, the "place" of black southerners to which whites so
frequently referred "was always more behavioral than spatial in nature. . . .
Valuing hierarchy more than they feared propinquity, whites casually rubbed
elbows with blacks in contexts that sometimes startled northerners."[1] In
Hancock public white supremacy went unchallenged over the first half of the
twentieth century. Simultaneously, interracial intimacy could be very close
indeed.[2] A tension existed in rural Hancock between, on the one hand, the
publicly unquestionable absolute of white supremacy, a truly solid South,
and, on the other hand, the wide range of socially ambiguous relationships

that rural white society allowed or could not prevent, an unexpectedly permissive South.

The Great Taboo: Interracial Dining

When white Hancock sharecropper A. J. Parker remembered race relations in his racially mixed community of sharecroppers, he chose to emphasize the way that isolation and shared poverty eradicated racial hierarchies. One of his black neighbors, however, remembered their community as somewhat less than egalitarian. According to the former sharecroppers on the Ray plantation, sharecroppers of one race sometimes invited those of the other race to share in their meals, but these moments did not bring black and white families together on equal ground. Mamie Washington claimed always to have resented the racial barriers erected at the dinner tables of her poor white neighbors. Occasionally the white family insisted on eating first. At other times "they would set out another table. Sometimes close together—other times, they'd separate the tables at dinnertime." Sometimes African Americans ate in the kitchen, while whites ate in the main room. Some white sharecroppers even insisted on these divisions when Washington was hosting them at her own house. She said, "It made me mad, but I had to go along with it." Nonetheless, Washington had one symbolic means of equalizing disrespectful social relations. Some white sharecroppers, like wealthier whites, had all African Americans—including guests—enter their homes through the back door. When they came to her home, Washington said, "I'd do them like they'd do me."[3]

Other rural Hancock African Americans used a similar system of reciprocation when responding to displays of social disrespect by individual whites. When Mary Hunt was a young girl, a few years before World War I, she grew up in an interracial rural neighborhood. Although she was an African American, she "used to play all the time" with a white girl who lived nearby. "One Sunday afternoon," Hunt remembered, "her father said, 'Come get some water, girls.'" They drank from the same container, using the same dipper. Then, without saying a word, the white man threw out the water and washed the dipper. She was six or seven years old at the time. "From then on," she said, "I wouldn't go back to play with them no more." When the white girl came over to her house, she refused to come out. Although she herself "didn't say a word to them" about her hurt feelings, her mother did. When the white girl's father asked her why Hunt no longer played with his daughter, she replied, "'Cause you insulted her. You made her feel bad." Her mother told her that he had responded, "Susie, I knew I was wrong, but I just wasn't used to drinking after them." Hunt said that "he didn't name the name 'Negro children,'" but her mother "knew what he meant." Finally, after the white girl persisted in asking her to play, Hunt relented. From then on, however, they would play only by her house, and Hunt told her, "I don't want you to drink out of our dipper." So from then on, the white girl had to go back to her own house for water.[4]

The taboo against black and white people eating together seems to have been second only to sexual relationships between black men and white women in terms of the consistency with which the racial prohibition was observed in rural Hancock. On many white farms black wage laborers, domestic servants, and (less often) lifelong resident handymen ate food prepared in the white kitchen. But the food—even when prepared in a common pot by black hands—was served to black people in the kitchen or outside the house, while the white people ate in the dining room.[5]

As noted by most southern sociologists and travelers through the South, the racial etiquette surrounding the consumption of food created some bizarre inconsistencies. Some interracial families did not eat together at one table. Some interracial couples that slept together did not eat together, even in the privacy of their own homes.[6] Perhaps these disjunctions suggest differences in the symbolic meaning of different spaces in a house. Whereas bedrooms are private and hidden spaces, dining rooms—often the central, largest room in a house—are more public, even when no extrafamilial visitors are present. The dining room is the space that private people present to the public. White men living with "black" families must have been pulled between two different ways of seeing and being, the one growing from their own experience of their wives' and children's humanity and the other pressed on them by the pervasive culture of white supremacy. Perhaps some white men felt uncomfortable ignoring the dominant ideology within the most "public" space in their own, private homes.[7]

Some white southern apologists tried to attribute the custom to white concerns over supposed black "dirtiness," but the custom was not rooted in white concepts of sanitation or an association between blackness and uncleanliness. Most white middle- and upper-class families employed African American women to stand in their hot kitchens, up to their elbows in the white family's biscuit dough. In many segregated restaurants, as everyone knew, all food was prepared exclusively by black hands. The cultural taboo against shared food lay not in white concerns over sanitation but in white fears over the destruction of one of the most potent symbols of white supremacy: a tangible delineation of caste. It revealed the extent to which whites distanced themselves psychically in many interracial relationships that were in other ways intimate.

Not for nothing have cultures around the world built elaborate rituals around shared food. The meaning of breaking bread together, eucharistic ritual, and cultures of hospitality throughout the world suggest that the consumption of food is fraught with as much inherent anthropological tension and significance as is sexual intercourse. The food on the table becomes part of the bodies of all who partake in it. This central sharing in a common humanity seems to resonate profoundly in the human subconscious. Unlike some other racial codes, the taboo against an integrated table almost always held sway in Hancock.[8]

Yet few absolute statements can be made about race relations in rural Hancock during this period without allowing for a number of exceptions, even in the case of this commonly observed taboo. White children, rich or poor, lived according to a set of rules separate from those that applied to white adults. Patsy Kennedy was the daughter of wealthy planters in Devereux. She remembered that as a child, she brought a black playmate to eat at her house. They "couldn't eat together in the dining room," so they ate together in the kitchen. Kennedy remembered thinking that eating in the kitchen was "an exciting change." Many other black and white Hancock interviewees spoke of white children eating with black children or their families. Apparently the actions of white children did not constitute socially significant disruptions of the ban.[9] Additionally, they inevitably took place in "black space"—inside the white kitchen or the black home.

A few other interviewees reported more meaningful breaks from the established pattern. Thomas Dixon, the son of a black county doctor, remembers the cordial relationship his family had with the white landowning family that lived next door in Springfield, in the northern part of the county. Occasionally, under the cloak of dark, their families would visit each other, entering through the back doors for dinners and conversations shared at the same table. He recalls these visits as festive and friendly occasions. Although not public challenges to the status quo, these neighborly dinners did seem significant to the participants.[10]

A. J. Parker remembered that when he was a child, the black and white tenants on the Ray place would go together into the swamp on one day each year. There they would take turns cutting wood. They "cut enough in one day to last the whole community the whole winter," Parker recalled. Those not engaged in cutting helped prepare a "big chicken and rice dinner" that all the families ate together. He further stated that he heard stories, passed down from his parents' time, of interracial pig barbecues that the tenants on the Ray place held in the woods. In the privacy of the woods, swamps, and fields, black and white sharecroppers again worked out their own way of dealing with race and leisure.[11]

Public codes of segregated eating had exceptions even in the towns. One wealthy white planter used to take his black grandson with him everywhere, including the restaurants of Sparta, where they ate at the same table. In this case, however, his unique behavior was the exception. In addition, there was another, more generalized infringement on the border of the interracial dining taboo. It occurred on the outskirts of the village of Devereux, where the rules of urban segregation seemed a bit looser than in Sparta. An African American couple, Mit and Rose Wallace, owned a meat market that functioned as the only restaurant in the vicinity. Rose prepared the food and served it to an interracial clientele. There were no tables inside the restaurant, possibly by design, so customers would eat their fish or chicken standing or take it outside and eat under a tree. In this way, they circumvented the general taboo.[12]

The manner in which food-related racial boundaries were transgressed raises new questions. The vague outlines of a pattern of exceptions seem to indicate that different spaces in rural Hancock conveyed differing meanings regarding the symbolic value of food consumption. The iron-clad rule against interracial dining bent only rarely indoors. The infrequent indoor gatherings in which all sat at the same table were small, private, and sometimes painstakingly screened from public view. Posing no challenge to public racial etiquette, they clearly posed no threat to public white supremacy. When a community of black and white sharecroppers ate together after cutting a supply of firewood, however, their numbers made their act a public one. Nevertheless, perhaps this breakage of the formal rules suggests an underlying anthropological meaning. The full answer may not lie in the relative political and economic weakness of the white sharecroppers, because, as Mamie Washington testified, some white participants segregated small interracial dinners in their own, private homes. Perhaps these white southerners understood the woods as lying beyond the bounds of "civilized" society. Picnicking there, instead of returning to their homes or to a church grounds, suggested an escape into the primitive—which is half the fun of eating and camping in the woods. Proximity to nature may have signified greater distance from human constructs, including the etiquette of white supremacy. The racial etiquette was contrived to symbolically reinforce an unequal division of economic and political power and of the surplus wealth and material goods that went with them. By entering into the woods, dressed in common workclothes, the black and white sharecroppers removed themselves from the physical symbols of their society, which possibly suggested greater distance from the rules that governed that society. Entry into space with clear, permanent, constructed boundaries such as walls and a roof, however, would be equated with entry into civilization and the rules that govern it.

Another exception to the food taboo suggests the existence of another symbolic demarcation within space. The Wallaces did not use chairs in their interracial dining space. Chairs, like walls, speak of the domestication of space. They signify culture and the conscious ordering of society. But chairs suggest more than civilization; they suggest power. Kings have thrones. Religious, political, and business leaders emphasize their positions of power with the notion of chairs. Honored university professors have endowed chairs. Chairs also formalize human interactions and demonstrate relative degrees of authority among the members of a group. One sits down to do business with equals but sometimes stands to do so with seated superiors. For black and white people to sit together for a meal in the South—or even to sit near one another—would formally imply their equality. By not placing chairs inside their restaurant, the Wallaces evaded the question of equality. Although sitting on the ground or standing also constitutes a sort of social leveling, it does so informally, almost accidentally. An arrangement of chairs and tables presents a static and stable structure. The ground or the forest offers a more free-flowing social space, one that feels temporary and unofficial. It seems that white southerners could live with this kind of ambiguity, because the Wallaces' place did good business for many years.[13]

The Sharing of Sacred Space

Outside of school—which occupied only a few years in most peoples' lives—the most important public rural institution was the church. Here, too, ambiguity marked the use of space that in the towns was clearly segregated by the twentieth century.[14]

In rural southern society, with its diffuse population, church was the primary place to trade news from beyond one's immediate neighborhood. The black civic leaders of the postdisfranchisement age, agricultural extension agents, home demonstration agents, Jeanes teachers, and Rosenwald School building agents all customarily spoke at black church services as the most efficient means of organizing their campaigns. Most churches hosted regular picnics, or dinners on the grounds, as they were called. After migrants began leaving for the cities, the churches helped maintain family and neighborly ties by having annual homecoming services. Even those not interested in religion were drawn by the crowds, the activities, and the chance for gossip. At some Sunday services the nonchurched of the neighborhood gathered by the parked wagons to talk and perhaps begin dinner a little early.

Black or white, farm people commonly spent more time at church than modern urban people felt necessary. But for African Americans in particular, the church paired with the family as the chief refuges against a hostile world. Speaking of life as an African American in rural Hancock during the first half of the twentieth century, Eugene Foster Jr. said: "The only time you really was free was when you went to church. You could relax. You were free. And time didn't mean nothing to you." Perhaps partly to maximize the time spent in this free space, African Americans held lengthy church services. According to Foster, "You'd go all day, from nine or ten in the morning to five at night."[15] Always filled with protracted preaching, as well as congregational and choir singing, Sunday services could be extended by special events such as "sings" or choir reunions, Mother's Day, Deacon's Day, and Pastor's Anniversary.

Sunday services began with an hour of Sunday school, in which people studied scripture and often sharpened their reading skills as adults. Additionally, until deep in the twentieth century, churches housed and often funded and administered the local school, especially in the African American community. Functions held on church-school grounds thus often overlapped in purpose and leadership.

Church also extended beyond Sunday. Church-based charities gave some aid to the destitute and organized missionary efforts. Beginning around 1946, some churches organized voter's registration drives. Once a year, moreover, each church set aside a week for prolonged revival services in which a visiting preacher and visiting vocalists drew people throughout the area and across denominational lines. Actually, denominational ties in the countryside hung pretty slack, allowing for a great deal of denominational intermixing. Religious crossover could occur in other ways as well.[16]

The segregated nature of rural churches is a complex subject. The past few years have yielded a strong literature about the shared and segregated religious cultures of the antebellum period. It is now clear that African Americans and European Americans shared membership in the same churches in many communities before the Civil War. Although seating during services was often segregated by race, gender, and class, many church responsibilities, including preaching, were sometimes shared. At least one white church in Hancock still has nineteenth-century records that list slaves as members.[17]

Some people living in Hancock, white and black, heard stories of antebellum religious interracialism and of the exodus of African Americans into independent black churches following emancipation. When they were free to go, blacks made clear that they had been dissatisfied with some of the discriminatory practices of the older integrated church. White church leaders had shown racial preferences at the picnic table and at the communion table.[18] Also, because African Americans historically used the church as a rallying point against white exploitation and cultural hegemony, they found it difficult to preach, pray, and sing freely, either under slavery or after, in the presence of whites. As slaves, they had maintained an independent religious tradition by supplementing racially integrated services with long, private ones of their own in the outdoors, under brush arbors. After freedom this hidden institution emerged to challenge the integrated churches for the loyalties of African Americans.[19]

Nonetheless, the movement of African Americans to their own churches did not completely sever all interracial religious ties. For a variety of reasons, some white Christians assisted their black coreligionists in establishing separate denominations and separate places of worship. When they realized that the blacks' decision to leave was irrevocable, the white leaders of the Methodist Episcopal Church, South, helped black Methodist members of their church—including Bishop Lucius Henry Holsey of Hancock—to organize the Colored Methodist Episcopal Church. Through much of the remainder of the nineteenth century, white Methodists exercised a great deal of paternal influence over the course of the new denomination. Eventually this church became fully independent of the white church, although it never appealed to African American Christians the way that the fully independent black Baptist and African Methodist Episcopal churches did.[20]

These churches found both help and resistance among whites. Many whites saw the black churches as threats to political and economic white supremacy, both during Reconstruction and after. During the Populist movement of the 1890s, one black preacher, Rev. H. S. Doyle, barely escaped Sparta with his life after a mob of white Democrats attempted to shoot him in front of the courthouse for campaigning for Tom Watson and the Populists.[21]

At the same time, some planters supported the churches to draw stable agricultural laborers to their fields or, if they could influence a black pastor, to hold some sway over the black community. Others did so as an expression of noblesse oblige. Possibly some did so out of a sense of Christian solidarity and fellow feeling.[22] In the years immediately following emancipation, many planters let the ex-slaves worship in groves on their land and sometimes contributed plots of land or even lumber for building black churches. Most rural black Hancock churches were organized in this way in the 1860s and 1870s. Some of the names of Hancock churches still point to their early history, such as Hickory Grove Baptist Church, Archer Grove Baptist Church, Powell Grove Baptist Church, and Pearson Chapel African Methodist Episcopal Church. During the decade of Populist challenge, white planters increased their support of black churches, selling local black communities plots of land for token prices in return for support at the polls. This pattern of white support continued through the twentieth century. Only rarely did white landowners charge Hancock blacks the market value of plots purchased for churches.[23]

In an interesting reversal of roles, one white woman born in 1908 remembered that the land for Pleasant Grove Baptist Church—her church—was donated by a black farmer named Bill Arnold. He was already old in her youth, but Francis Frazier remembered him coming regularly to the white services and sitting on the back bench. "After 'Amen,'" she remembered, "he tipped out." She figures that Arnold stopped attending when she was about ten or eleven years old. After that her church became completely segregated.[24]

The process of segregating religious institutions moved rapidly after emancipation. Soon after the Civil War the overwhelming majority of African American members of white-led churches transferred their memberships to autonomous black churches. Formally southerners were religiously segregated by 1870, yet as Francis Frazier's story indicates, religious people were not as easily segregated as their institutions. Informally regular visitations continued in both directions among farm folk at least until the 1940s.

Interracial church visitation illustrates class identity's tremendous influence on race relations. Whereas many people born in Hancock County before 1930 attended a baptism, a wedding, or more often a funeral across the race line at some time in their lives, few wealthy whites made a habit of going to ordinary black services. In the southeast section of Hancock, however, where a large number of black and white sharecroppers lived, many poor people regularly attended services across the racial divide.

White planters attended black church services from time to time to observe rites of passage for the black men and women who worked in their homes. Affection or a sense of duty may have motivated some to attend these services, but their visits also helped to enhance their status within the community. The large planters often employed many members of the church located nearest to their land. Sometimes they or their families had donated the land for the church. Some planters continued to support the churches their tenants attended. One black sharecropper, Mamie Washington, remembered a local planter nicknamed "the money man" who would put up to one hundred dollars at a time in the collection. Making an appearance at church helped labor relations within the context of the postslavery paternalism espoused—if not fully practiced—by the planters. At baptisms, marriages, and funerals the planters demonstrated—to their domestic help or tenants, to the black and white communities, and probably most importantly to themselves—that they were fulfilling the role of the benevolent patron.[25]

These same black men and women were invited in turn to observe their patrons' central rituals. At white churches they demonstrated to the white community the important position of the white family who brought them. Not only was their attendance allowed; it was expected. One white planter said that "it used to be a sorry funeral that didn't have any colored folks at it."[26]

Evidence suggests that through the 1920s some African American landowners chose to attend services at white churches for reasons of their own. Although he helped found the black Springfield Baptist Church, Zach Hubert, a prosperous landowner, also attended Sunday services at two white Baptist churches located in villages near his community. There, according to his children, he would ask successful white farmers about farming techniques or the cotton market. He also cultivated friendships with influential members of the churches—important assets for an independent black farmer in a culture of white supremacy. These ties later proved helpful to Hubert in a number of ways, especially in warning him against the most hostile and violent whites and in giving him a direct avenue of appeal when his family was threatened by white violence. Finally, his presence on the "black" bench at the back of the church, dignified but humble, probably helped reassure white farmers that Hubert "knew his place" even if he owned more land than they did.[27]

Hubert owned several hundred acres. Other black landowners with smaller holdings also attended white services. Erma Mae Quinn, who grew up in the white Island Creek Baptist Church, remembered that Minnie Watkins, a black landowner, and her daughter used to sit on the back bench of the church every service in the 1930s. Essie Mae Primer was born in 1916 to a black family that owned a small farm. They could almost see a white church, Zebulon United Methodist, from their home, and her grandfather would attend revival services there: "[He] would go on and be to their meetings, just like he was going to ours." She was too small to go at the time and often had to stay home to care for her ailing mother, but her grandfather did not always attend alone: "If Daddy wasn't too tired to go," she remembered, "sometimes he'd go with him."[28]

Black landowners had clear incentives to maintain close relationships to whites by attending their churches, but the majority of black farmers were tenants. Of those interviewed in this study—especially those who lived on large, all-black plantations, such as those around Devereux—most rarely or never set foot in a white church and did not often rub elbows with local planters if or when these men and their families dropped in on the black churches. At most they entered white sacred space briefly when a planter died. Sometimes these formalities of farewell were reduced to brief, assembly-line viewings of the corpse before the funeral began. One white woman whose family owned a small plot of land near bigger white planters recalled: "We would let blacks come in and see whites laid out at the funeral. They'd all come in at once and then out the door." In some communities whites wouldn't linger in black sacred space, either. Born in 1908, Eva Reese attended New Beulah Baptist Church all her life but has no memory of whites attending regular services or revivals. For funerals, though, they sometimes "just brought flowers" and left.[29]

Poorer white and black farmers attended the other race's religious services much more often than did wealthier farmers or townsfolk, particularly in areas that contained both black and white sharecroppers. Besides attending services to mark one another's personal milestones, they also invited one another to revival services and even to weekly services.

Until he left the Linton community in 1935, Kelly Brookins, a white sharecropper born in 1925, used to attend revival services at a black Baptist church. "Back then," he said, "we would go to black churches, and they would come to ours." He remembers that "three or four families would get together and go" at a time. Mamie Washington, a black sharecropper also from Brookins's part of the county, agreed: "We'd go to any church together." Mostly she attended choir reunions and revival services but remembers regular services, too.

Some white farmers spoke of just dropping in on black services from time to time. Sometimes, they came by invitation. Kelly Brookins remembered that the preacher of one black church used to "go to white people's houses and invite them to come to church." Mamie Washington said that sharecroppers of either race would ask croppers of the other race for leave to attend their churches. "We'd ask someone if we could go and they'd ask us [if they could go]." She described it as a fairly casual and conventional request, readily granted.[30]

At least one white landowning family—the Walkers of southeast Hancock—attended African American services with some regularity. The Walker family were semiprofessional musicians, and they found themselves irresistibly drawn by an appreciation of black church music. Dot Brown remembers that her parents and brothers "always loved to go": "We'd go every time. They'd have their revival—we'd go a night or two. Or to sings—on Sundays when they'd have different choirs from different places." They had no musical instruments, but as Brown remembers, "they could *sing*." She was especially moved by their complex harmonies. Although she went only when her whole family attended, her brothers used to go on their own and sometimes sat with the congregation. At other times, she said, "If [the white church] got out before the colored folks did, they would sometimes sit their car out beside the colored church and listen to them sing." But her family did not always have to go to the black church to hear the music. The church was so close that the Walkers "could hear them singing on clear nights" at their own home.

According to Brown, theirs was not the only white family in the neighborhood to attend this black church. "Several others in the community would go," too. Once, when her church was hosting a visiting preacher, the black church that they sometimes visited "was having a singing—and we wanted to go to it." So they invited the white preacher to come along with them. It turned out that he was quite comfortable with the suggestion. "He said he'd go and preach at colored churches that way. They'd ask him to go and preach. And, yeah, he'd go up with us to this one."[31]

This white family's appreciation for black church music raises a difficult question. Why were black and white sharecroppers and small landowners attending services across the racial divide long after formal religious segregation? The evidence offers only hints. Oral history does not work as well with distant motivations as it does with distant actions. Most regular visitors did not seem to improve their economic condition or social status by attending. Some stories suggest an appreciation of the personal style of a particular preacher or of the vocal range of a particular soprano in a church across the color line. Like Dot Brown, a number of white interviewees spoke of their admiration for the African American tradition of sacred music. A. J. Parker, a white sharecropper from the southern part of the county, said, "You never heard no good singing yet until you hear a bunch of black people that know what it's all about." He clarified, "I ain't talking about this young stuff, this rock and roll. I'm talking about those old black people. You get them in church, and you'll hear some singing." For some, the music was enough reason to go. Still, when asked directly, most people don't recall why they went. Perhaps interracial church visitation, for a long time, was an ordinary enough part of rural culture that it needed no special rationale.[32]

Sometimes visitors had mixed impressions. The enthusiasm evident in many rural black services put some white visitors off balance. One white sharecropper admired the black church music but found the more animated expressions of shouting and convulsing in the Spirit "kind of amazing to watch." Another white sharecropper whose mother brought her as a girl to black services in the 1930s was startled at the display and giggled afterward, until her mother told her that she should not laugh at other people's religion. Yet another white girl who attended the baptism of a black servant in the 1930s found the emotional tone of the service unnerving, although her parents seemed to enjoy the preaching. Years later she remembered it with uncertainty: "Mom and Dad said it was a good sermon. I didn't know if it was—it scared me to death." Other white visitors found the black celebration of the sacred not at all frightening. Speaking of black Christians' manifestations of "coming under the Spirit," A. J. Parker warned, "Oughtn't anybody say nothing against it, cause that's real, that Holy Ghost. That's real religion. It's the real thing. It can be overdone, now, you know—make somebody pay attention to you. But don't never say nothing against the Holy Ghost, cause that's real." A shared sense of the sacred became a powerful mediating feature in the culture—and perhaps sense of identity—of many rural black and white people.[33]

African American visitors to white churches seemed reluctant to praise or criticize white religion in the presence of a white interviewer. Most blandly stated that "it was nice." Some black visitors may have found the white churches uncomfortably restrained and dry. Although wild emotional displays were not uncommon among white evangelical churches in the first half of the nineteenth century, they toned down considerably after that time. One white sharecropper who remembered black Christians coming to his church said that they sat quietly through the service except for one or two who might offer up an occasional encouraging "Amen!" during the sermon. Some seemed drawn to the white preaching tradition. Essie Mae Primer remembers seeing her grandfather, a black landowner, regularly go off to attend revival services at a nearby white Methodist church in the 1910s and 1920s. "He'd come back, tell us what a good meeting they had, tell us what the preacher's texts were. He enjoyed it." Perhaps, despite the complex economic and status-related motivations many people had for attending, one can assume that most visitors chose to attend services across the race lines because they enjoyed them. In summary, these exchange visits—especially among poorer people—suggest a shared or overlapping interracial religious culture or at least the existence of individuals whose religious tastes overlaid two different religious cultures.[34]

Southerners generally agreed on the efficacy of prayer, especially the prayers of a man consecrated to the religious ministry. Both black and white preachers made themselves available and sometimes made house calls to counsel, comfort, and pray for their flocks. At least occasionally they served the spiritual or temporal needs of men and women across the racial divide. For example, a white preacher at a Green County Baptist church became the closest adviser of Zach Hubert, one of the county's wealthiest black farmers.[35] When power in the form of influence, information, or spiritual authority flowed in this direction—from white to black—it could be understood by whites as conforming to the paternalist ideal upheld by the conservative planter element.

When black preachers ministered to white Christians, however, they entered one of the most ambiguous zones in rural southern race relations. Whites did not automatically respect the authority of black clergymen. Because many preachers led their communities politically during Reconstruction, Populism, and later the civil rights movement, they could draw a high and lethal level of hostility from the white community generally. Because of their shared faith, however, some white southerners recognized the spiritual authority of some black preachers. Still, personal respect in things spiritual did not create generally egalitarian sensibilities in whites. One white man spoke of a black preacher who paid a pastoral visit to his house when his wife was critically ill. According to the man's testimony, after the preacher prayed for her, the woman recovered. The white man, with tears in his eyes, gratefully remembered the event and spoke out of the contradiction in southern race relations: "I don't know but that that nigger preacher saved my wife's life." By articulating this strange unconscious combination of respect and contempt, the white man showed that he believed that the minister possessed a kind of spiritual authority that drew his respect but that did not change his status as "nigger."[36]

A shared sense of religious identity may have brought black and white farmers together, but it did not fully dissolve racial conventions and the etiquette of white supremacy. Seating arrangements and picnics indicated the boundary lines. Seating in church buildings was always segregated. Black and white churches both reserved a separate row for interracial visitors; in white churches it was invariably located in the back, whereas black churches placed it sometimes at the back and sometimes at the front. When visitors were expected, the separate bench was kept open. One black woman remembered the special seating for whites as similar to the courteous treatment other honored guests received in the black church, to ensure they had a place to sit. Sometimes, however, visitors came late or unexpected, and a row would have to be cleared. One white sharecropper seemed to enjoy reminiscing about the deference that a bench clearing of the front row signaled to him.[37] Yet some white visitors declined this prerogative and chose to stand instead. On the Sunday when the white Walker family invited their preacher to come along with them to visit the black church for a "singing," they found a packed church with people already standing outside to hear. "We wouldn't take no seats," she remembered. "We wouldn't make none of them get up. They offered to get us some benches, but we said that we could hear just as good outside as we could inside." So they and their preacher stood with the other latecomers and listened in the yard in front of the church.[38] Racial etiquette did not require slavish conformity of rural people. It could be ignored in the interests of decency and good manners.

At one regular religious event in the southern part of the county, the rules of seating were thrown out the window. Each year in the fall a traveling black preacher would pitch a tent on a hill and hold forth for a one- or two-week camp meeting. "That was something to look at," A. J. Parker remembered. "Damn, if they didn't get down." Parker said that the big tent would be packed as full as possible: "People standing all around outside it, too. Go all night sometimes." The preacher was accompanied by a band and by choirs from local churches. "I mean it was something else to listen at," recounted Parker, laughing. "Man! You didn't know what kind of music they had. They had horns. They had a band. They had everything but a piano." A set of generator-powered lights let the meetings go on long into the night. Although it was "black run," "a bunch of whites" would come out for it. Parker remembers hearing the singing from the tent meeting as he worked in the fields. As the day went on, more and more people would be drawn by the sound. The meeting would start in the morning, and people would arrive with chairs and set them on the grass as close to the speaker as they could get. As a result, seating was ordered not by race but by a combination of religious fervor and the availability of leisure time.[39]

Perhaps this openness to randomness and racial intermixing was a product of denominational culture. Parker did not remember the religious affiliation of the black preacher, but if he was of the Holiness-Pentecostal wing of Christianity—which is suggested by the eclectic mix of musical instruments—his disdain of racial conventions would have flowed directly from his faith tradition. Environmental context might offer another way of understanding the flouting of seating customs. As I discussed earlier in the context of dining, interior spaces were readily segregated. The outdoors, only flimsily bounded by the tent, may not have offered itself as a "proper" space for segregated seating. Most of the time, however, religious celebrations took place indoors, and there segregated seating prevailed.[40]

The other point where convention structured religious interracialism in Hancock was the picnic table. Rural churches all had annual celebrations called "dinners on the grounds," basically potlucks for church members. These often followed homecoming services, which acted as a magnet for emigrants from the community—an opportunity to talk and eat at leisure over a long afternoon. Few interviewees mentioned these events when discussing religious interracialism, an omission that implies that these events were not integrated. Eva Reese remembered that she and other black women were sometimes invited to white churches to clean up after their homecoming dinners in the 1920s and 1930s. They were rewarded with the leftovers. One white sharecropper from a community that regularly exchanged interracial church visits said that whites "never did go to any of their dinners on the grounds because they didn't come to ours." There was no need to ask why blacks did not come to white dinners on the grounds. As I discussed earlier, the general taboo against sharing food at the same table seemed almost absolute within the sphere of religion. Essie Mae Primer's memories of her grandfather show that it was not quite absolute. When the white church he often attended "had dinner to serve, he'd eat with them, just like he would with another combination," Primer said. "Grandpa would go out and laugh and talk and eat with them." How the tables were arranged and whether he ate with them or merely near them cannot be known. Nonetheless, the idea that he, an African American farmer, was at a public meal with the white church in the 1910s and 1920s illustrates yet again that few rules were truly absolute in the rural South. The testimony of Hancock people argues that individual communities, like individual people, worked out their own pattern for race relations, especially through the first quarter of the twentieth century. The passing years, however, brought not an absolute closing of options but a persistent narrowing of them.[41]

The separation of black and white worshipers proceeded unevenly in rural Hancock. Most of the evidence of black attendance at regular white Sunday services comes from stories elderly people told about their parents and grandparents. Dot Brown, born in 1920, heard older people say that black worshipers used to come to the white church more often before the 1920s. In her day, Brown recollected, "they came more seldom—mostly funerals and such." African American sources generally confirmed her story. Zach Hubert, who died in 1926, had regularly attended the white Powelton Baptist Church and the White Plains Baptist Church a few miles away in Greene County. His children and grandchildren, however, stuck exclusively to the black churches. And although Essie Mae Primer's grandfather frequently attended white churches through the 1920s, she did not. Only four communities in the county described regular exchange visits through the 1930s, and three of those communities were in the county's southeast quadrant, which held most of Hancock's white sharecroppers.[42]

All of this suggests that a racial boundary in the rural religious sphere was crossed at the end of the 1920s. The timing presents a puzzle. It does not correlate with the black movement to establish separate churches in the 1860s, the white movement to segregate urban public spaces in the 1890s, or the rise of rabidly antiblack rhetoric in the 1890s and 1900s. Perhaps the change in attendance reflected the passing of the last generation that had attended the interracial antebellum services.

Alternatively, perhaps the decline of regular black visitation was a rural ripple made by the New Negro movement of the 1920s, in which middle-class young African Americans, led by W. E. B. Du Bois, among others, established a more self-consciously militant and self-reliant posture in race relations. A number of black men and women from Hancock did in fact study at Morehouse College and Spelman Seminary, respectively, where Du Bois was an influential figure. Some reported being influenced by the educations they received there. The black militant movement of the 1920s flowed through another channel as well—the Universal Negro Improvement Association (UNIA), led by Marcus Garvey. The Garveyite movement, although seen as northern and urban, was actually supported by the dues of rural southerners. Of 782 local divisions, 423 were in the South. There was no UNIA division in Hancock County or even in the east Georgia piedmont, but the movement was a powerful force in the black belt generally, preaching black pride, self-defense, and racial separation to the poor and uneducated. Whatever the cause or causes, regular black attendance at ordinary white church services declined noticeably in the 1920s.[43]

Yet a curtain did not fully fall between black and white worshiping communities even then. Rural white visitation of black churches in Hancock did not seem to slow for another decade or more, perhaps reflecting a social condition on which James Weldon Johnson commented in his 1934 treatise *Negro*

Americans, What Now? In this work Weldon encouraged African Americans to "cultivate friendly interracial relations" as a matter of "necessity and common sense" in facilitating economic advancement. He was, however, dismayed by the situation in the South, of which he wrote, "Interracial intercourse, when it does take place, is more often than not a one-sided arrangement." He explained, "In such instances, the whites come into our midst, but, no matter how sincerely they desire the closer relationship, they fear to offend public sentiment by having us go into their midst." Johnson recognized that the black community was more open and flexible than the white community in dealing with race relations, however flexible white individuals might be. As a result, he concluded, "the cultivation of social and intellectual intercourse between members of the two races in the South cannot progress very far until the whites are as free to act as we are."[44]

In the 1940s white visitation of black churches began to drop off as well. Again, we can only speculate on the reasons. First, World War II increased tension in race relations in Hancock. African Americans described whites as cooling in their attitudes toward them, and the southern newspapers reflected a white concern over the increased militancy and "insolence" among African Americans who had played a role in the war effort. Across the South whites feared that black southerners had been "ruined" by being treated as social equals in France or even having white French women as lovers and that they could never again fit into "their place" in rural southern society. One black soldier from Devereux, James Brown, attested that his experiences in France and Germany did lead him to question southern racial restrictions. Soon after being discharged from the army, he left Hancock for Detroit.[45] Yet many other black veterans stayed in the county. According to historian Orville Vernon Burton, these were "the most militant, aware, and active" members of their communities in the decades after the war.[46] In response, in Hancock and elsewhere, the Klan enjoyed a small resurgence, riding the crest of white anxiety.

Other structural changes may have influenced the pre-1950 rural culture in ways that made it less tolerant of racial ambiguity. In the 1930s and 1940s "modern" society established new ties with the heart of rural America, paving roads and running electric and telephone lines into places that had once been relatively remote. This does not mean that rural people had not earlier had access to towns and urban culture. Many went to town on Friday night or Saturday to see the sights. Most had relatives in a town somewhere. But they were aware of the differences between town culture and rural culture. What they chose to do in their own neighborhoods was their own business, and few people from town could pry into their private affairs. These innovations in travel and communications brought the separate rural and urban worlds closer together. The postwar upturn in the economy also placed cars within the reach of a larger number of people, speeding the flow of visitors up and down the newly smoothed roads. These alterations had to increase the visibility of rural relationships and heighten contrasts with "modern" race relations as they were structured in town. It is conceivable that, under the modern gaze, rural white people came to feel that their culture was "inferior" and "unsophisticated." It is easy to imagine the effect of scornful urban eyes on a rural culture with a lower standard of education or fewer symbols of modern life—a culture without flush toilets, fashionable clothing, gymnasiums, or strictly segregated churches.

Two Hancock churches unaccountably stood as bulwarks against the spread of strict church segregation in the 1940s. Mt. Nebo Baptist Church and Friendship Baptist Church, black and white, respectively, face each other across a road that divides Hancock from Washington County in the far southeast of the county. Groups of black and white Baptists were crossing that road, according to Mamie Washington, until the 1980s. In the late 1940s, according to one white sharecropper, they even endured a cross burning between the churches, locally attributed to the Washington County Klan. Still the visitors persisted, until the last generation that cherished an interracial approach to the sacred had all died or had become too old to attend on their own.[47]

The tradition of interracial church visitation attenuated as the years passed and rural folks moved to town. Indeed, after they had moved to town, not one person interviewed for this study ever entered a church across the race line for any reason except, rarely, for a funeral. Despite the increased social distance, however, some urban people still seemed capable of appreciating faith beyond "the veil." Robert Herndon was born in Milledgeville in 1930, after his father moved from Powelton. He heard black sacred music as he grew up in town, but only on warm days as it spilled out open church windows and down the street. He remembers enjoying the sound.[48]

Ironically, even as the culture of interracial church visitation and the other various manifestations of rural interracial intimacy leached away, memories of them began to be used more intensively to serve a new political purpose. Under the Truman administration, when new federal programs and court decisions promoted the civil rights of African Americans, the *Sparta Ishmaelite* and other southern papers began to run a spate of articles that sentimentally called on the "special relationship" between black and white southerners as evidence that white southerners knew the needs of their black neighbors better than "northern extremists" did. This kind of message had been featured heavily throughout the nineteenth century, first in defiance of northern threats to intervene in southern affairs and later as an appeal to black voters to elect "their friends and neighbors," the Democratic planters who "understood them best." Then, as the North became tired of "the Negro question" and black southerners lost their right to vote, the assertions of interracial intimacy became increasingly less frequent. The New Deal and particularly Truman reawakened the story, the retelling of which coincided with the loss of much that had given intimacy some shape and substance.[49]

Rural Health Care

Many rural Hancock interviewees described other points of interaction outside church. In southern cities such as Atlanta, hospitals, doctors' offices, and other health-care dispensaries were segregated. Like theaters and soda fountains, however, these segregated zones simply did not exist in the countryside. In fact, some did not exist even in Sparta: Hancock had no hospital during the first half of the twentieth century. According to Mae Warren, moreover, the doctors in this small town did not segregate their offices. Warren remembered that "they were good to black people. All patients waited in the same room." Overall, however, sick or injured rural southerners—especially those of small means—rarely encountered college-trained medical experts. When they did, the doctor frequently came to the house, even when the patient required potentially dangerous treatment. Kelly Brookins, the son of white sharecroppers, remembered when a doctor performed an appendectomy on his oldest sister, operating on the family's dining-room table; the family paid him with a forty-pound can of hog lard and a ham.[50]

Most of the time and for most people, home remedy, the root doctor, and the midwife met the emergencies of life. Many older people remember wild herbs that they and their parents gathered to help them deal with minor illnesses and the injuries often suffered in farm life. Hyndenberg and Eunice Dixon, black farmers from near Linton, said, "There wasn't no clinics in the country." As a result, all rural residents learned how to use such natural medicinals as wild sage, "salifaction" bushes, and peach-tree leaves in plasters or teas for common ailments such as fevers, coughs, headaches, and colds.[51]

When an illness demanded a medical expert, farm folk often consulted an herb-lore professional, a "root doctor." The black and white traditions of "root" are old in America, certainly intertwined, and apparently arose in part from Native American health arts. Both black and white root doctors plied their trade in early twentieth-century Hancock County and aided both black and white patients, taking payment in whatever form was available. One black woman remembers hearing that her grandfather, who died in 1926, "stayed up many nights working on sick people, white and black." Most root specialists had full-time jobs and worked root only as a community service or to supplement their income, but some became almost full-time root doctors. One white man, Tom Johnson, gathered large quantities of wild herbs and mass-produced natural remedies in any kind of bottle he could obtain. Many people of both races sought him for aid. Some of his patients—probably emigrants from Hancock—came from as far as New York City. A few other individuals became highly specialized root experts. One illiterate old black man occasionally called on a white man, W. J. Miller, who was then working at a service station in Sparta. He asked Miller to read letters from former patients in northern cities who had written to thank him for their cures.[52]

Root work was a fully developed interracial profession with a broad, interracial clientele. Miller, born in 1927 to a poor rural family, remembered one time in his childhood when his mother was quite ill with the flu. After a couple of days in bed, she asked her husband to "go get Aunt Leanne," their black neighbor. This neighbor knew root, and after listening to the sick woman's complaint, she went into the woods for a few minutes. She picked something that looked like rabbit tobacco, crushed it, and made an infusion of it. She told Miller's mother to drink the concoction three times that day and promised to return the next. Her fully recovered patient was up and about when she came back. It is interesting that the white Millers sought out a black woman for aid, because the county's leading white herbalist, Tom Johnson, lived only a few miles away. Apparently, in the selection of folk medical specialists, the issue was not race but proximity. "Aunt Leanne" was just a short distance away. In time of illness, the only concern was to end the suffering of the sick person as quickly as possible.[53]

Midwives completed the corps of health-care specialists working in the rural South. Although city folk and wealthier country folk had been seeking the obstetric services of medical doctors for decades, poorer country people still called for the midwife, or "granny-woman," in the last hours of pregnancy.[54] Usually these were older women who had long experience with delivery, but a few midwives started out young as apprentices of older women. Like root doctors, midwives could be either white or black, although the majority in

Hancock seemed to be black. Again like root doctors, they seemed to serve an interracial clientele. Some midwives helped entire generations of rural people in their neighborhoods to enter the world. Creasy Walker, the daughter of black landowners, was named for the ex-slave midwife who "caught" her. She was the last of five hundred babies her namesake had birthed in a long career of service to the local community. Unlike the doctors, midwives would stay through the whole labor process and sometimes for a period afterward to ensure that the mother recovered well. Instead of wielding clinical authority, tongs, and scalpels, they brought herb lore, knowledge of bodily manipulation, and the calming authority that comes from having been there many times before, perhaps at the pregnant woman's own birth. Some wealthier farmers called both the midwife and the doctor, trusting in a mixture of the old and the new, and often thereby in a mixture of the black and the white.[55]

When the medical expert had done his or her work, it became the responsibility of neighbors to help lighten the family's burden. As John Swint, a white farmowner, said, "Folks out in the country were really close together. They knew what was ailing each other." And it was not uncommon for them to extend aid across race lines. William Brookins, born in 1912 to white sharecroppers, remembered his parents sitting up with various neighbors—including African Americans—during illness, keeping watch over the sufferer so that the family could rest. John Roberts, the son of a white yeoman, tells a similar story. Sometimes the nurse could do nothing but offer the comfort of a compassionate touch. As young children, Myrtle Brookins, a white sharecropper, and her brother watched over an elderly black woman during her last illness. They each took a hand and held it as she died. Nor did death bring an end to neighborly service. William Brookins remembered black and white farmers assisting one another in watching over the dead, who were washed and laid out in their best clothes in private homes until burial. This last act was performed partly out of respect for the dead, shown by fanning away flies, and partly to ensure that a comatose person was not accidentally buried alive, as could happen without a modern medical exam. According to black sharecropper James Wilson, "there were no undertakers" among poor rural folk, "just brothers and sisters in Jesus Christ."[56]

After nursing the sick or sitting by the dead, rural folk would help the stricken family by working their fields or preparing food for them. "You'd watch all night," Brookins said, "and plow all the next day." Marvin and Mary Thompson, white farmowners from the southern part of the county, remembered that "if somebody died or was sick," neighboring black sharecroppers "would come and volunteer to cook or clean." When their turn came for neighborly reciprocation involving a sick black neighbor, the Thompsons said they "wouldn't cook and wait on them," but they "would cook and would carry it to them."[57]

Neighbors often found their own way of working through the complex and contradictory impulses of racism and neighborliness. Katie Hunt remembers a newly married and inexperienced young white woman coming over to her home for practical and personal advice.[58] One black woman remembered exchanging babysitting services—including wet-nursing—in the 1930s with a neighboring white woman. Both were small landowners.[59]

Sexuality, Family, and Kinship: The Most Intimate Interracial Relationships

Because of tension between the Solid South and the permissive South, breaches of interracial custom that could arouse a violent reaction in one neighborhood would be taken in stride in another. In some parts of Hancock and surrounding counties, interracial affairs between black and white people were broken up decisively. In others, monogamous interracial families were accepted without challenge by the white community.[60]

These relationships appeared in a number of different patterns. Under slavery many planters had sexual relations with slave women. Although the prevalence of interracial sexual intimacy proves that segregation was far from the minds of most antebellum planters, it does not indicate an egalitarian impulse. Most of these relationships were brief, entailed no commitment, and held little social significance; many, in fact, amounted to little more than rape. Other relationships were life-long and monogamous, however, and seem to have been maintained by deep commitments. Some of the children born to the more committed relationships were recognized by their white fathers and given special protection before and after the Civil War. Sometimes even extended kinship ties were recognized by black and white southerners.

Following emancipation the frequency of interracial sex declined sharply, as African Americans gained possession of their own bodies and the freedom to move. Still, antebellum kinship ties continued to be recognized by some families in the postbellum period. Additionally, some white and black southerners continued to initiate new couplings and new interracial families well into the twentieth century. Only recently have southern historians begun to examine this pattern, although southern sociologists in the early twentieth century clearly recognized it, and southern authors have lingered over the human dramas it produced.[61]

The largest number of interracial sexual encounters in the rural South after the Civil War, as before it, were not long-term attachments. Some planters continued to coerce sexual favors from black women, replacing legal privilege with economic leverage. Some of these men stabilized their relationships somewhat by maintaining black mistresses and black families "on the side." Poorer white men also pursued black women, offering them money or clothing. In his autobiography the Reverend James Brown, a black sharecropper born in 1926 in the middle of the Devereux plantation district, wrote with exasperation of the poor white overseers and sawmill managers in his community who paid black men to introduce them to black women. But one white sharecropper suggested that meetings between white and black tenant farmers need not hinge on material payments. He chuckled as he observed that, growing up beside one another, in relative isolation from many other people their age, some adolescents working in adjacent fields would "slip off in the woods" together and "think it all pretty natural."[62] Sexually, at any rate, there was no consistently enforced segregation in the rural South.

It is and was commonly understood that the great majority of interracial trysts and almost all long-term relationships involved white men and black women. As one black man related, in the South "the black man and the white woman were slaves and the white man and black woman were free to do what they liked." Nonetheless, as historian Martha Hodes proved for the colonial and antebellum South, and as many southern sociologists indicated for the Jim Crow South, more white women and black men were involved in interracial relationships than the white community later remembered. These relationships were, however, rarer and more carefully hidden from the public eye than were relationships between white males and black females. This secrecy was due to the danger they presented—social for the women; mortal for the men. Jean Toomer, the Harlem Renaissance author, wrote an essay about a white woman in Hancock banished by society for the two black children she bore. In Toomer's fictionalized account, she died alone and isolated, crushed under a fallen chimney. According to Katie Hunt, a woman who parallels Toomer's description lived quietly for many years in a black community on the rural outskirts of Sparta.[63]

Her relationship, although long-term, is difficult to reconstruct. The committed relationships of many white men and black women left much more evidence in the written record as well as in community memory. An examination of interracial families in Hancock and several surrounding counties showed that as young men, several planters and some poorer white men initiated relationships with black women, often mulatto, that continued through their lives. Their selection of mates is surprising in that many of these couples united on the heels of the Civil War, when the ratio of white men to white women was quite low.[64]

Some of these couples shared a house, with the black woman formally referred to as a domestic servant. Others lived in adjacent houses, or at least they told the census taker and other outsiders so. But as Ned Cobb, a black man from Alabama, observed in describing a rural interracial couple he knew, while they officially had separate residences in the same yard, they shared the same house during the day. And "at night, nobody there, no tellin where they slept at, the way they runned it when night come."[65] Usually such couples and their families lived in out-of-the-way places, invariably rural. Perhaps if such relationships remained discreet, local whites who may have disapproved chose instead to exercise "selective inattention." At any rate, the interracial families of rural white men and black women, even if generally known within a community, seemingly were allowed to remain a locally contained "open secret."[66]

Some of these families seem to have kept to themselves, as did the Skrine family, in the northern part of Hancock, or the Hills of Baldwin County, just west of Hancock. David B. Hill, one of the wealthiest planters in the county, built a private school and hired a teacher for his interracial children as an alternative to white and black public schools. Other families were apparently quite comfortable with their liminal position and socialized widely. The Guill family of Hancock County had an annual picnic and baseball game on the birthday of Frank Guill, which his white relatives and his common-law black wife's relatives both attended.[67]

All these monogamous interracial families were rural. Affairs between urban white men and black women no doubt occurred, but more committed relationships became socially untenable after the Civil War. This urban restriction had not always obtained, for in the antebellum period a leading Hancock judge and legislator, Nathan Sayre, had shared his Sparta mansion with his black family—apparently without sanction. But interviewees remember that by the late nineteenth century and through the twentieth, townsfolk would break up such couples by driving either or both of the partners from the county.[68] Sexually, the South had become solid in town even as it remained permissive in the country.

Additionally, interracial families needed economic independence. All the white fathers were at least small landowners. However intimate they were in other aspects of their lives, black and white sharecroppers did not possess the social leverage to build interracial families openly. Planters, however, had many resources with which to defend their families of color, and white yeomen with intermediate power depended more often on keeping a low profile—backed when necessary by the threat of personal violence—to protect their own.[69]

Interestingly, most monogamous interracial unions in the counties around Hancock were initiated between the end of the Civil War and 1890. Only a few of these relationships—which usually ended with the death of one of the partners—continued beyond 1921. This suggests that the rising tide of racism that characterized the decades immediately following 1890 directly inhibited the willingness—or the ability—of rural interracial couples to form common-law marriages. Nevertheless, a few of the most open families did stay together until after World War II. In addition, even if few rural interracial couples initiated their unions after segregationist rhetoric came to be expressed everywhere—in law, newspapers, and political stump speeches—the extended interracial kinship ties woven by earlier couples continued to hold people together far into the Jim Crow era.

It is likely that most "white" and "black" people who were biologically related simply ignored family members of the other race. Yet the frequency with which rural people recognized and maintained relationships based on consanguinity is surprising. Zach Hubert, the black grandson of an antebellum Warren County planter, maintained a close relationship with his white cousin, Matthew Hubert, for his entire life. The two visited each other and publicly referred to each other as "cousin." A gift of a cotton bale from Matthew's father to Zach's, in recognition of their tie as half-brothers, had assisted the black Hubert family's climb to the status of large landowners in the decades following the Civil War.

But the interracial kinship ties extended beyond the first cousins. Beautine Hubert DeCosta-Lee, Zach Hubert's granddaughter, related that annual family trips to the Powelton area to visit two "maiden sisters," her oldest white kin, "were usually anticipated with great joy," although in time the trips came to be marked by some ambivalence as well. One year her sister and a cousin completed their freshman years at Spelman and Morehouse Colleges, respectively. According to DeCosta-Lee: "They made it known that they were not going. They 'were tired of that old slavery stuff.'" She and several others of the younger Huberts agreed that they would not attend. Then, just before the trip, one of her other cousins began to remind them of the allures of the visit. DeCosta-Lee said: "We continued to be intellectual about the issue of 'the old slavery stuff,' but finally agreed . . . that we did not think the issue should cause us to miss the good food the sisters served."

She clearly remembered the sisters, after dinner, bringing out old family photographs "in velvet frames" or walking their "black" relatives around the cemetery behind the house and talking, in the best southern tradition of genealogical awareness, about their family connections. DeCosta-Lee admitted that as a girl she did not follow the conversations very carefully, because her mind was on playing with the other cousins, and she "was anxious to get outside as soon as possible," but her sister, Ophelia Hubert Taylor, remembered that the white Hubert sisters were quite direct in speaking about the interracial family tie. They "pointed" and "said, '———— was the father of ————. Therefore, he is your ————.'"

Sometimes these inherited ties stretched far from their place of origin. DeCosta-Lee herself "vividly" recalled one of the white Huberts writing her father at their home in Savannah to ask whether he could stay with them during a visit to the city. In a return letter her father "welcomed him" but added that a family of white Huberts also lived in Savannah and asked whether "he might prefer to stay with them." The man wrote back that "he knew there was a white Hubert family living in Savannah, but he did not know them well, therefore, he preferred staying with [Lee's father]." He did "and apparently enjoyed the visit," although Lee did not know "whether he visited the white Huberts or not."[70]

There are many other stories, similar in effect although ranging widely in form, told by elderly African Americans from Hancock. At least through the 1930s many whites seemed quite comfortable in quietly recognizing their black kin. Mary Hunt remembered a white man, Louis Tye, who lived near her. He had a half-brother, Will Tye, who often came to visit him, whom Hunt referred to as "a black white man." She recalled that "when Louis's children saw Will coming, they'd fly out over to go be with him." They "looked alike, one a little darker." They called each other publicly by their first names, and they did not try to hide the fact that they were family. "They were," Hunt stated, "good friends."[71]

Sometimes white southerners even took the initiative in introducing themselves as family to young African Americans who were born after their interracial forebears had died. Solomon Harper, an African American farmer near Devereux, shook his head as he remembered his surprise when a white woman—the sheriff's mother, in fact—explained to him the tangled weave of genealogy that made them cousins. He checked out her story and found that his own father, having been a bit closer than Solomon was to the original intersecting couple, had been given a first-rate education by a white school-teacher who had recognized him as a cousin. All in all, the rural South was home to quite a few white men and women who could refer to a black woman as "Aunt" without being condescending. Sometimes, as suggested in the story told by DeCosta-Lee, these ties became more socially embarrassing for black people than for the whites. As a young woman Otilia Edwards thought one older white man, a complete stranger to her, was entirely too indiscreet when he loudly announced their kinship when greeting her in public one day. If the primary purpose of segregation was to prevent miscegenation and the blurring of racially defined social caste, as many scholars have argued, then its effectiveness in the rural South was certainly far from complete.[72]

Sexuality, family, and kinship, the most intimate social bonds, drew together white men, black women, their children, and their extended families in many parts of the rural South. And in many local communities, they needed to exercise only a minimum of circumspection in shielding their relationship from public view. Clearly these relationships constituted only a small minority of monogamous relationships in the rural South, yet the fact that they existed with a degree of tacit social acceptance demonstrates the extent to which interracial intimacy was tolerated despite the reigning racial ideology. At the least, it shows again that segregation is an inappropriate way of conceptualizing race relations in the rural South and that this South was far from "solid."

Interracial Friendship

Friendship is perhaps the most difficult of these social relationships to document. Many other facets of social experience at least begin with tangible happenings that can be concretely described before any attempt to interpret them. For example, if rural black and white people commonly lived next door to one another or sometimes raised families together, direct evidence of such behavior can be found. Placed within proper geographic and chronological context, these data are fairly straightforward. They become difficult only when they are probed for social meaning. But friendship by its nature raises a question of a different order. Friendship assumes an invisible emotional tie that can be only sensed, never proven, even in present relationships. In the past, friendship left few footprints, especially when it wandered through racially charged terrain.

Furthermore, the word suggests a mutuality that is quite difficult to ascertain beyond doubt, particularly in the context of unequal power. How does one distinguish among friendship, patronage, and the face-to-face culture of neighborly assistance? In speech, Hancock people described all these relationships as "friendships," and their meanings frequently seem to have overlapped in ways that defy dissection. Terms of affection or affiliation meant many different things on the lips of different rural southerners. This chapter has explored some of the interactions between black and white people and has hinted at the range of emotional ties. Many white interviewees mentioned friendships between white families and their domestics. Fewer blacks did. John Rozier, in describing his family's relationship with a woman who stayed with them over the course of three generations, recognized the difficulty in reading these relationships from the other's perspective: "We felt that blacks were part of our family. I don't know how they felt. They might have felt differently, but they invited us to weddings and funerals and we'd go. I suppose they wanted us—because they invited us." Mae Warren, who spent some time working as a domestic and who had relatives who did so as well, agreed that domestics and their employers in the Jim Crow South never knew exactly how the other felt. Both had an interest in exhibiting at least a show of friendliness. Still, she "felt friendly" toward one family she worked for and thought that black domestics attended white events sometimes out of duty and sometimes because they wanted to do so. It was a case-by-case situation that could not be generalized.

Other interviewees spoke of the tie between some black men and women—particularly those of the black elite—and the white elites who sponsored them. These were tacitly acceptable relationships, even conventional ones. Sanford Butts, a leading Sparta merchant, spoke of feelings of "affection" and "trust" between "an honest black and a decent white." However, Butts hinted that public pressures limited the ways he could express his feelings: "It didn't show except in my store [helping some people with their credit] and in the middle of your heart." But there were many ways to express this relationship quietly. James McMullen, a leader in the black community and a sharp critic of the Jim Crow regime, recognized certain white men and women who "accepted" him, met with him privately, and advised him financially. "They'd take me into their homes. . . . I'd just sit on their sofas and all."[73]

A number of people interviewed spoke directly of lifelong relationships with neighbors across the race line. Some of these people described intimate and emotionally meaningful sharing that developed over decades as families gave each other assistance in times of sickness or economic hardship. Sometimes the relationships transferred to children and grandchildren; several of the elderly people interviewed—black and white—said that they are still regularly visited by the children and grandchildren of ex-neighbors or old friends from across the race line. Once, when I was interviewing an elderly black landowner, Katie Bell Hunt, in an isolated area near Linton, an elderly white woman who was her only neighbor called to make sure I was harmless.

A few white people made their interracial friendships public. A very few actually seemed to make a game of chicken out of making minidents in the edifice of public segregation by insisting that their black friends eat with them in restaurants or share some other segregated facility, or else they would make a scene, refuse to patronize the facilities, punch out someone's teeth, or foreclose on someone's daddy, depending on the personal social standing of the white person in the relationship.[74]

In a few cases quite remarkable friendships developed. Creasy Walker, a black landowner, said she grew up in a neighborhood in which black and white farmers "were mixed about." Her closest friend in childhood was a white girl, Irene Gladden, who also came from independent farming people. "We were close neighbors, and we were just like that," Walker said, holding up two fingers pressed side by side. Their relationship remained close after both women married. "She told me," Walker remembered, "that anything she had, I had part of it." In 1953 Gladden, who had become a nurse, helped Walker get a job with her at the state hospital in Milledgeville, where most jobs were reserved for whites. She was the first black woman to work in the kitchens there. Because Walker had no money, Gladden bought her a uniform with which to begin work. Every day they rode together out to Milledgeville in Gladden's car. When Walker's mother was sick, Gladden drove her to a hospital in Augusta. "She was a lady," said Walker; "Oh, that was a good woman."

Walker remembered how they used to defy segregation codes. They would enter a restaurant together but not stand too close to each other. Gladden would step to the counter first and ask for two plates of food. When they were made, Gladden would pass one plate to Walker. When the server began the inevitable complaint, Gladden would answer, "Well, give me my money back and carry the plate back where it come from. If I eat here, she eats here." They usually ate. They did the same at a motel—and shared a bed. They repeated the strategy at an all-white pay-to-fish pond. Faced by Gladden's fait accompli ultimatum, the pond's ticket taker "didn't know what to say. He stood there and stood there." Finally, wordlessly, "he turned around and walked on back." "She brought desegregation in here," said Walker of her friend.[75]

In the presence of other whites, however, most interracial friendships seem to have faded into the background. George Lott worked for many years at an automotive repair shop with a white man whom he viewed as a good friend. They talked, he remembered, about all aspects of their lives, weather, politics, children, and religion. Yet Lott also remembered that they had to readjust the intimacy of their conversation when customers walked into the shop. In front of some men, they could be themselves. In front of others, they felt that they had to censor their conversation—and the familiarity and friend-ship that it suggested. Mamie Washington stated that many white men and women often pretended that they did not know their black rural "friends" in public. She said that she simply learned to reciprocate, to ignore those who ignored her and to speak with those who spoke with her.[76]

The rural isolation in which these relationships developed and in which white and black farmers visited one another's churches and played baseball together raises questions about the social significance of such interactions. How substantive were these experiences if they could not survive the light of white public scrutiny? What, finally, was the value of private acts and private relationships if they were not witnessed publicly? Were they merely personal anomalies, irrelevant exceptions that tell us little about southern culture? Their significance seems to turn on the definition of the term *public*. If one thinks only of the larger, assembled white community or of the conversation white people carried on publicly through law, politics, and the county news-paper, then the significance of rural interracial intimacy is slight. If, however, one considers that most rural social circles were small and held only a few people at a given place and time, then individuals in private relationships became the audience to their own actions—and did so in significant num-bers. Although they seem to have been "merely" personal, these relationships together formed a web that shaped the larger social structure. These ties often gave real practical assistance to struggling individuals. Nevertheless, they also humanized white supremacy without effectively diminishing it—certainly not for the majority. In the rural South these personal ties moderated the harshness of white supremacy even as they undermined black solidarity. Perhaps personal relationships acted as a pressure valve, keeping the entire system from boiling over. Later, in the 1960s, Stokely Carmichael tried to expose these relationships as barriers to the black power movement. They were significant.[77] Overall, in rural neighborhoods, the daily experienced economic, social, and psychic impact of interracial exchanges and relation-ships could be profound. In addition, when rural people left for the cities, as most of them ultimately did, many carried with them at least the memory that interracial intimacy is humanly possible and not "unnatural," even if the segregationist social and demographic realities of the urban context made that experience difficult to recapture.[78]

Racism and Intimacy in a Culture of Personalism

This chapter has not argued that white supremacy was peripheral to rural southern culture. It was clearly central. Rather, I have argued that in the rural South, physical segregation was not an important agent and symbol of white supremacy, as it obviously was in the urban South. In the rural South white supremacy took other forms: economic exploitation, paternalism, and an etiquette of subordination (discussed earlier), and violence, disfranchisement, and civic nonpersonhood (to be discussed in the following chapters). Rural whites in Hancock quite successfully established a truncated opportunity structure for blacks, despite the absence of enforced segregation. Moreover, although some evidence indicates that African Americans experienced a wide range of relationships with white southerners, including relationships that they themselves characterized as "good" or as "friendships," even the best personal relationships between black and white individuals were influenced—at least to a degree—by white supremacist codes of etiquette. For example, despite their unusually close friendship, Creasy Walker addressed Irene Gladden formally, and the white woman reciprocated informally. Furthermore, a lack of distance between black and white southerners meant a lack of privacy for African Americans and in some places white interference in the personal affairs of black families. In many southern counties there are stories of white planters who practiced peonage long after the legal end of slavery or who casually and personally employed physical violence to "discipline" black dependent laborers. The close, personal contacts of the rural areas had the potential to be as oppressive as the distant, impersonal ones of the city.[79]

So, again, I have not argued that black farmers experienced a more benign form of white supremacy than did black urbanites. I have argued that significant variation in race relations occurred in the rural South. In addition, I have argued that because the rural system was frequently marked by interracial intimacy, systematic segregation makes an inadequate model for describing rural race relations.

To summarize, a number of factors contributed to the difference between rural and urban race relations and the relative absence of segregation in the rural spaces. First, the demands of the plantation labor system discouraged segregated patterns of housing and nurtured a culture that promoted personal ties across race lines. Second, the wooded isolation of many rural homes and the slow and uneven transportation and communication networks that connected them to the "outside world" created a diverse patchwork quilt of highly localized and personalized racial customs. Third, various overlapping identities of religion, neighborhood, and especially class complicated and sometimes diluted the significance of rural racial identities.

It should be clearly understood, as I attempt to categorize the social relations of rural Hancock County, that rural whites there who experienced close contact with blacks were not acting as modern "liberals." Far from it. They were acting more as premoderns, uncoerced by the influences both of modern, scientific racism (whose urban expression was segregation) and of the modern liberalism that articulated egalitarian racial integration. However we understand them, historians need to develop a new paradigm for rural spaces to stand alongside the modern, "progressive" one that describes urban race relations.[80]

Segregation was, after all, the creation of urban, middle-class Progressive reformers. Although these urban reformers succeeded in regulating behavior in the towns, their plans for rationalizing and systematizing the South were often opposed or ignored by rural southerners. As was noted previously, many rural black interviewees described their awareness that a completely different set of racial codes operated in the towns. Willie Butts, an African American, grew up in a mostly black neighborhood on the rural outskirts of Milledgeville. The only white family nearby had a boy Butts's age, Bill Massey, who used to join in all the activities of young Butts and his other friends. Butts recounted, "We fought, played and swam together." The two kept in touch even after they grew up and Butts left for a lifelong journey through northern cities. On one of Butts's more recent trips to Milledgeville, the two caught up with each other, and Massey, thinking back on his family's experience, told him, "The only time we were white was when we went to school and went to town."[81]

David Harper, born in 1935 to a black farmowner, remembered the social difference between rural and urban spaces even into the early 1950s. As a boy Harper had a white friend named Billy with whom he picked cotton, fished, and killed time. Often on Saturdays the two would catch a ride for the fifteen or so miles to the county seat. There they would separate. Billy saw movies on the main floor; David, from the balcony. Billy walked into restaurants for food; David ordered out the back door or a side window. Billy walked up and down the streets or loitered on corners with knots of white friends; David did so with his black friends. When they passed, they did not speak, although sometimes they recognized their rural friendship with a slight urban nod.[82]

Race relations in rural Hancock County in the first half of the twentieth century were in some ways simple. White supremacy, like the Democratic Party and low cotton prices, seemed inexorable. Yet in other ways race relations were extremely complex and fluid. Although individuals' social relations across the race line always exhibited some ritual reference to white supremacy, that ritual did not usually involve segregation. Propinquity rather than distance was the identifying mark of rural race relations.[83] In the locally isolated spaces of rural Hancock, interracial intimacy could appear in many different forms. The fact that intimacy could appear as easily in the form of savagery as it could in that of friendship will be explored in the following chapter.

A. J. Parker and his aunt Minnie Parker about 1950

Dave Dyer as an officer in World War II

Eva Reese in the 1940s

Katie Hunt around 1990

Mae Warren around 1935

Marshall Boyer with a grandson around 1995

Samuel Williams as an agricultural extension agent, 1940s

Rev. Robert Edwards, 1950s

Dr. Carlton Morse, around 1980

5

Race, Violence, and Power
in a Personal Culture

THROUGHOUT AMERICAN HISTORY, violence and the threat of violence have been the ultimate means by which European Americans have subordinated African Americans. Violence was, of course, the cornerstone on which slavery was built. After the Civil War white northerners and southerners alike used it to repulse African Americans from desirable jobs and neighborhoods and to deprive them the exercise of their civil rights. White southerners in particular employed it to throw down Reconstruction, to secure the region's inequitable labor system, and to maintain regular observance of the social etiquette of submission and dominance.[1]

In rural Hancock County the palpable threat of violence made segregation irrelevant. At bottom, white supremacy was maintained not by increased distance between black and white bodies but by paternalism and racial etiquette backed by the regular, physical threat that white bodies posed to black bodies. Not separation but intimacy drove home the message of power and racial hierarchy. Physical violence could flow through a number of different channels. White antiblack violence most famously entailed mob action. Additionally, when members of a white community desired more respectable processes, they could initiate official state violence through law-enforcement officers and the courts. For the most part, however, rural southern violence took neither of these forms. The planters of rural Georgia preferred direct, personal control to public, institutional control. Although the white community could commit violence as a group, either inside or outside the law, interracial violence typically meant one individual assaulting another on the isolated farms and fields of the South.

Accordingly, rural African Americans—although circumscribed by white violence in many ways—were not as impotent to defend themselves as is often currently assumed. Because violence was largely the domain of individuals, it could be an unpredictably democratic vehicle of individual power. Whites who lived in this intimately interracial, rural society employed a culture of violence to intimidate African Americans into a subservient position economically, politically, and socially, yet because of rural isolation and their own culture of violence, Hancock's African Americans never became mere rabbits pursued by hounds.

Although the politically motivated violence that brought down Reconstruction was far bloodier than anything afterward, Jim Crow–era lynchings have become the most powerful symbol of southern antiblack violence.[2] It has been reported that during the height of lynching in the United States, from 1889 to 1918, 3,224 persons died at the hands of mobs. Of that number, 2,834 were murdered in the former states of the Confederacy. And among southern states, Georgia was long recognized, both through folk lore and statistics, as the land of the lynch mob. According to statistics compiled by the National Association for the Advancement of Colored People (NAACP), of the six southern states that lynched more than two hundred people between 1889 and 1918, Georgia led the list with 386 victims. The level of recorded Georgia violence peaked with 137 lynchings in the 1910s, as the dislocations of World War I intensified white fears. Then the numbers plummeted. During the 1920s, 41 people were reported killed by mobs. Another 5 black men were lynched in 1930, and then 15 more before that decade ended, signaling the end of the wholesale wave of murder.[3]

Three recent students of lynching, historian W. Fitzhugh Brundage and sociologists Stewart E. Tolnay and E. M. Beck, have argued that white Georgians in the plantation belt were more prone to lynch African Americans than were whites of any other part of the state. They base their claims on the absolute numbers of southern African Americans lynched, which were indeed highest in the plantation belt.[4] Others follow sociologist Arthur Raper in arguing that, next to the Atlantic coastal region, the plantation belt actually had the lowest level of lynching when understood as the ratio of lynchings per thousand African Americans living in the area.[5] Both answers are correct, so the question is wrong.[6] It might be more productive to shift the debate from a quest to find the "safest" and "most lynch-prone" sections of the state to a search to better understand the distinctive social contexts of violence in each section.[7]

The relative safety of African Americans in the cotton belt is thus still debatable, but other aspects of cotton-belt violence are not. The cotton belt led Georgia in the percentage of lynchings carried out by "mass mobs" of fifty or more people (sometimes thousands). This means that individual whites in the cotton belt were more disposed to participate in public murder than were whites in any other section of the state. It has also become clear that, although they were quite willing to take part in lynchings, whites in the cotton belt also aimed their violence at individuals whom they held responsible for particular crimes or offenses. This distinguishes them from poor upcountry whites who launched sweeping attacks against all blacks in their communities and from northern and southern urbanites who participated in bloody but impersonal race riots. In the cotton belt, interracial violence was deeply embedded in the culture of personalism.

Written sources suggest that, although it lay in the middle of Georgia's plantation belt, Hancock County had a relatively low level of lynching. Furthermore, African Americans from Hancock and neighboring counties generally stated in interviews that Hancock had a relatively good record—especially compared to the bloody reputations of Warren County to the north and the equally violent Washington and Wilkerson Counties to the south.

Yet violence formed an important part of race relations as experienced in Hancock as well. During Reconstruction many black Hancock men and women were beaten by whites, and some were killed, for attempting to claim their legal rights under their newfound liberty. A few decades later, during the bloody Populist movement of the 1890s, both Democrats and Populists mixed aid to supporters with violent retribution for political opponents.

After the defeat of Populism, both poor white ex-Populists and wealthier white Democrats redirected their political frustrations at their former African American allies. Seemingly with one voice, white southerners called for black disfranchisement, for lynch law, and for a wall of Jim Crow laws. These measures were necessary, white leaders argued, to defend white civilization—and especially white women—against the threat that black men posed. Political opportunists such as Hoke Smith and popular writers such as Thomas Dixon whipped up white southerners, bestializing the image of black men in their minds. Like Democratic newspapers all over the South, the *Sparta Ishmaelite* helped fan the flames of race hatred at this critical time. When demagogues shrilly decried the wave of black crime they said was sweeping the region, the *Ishmaelite* obligingly and prominently featured articles on black crime. Because Hancock's African Americans uncooperatively declined to run wild in the streets, however, the local crime wave looked fairly anemic. As a result, the *Ishmaelite,* like other southern papers of the time, began to cull stories occurring farther and farther away. In the last few years of the nineteenth century and the first few years of the twentieth, the *Ishmaelite* routinely printed black crime stories from all over the country. This media-made crime wave inspired an all-too-real retaliatory wave of white violence against African Americans. The most famous of these struck Atlanta, sixty miles away, in 1906. No comparable paroxysm of mob violence ever struck Hancock, but the climate of racial tension that the newspapers and demagogues nurtured set the stage for the violence that did come there.[8]

Context: The Southern Culture of Violence

Interracial southern violence should be contextualized within the generally violent society of which it was a piece. In the early years of the automobile, for example, the pages of the *Ishmaelite* related periodic misadventures involving horse-drawn buggies and motorists that read like metaphors for the collision of premodern and modern dangers. There were many ways to be killed or disfigured in rural Hancock. One boy's face was gored by a hog. A man had both legs and an arm severed by sawmill. Others were accidentally shot with firearms, kicked by mules, or trampled by runaway teams of horses. In the rural South violence and injury could befall anyone at any time during this period.

Within this context intentional violence bristled as one more variety of the hazards of life. Rural southern men, black and white, were frankly dangerous people in the early twentieth century, a fact in which they took pride. Most had firearms for hunting and self-defense.[9] Ordinary conflicts, or even trivial ones, frequently turned bloody with so many guns handy. For example, James Wilson, a black sharecropper, remembered a time in the 1920s when another black Hancock man shot Wilson's cousin dead at a Georgia skin card game near Warren Chapel. The two men had been arguing over the possession of a single penny.[10] The abundance of guns merely made killing easier, however; it does not satisfactorily explain the vastness of the culture of violence. A number of Hancock people killed without recourse to guns. In 1910 one white boy in the southern part of the county killed his father with a knife to stop him from beating his mother. The father exonerated his son before dying, and no charges were pressed. This was understandable, even expected violence. Although Hancock people usually regretted violence, they just as often accepted it as an inevitable part of life. In the late nineteenth century and through the first decades of the twentieth, the *Ishmaelite* reported case after case of stabbings, shootings, and beatings by Hancock residents. It related violence with casual interest, amusement, or outrage, depending on the social standing of the individuals involved and the reasons given for the attack.[11]

In the rural South violence was almost always committed within the context of personal relationships. People killed their neighbors, employees, employers, and family members. Anonymous, impersonal violence was an urban phenomenon. In this world both the killer and the victim could call each other's names in the middle of the homicide, with both understanding perfectly the reason for the murder.[12]

In large part this culture of violence filled a crucial place in rural southerners' understanding of manhood. Men by definition had to possess the physical power or firepower to defend their honor violently, as well as the will to do so. Historian Bertram Wyatt-Brown has demonstrated how a premodern culture that emphasized shame and honor—the publicly imposed perceptions of an individual's worth—united the North and South in the colonial period. As the North industrialized, its culture modernized as well, shifting to an internalized, self-possessed mode of daily social control: guilt and pride. Well into the twentieth century, however (and in some ways to the present day), social pressure and a winking legal system often compelled rural southern men to take their own extralegal action on the bodies of individuals who had transgressed recognized boundaries. Scholarly attention has already been paid to the white culture of honor and the routine violence that arose from it.[13] Nevertheless, many aspects of this culture applied to black and white southerners alike. This can be seen by considering same-race violence—the majority of violent confrontations, which did not cross the race line.[14]

In some times and places in the South, county law-enforcement agencies assiduously prosecuted all black criminal offenders to make them available to planters as cheap convict labor; in Hancock, however, black men were often forgiven for violent acts that whites interpreted as justifiable defenses of honor.[15] In 1916 the *Sparta Ishmaelite* reported that a black man had shot another black man with two loads of birdshot. "The nigger that did the shooting is considered to have had somewhat of a provocation," wrote the editor, so "no steps have been taken to apprehend him." Even fatal shootings could be taken in stride in some situations, with community approval and short sentences. Johnny Evans Johnson, a white merchant-planter, enjoys replaying a conversation he had with a black man, Raymond Harper, who once worked on his land. After buying him out of prison by paying his fine for moonshining, Johnson found Harper back in jail. He went to see about getting him out again: "What'd you do?" asked Johnson.

"Killed a man."

"Why?"

"Had to kill him. We had an argument [over] a skins game. The nigger cut me. I wanted to fight fair and got mad. Said I was going to my house to get my gun. I did and he was still there. So I had to kill him."

"Yup," Johnson agreed. "You had to kill him." Satisfied, Johnson paid the man out of jail again.[16]

Memory and Violence: The Early Twentieth Century

Despite the alarming frequency with which blood was spilled in the county, most people I interviewed claimed not to have lived in fear of violence—and pointedly not of interracial violence. Again, the great majority of violence was white on white or black on black. Furthermore, violence usually occurred within socially sanctioned boundaries, such as insulted honor or marital infidelity, or at "enter-at-your-own-risk" gatherings such as gambling dens and blind tigers. Hancock's people did not consider such violence to be random. When interviewed, most elderly African Americans stated that they "didn't fear whites."[17] Most white Hancock natives, even those completely surrounded by black neighbors, now state that they reciprocated the feeling: "We had no fear of black folk," said one. "We never locked our doors."[18]

Yet memory tells only part of the story here. The wave of southern white newspaper editorials and political speeches that generated both disfranchisement and segregation around the turn of the century reveals a white fear of blacks that sometimes bordered on the hysterical. During the two economically depressed and politically turbulent decades surrounding 1900, white Georgians invented a novel terror: the myth of the black rapist. They believed that African Americans, freed from the civilizing school of slavery, were degenerating into barbarism. Most white newspaper editors responded to this rising radical sentiment by calling for lynching as a tool of counterterror. Even the generally conservative Sparta Ishmaelite capitulated to radical racism in the 1890s out of fear of the "black beast" and called white lynch mobs a natural, if regrettable, reaction to what whites came to see as the most terrible of threats to white civilization. In Hancock this paroxysm of racial radicalism had begun to ebb by the end of 1910 as the racial conservatives reasserted their hegemony. Accordingly, by the time that most of the white interviewees in this study had become aware of their worlds, the Ishmaelite had ceased to fan the flames of race fear. By the 1920s the world again seemed well ordered to the whites of Hancock. The threatening "bestial" aura seemed to melt away from black men, leaving familiar figures who—whites were eager to believe—humbly accepted the newly established "natural order of things." Once more black people seemed to evoke a warm and homey, if condescending, response from white farmers. After World War I what fear remained was pressed into the background, reserved for the "strange Negro" or the returning black military veteran and only rarely directed toward the black tenant family who lived within sight.[19]

The oral testimony of African Americans in Hancock also seems to reveal a minor theme of fear beneath the general chorus of assertions that whites posed no physical threat. Some of the oldest African American respondents spoke of an earlier time, a time related to them by members of their parents' generation, when blacks had a great deal to fear from whites. Some seemed frightened to talk about this period, as though they would again be subject to white violence if they spoke out.[20] Others acknowledged that white men had killed many black men from the 1890s through the 1920s but said that most adults during those years had tried to hide the information from their children and never spoke of it afterward. Mary Worthening, born in 1922, heard occasional whispers of murders when she was a child, but little more: "It was hushed up pretty good. Folks seeing it, but they weren't talking, 'cause they were scared." Essie Mae Primer, of southern Hancock, said, "Daddy knew about mobs killing folks," but she added, "People would be scared to say who did it." Accordingly, even black Hancock interviewees who were no longer afraid to speak about white violence generally knew few details surrounding these events.[21]

Interviews with white Hancock senior citizens suggest that few of them have heard stories of organized local violence against blacks. One elderly Democratic merchant did remember stories of Populist violence against black Democratic voters.[22] Another farmer, born just before 1900 to small farmers in the northeast part of the county, spoke with bitter nostalgia of his childhood days; back then, he said, the white community "wouldn't put up with all the killing that the colored do. They'd take them out and hang them."[23]

It seems that Hancock's whites copied their African American neighbors in not discussing interracial violence publicly, especially in the presence of children. One woman from the Powelton community remembered an incident her father had described from his own childhood at the turn of the century. As a boy he had heard that a black man had attempted to stop one of his older cousins, a woman from Powelton, while she was driving a buggy on a secluded road. According to the snippets of the story her father had picked up, the man "had grabbed those reins on that horse and was going to get [her] out of the buggy." She fought him off—a man she knew—and made it home. "That night, after the evening meal, all the men in the community left for a little while; . . . a sawdust pile burned, [and] they didn't see the black man anymore." Her father had put the pieces together by himself, because, according to his story, no one would talk about it, then or later.[24]

Interestingly, the three white interviewees who spoke of organized white violence against black men all came from the northern part of the county, around Powelton. The Powelton community was composed of long-established small white yeoman farmers and a growing number of black yeoman farmers. Powelton was also located at the border of Warren County to the north. Dominated by small white farmers, Warren County had a bad reputation among Hancock African Americans. They believed it had a long and violent tradition of Klan activity. One woman reported that well-dressed blacks who passed through Warren County in cars were sometimes stopped and robbed of their possessions and clothes by jealous whites. These small white landowners seem to have been the least secure in the superior status that white supremacy bestowed on them and the most willing to resort to organized violence in its defense.

A few African Americans did remember snippets of stories passed down from the "old days." One woman born in the early 1920s believed that white-on-black violence was common "before her time." She heard the outlines of only one such story, told to her by her mother. When her mother was a girl, in the 1890s, she knew a black woman who worked in town as a maid and brought her young son to work with her. According to the story her mother heard, the boy was playing with a little white girl one day when the girl innocently asked him to "fasten a button on her bloomers": "[He] didn't know nothing and did. . . . the whites hung up that little child and shot him to death."[25]

This story, like that of the man who tried to stop a woman's wagon near Powelton, probably reveals more about the oral culture of violence of Hancock County in the early twentieth century than it does about concrete experiences. Whereas almost all other stories reported in this study were told to me as firsthand experiences, these were related third hand. Neither story is corroborated by any newspaper accounts in a time when newspapers, including the *Sparta Ishmaelite*, brazenly published accounts of lynchings as warnings to African Americans. Neither was cited in any of the three major indexes of U.S. lynchings compiled by the NAACP, the *Chicago Tribune*, or Tuskeegee University. The first story was passed on to the interviewee with whom I spoke sometime after the screening of *Gone with the Wind*, which contained a strikingly similar scene. As to the second story, an event as sensational as the lynching of a child in town would surely have attracted media attention. The stories were probably borrowed from other locations and personalized as object lessons for black boys. This does not necessarily diminish their fearfulness, certainly not for the young people to whom they were told as truth. After all, these kinds of things could happen, and they did in other places.

But other interviewees reported stories that more plausibly happened in Hancock. James Wilson, born in 1917, remembered two episodes that took place in his lifetime not far from his home in the western part of the county. Walking down a public road in the 1920s, one black man was shot dead by a planter who had previously told him "he'd better not be caught on his plantation." The unfortunate man had been visible from a window in the planter's house. Nothing came of it. According to Wilson, the man's family couldn't object, because African Americans did not dare go to the sheriff to accuse a white man of a crime. Later, in the mid-1930s, that same planter's son, then employed at the state hospital in Milledgeville, killed a second black man, Charlie Smith, in a dispute over a black woman. Wilson reported, "The white man was going with all the black women in Smith's family—the mamma, the daughter . . ." When Smith protested, he was shot, and "the whole black family had to move from the county." The authorities were again silent: "Wasn't nary thing did about it." The white man did not have to answer for his actions in court, although, Wilson cryptically added, "something bad happened to him soon afterward."[26]

From the 1890s through the late 1920s the *Sparta Ishmaelite* echoes the shadowy stories whispered down through the years in the African American community. According to the *Ishmaelite*, during these years black men from time to time suffered injury or death at the hands of white private citizens. Although the reports almost invariably speak of the dead black man as having first acted in a "threatening" or "aggressive manner" toward the white man who killed him, there were almost as inevitably no witnesses to the killings to either confirm or dispute them. Often the black men were unarmed. Sometimes they were shot from behind. Taken together, the separate newspaper accounts form the constellation of an obvious lie. They bring to mind the author Harry Crews's description of the frequent white-on-white violence occurring in his South Georgia community around the same time. According to Crews, "a man could shoot you with impunity if you were on his property and he managed to get you dead enough so you couldn't tell what actually happened."[27] This pattern illustrates the sinister side of rural isolation. While rural white people in Hancock could ignore Jim Crow codes free of public censure, they could also kill African Americans without answering for their actions.

A Year of Violence: 1917

The *Sparta Ishmaelite*'s stories roughly sketch the nature of interracial violence in and near Hancock during the early twentieth century. This subsection lists all reported interracial violence for 1917, an especially bloody year but still representative of the shape, if not the intensity, of interracial violence in early twentieth-century Hancock. From 1917 to 1919, when the United States engaged in World War I, violence against blacks sharply increased nationally after having declined considerably during the previous decade.[28] The war created new tensions as hundreds of thousands of African Americans joined the military and even more fled the poverty of southern farms toward better paying jobs in the urban North. The experience of the war created rising expectations for blacks across the country and elicited a violent backlash from whites fearful of losing the status quo. The violence played out in Hancock as elsewhere: over the course of 1917 one man was shot and killed west of Sparta, one man was shot and killed just north of Sparta, one man was shot at in downtown Sparta, and several boys were injured by a car that struck them on the sidewalk in Sparta. In all these cases the victims were black and the white men responsible were never prosecuted. I will examine the incidents in the order in which they were reported.

On July 28 Percy Moore mishandled his gear shift, causing the "big Paige touring car" Moore was driving to jump the curb in downtown Sparta, "injuring several negro boys standing there." One boy "had his leg and ankle badly crushed." Whereas Moore was identified as white by the application of "Mr." to his name, the editor did not deign to name any of the boys, nor did he state the number injured or the extent of their injuries. The editor did find space in the brief article to assure readers more concerned with white property than black suffering that "the car was only slightly damaged." Although there is no reason to doubt, as the *Ishmaelite* emphasized, that the incident was a tragic accident and that Moore regretted it very much, it is worth venturing a guess at what would have happened had the races of injured and injurer been reversed. Moore was a wealthy planter. No charges were pressed, and according to the *Ishmaelite*, "no special blame [was] attached" in the case. By contrast, on a number of occasions across the South, African Americans were lynched for being involved in ordinary car accidents with whites.[29]

A couple of near misses of this sort happened just outside Hancock during the same period. In the first, several years before the Moore incident, Moses Hubert, a member of one of Hancock's wealthiest and best-connected black families, was driving a horse and buggy in White Plains, a small town a couple of miles north of Hancock. According to the Hubert family history, he "accidentally brushed against a white woman and injured her slightly." He was beaten and nearly lynched before the sheriff arrived to take him into custody. Moses Hubert might still have been lynched had his brother, Zach Hubert, not interceded on his behalf with some of the influential white men with whom Zach had cultivated close paternalistic relationships. Moses Hubert was ultimately released unharmed.

The second incident occurred when Georgia soldiers returned from World War I. One black veteran, Hank Boyer, who lived just outside the county line to the west of Hancock, bought a car with money he had made gambling overseas. A white man he knew—also a veteran—did likewise. After a rain their cars met on a slippery, rutted country road. Afraid to pull to the side, as etiquette dictated, lest he lose his car in the ditch, Boyer stayed on the road and clipped hubcaps with the white man's car. When the black veteran reached home, his younger brother, Marshall Boyer, remembers that the black veteran had another brother drive him immediately to the train station, where he boarded a train north. When the car returned from the station, the driver found a group of angry white men gathered at the veteran's home—a few hours too late. Marshall Boyer is sure to this day that they would have lynched his brother for the offense. Considering the well-documented, widespread violence that greeted returning black soldiers after their service in World War I, he may be right.[30]

Boyer's story touches on the role of the automobile in undermining the traditional ordering of race relations in Hancock. Besides being a conspicuous symbol of wealth, cars offered concrete advantages to tenant farmers, who could use them to drive to town to furnish themselves more cheaply than they could at the rural general stores. Planters certainly would not have welcomed such an enhancement of black autonomy. But the symbolic power of cars posed an even greater challenge to the traditional social order.

In the early twentieth century automobiles evoked a sense of wonder at their speed and sleek, modern appearance. The *Sparta Ishmaelite* repeatedly described dozens of Hancock's wealthiest and most fashionable citizens joy-riding in convoys to such distant cities as Athens and Augusta. The newspaper would announce the departure times, and crowds formed to view these symbols of progress as they passed. Yet not all southern folk welcomed the coming of the car. Some worried that such rapid and anonymous means of transportation would disrupt community traditions of courtesy and ritual deference. By the 1910s some editors complained about the tendency of rapid, noisy cars to frighten the horses and mules drawing the wagons of poorer neighbors, putting their passengers in real jeopardy. Others noted the declining willingness of hermetically sealed automobile drivers to stop and offer rides to rural pedestrians, as slower and more easily recognized wagon drivers had traditionally done.[31]

African American ownership of automobiles proved threatening to white sensibilities of order, and rural African Americans had began to purchase cars in large numbers by the 1930s. In Greene County, just north of Hancock, about half of black renters and even a third of black sharecroppers had purchased cars by 1935.[32] Cars had arrived in the South just after the traditional, paternalistic, and highly interpersonal system of race relations had given way—at least in the towns—to the newer, impersonal, and segregationist mode of race relations. These newly arrived cars raised difficulties for both systems. The impersonal nature of the automobile placed it beyond the reach of traditional means of control. A black man in a fast-moving automobile could not reasonably be expected to doff his cap and call "Morning, sir" to each white man he passed. The steel-and-glass cage removed the passengers from the public space of the roadways and sealed them in a private space—removed psychologically from the presence of others—and thereby from the demands of ritual deference. Nonetheless (the experience of Boyer's brother notwithstanding), the demands of efficiently ordered traffic flow rendered the "modern" racial solution of segregation impractical on roadways. Whereas segregated train, theater, and restaurant seating symbolized to whites the progressive, scientific use of public space, the car—another powerful symbol of modernity—worked at cross-purposes with the logic of racially separate spaces. Segregated city streets obviously would have created an unthinkable tangle as well as a ridiculous city expense.[33]

Arthur Raper thought he saw in the automobile a powerful force for egalitarianism in the midst of a race- and class-conscious society. "In his car," wrote Raper, "the tenant has a right to half of the road whether he is meeting another tenant, a traveling salesman, or his own landlord. Only in automobiles on public roads do landlords and tenants and white people and Negroes of the Black Belt meet on a basis of equality," whereas in the past, "when master and slave met along the road . . . , each acted in keeping with his station." Raper hoped that the automobile would provide for a new morality "more fundamentally democratic than anything the world has known."[34] As white southerners came to recognize the revolutionary impact of the automobile, the level of tension in areas such as Hancock must have risen, and with it the potential for violence, as described by Marshall Boyer.

On August 2, 1917, the same day that the *Sparta Ishmaelite* went to press with the Moore story, it printed a brief notice of the second incident that year in Hancock. This one occurred near the village of Culverton, a little to the northeast of Sparta. The son of a white farmer "engaged in a difficulty" with a black man. "While backing away from him, with his hand in his hip pocket," the black man was shot and killed. The *Ishmaelite* editor opined, "The case seems to be one of self defense," adding, "at this hour no warrant has been sworn out." The "I-thought-he-might-have-a-gun" defense used in this case could be tailored to fit almost any situation. If self-defense could be used with respect to an unarmed man, as it seems to have been in this case, there was legally nothing to prevent any white man from shooting almost any black man, for any cause, in almost any private situation.[35]

Next came a case that the *Ishmaelite* reported had "attracted some attention in Sparta, and in fact, throughout the county, among both white and colored races." At nine in the morning of October 14, T. L. Davis shot and killed Tom Dunn on the Davis farm, about five miles west of Sparta, and offered the usual story of self-defense. The physical evidence made his story considerably less than credible, however. The white farmer claimed that he had killed the black man "only after the dead man had made an effort, apparently, to draw a weapon and advance on him." There were, as Davis admitted, "no witnesses." He had shot Dunn twice, once in the front of the head and once in the back of the head. Whereas the wound to the front of the head had been fatal—probably immediately so—the wound to the back of the head had not; indeed, it had not even penetrated the man's skull. Apparently Dunn had first been shot from behind and then turned to receive the fatal bullet. An all-white grand jury weighed the evidence and found themselves unable to avoid the opinion that Davis "was not acting in self-defense." Nevertheless, they did not recommend that he be taken into custody. The following year a grand jury declined to pass the case on to trial. The *Ishmaelite* had nothing more to say on the matter in later issues, despite the interest it admitted the case had generated. Apparently, although shooting a man in the back of the head could not be called self-defense, neither was it illegal in 1917 Hancock, as long as the killer was white and the victim was black.[36]

Finally, on November 13, at ten o'clock at night, Charlie Dunn (white) and Frank Battle (black) "became involved in a difficulty" over right of way on a sidewalk along Sparta's Broad Street. The stores had closed, and "a very few people only were on the streets at the time." According to the story that the *Ishmaelite* repeated, Battle, "accompanied by a few others of his race, was parading Broad street and indulging in loud talking and whistling." Battle and his friends may have been creating a public disturbance, or they may simply have been walking and talking with open self-confidence in the county seat, where whites expected them to appear deferential and subservient. Either way, they would have angered white Spartans and placed themselves beyond any flimsy protection the law might offer them. It is unlikely that the men had been drinking, because the *Ishmaelite* would have delighted in providing that bit of information if there had been reason to suspect it. Battle "passed" Dunn and, said the story, "ran into him, almost pushing [him] off of the sidewalk." Again, it is difficult to accept the story at face value, because contemporary sources indicate that African Americans in town had to step to the side, sometimes completely off the sidewalk, to let whites pass. This rule was one more example of the racial separation of space that was implemented in southern towns and cities. There is evidence that this particular form of segregation—in which blacks could occupy a space only as long as a white person did not claim it—predated the other components of urban segregation. Elderly African Americans from Hancock testified that the practice was still enforced decades after this particular conflict. Battle, conceivably, simply neglected to step off the sidewalk to let the white man pass. Back to the newspaper story: "When called to account for his conduct, the negro became impudent and assumed a threatening manner." As in the previous cases, "a threatening manner" by a black man offered a believable excuse, if an undefinable and therefore a readily available one, to allow whites to use violence. Additionally, the editor of the *Ishmaelite* accused Battle of being "impudent," a significant choice of words. Speaking to a white man without displaying clear deference through verbal and postural cues could bring this charge on any African American.[37] In his encounter with Dunn, Battle was apparently not deferential. According to the *Ishmaelite*, "using an oath, [Battle] informed Mr. Dunn that he must not be aware of the character of the man he was fooling with. Battle was correct in that statement because

Dunn reached for his pistol which he fired twice at the darkey, following which the latter took to the tall and uncut timbers."

To ensure that the sympathies of his white readership were solidly with Dunn, the editor added that Battle, while riding a horse sometime earlier on the same Sparta street, "ran down" Sam Hollis, a leading planter-merchant. Maybe he did—and did so recklessly. Alternatively, the affair may have been an accident, like the bloody one that had happened to Moore earlier that year. At any rate, the incident with Hollis was not severe enough to have merited any write-up in the *Ishmaelite* when it had taken place. The entire story of the conflict between Dunn and Battle, related in a humorous tone, was designed to reflect credit on Dunn's "manly" character and to present his behavior as an exemplum of the proper way to deal with assertive African Americans who challenged Jim Crow codes. There was, of course, no mention of any possible charges against Dunn or even a hint of rebuke for the impropriety of an assault with a deadly weapon and the discharge of a firearm within city limits.

The Causes of Hancock Violence

Although most African Americans escaped personal attacks, the cumulative effect of these acts of white violence touched everyone. They demonstrated the lengths to which whites could go to punish encroachments on white supremacy in any area, whether etiquette, labor relations, or political participation. Not all whites responded to black challenges with violence, but the threat clearly hung in the air. In some areas of the South prosperous blacks were physically attacked by jealous whites for no cause other than their prosperity. Outside the cotton belt large numbers of poor whites resented the success of black landowners and competition from poor blacks for sharecropping positions. In these cases organized violence typically manifested itself in terrorist mobs, or whitecappers, striking not against individuals but against entire classes of people. Over the protest of planters, who saw their labor supply diminished, these terrorist mobs attempted to drive all blacks from large sections of northern Georgia, succeeding completely in Forsyth and Dawson Counties in 1912 and 1913.[38]

There is no evidence that any black landowner was ever attacked in Hancock. Planters there were not threatened by the area's few black landowners, and they held far too much control to let poor whites attack their primary laborers at will. Nonetheless, the consciousness that such attacks did happen elsewhere and so might conceivably happen to them pushed Hancock's better-off African Americans to act with assiduous deference toward whites generally and to develop patronage ties with influential whites. Because interracial violence in rural Hancock was personal, Hancock blacks understood its remedy to be personal as well.

Although the planters clearly did not want to drive away blacks generally, as did the whitecappers, the threat of violence offered them other benefits. Fear of attack forced most black southerners to accept the daily snubs and insults of white supremacist social etiquette. It kept most blacks from approaching the courthouse, whether to vote, sue, or do anything else. Most significantly, fear of violence made Hancock's African Americans accept the economic decisions of landowners. As black interviewees attested, it forced them to accept settlements with landlords that they themselves knew were fraudulent.

In Hancock shootings involving black and white men seem to have been frequently connected with disputes over crops. This pattern dovetails with Tolnay and Beck's discovery that lynching rose and fell with the crop. Lynchings peaked each summer and fall and declined in the winter and spring. Planters clearly did not want to scare away their labor force. However, by targeting individuals suspected of crimes and making public examples of them, planters could render the rest of their labor force more pliable to direction and exploitation.[39]

The examples that some whites made of some blacks who challenged white supremacy affected all aspects of race relations in the South.[40] The apparent impunity with which whites attacked blacks also demonstrated the connection between public white power and private white terror. The "better sort" who held office winked at these individual acts of violence—even when committed by poorer men—as long as they helped to keep African Americans from challenging their power. Across the South violence was, as historian Neil McMillen called it, "the instrument in reserve" to defend white supremacy.[41]

The previously described cases are fairly representative of the kind of violence occurring in Hancock during the Progressive period. They differ considerably, however, from the popular image of antiblack southern violence. First, contrary to popular white perceptions then and now, relatively few black men killed by whites were thought to have assaulted white women. As the black activist Ida B. Wells argued at the time, only 20 percent of all black lynching victims were accused of rape (much less guilty of it). Using a larger database W. Fitzhugh Brundage found that accusations of rape approximated Wells's findings. Between 1880 and 1889, when lynching was still relatively infrequent, 60 percent of all lynch victims in Georgia were accused of rape. Then, when the numbers soared in the following two decades, rape was alleged in 27 percent of all lynchings, and only 17 percent thereafter. The "usual crime," as it was then called, was actually unusual. Brundage found that Georgia's black lynch victims in the decades after 1890 had been accused of murdering whites more often than they had been accused of anything else.[42] In Hancock violent interracial incidents seemed to arise from conflicts between black and white men: over debts, over white demands for deference, and over black women, but only very rarely over white women. The Harlem Renaissance author Jean Toomer, after briefly teaching school in Hancock County in 1921, pointedly made an interracial contest for the affection of a black woman the cause of a lynching he described in his short story "Blood Moon Rising." After the white man is killed in a knife fight that he initiates with the black suitor, the black man is burned in a warehouse by a mob of enraged whites. By standing the reigning myth on its head, Toomer brought his story closer to the historical causes of violence.[43]

It seems that the *Sparta Ishmaelite* accused only one black man of assaulting a white woman in Hancock during the first half of the twentieth century. In 1903 eighteen-year-old John Dixon was sentenced to twenty years in the state penitentiary after he pleaded guilty to attempting to assault two visiting white women in Sparta. The oral sources describe another, private accusation that never received public mention: the previously described dubious assault and subsequent burning near Powelton, which, if it occurred, would have taken place a few years after the Dixon incident.[44]

The reserve that Hancock whites demonstrated in the case of John Dixon raises some questions about the power of the black rapist myth. Recently historians Nancy MacLean and Glenda Gilmore have argued separately and persuasively that the wave of antiblack legislation and violence that marked the late nineteenth and early twentieth centuries can best be explained as an attempt by young white men to render harmless the supposed threat black men posed to white women. This rising generation of late-nineteenth-century white men, denied the opportunity to seek heroism as their fathers had in a great war, defined their masculinity in terms of the ferocity with which they defended their women.[45] In Hancock the *Ishmaelite* reported lynchings and antiblack riots from around the South and often defended them as the only way to prevent black "outrages" against white women. In the midst of the disfranchisement crisis, however, with Dixon providing the perfect opportunity for Hancock men to demonstrate their "manliness," they calmly turned the offender over to the courts.

Three years later white Georgians' fervor to use violence to defend white women against the "black beast" led to the vicious Atlanta race riot of 1906. After Atlanta papers competing for readers manufactured increasingly lurid articles about rapes, including stories invented out of whole cloth, a white working-class mob ran amok, killing twenty-five blacks and injuring countless more. Although the *Ishmaelite* intoned that the mob violence was a regrettably "natural" response to black crime, it ultimately held the Atlanta newspapers responsible for "having aroused the fickle mob to acts of frenzy by lengthy, threatening editorials, as well as sensational headlines." While explicitly "not disclaiming our own adherence to" mob law, the *Ishmaelite* rebuked the irresponsibility and unsteadiness of the sensationalizing urban papers in tones of aristocratic disdain.[46]

A few decades later some Hancock elites continued to demonstrate a measured response to the supposed threat black men posed to white women. Gay Andrews, the daughter of a leading Devereux merchant planter, grew up in a mostly black section of Hancock. During her youth, when her parents were away, an African American man who worked for her family routinely spent the night on her family's porch, a shotgun ostentatiously across his lap. How does one read this? The conservative, personal culture of Hancock allowed one black man to play the role of trusted guardian against the possible sexual threat of other black men. This hardly fills the psychic need, demonstrated by many white southern men, to homogenize all black men under bestial masks and to personally drive them out of all positions of power from which they might threaten white womanhood.[47]

Black-on-white sexual assault was rare, but the real "usual crime," the sexual assault or coercion of black women by white men, was far more common. There is considerable evidence that female slaves stood in danger of sexual assault by the white men who had control over them.[48] This threat diminished greatly at emancipation, but it did not disappear.[49] Some older black Hancock women spoke of the difficulty that female friends and family members had experienced with white men who held economic power over them. According to their testimony, one planter with personal control over the selection of the black schoolteacher in his area regularly attempted to coerce sexual favors in return for the job. Another white man, the owner of a country store, had a reputation for accosting or assaulting black women who entered his store alone. Black women were also sometimes in danger of sexual assault in the homes of the white men for whom they worked as maids. A number of black women stated that their parents had refused to allow them to work as maids to keep them from just such a trap. Unlike white women, they had no recourse to the law when assaulted, and their men risked death if they attempted to defend or avenge them.[50]

Personalism, Planter Dominance, and Demography in Hancock

The examination of Hancock violence further suggests that southern anti-black violence was less dramatic, although much more common in the late nineteenth and early twentieth centuries, than is generally thought. Many locations across the South witnessed a kind of furious carnival of violence in which white crowds gathered to watch and participate in the ritualized torture and murder of African Americans. Sometimes organizers openly prepublicized these spectator events, and train lines offered discounted fares to the site. Venders hawked wares. Men, women, and sometimes children attended these events, especially if they were held in public settings. In Oglethorpe County, two counties to the north of Hancock, five thousand people crowded together to watch a man tied, shot repeatedly, and burned in 1919.[51] On occasion the audience took home fragments of the victim's clothes and body parts as grisly trophies of the lynching. There were country stores across the South that openly displayed these relics of savagery. Although this kind of violence did in fact occur, it has grown to seemingly mythic proportions through art and literature, until it has obscured the more prevalent, though more prosaic, brand of murder that dominated the region.[52]

In almost all cases of intentional violence reported in the *Sparta Ishmaelite* or mentioned in oral interviews, the lethal weapon was a pistol in the hand of a lone assailant, not a rope or torch in the hands of a mob. Additionally, these shootings usually took place in secluded places with few witnesses, if any.

The only clear, publicly known lynching in Hancock occurred in 1885, just before the lynching craze began to take hold of the region generally.[53] On November 25 a mob of about fifty "disguised" horsemen rode into Sparta from the direction of Linton and seized the sheriff at his home around midnight. They brought him to the jail and compelled him to hand over Alec Etheridge. Etheridge was accused of having burglarized homes from Linton, in Hancock, to Bibb County, forty miles to the southwest. When arrested in Bibb County, he pleaded insanity and was committed to the asylum in

Milledgeville. From there he escaped, reportedly shot an officer in Milledgeville, and was recaptured in Hancock. Before they carried Etheridge away, the riders choked him when he tried to scream and roughed him up. His body was never recovered. Although the *Ishmaelite* editor Sydney Lewis noted that "the affair is to be regretted because of its lawlessness," he explained the lynching as a case of self-defense.[54]

According to another story, missed by the national antilynching organizations but passed down orally through the victim's family, a young black Hancock man named Hervia Ingram was castrated and thrown to his death from a speeding wagon sometime in the mid-1930s; the attack followed rumors that he said "something complimentary" to the daughter of his employer, a white sawmill operator. Reportedly the men of the woman's family abducted and killed him. The victim was the son of Sherman Ingram, a wealthy black sawmill owner.[55] The incident is unusual in that it is the only story in Hancock of the murder of someone related to a black landowner.

So in the end, Hancock's whites probably carried out two lynchings, once by a mass mob in 1885 and once by an unreported private group in the 1930s. According to the indexes compiled by antilynching organizations, this places it below the cotton-belt average of three reported lynchings per county and well below the ten to eighteen lynchings of the most lynch-prone counties. Comparisons between counties are difficult to make because doubtlessly many other quiet lynchings, such as the Ingram incident, escaped notice elsewhere.[56]

Although dramatic public lynchings gained much more attention from reporters, social activists, and the historians who traveled in their wake, they made up only a slim fraction of the untallied sum of interracial killings in Hancock and the South. The NAACP, Tuskegee University, and the *Chicago Tribune* investigated lynchings in the South in the late nineteenth and early twentieth century. To raise public awareness of the extent of the problem, they attempted to make annual enumerations of these killings—as high as a hundred a year. Yet their statistics show only the tip of the iceberg. These organizations probably learned of all large, public lynchings, but most lynchings, even in Georgia, were perpetrated by smaller, more secretive groups, such as the one that murdered Hervia Ingram.[57] Except for the 1885 Etheridge lynching, none of the murders discussed in this chapter came to their attention or qualified as lynchings. Nevertheless, black men were quietly killed by white men in Hancock during this period. Murder, though not turned into a spectacle, was still a tool of social control in Hancock as elsewhere through the 1920s.

One should not, therefore, overpraise white Hancock citizens for their chosen mode of violence. Being shot in private was perhaps only a relatively better fate than being burned in public. Yet the form that interracial violence took has some social significance. Brundage has argued that mass mobs, comprising sixty to thousands of members, accounted for 34 percent of all lynchings in Georgia. Cotton-belt whites, Brundage found, were particularly apt to form mass mobs, indicating widespread popular support there for lynching.[58] But Hancock whites usually employed violence against blacks without mobbing them. Additionally, on several occasions that in other places would likely have led to mob action (e.g., a slave revolt in 1863, John Dixon's assault on two white women in 1903, or a black man's murder of a white policeman 1935), Hancock whites allowed the court system to act for them. This suggests that the white people of Hancock did not share the psychic need of many white southerners to transform race murder into a lavish public ritual. Why not? To attempt an answer, we must enter into a still-unresolved discussion in southern history. Why were people in some areas more willing to lynch than were those in other parts?

According to the school of thought promoted by historians Edward Ayers and Roberta Senechal de la Roche, the southern counties with the highest levels of lynchings per capita had extremely sparse, rural populations and experienced sudden and large waves of black in-migration. These counties tended to be especially isolated, with weak government and high levels of transiency. Whites under these conditions seemed to fear losing control to a supposedly "primitive" black population. By making examples of perceived criminal elements in it, they attempted to terrorize all African Americans into cringing servility. Hancock's population, however, was characterized by a stable black majority. Lynch-prone counties further differed from Hancock by having few ties between members of the black and white communities, few whites who knew the character or family of a threatened man, and thus little mercy. This line of reasoning suggests that intimacy brought security and distance brought danger.[59]

Sociologists E. M. Beck and Timothy Clark have countered this argument through a statistical study indicating that local residents outnumbered strangers as lynch victims by three to one.[60] Beck and Clark then considered lynch victims whose history of crime or deviant behavior had marginalized them within the community. They found that strangers and the marginalized together still composed only 45 percent of the victims. Most lynch victims were integrated members of their communities. More often than not, then, lynch mobs murdered men whom they knew, men who were, by most definitions, members of the community. Most lynchings were personal. In a society in which landowners exercised personal control over the economic life of the county, lynching functioned as a tool to maintain the framework of white supremacy, which had been constructed to harness black labor. Where blacks were most needed in the economy, they reason, that tool was most needed and most employed by planters. After all, African Americans were lynched more often in the cotton belt than anywhere else, and that region also had the highest percentage of whites who participated in lynchings.[61] Yet all is not settled.

Despite the statistical evidence suggesting that no African American was truly safe from lynching, anecdotal evidence suggests that African Americans believed themselves to be made safer by personal connections with white "patrons." To reside in an area is one thing; to construct a safety net of relationships is another. The fact that few black landowners were lynched illustrates this point. African Americans could not get land unless they were backed by the leading whites of their community. Apparently the relationships that opened the doors of landownership also held back the lynch mobs. In addition to the oral testimonies of Hancock County blacks presented previously in this study, several published autobiographies by rural African Americans tell of men and women appealing to white "patrons" to assist them in conflicts with other whites. Hosea Hudson, who grew up in Oglethorpe County, about twenty miles north of Hancock, remembered a black man who was saved from a hostile mob by white neighbors who spoke for him. "We know him," they said; "He's alright. Leave him alone." And the mob did.[62] Ed Brown, who lived in Wilcox County, about seventy miles south of Hancock, was a chameleon-like survivor. Ned Cobb, a sharecropper in Alabama, was a forthright hero. Nonetheless, both men repeatedly told of white "friends" who took their part to rescue them from the economic or physical threats of other, hostile whites. Simultaneously, both men described betrayal by white men from whom they expected assistance.[63]

These betrayals testify that personal relationships were no substitute for the right of equality before the law. Whereas civil rights are assumed to be embodied in an enduring body of law, personalist protections were invested in the changing shape of personal relationships. Like the ties of any human relationship, the cords of paternalism were fragile and could snap at any time. There was no way of being sure how much weight they would support in a time of need. Additionally, to gain the support of white protectors, African Americans had to accept their personal authority over their own lives.[64]

Roberta Senechal de la Roche has added one other argument to the discussion. She proposed that collective violence could be divided into two

categories: violence in which entire groups are held responsible for the supposed action of individuals, as in race riots, pogroms, and vigilanteeism,
and violence in which only the individual believed personally culpable of an
offense is held responsible and attacked. Drawing on evidence from around
the world, she argues that indiscriminate collective violence is most common where members of the two groups involved have unequal status, where
they are culturally distant, where they are not mutually interdependent, and
where they share little personal intimacy.[65]

Interestingly, the characteristics that define Senechal de la Roche's context
for indiscriminate violence best describe racial tension in urban America,
North and South, particularly in the first decades of the twentieth century.
Urban whites witnessed rapid demographic change, transiency, and anonymity and perceived a loss of social and racial control. Whereas whites in rural
southern counties lynched individual African Americans to regain a sense of
control, those in urban settings responded in a different way: they rioted. The
difference may be primarily due to the divergent economic sources of racial
tension in urban and rural settings. In the cotton-belt South black people were
the indispensable engine whose cheap labor drove the economy; in northern
and southern cities they competed against poor whites for jobs at the bottom
of industrial society. As a result, efforts at social control in the cotton belt
revolved around exploitative violence to keep blacks close but docile, while
urban efforts employed aversive violence to drive them away.[66]

Urban communities responded to racial tension with race riots, segregation, and the professionalization of violence. Although the 1863 New York
draft riots may spring quickly to mind, these were only the bloodiest of
many instances when northern white mobs took out their frustrations on
black communities in the eighteenth and nineteenth centuries. At the turn
of the twentieth century, race riots broke out in Wilmington, Atlanta, and
other southern cities as media-driven "black rapist" scares coincided with
the final measures of disfranchisement. Next came the Great Migration,
and in response white urban violence swept the nation. In East St. Louis,
Springfield, Chicago, Omaha, Knoxville, Tulsa, Houston, Longview, and other
places, white mobs invaded black neighborhoods, contesting for jobs and
living space. The violence broke out anew in some places during World War
II. In 1943 Detroit, white laborers furious at competition from blacks poured
into black neighborhoods and began mobbing all blacks they encountered,
leading to the deaths of twenty-five blacks and nine whites. In these riots
scores of people were murdered not as identifiable individuals accused of
individual crimes but anonymously and randomly, simply for being members

of a community that stood in the way of white people who wanted their jobs and their homes.[67]

But frequently these race riots led to the widespread destruction of property, disruption of business, and discomfiting of elites, who called for state protection of their interests. One typical urban answer was segregation to create a safe distance between members of competing groups. The North had earlier pointed the way by inventing racial segregation in the antebellum period. In the late nineteenth and early twentieth centuries, southern urbanites self-consciously developed the same modern system to limit racial friction.[68]

Urbanites also dealt with racial threats to civic peace by creating more efficient, modern police forces to maintain peace and administer violent social control carefully, impersonally, and professionally. With a greater investment in concentrated property interests than rural elites had, and more to lose from the kinds of disturbances that unpredictable mob action brought, urban elites gave the state a monopoly on legitimate violence. Policing labor disputes and using force to maintain white supremacy became two of the many expanding bureaucratic functions of the state. Black men were still subjected to beatings and shootings in northern and southern cities, but the men who committed these acts were usually professionally trained to do so. In the cities antiblack violence was not a private concern; it was "good government" in action.[69]

Although whites in North Georgia responded to black competition with the same indiscriminate terror tactics that whites employed in cities, Hancock whites felt themselves in a different situation and responded with different measures. They certainly did not want to drive African Americans from their fields and did not employ random, mass violence, regardless of the provocation. Taken as a whole, Hancock whites held unambiguous public power in the county, economically, politically, and socially. They may not have felt the need for further, public proof of a control that was no longer publicly contested. The wealthier rural whites still maintained direct power over African Americans through paternalistic ties—direct and very personal.

Additionally, as in other old plantation counties, the racial ratio of Hancock's population had remained fairly steady for decades. In the first decades of the twentieth century whites in the county found themselves outnumbered approximately two to one. But they had been raised in a demographic context similar to that of their parents and grandparents. Living among a black majority was neither novel nor, apparently, frightening to the white people of Hancock.

While black anonymity seems to have heightened white fears—and increased the likelihood of lynching—few black faces were unfamiliar to local whites in Hancock. Hancock's World War I draft cards reveal that 90 percent of the county's young black men had been born in the county. An additional 6 percent had been born in a bordering county. Only 20 men out of a sample of 502 draft-age black men had been born more than one county away from Hancock. In fact, the majority of unfamiliar faces in Hancock were white. Only 70 percent of young white men were born in the county, and 10 percent more were born in a bordering county. Fully 20 percent, or 37 out of 182, were born more than one county away from Hancock. The draft-card data also show that the areas in Hancock with the highest proportion of African Americans were also those with the highest stability in that population. In the most planter-dominated section of the county, Devereux, 71 percent of the resident black men of draft age had been born in the Devereux area. The respective figures for other rural areas with large numbers of African Americans were 75 percent for Mayfield and 71 percent for Culverton. The figures are rather different for whites living in the same areas: only 40 percent of draft-age whites living in Devereux were born there, with Mayfield weighing in at 54 percent and Culverton showing only 24 percent. Even in Sparta, Hancock County's seat and only truly urban space, 74 percent of black draft-age males were born in or near the city, but only 44 percent of whites were.[70] To Hancock's native whites, blackness communicated familiarity, not strangeness. Unlike whites in cities or lynch-prone rural counties, those in Hancock personally recognized most of the black people they saw on the walking paths and in the fields around their homes. They would, moreover, likely be familiar with each person's family and reputation.

Because most Hancock families, black and white, had lived in the county for generations, there were many interracial ties among them, some inherited from slavery, some arising spontaneously among neighbors, and some consciously constructed by African Americans who hoped to find security in them. As was argued in the previous chapter, many rural black and white people spent time in one another's company at church, recreation, or work. A number of interracial families spun ties between two theoretically separate communities. A web of interconnectivity held together the interracial, rural world of Hancock, fostering, if not justice, at least a climate less conducive to rule by lynch mobs.

Finally, and perhaps most important, the restraining influence of the conservative planter elite played a strong role in county affairs. Under their leadership, Hancock whites generally acted with moderation. In this way Hancock resembled Virginia, where conservative elites, valuing the calm majesty of the law and fearing anarchy more than black crime as a threat to order, kept lynching at relatively low levels.[71] The county's history clearly shows the influence of this aristocratic class. For example, Hancock citizens steadily supported the Whig Party in the antebellum period and then shifted their support to the Constitutional Union Party instead of the Southern Democratic Party during the polarized election of 1860. When Georgia began to tilt toward disunion and Civil War, Hancock legislators and delegates opposed secession until it had been passed despite their objections.[72]

These conservative elites found their control tested during the Civil War when a group of slaves organized an armed militia and marched to attack Sparta, with the intention of then joining the Union army. The men were captured, after which two leaders were hanged and two were whipped following a careful trial; the others were released to their owners. The restraint shown was remarkable, considering that thirty-four men were involved in the revolt and that some of these men fired on white men before being captured.[73] Judge Thomas W. Thomas of Elberton, north of Hancock, wrote a Hancock judge, saying: "[How] fortunate for the country that if we were to have an attempted negro insurrection it should first develop in Hancock County where it would be met and managed by sensible, firm and discreet people."[74] This response can be appreciated only in comparison with the hysterical and merciless manner in which other areas handled slave revolts during peacetime, much less wartime.

As in most southern counties, white men in Hancock used violence against African Americans in the years following emancipation. Hancock's black state legislators testified before Congress to the suffering these attacks caused.[75] The violence seems to have been due to several causes, all stemming from a general rejection of the implications of black emancipation. Some attacks were attributed to white outrage at blacks who refused to offer customary deference; others, to labor disputes; and still others, to the terrorism inflicted on politically active blacks. These attacks undoubtedly weakened the organized resistance of Hancock's black citizens when county whites used a legal maneuver to bar them from the polls and end Reconstruction locally.[76]

Finally, the last governor elected from Hancock, William J. Northen, attempted to make his county's generally Whiggish tradition into state policy by actively pursuing the prosecution of lynch-mob members throughout Georgia during his two terms, in 1890 and 1892. Besides being a Civil War veteran, Northen had been an educator and the president of both the Southern Baptist

Convention and the State Agricultural Society. As governor he successfully promoted legislation that made members of lynch mobs individually liable for murder. He posted two-hundred-dollar rewards for information leading to the arrest of any member of a lynch mob and used state resources to protect potential victims of mob violence.

After he left office, Northen continued to work for a kind of justice for Georgia's African Americans. Although in 1899 he blamed black crime for southern lynching while giving a nationally conspicuous speech in Boston, he committed most of the rest of his life to eradicating that form of violence. Galvanized by Atlanta's bloody 1906 race riot, Northen began a statewide campaign to organize popular white resistance to lynching. In each county he spoke before crowds, calling on responsible members of the community to form Civic League committees devoted to combating crime and lawlessness—in particular, lynching. When he spoke in Hancock in December 1906, "in the interest of the new movement to bring about a better understanding between the races," the *Sparta Ishmaelite* reported that he "was greeted on all sides with smiles by his many friends." Even as they smiled at him, however, Hancock's elites declined to assist Northen in his public campaign for racial cooperation. Northen's idea of sitting at committee meetings with black businessmen and professionals may have run counter to their premodern sense of planter prerogative and the "place" of black petitioners. Looking out for "their people" was a private task, anyway. White conservatives simply did not come together to deal with such personal issues publicly, at least not since the Populist threat had been defeated. John D. Walker, Hancock's leading businessman and banker, had to write a letter to excuse himself from Northen's personal appeal. He pleaded that, because he was too busy, "the matter of organizing the committee [would] have to be deferred."[77] Perhaps Walker could read the tenor of the times better than could the ex-governor. In the early twentieth century the South slipped from the control of the old conservatives and into the hands of such demagogues as "Pitchfork" Ben Tillman and Theodore Bilbo. These radical racists and their following won control of the public rhetoric of race and imposed a virtual ban on public dissent from any aspect of white supremacy—including the righteousness of lynching. The southern journalist W. J. Cash famously referred to this demand for public conformity as the "savage ideal," and ultimately it silenced even Northen. Still, although Northen and his lonely crusade were crushed by the onslaught of Georgia's radical white racists by 1911, it seems that pressure from such conservative men of means discouraged mob rule in Hancock.[78]

The Klan

Interestingly, the Ku Klux Klan, in its twentieth-century incarnations, kept a fairly low profile in Hancock County, likely because of the influence of these same Whiggish elites. Yet the Klan was not wholly absent there. It earlier had played a role during Reconstruction, when wholesale violence broke out against black people. A black state representative from Hancock, William H. Harrison, stated before Congress that more blacks were whipped after the Civil War than under slavery. Many others were murdered. In Hancock the Klan came to play a role in this violence, although most of the mayhem appeared diffuse and disorganized, the work of white men acting alone. In many counties white elites led the Klan, but in Hancock the aristocracy seems to have opposed the bloodshed and anarchy represented by the secret organization. When a Klan leader in a nearby county wrote his autobiography, he stated that the Democratic political leadership of Hancock had not been Klan dominated. He noted that Linton Stephens, an ex-Whig who orchestrated the bloodless coup that ultimately ended Reconstruction in Hancock in 1870, held a "prejudice" against the organization. Still, Hancock's African Americans had much to fear from Klansmen from other counties, especially Warren County, to the north. One white man from Warren told Congress that the Klan had used threats of violence to force him to join. He also stated that Warren County Klansmen used to make expeditions to Hancock, a point corroborated by black Hancock sources.[79]

After Reconstruction the Klan died across the South. Then, in the 1910s and 1920s, white American Protestants reinvented the Klan to defend their provincial worlds against the perceived threats of modernization, including the increasing presence of women in the workforce; immigrants from eastern, central, and southern Europe; communists; Catholics; and African American veterans who had learned something about fighting and integration in France.[80] The second Klan was founded in Georgia in 1915 and received a great recruiting boost from D. W. Griffith's film *Birth of a Nation,* which exalted the Klan as the defender of white civilization against black "primitivism," and especially of white womanhood against the "black rapist."[81] The film was not shown in Sparta's movie theater, however. The nonappearance of the movie received little comment in the *Sparta Ishmaelite,* which had been under the sedate editorship of T. C. Moore since 1910. Nevertheless, the outspoken style of the previous editor, Sidney Lewis, in commenting on an earlier, stage version of the story reveals the conservative attitudes that held sway in Hancock. The movie was based on a novel by Thomas Dixon, *The Clansman*. In 1905 Dixon had rewritten the novel as a play that toured the country before packed houses almost everywhere—but not in places such as Hancock, where Lewis, writing in the *Ishmaelite*, called Dixon a "firebrand." When the theatrical version of *The Clansman* launched on a second tour in 1906, Lewis warned his readers: "'The Clansman' is coming South again with Dixon, the fanatic, still shaking the red flag. The play will do infinite harm to our conditions in Georgia." Although Lewis mused that "there was a time when it would have been appropriate," probably referring to the periods when blacks and poor white farmers posed serious challenges to the planters' position during Reconstruction and the Populist movement, he commented that "the play possesses no remarkable literary [or] scenic qualities" and expressed hope that "this trip [would] be the last." Firmly seated in the saddle of power, Hancock's conservative leadership had no desire to inflame the unpredictable passions of the middling white men who did not depend on black labor and who made up the majority of the 1920s Klan.[82]

Accordingly, the hooded brotherhood seems to have had limited appeal in Hancock during the second Klan movement. When two Klan organizers called a "mass meeting" at the Sparta courthouse in February 1921, fifty-three men attended, some of whom applied for membership. Still, Hancock's klavern during the 1920s appears to have been a small, inactive, and insignificant group, apparently more interested in social activities than terrorism. It seems to have left no mark in the memories of black or white Hancock people and attracted little attention in the *Ishmaelite*.[83]

The third and most recent Klan movement began during World War II. For reasons similar to the ones that prompted the second Klan, a group of men in Hancock reorganized the klavern. According to African Americans, who established an organization to watch the Klan, it was resurrected by whites who worried that, with most young white men off at war, white women were in danger of imminent attack by black rapists. Of course, as usual, no rapes occurred. After the war the Klan organization continued, not knowing that it was being regularly monitored by the black community through black maids whom whites customarily ignored. Although he declined to provide a detailed account, one member of the anti-Klan organization stated that black men and women were prepared to take action if the Klan attempted anything too threatening.[84]

They did use at least one weapon against the Klan. G. Lee Dickens, who began his law career in Sparta shortly after returning from World War II, remembered that the Klan was rebuffed by all local white politicians and most merchants. When they organized a hooded march through downtown Sparta, however, one merchant's heavyset figure betrayed his identity. According to Dickens, "he didn't last six months after that. The black community completely boycotted his store." In a county with a 70 percent black majority, all downtown businesses were dependent on black patronage, and this fact gave the black community meaningful retaliatory power.[85]

The reputation of the third Klan among Hancock leaders may best be summed up by David Dyer, a white teacher, the director of agricultural extension in the 1940s, and a World War II veteran. "They were just riffraff that had dodged the draft and felt guilty about it," Dyer said in his breathy, whispery voice. "They asked me to join up—tried to get all the county leaders. I told them I didn't want anything to do with them. They wanted to show that they were men, so they burnt down an old colored woman's house." They did indeed. As their fellow Klansmen did elsewhere, the Hancock Klan attempted to police the sexual and racial codes of their communities. Perhaps fortunately for race relations in Hancock, their first victim was a mulatto woman, the lifelong consort of one of the wealthiest white planters in the county. The couple had for decades made no secret of their apparently monogamous relationship without arousing attack or even ostracism. When the third Klan burned down the woman's home in the 1940s, they overreached themselves and were quickly brought to heel by the county's conservative leaders. In retaliation for the burning, the planter, who happened to be a leading subscriber in a drive to build a new county hospital, withdrew his pledge, and the project fell through. The county's conservative elite reminded the Klansmen who paid their salaries and held the mortgages for their daddies' businesses and homes. Thus ended the third movement of the Klan in Hancock.[86]

The Decline of Southern Personal Violence

During the 1920s personal white-on-black violence declined in Hancock County and the South in general. The *Sparta Ishmaelite* reported diminishing incidents of "justifiable" violence against African Americans. Although a few incidents of interracial violence occurred in the following decades, they had an anachronistic air. Certainly white supremacy remained, but personal interracial violence was no longer a casual, central component in its maintenance.

The decline in personal interracial violence coincided with that of lynching. When southern mobs did take black lives, they increasingly came to do so in small, furtive bands and rarely through the brazen spectacles that had formerly been believed to cover the murderers with honor while providing a public lesson to the black community. Somehow white southerners came to see lynching as dishonorable. Indeed, the *Ishmaelite* stopped reprinting lynching stories from elsewhere in the South, as if the less said about these sorry affairs, the better.

The sharp decline in lynching during the 1920s is well documented but not yet explained in a fully satisfactory way. Most of the forces offered as causes postdate the decline of lynching. Jessie Daniel Ames's Association of Southern Women for the Prevention of Lynching, while important, was founded in 1930. The New Deal subsidization of cotton, which in many places relieved planters from reliance on the labor of their black tenants, might have exacerbated interracial tension instead of relaxing them, and at any rate it came too late to have affected lynching trends. The Progressive reformers' craving for rationality, order, system, and control by educated elites might offer an strong explanation had the drop in lynching come during the lynch-crazy Progressive Era instead of a decade or two later.

Other proffered causes, such as mounting pressure by a handful of crusading social scientists, journalists, and politicians, although at least antedating the shift, seem somewhat epiphenomenal. What shaped their opinions, and for whom did they speak? What is more, how do we know whether anyone listened? For example, the religious reformers and civic boosters who founded the Commission on Interracial Cooperation in 1919, although well intentioned in attacking lynching, were neither bold nor influential. At most these antilynching reformers subtly shifted the public rhetoric used to describe lynching and made whites—particularly middle-class urban whites—more conscious of black grievances. The NAACP, too, launched concerted antilynching campaigns in the 1920s, publicizing and condemning each lynching as it occurred, but how their message played in the lynching grounds of the rural South is far from clear. Nonetheless, interracial violence did decline. To a degree the threat of a national antilynching bill motivated some southerners to attempt to police themselves, but the federal government did not attempt to investigate and prosecute lynchers until 1942. A cultural shift toward modernity, best described by J. William Harris, might provide the solution, yet cultural change is difficult to pin down, and in any event, we need full-length studies to substantiate Harris's brief arguments.[87]

The event that coincides most plausibly with the decline of lynching is the Great Migration of the 1920s. Although this mass movement was launched by the employment opportunities in northern factories that World War I opened for blacks, the migrants' personal motivations were various and mixed. Many migrants spoke of their disgust with southern white supremacy in general and the scandal of lynching in particular. Planters, fearful at the loss of their cheap supply of labor, first tried to use anti-enticement laws and the threat of personal violence to keep their tenants off the northbound trains. Failing at that, they offered improved conditions on the farm. Most visibly, they began to promote the public funding of black education. Less visibly, they seem to have used their influence locally to check antiblack violence. Some newspaper editors seem to have become more outspoken against lynching. The *Atlanta Constitution* warned that Georgia's "indifference in suppressing mob law" was depriving the state of its "best labor." Overall the evidence for the impact of the migration on violence is quite slender, but the sharp decline in violence both by mobs and, at least in Hancock, by private individuals makes the linkage likely.[88]

With private white citizens playing a rapidly diminishing role in interracial violence after the pivotal 1920s, law-enforcement agencies came to hold primary responsibility for enforcing white supremacy, even in rural communities. The rural culture of personal violence thus gave way to the modern, bureaucratic culture already established in southern cities. This transference of responsibility did not necessarily ensure greater justice in the administration of violence. African American testimony meant little in court before white accusers, white prosecutors, white juries, and white judges. For years southern juries felt compelled to convict any blacks accused of a serious crime against whites so as to forestall possible lynchings and demonstrate that "the system worked."[89]

When asked whether they could appeal to the law if a family member was killed by whites, almost all black respondents laughed before saying anything. In the pre–civil rights South, a white man who murdered a black man rarely went to trial, much less received a sentence. The *Sparta Ishmaelite* appears to have described no incidents of serious legal consequences for such an act throughout the late nineteenth century and the first half of the twentieth.[90] At the same time, any violence a black man directed against a white man, regardless of the provocation, usually resulted in court action or an extralegal attack. "A white man could kill a black man and wouldn't be a thing in the world done about it," James Wilson stated, "but a black man couldn't show a white man's blood. They'd kill a black man for getting blood out of a white man." Nonetheless, the court system did allow tempers to cool, set a legal standard for evidence, offered a chance at appeals, and allowed an accused African American to seek help from white friends, if he had any. The Jim

Crow legal system, however unjust, was still more equitable than the previous system—which as often as not had amounted to an impulsive backwoods bushwhacking.[91]

Striking Back: Black Interracial Violence in a Culture of Personalism

Although the balance of violence and power was decidedly uneven, African Americans were not utterly defenseless.[92] Whites had most of the guns, the greater will to kill, and the official violence of the state to back them. But blacks, too, had rifles for hunting and pistols for self-defense, as well as the physical power that hard labor builds. They knew the terrain and people who might shelter them in an emergency. Finally, they, too, were members of the southern culture of honor and violence, and although white society attempted to intimidate them into passivity toward whites and held them as ritually "dishonored," the desperation of long frustration or momentary fury could override concern for consequences.[93] Also, an aspect of the southern culture of honor directed much violence, including interracial violence, into one-on-one confrontations. According to southern codes of honor, a man was expected to defend his personal honor personally. His manhood was diminished in the eyes of others if he had to ask for help.[94]

Black men shared with white men more than just this culture of honor, however; they shared the transforming personal experience of war, too. In World War I, 248, or 62 percent, of Hancock's 400 enlisted men were African American. Hundreds more served in World War II.[95] While many black World War I soldiers were not given an opportunity to enter combat, white southerners seemed unwilling to take any chances with their new militancy and organized to beat them back into submission. Although no black veterans were lynched in Hancock, black sharecropper Eva Reese remembered that "some veterans were not able to find work and had to leave for the cities." Apparently whites were worried about what these men might do. Far more black men saw action in World War II. After testing their physical courage in the carnage of that conflict, some black southern men returned home radicalized and resolved never again to accept white southern violence. Grover Thomas, a Hancock native, said that his tour of duty led him to a decision: "You can kill me, but you can't beat me." Some other interviewees from his generation used the same phrase in expressing their refusal to be bullied in the years after World War II. One Communist organizer in the

South remembered that World War II veterans were the most militant African Americans in rural communities. Many black veterans, however, decided to leave the region. After staying in Georgia for a few years, Thomas moved north believing that he was thereby avoiding a bloodbath.[96]

Richard Wright, the black novelist, knew a number of rural black men who wouldn't surrender their dignity to anyone and who dared whites to attack them. He created his most famous character, Bigger Thomas, as a composite of these men. Some of them, and perhaps most, ultimately paid a steep price for their direct challenges to white authority. One such man whom Wright knew was sent to an insane asylum, and others were killed. In Hancock some died too, although others escaped, and still others, within the highly personal and local context of the rural South, were tolerated unmolested. Taken together, their daily example of challenge and their widely varying fates exposed some of the seams and tears in the fabric of white supremacy.[97]

A southern white man confronting an unyielding, dangerous black man might have found some satisfaction knowing that the white community would avenge his death if he was killed defending white supremacy, but he would still have been dead, a perhaps less than acceptable trade-off.[98] Speaking of Winston Boyer, Marshall Boyer said, "[He] wouldn't ever back down—from whites either—and everyone knew he carried a gun. He was a bad negro." Marshall Boyer believed that "he had many white relatives on his side—and that made a difference, too." Eventually Winston murdered a white policeman and was executed, but not before he had lived for years by his own rules.[99]

Mary and Elizabeth Thornton, white sisters in a Devereux landowning family, were born shortly after 1904, the year that their uncle, L. Delma Thornton, was fatally shot by Buck Devereux, one of his black tenants. Few details remain of the incident, but the Thornton sisters remember that the shooting followed a dispute between the two men. According to the *Sparta Ishmaelite*, "the difficulty between them grew out of the refractory conduct of Devereux and his refusal to carry out the instructions of his employer." Thornton's nieces remember hearing that the black man had spoken insolently to their uncle. "Devereux left the field and went into his house, and when Thornton approached it, Devereux shot him with a shotgun." After eluding the law for several years, Devereux was captured, tried, and executed by the state for Thornton's murder.[100]

Not all the Nat Turners of the South were captured or killed, however. Willis Walls, a black World War II veteran, remembers an incident that occurred near his Devereux home in the 1940s. A black sharecropper who worked for one of the county's wealthiest planters got into a dispute with the planter's overseer about the crops. Outraged, the white man got his gun and came to the black man's house. He gave chase and seemed intent on killing the black man. After evading the overseer, the sharecropper slipped into a house and behind a window, shooting the overseer dead as he passed by. He had acted in self-defense, but it was doubtful that the white authorities would see it so. A manhunt was organized, but before the man could be apprehended by the white community, black friends laid him in a casket and, according to the story, shipped him out of state to other friends, who released him.[101]

The tradition of violent African American resistance is probably much more extensive than is currently known. In the private, rural contexts of slavery and sharecropping, most conflicts took place out of the public view. Slaveowners disciplined their slaves personally, or through overseers, their personal employees. Master-slave conflicts rarely became public affairs except in unusual situations, such as general slave uprisings. In their day-to-day dealings with their slaves, white farmers were on their own. As can be gathered from the Works Progress Administration (WPA) slave narratives, the slave experience varied according to a number of factors, including the kind of crop grown, the size of the plantation, and the personalities and outlooks of individual masters and slaves. In this highly personal world, physical strength and the will to use it—certainly by masters but sometimes also by slaves—determined the final balance of their relationship.

Perhaps the most famous example of the successful use of violence by a slave is that of the abolitionist Frederick Douglass in his youthful struggle with Edward Covey, a farmer to whom his master had rented him specifically to break his will. According to Douglass's autobiographies, Covey beat him repeatedly and severely. Finally Douglass—who would soon become a powerfully built man—could take no more. When Covey attacked him, he took the older man by the throat. Covey immediately called for help, but after Douglass disabled Covey's cousin, and two other slaves refused to help the slavemaster, Covey was left to his own strength. It was not sufficient. The match ultimately ended in a draw, with both combatants too exhausted to continue, and that was the end of the matter. Douglass himself believed that he had escaped punishment because the older man was too embarrassed to admit to other white men that he could not handle his slaves, and he could not in fact overpower Douglass by himself. Covey did not strike him again. Physical power and courage allowed Douglass to place some boundaries around his own servitude.[102]

A few African American families in Hancock passed down similar stories of slaves whose physical power and intransigence let them carve special niches in the master-slave relationship. Willie Butts retold family stories about his great-grandfather, Wednesday Butts, who said he beat up the overseer and escaped punishment partly because of his imposing stature and partly because he was a favored slave of his master, Dave Butts. Dollie Walls's great-grandfather, Tuesday Walls, told him that he had told his master: "I won't be whupped." Big, powerful, and forceful, he could outplow everyone else on the plantation. "He was all man," remembered his great-grandson with admiration, and according to his own story, he never was beaten a day in his life, despite stretching and personalizing plantation rules. Tuesday Walls's stories of slave resistance became the central motif for race and labor relations for his descendants. For generations the Walls family traded on their reputation for hard work in order to demand—and according to them, receive—good treatment. At one sawmill where he worked, Dollie Walls heard the owner tell his son, the overseer, not to do anything to antagonize Walls, because he was a good worker and the owner did not want to lose him. Walls stated his philosophy repeatedly and emphatically: "I'm going to treat them right. And they're *sure* going to treat me right." He said he told white employers in the 1930s and 1940s, "I'm a man, and you're going to treat me like a man." He added, "I didn't have no problems when I'd tell them that. I'd say if I ain't working to suit you, just let me know. I'll move on to another place. . . . It was always easy for me to get jobs. They always wanted me. I didn't have to stay there."[103] The Walls family, a group of quiet, serious, hardworking, and physically imposing people, let whites understand that it would be in their best interest not to molest them verbally or physically.[104]

Yet some black men had white violence brought to them despite their best efforts. James Wilson, a wiry, dark, animated man, greatly enjoys telling a story about his father, Dave Payton Wilson. While working as a sharecropper near Devereux in the 1920s, the senior Wilson "had a run-in" with the landlord's son "over mowing some grass." The white man grabbed a hammer to discipline the black man. "When [he] pegged my daddy with that doggone hammer, my daddy ran and got that damn pitchfork. They had a footrace then. He couldn't catch [him]," Wilson recounted, laughing, "so they let him go off the place." That same day the Wilson family, including young James Wilson, packed up everything to start again with another planter. He soberly added that if the family had stayed on, problems would have arisen again, and he knew that both men had narrowly escaped harm that day. Perhaps the white planter family saw the incident as an understandable heat-of-the-moment tangle between men, and as long as word didn't get out about the outcome . . . well, the less said, the better. At any rate, no lynching or retaliation occurred, although James Wilson said he knew of black men who were killed for lesser offenses. In rural Hancock there was no clear, unchanging code for race relations. Rather, men and women with different personalities and different views of the "proper" place of blacks in society invented "the rules" to fit different circumstances in each isolated neighborhood.

If they killed a white person, blacks could expect little mercy in the courts, whatever the provocation. Even nonlethal force, if used by blacks against whites, seems to have been legally inexcusable. As one south Georgia sharecropper, Ed Brown, wrote after telling of a black man who had knocked out his white tormentor with a whiskey jug, "In them days if you hit a white man, you had to take to 'Mr. Bush' to stand your bond. I mean you had to move on."[105] I found no case from early twentieth-century Hancock in which a black won and a white lost when their stories were pitted against each other in court. So the white supremacist deck was stacked if a conflict was brought to the public space of a courtroom, but in the more level playing field of private space, no end was predetermined. If a black man could win on that field and flee the region, he could get away with his use of violence.

In November 1906 Jeff Lundy shot and killed Eugene Binion in the western part of the county. Binion, a white man, worked for W. H. Rives, a wealthy planter, who had sent him to collect a bale of rent cotton from Lundy, a black man. From there versions of the story diverge. Although the *Sparta Ishmaelite* admitted that there were "no responsible eyewitnesses" (meaning no whites), its editor, Sidney Lewis, stated that Lundy had tricked Binion into turning his back, "whereupon the negro, who had stepped into the house and got his shotgun, emptied the contents of it into the back of the white man." It was several hours before anyone white learned of the killing, and by then Lundy was gone. A posse went to see Lundy's brother "and found that he had his gun loaded with cut shells and himself in a belligerent mood." There the posse heard a different story. According to his brother, Lundy had fired in self-defense after being "severely wounded from a shot from the dead man." Although the editor conceded that "this is the account given out by the negroes," he found it "hardly probable" that a man would "turn his back on a man with a shot gun after having shot at him." Running away from a black man apparently seemed too undignified an option for the white editor to admit publicly.[106]

A week later Lundy was located in Rockdale County, about fifty miles from Hancock. When he tried to run, law-enforcement officers shot him in the back and arrested him. He had pistol wounds in the head and neck from his shootout with Binion. In retrospect, it seems most likely that the man who was physically able to flee was the last to shoot and not the initiator of the violence. As Lewis wrote, however, "the stories are somewhat mixed." Lundy repeated his brother's story, saying that he and Binion had become "involved in a dispute about some cotton which he was unloading, . . . that . . . Binion had endeavored to kill him[,] and that in self-defense . . . he had killed his adversary."[107]

Nearly one hundred armed men assembled at the Sparta depot to meet Lundy. Lewis hastened to attest their good intentions, writing, "They were there to protect the prisoner"; nevertheless, he admitted, "The rumor went to Warrenton that a mob was waiting for the negro and he was held over there." In his first report of the story, Lewis had openly assessed Lundy's chances: "[If he] ever comes to the County again, it will go hard with him." Apparently Hancock barely missed its second mass lynching.[108]

But this is not the end of the story. Two weeks later, according to the *Sparta Ishmaelite*, a black man from Sparta visited Lundy in his hospital room in Augusta, loosened his chains, brought him outside to a waiting hack, "and carried him rapidly away to some place in the city, where he [was] attended while convalescing from his injuries." Lundy did not reappear in the *Ishmaelite*. Apparently he either quietly died of his wounds or slipped away, scarred, but alive. Perhaps this time he was wise enough to leave the state.[109]

Considering the risks for blacks, the best-case scenario in a standoff with whites was to threaten violence but not resort to it. Knowing when and how far to push involved a good deal of brinkmanship. Some black Hancock men and women showed great nerve in carefully holding out the threat without being pulled into actual violence.

One black Hancock family told a remarkable story of armed resistance to a white posse in November 1935, the kind of story that was not supposed to happen in the white supremacist rural South but did. Katie Hunt, born in 1891, and her husband, Wilkins Hunt, rented a small but relatively prosperous farm near Sparta. One day the lone Sparta policeman, Morris Stafford, stopped a group of young black men in a car and searched them. When one of the men, Winston Boyer, refused to be searched, the policeman reportedly pulled a revolver and fired it at the ground between the man's feet. The black man pulled his own concealed weapon, shot the policeman dead, and took to the woods.[110]

The white community of Hancock reacted quickly. They organized a posse to capture the man and placed all African Americans under house confinement until he was found. Believing that the fugitive was being sheltered by

African Americans, groups of armed white men began roughly searching black homes. Some took advantage of the situation to vent frustrations toward the black community by tearing up houses and destroying or stealing property while searching. The Hunt family got word from a friend that a search party was coming to their house soon. (They later learned that a black man, jealous of their economic security, had lied to whites about seeing the fugitive by their house.) When the search party came, it had grown to a heavily armed, disorganized, and potentially dangerous mob.[111]

Having had advance notice, the Hunts and their eleven children deployed themselves for armed resistance. Wilkins Hunt sent one son running to get the sheriff, a man who Hunt hoped could control the mob. He positioned three other sons with shotguns in the cornfield behind the front yard, where he expected the crowd to gather. Wilkins and two more sons stood ready at the home's upstairs windows, guns in hand, while his daughters prepared to reload the weapons and pass them to the men should shooting break out. The Hunt family, even in Georgia's plantation belt under white supremacy, was not about to surrender the sanctity of their home to ruffians without a fight. Katie Hunt, a fiery, proud woman who was not used to backing down to anyone, met the mob in the doorway of her home. She attempted to stall to give the sheriff more time. "Pump ain't here!" she declared to the ringleaders, using her husband's nickname. "Let us in!" they demanded. "You are not getting in until my husband gets here," she declared emphatically. And in the yard they stayed. At one point in the standoff, after nightfall, Wilkins slipped his lightest-colored son out the back, with a hat pulled low over his eyes, to circulate among the white men and report back if they were planning to rush the house. Finally the sheriff arrived, and Katie let him in, along with a few of his men. They did not find the fugitive, of course, although Katie made a number of sarcastic suggestions, including that they not forget to look up the chimney over the fire burning there. In frustration a couple of the men grabbed handfuls of flour from Katie's flour barrel and threw them in the yard—as if to assert in a petty, spiteful way that white men ruled Georgia, even if black men and women sometimes successfully resisted that rule.

At the Hunt house, as if in a scripted drama, the white supremacist South offered a glimpse of the highly personal nature of its conflicted soul. The Hunts knew most of the men arrayed before their door. Some were wealthy, and some were poor. Some were even neighbors. Under the summons to protect white civilization and assert white authority, ordinary white men set themselves loose to terrorize their black neighbors, people they knew personally, people with whom they often worked and sometimes fished and worshiped. Any trust that had been earned in private relationships was often sacrificed at public moments such as these. Yet somehow the Hunt family seemed to respond to the incident with surprising equanimity. Charlie, the young man sent out to mix with the crowd, later talked to a white man his age who had been in the posse. When the man bragged that he hadn't been frightened before the garrisoned house, Charlie laughed and said, "Yes you were. I was standing right behind you, and you were shaking like a leaf." According to Charlie, the two men teased each other good-naturedly about their opposing roles in the potentially bloody incident and resumed a relatively friendly relationship. When asked how he could continue relationships with people who had threatened his family, Charlie and the other Hunts simply shrugged and looked at one another. "It's just the way it was" is about all they said. They did not forget, but they apparently learned to take hateful actions in stride and go on.[112]

The Hunt family story also tells us something about the power that individual African Americans had in rural southern society. If shooting down one white officer in self-defense was a high offense against Jim Crow codes, what can one say of the steady-handed threat to mow down a whole posse of deputies and tagalongs? Their house was finally searched, but in the end, it was done on their terms. They risked a great deal to protect their dignity, but protect it they did. One wonders how often other African Americans were able to assert their dignity in the face of white oppression in the rural South. The written sources are largely silent on the matter, but this absence of information proves nothing. Newspapers would simply not have reported such events. It would have been embarrassing for whites to admit publicly the lapses in their supposedly unchallenged rule. So what can we learn from the oral evidence? The Hunt family story tells us that in Hancock, long before the dawning of the civil rights movement, white supremacy was not always supreme.

When the Hunt family trained guns on a white posse and set the terms under which they would submit to search, the white community overlooked their act of defiance. After all, no shots had been fired. But what might have happened if the threats of violence had escalated? Would there have been certain retribution by the white community? Not necessarily, as shown by the testimony of another African American family that lived on the line between the west side of Hancock County and Baldwin County.

Although Alma Dixon Smith was raised in Chicago, her parents sent her to spend each summer on her grandparent's prosperous farm midway between Sparta and Milledgeville. There she played with her cousins—most of whom had also been sent down from northern cities for the summer—and, best of all, got to know her grandparents, Annie and Frank Dixon, the powerful forces that had shaped her father's life. Frank was a quiet, hardworking man with a reputation as an excellent farmer. Annie (or "Sweetness," as she was usually called) was a warm, strong, generous woman. She was also, as they would learn, a proud woman. Smith reported that everyone around knew and respected her grandparents, but as she heard one white person say, "You didn't mess with Miss Sweetness's young'uns." As Smith recalled it, life on the Georgia farm was heaven to the children. During the day her grandparents taught them about animals, trees, hard work, and self-sufficiency; later, after dinner and before the children's bedtime baths, they told them stories about their family and life in the South. The old couple also taught their grand-children about courage, honor, and the contradictions and highly personal nature of southern race relations.

Although their parents had sent them south "so they didn't have to worry about them getting into trouble" on the streets of Chicago, New York, Phila-delphia, Detroit, or Washington, sometimes southern-style trouble stalked up to the door of their grandparents' home. Once in the late 1930s, while Smith was staying there, a white neighbor who had grown up next to the Dixons and was well known to them came over and accused one of the Dixons' sons of trying to steal a cow. It was Miss Sweetness who met him on the porch. She said, "Why would he do that with all these cows here that we have?" But the man would not leave and continued to shout at her and her son from the front yard. Finally, Smith relates, "she went for the shotgun" and fired it over the head of the rapidly retreating man. He went to the sheriff to complain, but instead of arresting Mrs. Dixon, the sheriff told him that "if she did that, you must have been messing with her." The white neighbor, perhaps having located the missing cow elsewhere, later came back to the Dixon's house to apologize for his behavior. Apparently the apology was accepted, and life went on. Besides some new stories to tell her grandchildren, the only result of the incident was that Annie "Sweetness" Dixon picked up her second nickname, "Annie Oakley."[113]

The stories of "permissible" black violence against whites, or rather the threat thereof, raise questions about the role gender and class played in white perceptions. Perhaps events would have developed differently if, instead of his wife, Frank Dixon had fired the shotgun. W. Fitzhugh Brundage, the leading historian of lynching, believes that black women were given more latitude than black men in challenging white supremacy. They may have been allowed to challenge white authority because their assertiveness could not have been misconstrued as a sexual threat to white women. Perhaps this is also why Katie Hunt met the white mob at the door, represented her family at the height of the crisis, and felt free to make personal insults to the white men searching her home.[114]

Class also played a role in shaping white perceptions of black resistance. In the eyes of the white elite of Hancock and Baldwin Counties, the Hunts and Dixons were respectable people. They were renters and landowners, respectively. They were sober, hardworking people who stayed out of trouble, paid their bills, and to some degree shared with whites the right to defend not only their lives but their outraged honor. Their stories reveal that not all white southerners felt that all African Americans had to be "kept in their place"—or more accurately, that not all African Americans were thought to belong in the same place. This does not mean, of course, that the outcomes would have been the same in other parts of the South. Even in Hancock and Baldwin Counties, moreover, if Annie Dixon had been a poor sharecropper, had previously been arrested for moonshining, or had lacked a good relationship with the sheriff, her use of a lethal threat would probably not have been tolerated. But that is precisely the point. Across the South, white supremacy rested on white violence, yet because of the highly personal character of rural culture and the divergence between separate rural areas, communities differed in the use of white violence and the degree of violent black retaliation that whites allowed. In violence, as in interracial social relations, there was no "Solid South."

It also must be stated clearly, however, that the overall economic, political, and social structure of Hancock was not threatened by the black retaliatory violence that whites (or some whites) allowed some blacks. Annie Dixon's successful defense of her family's honor against a white neighbor's accusations in no way altered the power relationships between the county's two racial groups. Drawing as they did from an old conservative tradition, the governing elites understood this. Unlike planters in many other, more racially radical parts of the South, they would not be panicked into releasing waves of dangerous, anarchic violence into the community simply to ensure that all Hancock's blacks consistently deferred to the higher status of all Hancock's whites. Confident in their control, the planters allowed the development of a rural culture in which the threat of violent retaliation by respectable blacks was tolerated and sometimes condoned. Although gendered identities, class interests, and intellectual traditions help us understand these general patterns in the county, many interracial incidents can be understood only within the context of the highly interpersonal culture of rural Hancock.

Another story illustrates this point. It comes from an interview with a black man who also grew up on the line between Hancock and Baldwin Counties, not far from Annie Dixon. In 1923, when Marshall Boyer was fourteen, a deputized posse of white men met in the yard in front of his house to scour the surrounding woods for a black man. The man, who was armed and dangerous, had fatally shot a white farmowner in a field a short time earlier. Each day the men came at dawn to start their search; each day, as Boyer heard, they came up empty. Finally the word reached the county that the man had somehow evaded the dragnet and escaped to Detroit. As Boyer grew up, he came to hear more and more from the men involved in the incident, filling in more pieces of the puzzle. Life eventually took him to Detroit, where he met the fugitive himself, Tommy Ray, and heard the rest of the story from the man's own mouth.

Ray had sharecropped for a white man, Winton Edmund, and had developed a friendship with him. One day a white man with a reputation for meanness got into an argument with Ray and left enraged. Edmund, hearing that the man was coming to shoot Ray, went to warn him, but he did much more than that. Edmund asked Ray, "What kind of gun do you have?" "A .32 pistol," was the reply. Edmund had a .38 and swapped weapons with his friend. Both men then went to the field to work. Edmund later told Boyer that, as he worked in the field adjacent to Ray, he heard a pop from a small-caliber gun, followed by two booms from his own gun. He told Boyer that he had thought to himself, "Oh God, Tommy Ray done kilt him now." Sure enough, the white man, who had shot at Ray through some bushes and missed, was laid out dead from Ray's return volley.

According to the story Boyer heard from Edmund, the landlord then went to the sheriff to help organize a posse, but before he did so, he hid Ray in a dense section of woods. Each day he set out from the Boyers' yard, gun apparently at the ready. When the line of men would approach Ray's hiding place, he would call out, "I got this section! I think I'm going to find that black so-and-so over here!" Then, as he passed Ray, he quietly dropped some lunch and walked on. After a few days of this maneuvering, Edmund got a trusted white friend to bury Ray in his wagon under a load of hay and haul him to the opposite side of Milledgeville. There Edmund met Ray in a car, drove him to Atlanta, and put him on a train to Detroit. "That's all I can do for you," he said. Indeed, what else could he have done—either for his black friend or to challenge the modern assumptions of universal white solidarity against African Americans? Racial identity drew lines that separated people from one another. Yet there were other ways of "picking sides," other forms of identity. Friendship, clearly, could be one such form of identity. In this case, the self-interest of an employee in protecting his labor does not begin to explain Edmund's actions. First, the white man took considerable risks on Ray's behalf. He did not just "speak a good word" for him. He gave him a weapon with which to kill a white man. Then he shielded the black man from the law and transported him out of the state. All were clearly criminal acts for which Edmund would have paid a price had he been discovered. Second, what did Edmund gain? He lost a good laborer by aiding Ray's flight as surely as he would have if Ray had been killed. Economically he had no stake in the outcome of the event. But personally, in ways that are not easy to categorize, he seems to have felt that friendship and justice were sufficiently important to warrant siding with a black man on the run.[115]

* * *

An intrinsic aspect of the culture of personalism, interracial violence remained the ultimate weapon for maintaining white supremacy. In the rural context of secluded settings and private relationships, however, black people were not reduced to helpless pawns, and their anger and capacity for violence also had to be acknowledged in the racial balance of power. Although white supremacy held constant as a public reality, its different private meanings to different people in Hancock County reveal a distinctly unsolid South. Different traditions of race relations—including the use of violence—existed in different parts of the South. Furthermore, various standards were set for black men and women depending on their gender, their economic status, and their personal ties to members of the white community. In the following chapter I will show that within the culture of personalism, whites also extended limited political rights to a small number of well-connected black voters throughout the first half of the twentieth century.

6

Paternalism and Patronage: Public Power in a Personal Culture

OLD NEGRO DEAD

On Monday of this week Uncle Eli Barnes, an aged negro well known in Hancock County, died very suddenly. He was a familiar figure for many years, and during the days of the Reconstruction represented Hancock County in the house of representatives.[1]

In 1910 this brief message in the *Sparta Ishmaelite* notified the people of Hancock County that Eli Barnes had passed away—and with him, their link to an earlier era in which African Americans had been public, independent actors. After having helped shape the course of government in the 1860s and again in the 1890s, the African Americans of Hancock County had essentially lost their citizenship, and Representative Barnes was merely a "dead Negro." In losing independent political power, they had lost all claim to legal protection. In losing legal protection, they had lost leverage for economic security. Along with these tangible losses came a significant symbolic loss. Self-directed voting is a sign of full membership in the public community. Black southerners at the turn of the twentieth century largely lost this sign of adulthood, competence, and—given that the franchise remained largely a male prerogative through the first half of the twentieth century—manhood. They were by and large falling into civic nonpersonhood. The manner of their doing so in Hancock, however, is a complex story.

Rural white elites across the South concurred in keeping state and local government small and weak. They thereby ensured that little power would be delegated to the public sphere; most power would remain as personal wealth, personal connections, and personal capacity for violence. In the cotton belt the elite consolidated its grip on this small government by supporting the disfranchisement of first African Americans and then poor whites. It is widely believed that rural black disfranchisement had been fully accomplished by the early twentieth century and abated only with the civil rights movement. But in Hancock, and perhaps in other demographically similar counties, the security of the planter elite led to a somewhat different course. Because of their firm economic and political control of the county, Hancock's twenti-eth-century leaders continued to allow a degree of black involvement in the "for-whites-only" political process. For the first two decades of the twentieth century, however, most of the county's African Americans who remained eligible to vote seem to have served largely as political tools in the hands of the planter class. Later, as long as African Americans did not constitute an organized threat to the political order, the white citizens allowed a select few self-sufficient blacks the privilege of directing their own votes. This was the political face of the paternalism described in earlier chapters. Whenever independently organized African Americans had constituted a threat, as during Reconstruction and the Populist movement, the planter elite moved decisively to crush the challengers. In politics as in economics, social relations, and personal violence, Hancock's racial order was based on the distinctively personal nature of power relations in the county.

The two leading studies of the restriction of African American voting rights in the South both end in 1910 with the decimation of black voting strength. By the early twentieth century, white supremacists across the South had essentially reduced the franchise to a small portion of the white population. After official black disfranchisement, black political activity survived—to the extent that it did—largely in the cities. Surprisingly, however, some rural African Americans did continuously participate in the county's political process, from Reconstruction to the present. We know little about this politically active black remnant and the context in which its members acted. Their story, between the end of Populism and the beginning of the civil rights movement, deserves some investigation.[2]

The Traditional View of Disfranchisement: Hancock's Newspaper Records

The question as to who would share in the franchise was largely settled before 1900. Therefore, this chapter will reach back to examine the nineteenth-century events that profoundly shaped Hancock's political landscape through the first half of the twentieth century: the defeats of Reconstruction and Populism and the rise of the white primary. During Reconstruction most African American southerners voted with the Republican Party—partly in gratitude for emancipation but also because the Republican Party proved itself somewhat sensitive to their concerns. The freedmen asked for and received some innovative government measures. They wanted, among other things, universal education, some protection from white violence, federal arbiters to assist them in drawing up contracts with landlords, and state recognition of property rights for married women. Most of this legislation, passed under so-called Radical Reconstruction, was so measured and moderate that it remained on the books even after the Democratic coups thrust the Republicans from power.[3]

Across the South, African Americans faced assassinations, rapes, and beatings at the hands of whites as they attempted to exercise the rights of citizenship. Again, Hancock's Whiggish, conservative elites did not prevent local African Americans from suffering a series of these violent attacks. Paternalism and protection operated during "normal" times, but when blacks seriously challenged the status quo, the planters of Hancock regained control by heightening personal violence and augmenting it with organized violence. During the first four months of 1866, three black men were murdered by white men, all of whom were released on grounds of justifiable homicide. Hancock blacks were subject to regular violence over the next several years, and in each case the white murderers escaped justice.[4] When blacks tried to organize privately to avenge these attacks, however, they were arrested and sentenced to prison. As long as African Americans contested for political power within Hancock, the pattern of violence continued.[5]

Political Reconstruction had a brief life in Hancock. In a state special election held in April 1868, over 1,900 Hancock men cast ballots and by a large majority sent two black Republicans, William Henry Harrison and Eli Barnes, to the state legislature, where they were denied seats. Halfway through their terms they were restored to office, but by then Democrats had already reasserted control over the county. Before the presidential elections of November 1868, the Republican Georgia governor tried to bring in the widest vote possible by signing an executive order to set aside the constitutionally mandated collection of the poll tax for that election. In Sparta, Democratic election managers ignored the governor's order and turned away all who had not paid the tax, thereby ensuring a large Democratic victory for Horatio Seymour over Ulysses S. Grant in the county.

The process was repeated two years later. In 1870 the governor had secured passage of a state law suspending the collection of the poll tax. Hancock also had new, Republican election managers, including two African Americans. Linton Stephens, who was a Hancock native and the chief justice of Georgia's Confederate Supreme Court, protested to the managers that the law was unconstitutional and therefore invalid. When they decided to ignore his protest and allow anyone to vote under the new law, Stephens secured the cooperation of a justice of the peace and the sheriff, who arrested and jailed the Republican managers. Democrats quickly replaced them and refused to open the polls to those who had not paid the tax—mostly African Americans. When Harrison, the black state representative, tried to lead a black crowd to release the Republicans from the jail, a white militia—which had been training for such a situation—broke into stores to seize guns and headed off the would-be liberators as they approached the courthouse. Because years of white violence told them that the threat was real, the black men backed down. Few African Americans voted in that election, and the Democrats won. Hancock's African Americans would not run for office again for nearly one hundred years. In the end, political white supremacy in Hancock County was won by a legal maneuver backed by the threat of violence.[6]

During Reconstruction Georgia's white Democrats tried to reidentify their faction as "the white man's party." In reality, however, white men in Georgia divided their loyalty among many competing parties: the old Democrats, the fading Republicans, and a rising series of independent challengers such as the Greenback Party. During the 1870s and 1880s these independents proved a serious challenge to "Democratic unity," electing two congressmen and nearly electing a governor. Nevertheless, Georgia's Democratic elite held enough economic and social influence with black and white voters to carry most elections.

Then, in the 1890s, poor white farmers, hard-pressed by a decade of economic decline, revolted from the Democratic elites' hegemony. Under the leadership of Tom Watson, they made overtures to black voters, seeking to unite with them in a sweeping reform of capitalist monopolies and unrepresentative government. As the Republicans had before, Populist rhetoric openly recognized African American rights and interests. Watson consistently addressed both black and white farmers, offering to both the rewards of an interracial class movement. He declared his intention to "put every man on his citizenship, irrespective of color."[7]

The Democrats exploited the frankness of the Populist appeals to blacks, decrying the challenge they posed to the united front of white supremacy. Yet their appropriation of the term "white man's party" is misleading, because the elites, too, appealed to black voters. They did so, however, within the rhetoric of paternalism. Whereas the Populists offered no specific, concrete benefits to black voters but only the more hypothetical rewards of a classwide victory over "the money power," the planters offered material assistance to rural blacks. Sidney Lewis, the stridently Democratic editor of the *Sparta Ishmaelite*, reminded black voters of their position: "[It is the Democratic planters] on whom the colored voters depend for employment ... and to whom they go for assistance when in trouble." He added, "The men who have helped them to build their churches, and who have established schools and employed teachers for the education of their children, are Democrats." Furthermore, Lewis argued, it was the Democratic planters who protected them from the violence of mobs, although he simultaneously hinted at economic and violent retribution should African Americans side with the Populists. The editor then demanded votes as a sign of gratitude for these tokens of "friendship."[8] That was the paternalists' offer: private assistance in return for public votes. A number of articles in the *Ishmaelite* written by black Hancock men showed that these appeals hit home. They referred to the planters as "the race's true friends." Several wrote testimonials to the solicitude of individual local planters. "When I was in trouble," said one Hancock black man, "no one helped me but a Democrat."[9]

The contest was especially heated in Hancock because the state's Democratic leadership gerrymandered the county onto Watson's tenth congressional district, expecting the Hancock planters' firm control over black voters to decide the race for their party. In the end, the Democrats did carry Hancock and the district overall, apparently with a majority of the black vote. The best estimate is that in the three contested elections from 1892 to 1896, an average of 45 percent of white voters supported the Populist Party in Georgia, with an average of only 30 percent of black voters doing so. Just to make sure of victory, the Democrats in Hancock and elsewhere in Georgia threw out Populist votes and stuffed the ballot boxes with illegal ballots. In nearby Augusta, the largest city in the district to which Hancock belonged, the number of votes cast—mostly Democratic—was twice that of registered voters. Over the following years the outraged Populists, again led by Tom Watson, turned on their erstwhile allies for vengeance. The Democrats, recognizing their narrow escape, helped direct poor white outrage into a crusade ostensibly "to clean up campaign corruption" by disfranchising African Americans.[10]

During the first years of the twentieth century, "Progressive" campaign reform in the South was formulated as a crusade to disfranchise economically dependent men, who could be influenced by wealthier men. In nineteenth-century America many poor men, black and white, exchanged their votes for bribes. Sometimes planters or mill owners threw parties for their workers, giving them food and liquor and then passing out ballots and driving or marching the men directly to the polls to vote a straight ticket. Although Hancock's Democratic planters apparently used their influence—both paternalistic and coercive—over their tenants to vote them for the Democratic Party, some independent-minded black voters supported the Populists instead. The *Sparta Ishmaelite* noted in annoyance that many African Americans resisted election bribes when offered candidates whom they believed were worth voting for. In 1892, to draw Populist voters from a campaign speech delivered by Tom Watson at the Sparta courthouse, the Democrats threw a free barbecue a short distance away. The editor of the paper noted that although Watson's crowd thinned somewhat, his black followers stood by him to the end of his speech and refused the free meal.[11] One bewildered white newspaperman wrote that he "heard of a hungry and destitute colored man, the head of a family," refusing ten dollars to vote Democratic. Apparently paternalism had its limits, at least for some.[12]

After Populism's defeat, however, African Americans faced disfranchisement when white Populists blamed them for the election's outcome and urban reformers scapegoated them for the general corruption of politics. Georgia had been the first southern state to impose a poll tax in 1868 and the first to make the poll tax cumulative in 1877, yet white Georgians restricted the franchise even further around the turn of the twentieth century. In 1898 the state Democratic Party implemented the white primary. A few years later Tom Watson pressed Hoke Smith to make the constitutional disfranchisement of African Americans the central issue of his 1906 gubernatorial campaign. After winning the election, Smith proposed an amendment to the Georgia constitution to further restrict the franchise via property and literacy tests.

Blacks did not accept the movement uncritically, although the *Sparta Ishmaelite*'s coverage of these events rendered black people and their perspectives largely invisible. On May 15, 1908, however, its editor did react sharply to two public condemnations of the disfranchisement amendments voiced by African Americans in Sparta, the first by the state grand master of the Colored Odd Fellows and the second by Dr. B. W. S. Daniels, a Hancock delegate to the Tenth District Republican Convention in Augusta. Because the two men, speaking before black audiences, dared to criticize these patently unjust actions by white politicians, Lewis reproved them for being disrespectful. Little more than a decade earlier the same editor had reprinted several political statements from African American Democrats, either in criticism of white Populists or in praise of white Democrats. At the time Lewis had flatly stated that white southern Democrats "would never allow blacks to be disfranchised." But times had changed. By 1908 Lewis wholeheartedly supported the disfranchisement movement. In his eyes, African Americans had no right to speak publicly on public matters—no right to a public presence. For Lewis, they were no longer even marginally independent citizens.[13]

Yet African Americans in Hancock continued their public resistance to disfranchisement up to the day of the 1908 referendum on the constitutional amendment. They conducted a voter registration drive and, much to Lewis's distress, registered over three hundred black voters to oppose the amendment. Despite these efforts, few actually turned out to vote, which suggests that the African Americans feared violence at the polls. Hancock voters carried the amendment 531 to 66. Although turnout was light across the state, white voters as a whole—particularly in the black belt—joined the Hancock majority in ratifying the amendment. The disfranchisement amendment contained understanding and grandfather clauses providing loopholes for poor whites, if election managers wished to use them. Frequently they did not so wish. Whether they recognized it or not, many poor whites watched themselves being voted out of the franchise. By the 1920s and 1930s only one-quarter of adult white men still voted in Georgia.[14]

Disfranchisement, Small Government, and the Culture of Personalism

While African Americans were clearly the publicly advertised targets of disfranchisement, most Georgians lost something from the restriction of the franchise. After most of the voting base had been disfranchised, there came to be little difference between candidates and few meaningful choices for voters. The South had enjoyed healthy contests among opposing political parties during the nineteenth century, offering choices among Whigs, Democrats, Republicans, Populists, and some minor parties. Hancock lost its earlier political flexibility in the twentieth century as politicians came to compete for the votes of a diminishing portion of the population. Without an electorate representing truly diverse views, southern elections shifted from an issues-based to a personality-based format. Politicians became stand-up comics who aimed their hee-haw jokes at the lowest common denominator of voters, snapped their suspenders, offered barbecue dinners, and assailed, in terrible terms, the "Negro threat." After having sent men of substance and learning, such as their own William Northen, to represent them in the nineteenth century, Hancock voters in the first half of the twentieth century wholeheartedly gave their votes to demagogues, the clown prince of whom was Eugene Talmadge. As governor in the 1930s and 1940s Talmadge distinguished his terms of office by canceling the state tax on dogs and by fighting against the New Deal until the federal government took over the administration of its programs in Georgia. In 1941, after he interfered with the administrations of the state's white colleges, accusing them of being soft on segregation, the regional accrediting board stripped accreditation from all ten of them. As a symbol of his commitment to the rural and small-town folk who sent him to "cosmopolitan" Atlanta, he put a cow and chickens on the lawn of the governor's mansion. Talmadge promised to bring prosperity to Georgia's farmers while maintaining the status quo, especially local autonomy and white supremacy. Marshall Boyer, an African American farmer who grew up just beyond the western edge of Hancock, remembered him promising, "If you elect me, I'll get your cotton chopped." Then, when asked to deliver, he replied, "I don't got no niggers." Such was the state of politics in Georgia.[15]

Most Georgians were poor during the twentieth century's first fifty years. Those who voted and controlled state government under the state's regressive county unit system tended to be middling farmers and small-town merchants who were unwilling to tax themselves and proud of their personal independence.[16] As a result, government was relatively weak in the urban centers and even weaker in rural areas. Public support for education, mostly in the form of paltry teachers' salaries, took up the lion's share of government expenditures. Half of the remainder went to the upkeep of roads and bridges. The small sum left over was used to pay judges, juries, bailiffs, sheriffs, and a few other administrators, and for maintaining paupers, the insane, and convicts, the last of whom earned their keep by repairing county roads. This list nearly exhausts the role of government in early twentieth-century Hancock: educating the children up to sixth grade or so, adjudicating legal disputes, protecting the community from criminals, and keeping the roads somewhat passable. Overall, government barely touched the lives of rural Hancock people until late in the 1930s and did not make a serious impact until World War II. Dave Dyer, who began his career in Hancock politics in the late 1930s, remembered that "the old men" who ran the county then "didn't want any expansion on government. They were very tight businessmen."[17]

For decades the political structure of Hancock served the interest of the planters and merchants. Sometimes it did this directly, as when it enforced segregation laws in downtown Sparta or collected the poll tax. More often it did so indirectly, by underfunding black schools to keep the school terms short or by looking the other way when white men shot black men. Most often, however, county government served the planters simply by being small and ineffectual. The impotence of local government created a power vacuum that the planters filled with their own personal power. The planters, through their court-sanctioned use of personal violence to settle conflicts with tenants, eliminated their "need" for the services of modern-sized law-enforcement agencies. In addition, the planters and merchants partially filled the function of welfare agencies through their springtime furnishes and personal acts of benevolence. One man from an elite Sparta family remembered that "through that awful summer of 1922," when the boll weevil closed farms and diminished the furnish, "there was no welfare, no food stamps, no social services." In town his devout Methodist aunt, Fionne Rozier Miller, tried to fill the void, daily carrying food and attending to the bodily needs of sick and elderly African Americans who had moved into abandoned mill houses on the outskirts of Sparta. He remembers that they "would call out blessings on her name." Ten years later Louis Yaffe, a Jewish merchant in Sparta, collected used clothing to give to the needy. These personal kindnesses were small attempts to fill the void left by the local government's callous unresponsiveness in the face of Hancock's sharpest humanitarian crises.[18]

The smallness of local government gave each planter great leverage over labor. In this system black tenants and anyone else in the county who held little personal power needed to cultivate relationships with a more powerful patron. In Hancock County the personal was truly the political. This is why many southern voters opposed New Deal programs, even though they would have received most of the benefits from the programs. They recognized the threat that a powerful national government posed to their own unimpeded exercise of personal power.

In fact, as I will discuss in the epilogue, most Hancock people passed through the 1930s without being greatly affected by the great federal expansion of the period. While the Red Cross handed out a small amount of food, the government apparently did not. For those with connections (almost exclusively white), the Civilian Conservation Corps, the Works Progress Administration, and the Public Works Administration provided employment during a critical time. As the planters had feared, these programs began to create a new sense of the government's role. Those who had personal experience with the Farm Home Administration often found that the government could provide practical benefits, but few people were involved in this program. The Agricultural Adjustment Administration taught farmers about both the benefits of federal largess and the drawbacks of federal regulations. Of course, the wealthier farmers received most of the former and complained the most over the latter. Later the Wages Equalization Act nudged up the wages of sawmill workers in Hancock—and indirectly, the wages of agricultural workers. These federal interventions did alter rural people's experience of government, but for most of the dependent farmers who followed the mule, life seemed to continue from the 1920s through the 1930s without passing over any memorable civic landmark. Most poorer farmers said that they had heard about the New Deal but did not know much about it firsthand and certainly had not benefited from it directly. Several spoke with gratitude of the one memorable exception, the few dollars of Social Security benefits that their parents or grandparents received before dying. Their clear recollection of this program lends credibility to their general story of government neglect. For most of them, the great bustle of the New Deal was largely a rumor.[19]

Much more significant for the lives of rural Hancock people were the side-effects of war mobilization in the 1940s. Most who lived through those years remembered the rationing of rubber, sugar, and fuel. Many poor farmers remembered the war-work industry and the shortages of labor it created in other industries as their first chance at a decent wage and the G.I. Bill as their first chance for an education. Whether Hancock people went abroad for the war, or simply heard about the outside world from others, what they learned during the war raised their expectations. Afterward they demanded and received more paved roads, better schools, and a more activist government. World War II—a federal program on a massive scale—permanently altered the role of government in Hancock. But until it did, government was kept small, and power remained personal.

Another View of Disfranchisement: Deciphering Hancock's Poll Tax Records

When the poll tax was first enforced in 1868, it diminished the black vote and ended Hancock's experience of Reconstruction. The 1899 white primary and the constitutional disfranchisement of 1908 were designed to sweep any remaining African Americans from political involvement. As figure 8 indicates, however, the Hancock County tax digest seems to complicate this thesis. Under the heading "poll tax for whites," the digest reveals that more blacks than whites were listed as having paid their poll tax in every year from 1874 to 1911. From 1874 to 1898 an average of 847 whites and 1,451 blacks were annually listed as paid. Whites did not achieve their first, temporary majority in poll-tax payment until 1912, when 879 whites and 761 blacks were listed as paid. Even after that date African Americans seemingly continued to pay the tax in large numbers, sometimes in majorities. Not until 1921—fifty-three years after Georgia's poll tax had been established and thirteen years after the final barriers to the vote were raised—did whites in Hancock County achieve what was to be a permanent superiority in poll-tax payment. How was this possible?[20]

The dates of declines in the black payment of the tax may offer some hints. There were two great drops in black payment of the poll tax in Hancock. The first came in 1899, when payment of the poll tax for African Americans fell by 42 percent, from 1,677 to 971. Payment of the poll tax by whites fell that year as well, from 906 to 800, a drop of 12 percent. This drop seems due to two factors: the decline of Populism and the rise of the white primary. In 1898 the Democratic Party in Georgia had ruled that coordinated statewide primaries would be mandatory for the selection of delegates to Democratic conventions. The following year Georgia Democratic leaders excluded blacks from participation in this new state primary.[21]

The second drop in black payment of the poll tax came in 1921, arguably the most significant date in the county's economic history. That year the boll weevil came and devoured Hancock's economy. There was simply little money in the county after 1921 for life's essentials, much less the poll tax. As figure 8 demonstrates, the number of blacks who are listed as "paid" fell from 1,029 in 1920 to 680 in 1921 and 378 in 1924. Over the course of those four years, the number of African Americans eligible to vote by payment of the poll tax fell to a little over one-third its 1920 strength. Whoever was paying the poll tax of African Americans seems to have quickly decided that the benefits no longer balanced the considerable expense. Until collection of the poll tax was discontinued in 1945, the number of those paying it in Hancock fell almost every year. After 1930 fewer than 300 blacks paid the tax; after 1936, fewer than 200; after 1941, fewer than 100. In the last year of the poll tax only 27 African Americans paid it. Although white payment of the poll tax did not fall significantly after the coming of the weevil, it too began to decline after the first couple years of the Great Depression. Between 1932 and 1944 the number of whites paying the poll tax fell by roughly one-third, from 828 to 505.

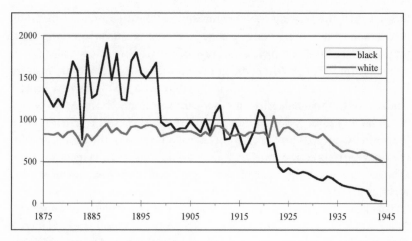

Figure 8. Payment of the Poll Tax in Hancock, 1875–1944 (*source:* Hancock County Tax Digests, 1874–1944, Georgia State Archives, Atlanta).

Although the poll-tax payments in the annual county tax digests seem to tell a straightforward story, it is impossible to determine voting behavior based on this evidence. Mere payment of the tax did not mean that people listed as "paid" voted or, if they did, that they themselves determined for whom they would vote. One black educator in Hancock said that many were paying the poll tax and not voting. He speculated, "They may not have known what it was for," adding that they may have seen it as just another tax they had to pay.[22]

Another explanation seems more likely for the period before 1899. In many parts of the nineteenth-century South, wealthy whites paid the poll tax of poorer folk—both black and white—and directed their voting behavior. Some Hancock interviewees stated that some planters and sawmill operators continued this practice and "voted" their white tenant farmers and employees well into the twentieth century. The planter J. E. Johnson remembered that county leaders would "have fish fries and barbecues by ponds." Before that, they "used to buy a man's vote with whiskey." Johnson continued, "Plumbers, mechanics, carpenters, and clerks would take money for their vote. Vote how the employer said." When asked how a vote-buyer would know whether his man would vote as directed, he said, "You'd know because all the ballots were numbered—you'd hear how they voted." Oversight of purchased votes would have been even simpler before 1922, when Georgia adopted the secret ballot. Actually, the former system may have persisted even longer in Hancock, for the *Sparta Ishmaelite* reported the first use of the Australian ballot in 1924, and Johnson did not remember seeing screened-off booths until the New Deal. Another planter explained how Hancock elites controlled the vote. "Many folks couldn't read and write, so they had a friend fill out the ballot for them." When asked whether a literate friend would accompany the voter in the booth, he said no: "It would get too crowded. They'd take the ballot and go." Some of these ballots came his way. "I'd give them advice," he said and then corrected himself: "Well, they let me fill it out how I wanted, but that's what I paid them to do." For helping elect members of the county commission, he said, "you'd get a favor back from them" when they decided, for example, where the chain gang should repair the roads and bridges. "They say one man, one vote," he summarized. "I don't believe that. A poor janitor doesn't have responsibility."[23] In the eyes of such men, the poor were resources to be exploited politically as well as economically. In all likelihood, most blacks voted as directed before 1899, as many poor whites apparently continued to do after that date.

Until 1923 the poll tax showed wild fluctuations in payment by African Americans. Seemingly, men would let the tax lapse every couple of years and then pay it off. Because the tax was cumulative, they would have to pay off the skipped years as well as the current year. Who was doing this? Figure 9 shows that during these years the vast majority of eligible black voters were dependent farmers. It is improbable that poor men would pay off two or three

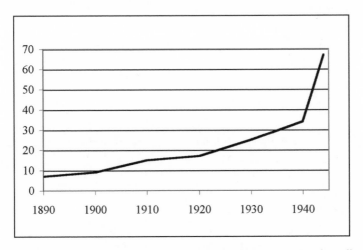

Figure 9. Black Landowners as a Percentage of All Blacks Paying the Poll Tax (*source:* Hancock County Tax Digests, 1874–1944, Georgia State Archives, Atlanta).

years of tax at a time. Seemingly, political patrons were paying these men's poll taxes. Perhaps the merchants and planters, having decisively crushed any significant challenge to their power, continued to hold some voters in reserve in case a new independent party once again turned the general election into a meaningful contest.

On the other hand, the tax digest shows black landowners paying their poll tax steadily, year after year. In 1890, 54 percent of black landowners were marked as "paid" (see fig. 10), but they accounted for only 7 percent of all African Americans so marked—about proportionate to their numbers in the population. Over the ensuing decades, as Hancock's electorate shrank, black landowners comprised an increasing segment of those still eligible to vote. By the 1940s, just before the U.S. Supreme Court struck down the poll tax, they made up a majority of the small band that persisted in paying it.[24]

Figures 9 and 10 show that while black landowners increased as a percentage of black eligible voters in Hancock during the first half of the twentieth century, their absolute numbers diminished.[25] Furthermore, figure 10 indicates that many in this category—those who had most probably paid their own poll taxes—quit doing so after the rise of the white primary. They later returned, apparently in an attempt to block disfranchisement in 1908, and then dropped off again, most precipitously during the hard-time 1920s. Seemingly, after decades of withering political turmoil without a sign of any progress, most of Hancock's politically active African Americans had

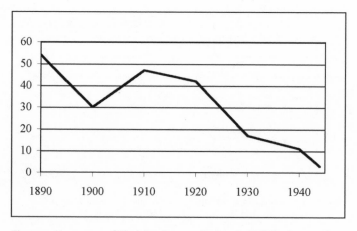

Figure 10. Percentage of Black Landowners Paying the Poll Tax (*source:* Hancock County Tax Digests, 1874–1944, Georgia State Archives, Atlanta).

decided the dollar required each year for the poll tax might be more profitably spent elsewhere.

Oral History and the Persistence of Independent Black Voting in Hancock County

We can count the numbers of those who are marked as having paid the poll tax, but we cannot know how many black Hancock voters cast ballots in the first decades of the twentieth century. Although voting boxes were segregated at the polls, the returns were reported together, so there is no way to know who voted for whom. Ultimately, the relatively low level of voter turnout and the increasingly racist cast of elections suggest that most eligible black voters stayed home on election day. Furthermore, even though it seems that the majority of black men, and later women, who were marked as having paid their poll tax did not vote after the decline of the Populist movement, the oral evidence indicates that a remnant did vote—and in doing so, made their own decisions.

Emmie Mae Harper was born near Linton in 1910 to African American landowners. She related that she and her father, George W. Harper, had voted all their lives. No one ever told her how to vote, and she consulted only her father in political matters. Besides being economically independent, the Harpers were well educated. Like her mother, Nancy Butts Harper, who died young, Emmie Mae became a schoolteacher. Her father, a hardworking, self-made man, read the *Atlanta Constitution* and the *Progressive Farmer* and talked about politics with anyone who would listen. He also kept a shotgun handy on the family's isolated farm in case of trouble. He reassured his daughter that he would fight if anyone came to threaten the family. "Don't worry about me or yourself," Emmie Mae remembered him saying to her, "'cause ain't nothing going to happen to you." Trusting her father, Emmie Mae began voting as soon as she was old enough to do so. Many others, whom she described as "afraid to vote or illiterate," used to ask her whether she was afraid. "No," she would reply, true to her family roots; "I'm not scared of anything." According to Emmie Mae, however, her right to vote was never challenged. "Nobody never said a word." She believes that their level of education made the Harpers acceptable active citizens in the eyes of local whites. Perhaps so. Perhaps her father's tradition of shooting off his shotgun every Christmas also deepened white neighbor's sense of respect for the public-mindedness of this black family.[26] More likely the white elite of the county felt secure enough in their position not to be threatened by a relatively small number of independent black voters. Whatever the reason that the Harpers went unmolested, their voting tradition—which extends for decades through the years when all rural southern African Americans were supposed to be disfranchised—testifies to the personal exceptionalism that marked race relations in Jim Crow Hancock.[27]

Emmie Mae Harper and her father were not the only African Americans who made their own decisions when voting in Hancock. In the northern part of the county many of the black landowning families of Springfield were voting long before the 1960s. Similarly, north of Devereux was another established community of black landowners, Warren Chapel, where some people also speak of black men and women who quietly voted in the first half of the twentieth century.[28]

According to white planter J. E. Johnson, blacks voting in Hancock before the end of World War II did so as Republicans in the general election. He believed that the white Democratic primary—and thus the real political decision making—was closed to them. As a result, according to Johnson, they had little influence on local government. This is as one would expect. In the decades after Reconstruction black men from Hancock, such as Eli Barnes, Allen Grant, and Aaron Spencer, continued to play leading roles in the state Republican Party, and large numbers of the county's blacks continued to vote Republican. In the 1888 general election, for example, 173 Hancock citizens gave their votes to the Republican presidential candidate, Benjamin Harrison. Nonetheless, by 1900, the first presidential election after the establishment of the white primary, only sixteen Hancock votes went to William McKinley, the Republican. The *Sparta Ishmaelite* noted that these sixteen voters were "mostly white." When Theodore Roosevelt ran in the following presidential election, the *Ishmaelite* crowed, "The negro voters ignored the negro candidate for president, preferring grub to glory." Thus relatively few of Hancock's black Republicans remained active into the twentieth century.[29]

Still, the allegiance of a few of Hancock's African Americans to the Republican Party gave them some shred of institutional power through the Jim Crow years. J. E. Johnson remembered that because of the patronage system, when Republicans held the White House in the 1920s, "you had to go through a black man in Atlanta, Ben Davis, to get a job in the Post Office." Because the job paid well, Johnson remembered, men would shell out quite a bit of money to be selected. For a while in this period, a black man, J. W. N. Clay, headed up the Republican Party in Hancock. Then the Republicans adopted a lily-white policy, and Clay was replaced by a white man from an adjoining county. According to Johnson, Clay was a "tall, lanky" man who "owned about thirty acres and drove a blind horse to his buggy." "He didn't ask for much," Johnson remembered, "and we got along with him."[30]

Whereas Clay held on to the "party of Lincoln," it seems that some portion of Hancock's remaining black voters were voting Democratic not merely in national general elections but in the local elections as well. Arthur Raper found that in Greene County of the 1920s and 1930s, "some few" blacks had "been voting the Democratic ticket in the national election and occasionally in the local election." To the extent that he could recall these matters, Forrest Shivers, who was born in Hancock in 1918 and wrote the county history, agreed with Raper. Republicans never ran in the local elections, so a small number of African Americans seem to have been allowed to select county commissioners and superintendents of education from the various Democratic contenders.[31]

Most of Hancock's black voters before World War II seem to have been similar to Clay—humble, conservative property owners. Raper noted that most in Greene County were homeowners who had "already proved themselves acceptable to the white people." Forrest Shivers remembered Hancock's black voters of the pre–World War II period as being schoolteachers and skilled craftsmen. Marshall Boyer's father was one of the few black voters in neighboring Baldwin County during the 1910s and 1920s. Some, like Boyer's father, were landowners. Others were doctors, pharmacists, or prosperous carpenters. Boyer asserted, "Just a few were recognized for what they stood for. They were independent—didn't need to borrow from anyone." And as always, personal connections helped. Boyer's father had a white patron who smoothed the way for him. Finally, many members of this privileged group had the additional advantage of light complexions and kinship ties to whites. According to John Rozier, the usual rules did not hold for these men and women. "They didn't have to come in the back door"; segregation rules were suspended for them in the soda shop; and they could vote. As Rozier summarized, "high status, blood connections and money" made the difference.[32] These few active voters casting ballots for national Republican and local Democratic candidates were less the precursors of the civil rights movement than they were the embodiment of patronage ties between the white elite and the "respectable" black men whom they trusted. Nevertheless, this band formed a bridge of political memory between nineteenth-century black political activism and the political explosion of the civil rights movement. They were living reminders that black people could vote.

Then, during World War II, the legal context changed, and a new kind of black voter entered the arena. First, the U.S. Supreme Court declared the white primary unconstitutional in 1944. Two years later a federal district court struck down Georgia's version of the primary. That year, too, Georgia governor Ellis Arnall pushed through the ratification of a new state constitution that abolished the poll tax. Immediately the numbers of black and white voters began to rise. Across the South the number of African Americans voting quadrupled between 1944 and the end of the decade, rising from 150,000 to 600,000. The majority of this increase occurred in the Upper South and in the larger southern cities, yet by 1946, 100,000 had registered to vote in Georgia alone. Even in a county as decidedly rural as Hancock, the African American movement to retake the franchise was noticeable. One Hancock politician of the 1940s and 1950s estimates that blacks "were voting heavy" by the 1952 elections. Indeed they were. The *Sparta Ishmaelite* reported that, in the 1946 state Democratic primary, "over four hundred colored citizens voted at the Sparta precinct and there were 1,300 registered to vote." The new voters formed a line early in the morning "on the west entrance to the courthouse where a separate table and booths had been arranged for them to vote." According to the *Ishmaelite*, "they were voting in orderly fashion, and no trouble of any kind was expected."[33]

After this quiet revolution, black voters became a fixture in Hancock politics. African Americans celebrated their newfound citizenship rights, causing the *Sparta Ishmaelite* to grumble as the 1948 election loomed: "From all the bragging of the minorities in this county, it seems like it might have been a fine thing if they had been allowed to take over a hundred years back." But while he met this new challenge with relative calm, still the editor hoped that new legislation would prevent blacks from freely voting in this black-majority county. He concurred with the editor of the *Sylvester Local,* another small Georgia paper, in calling for a new voter qualification law now that "the primary can no longer be used as an instrument to keep the colored brother out of the voting booth." Simultaneously, the Hancock County Grand Jury, in its presentments, urged their state representative to introduce a bill that would require payment of a three-dollar fee before a person could register to vote. The jurors also called on the board of registrars to, "as near as possible, remove the names of all persons from the lists who do not qualify in the full sense of the law." In many counties these measures and others like them, such as literacy tests and "good citizenship" tests, held down black voting for another two decades. In other places a cruder solution was found. In many communities across the South, voting-rights activists were routed by violence and terror. In Hancock some whites gave this a try. On September 9, 1948, the *Ishmaelite* expressed surprise that the KKK had paraded in Sparta with lights on in their cars. "A small electrically lighted cross was attached to the front of the lead car, and they visited the Negro settlements on the outskirts of town." According to the *Ishmaelite*, no one was personally molested. There is also oral evidence that around this time the police harassed a black activist preacher for encouraging his entire congregation to register to vote. These seemed to have been final, half-hearted, and ultimately unsuccessful attempts to bring organized white terror to bear on the black community. Neither legal barricades nor terror succeeded in turning back the tide in Hancock. Through the 1940s and 1950s, blacks continued to vote in large numbers, and whites seemed to take the event largely in stride. As a symbol of their outlook, they followed the lead of the *Ishmaelite* in supporting the Democrat Harry Truman and his civil rights planks instead of Strom Thurmond and the States Rights Party. Perhaps Hancock's paternalistic elites did not press the issue, confident that they could manipulate the new masses of voters through old methods.[34]

However, the new waves of voters did not try as hard to win white approval before showing up at the polls. Instead of working as individuals through patronage ties with influential whites, they organized within the black community. With the Supreme Court behind them and the opportunity to crash the Democratic primary before them, they plunged ahead assertively. They were organized by politically outspoken preachers and schoolteachers—a new, better-educated generation whose memories of the turn-of-the-century lynching craze were more distant. Some were also shaped by their participation in World War II. As Carlton Morse said of returning veterans and social change during the postwar period, "Black folks had fought like hell. They weren't going to take the kind of junk they had before. They had become more militant." At the same time, "the whites in power had a kind of broad enlightenment" that the previous generation had not evinced. Times and people had changed.[35]

Yet for all their boldness, this new wave of black voters was neither politically equal to whites nor entirely free of paternalistic ties. While they could vote, they could not run for office. A small number of black political leaders were made jury commissioners, and a few served on juries. These were big landowners, funeral directors, and general-store owners, who had influence over large numbers of potential voters. Their influence became the channels through which white elites directed their new brand of paternalism. G. Lee Dickens, who came from a politically active white family, began serving as an attorney in Sparta two years after he returned from service in World War II.

Throughout this period, between World War II and the mid-1960s, African American voters determined local elections in Hancock. When asked how white politicians campaigned for black votes, Dickens said: "They didn't campaign. They had conversations with black leaders with whom they were close." The relationship worked both ways. "A black leader, if he needed help, would come to a white leader to whom he was close. And if it was reasonable, [the white leader would] try to help him." There were two white political factions in the county, and each cultivated the support of some black leaders. According to Dickens: "When politics started after World War II, the principal black leaders were the country preachers. Before an election, they'd have a meeting—a political meeting. If you wanted to win an election, you had to have a black leader willing to stand up and speak for you. Then the supporter of the other white faction would speak. They'd debate it and take a vote. Whichever side won the vote, that's how they'd all vote. If you knew how their vote turned out, you'd know who was going to win the election." Earnest Jack Ingram, a black mortician, remembered that this body called itself the Democratic Club. Sometimes they even put out fliers to disseminate their endorsements. Yet for all their influence as a voting bloc, black men and women got little for their vote, entangled as they were in the ties of paternalism.[36]

How did white politicians feel about their rising black constituencies? According to Dave Dyer, who seemingly held most elected positions in the county over a long career, they eagerly sought their votes. Dyer was born in Calhoun County, Georgia, eighty miles south of Sparta. He came to Sparta to do his practice teaching in 1939 and stayed on. In 1940 he was appointed county extension agent. Then he went to fight in World War II. After returning, he won elections as mayor pro tempore, superintendent of schools, city councilman, and county commissioner. He is quite proud that every time he ran, he won a majority of both white and black votes. He said that white politicians certainly did not spurn black support in Hancock. They "solicited them as hard as the whites," Dyer explained, "if not more so, because they tended to vote in a bloc."[37]

There were three separate clusters of black voters: the Warren Chapel community, just north of Devereux; the Springfield community; and the county seat of Sparta. A few voters, such as Emmie Mae Harper, were sprinkled near Linton. Two of the voting blocs, Warren Chapel and Springfield, were organized around charismatic black preachers: Rev. Willie James "Battle-ax" Davis and Rev. Robert Erskine Edwards, respectively. Each man acted as an intermediary between his community and white county leaders. Because each man's word was highly influential in his own community, white candidates would visit the men to ask for their support. Davis told Dyer, on meeting him during one election, "These politicians are about to worry me to death!" Dyer chuckled when he recalled that Davis would sometimes remove himself from the area after he had made up his mind whom to support to avoid contact with beseeching white politicians.[38]

One black educator, Carlton Morse, wondered whether there were payoffs involved in the negotiations between black political organizers and the white politicians: "I always wondered how much money those guys got who carried around votes in their back pocket." He believed that the votes had yielded little benefit to the black community as a whole. "It was mostly cheap politics," he summarized. Dave Dyer, who had solicited the support of Davis and Edwards, denied that there were any bribes involved. He agreed that the political stakes for all were fairly low in the 1940s and 1950s but disagreed that the preachers gained materially from their political support. He believed that the men simply enjoyed the prestige of being power brokers.[39]

According to his daughter, Ruth Davis Robinson, the Reverend Willie Davis was born in Jacksonville and took quickly to the ministry. He began preaching at thirteen and joined the Florida Conference at fourteen. After studying at Morris Brown College, in Atlanta, he pastored in Monticello for a while, married in 1935, and soon afterward came to Warren Chapel, in Hancock County, where he spent the next thirty-three years of his life. He was a gregarious, warm man with a fine singing voice. Around the time he came to Hancock, he wrote a gospel song, "Battle-ax," that is still sung in rural black churches all around Georgia. Ringing, rolling, and joyful, the song was hardly a hymn for a broken, defeated people. It is a song of militancy and hope: "He's a battle-ax in the time of the battle / And a shelter in the time of the storm." Affable though he was, Davis became known as "Battle-ax" for the rest of his life. For thirty-three years he took the tour busses north to preach and sing his song at church revivals in New York City.

"Battle-ax" Davis was something of a justice of the peace in his community. He carried a great deal of charismatic authority, and people came to him regularly to settle personal disputes. They also came to him for political advice. According to his daughter, Davis himself voted from the 1930s on. Furthermore, "folks would talk to him about voting," she said. "People obeyed him. They depended on his advice." She remembered him preaching in church about voting and driving people to the polls long before the 1965 federal Voting Rights Act. She does not remember him encountering white resistance, despite being an active voter and a man of influence in local elections. Perhaps planters perceived him as "safe," a man who could be accommodated, whether with personal patronage or with limited patronage to the community he represented.

The northern part of the county, too, was led by an energetic black minister. Less than a decade after he came to Hancock County in 1935, Rev. Robert Edwards, who preached at the Springfield Baptist Church, began to openly encourage the people of his community to register to vote. Edwards had been born north of Hancock, in a rural community near Crawfordville in Taliaferro County. He was the son and the grandson of hardworking landowners who wrested a subsistence—but not much else—from the soil. Serious, tall, and precocious, he excelled in school but could not often be spared from fieldwork. He caught a week of schooling here and a month there. After attending a nearby one-teacher school for five years, he began to raise money on his own to slowly continue his education. At the age of twenty-two he graduated as valedictorian from a Negro academy in Athens. He graduated from Morehouse College in 1931 and completed seminary training at Oberlin College in 1934, earning the rank of salutatorian at each school.[40]

His wife, Louise Edwards, remembered that around the time when the poll tax was discontinued, in 1944, her husband got a sample ballot and used it in church to explain the voting process to his congregation. "You are citizens," he told them. "The power to vote is great! People will recognize you when you vote for them." Yet she added that the people were still afraid. Although some of them had been voting in the past, they had reason to be frightened.[41]

One Sunday after church in the mid-1940s, soon after Edwards had preached on voting, the Sparta police came to pay him a visit. According to his wife, they intended to lock him up. Although Hancock's paternalistic white leadership had long accepted a few carefully selected elite black voters during the first half of the twentieth century, they apparently intended to resist an open call for the masses to take up their citizenship rights when the U.S. Supreme Court and Georgia's governor united in striking down old voting barriers. But Edwards stood his ground. According to his wife, he told them that "they couldn't lock him up." He was within his rights and knew it. When they persisted, he demanded a lawyer. Although he stammered, as he always did when excited, the police backed down and left. Later a group of unidentified white men burned a cross on the family's front yard. But again they were trying to terrorize a proud and fiercely independent man and a community that matched their preacher in temperament. A group of young Springfield men organized a line of defense around the man who had taught many of them in school. Groups of them took turns sitting up at night in front of his house, shotguns across their knees. The would-be intruders did not return, and Edwards continued his voter registration drive. He encouraged his students to drive to Sparta—always in groups—to register, and he continued to offer guidance in political matters to the people of his community.[42]

It is no coincidence that the two most important black political leaders in Hancock in the 1930s and 1940s were preachers. From slavery to the present, African American ministers have taken a prominent role in leading their communities and representing them in public. It is well known that black preachers emerged as political leaders during Reconstruction and the civil rights movement. Their activity between these periods has been less studied, but as Lee Dickens stated, they seem to have continued as vote brokers during these years. In his 1903 study *The Negro Church* W. E. B. Du Bois wrote that "the announcement for candidates for justice of the peace" was given at the black church. "In fact," he wrote, "the white office seeker has long since learned that his campaign among Negroes must be begun in the Negro church, and by a Negro preacher."[43]

Much like these ministers, some teachers used their positions of authority to encourage young people to assert themselves as citizens. In the late 1940s and early 1950s at the Sparta Agricultural and Industrial School, Principal Carlton Morse had his social studies teacher take high-school students to the courthouse to register them to vote. Morse himself voted. He reasoned that "if you were black, your life was like a rabbit anyway, so you might as well take a stand and do something good."[44]

Female schoolteachers, too, were encouraging their students to take daring steps for civil rights well before the civil rights movement. Emmie Mae Harper began her long career as a teacher in a small rural school in the late 1920s. In class she actively encouraged her students to vote. She talked about current events every day and used the *Sparta Ishmaelite* to illustrate civic and social issues. To encourage her students to apply themselves harder to their studies, she told them that not all people could vote. When they asked why, she replied that some people "had been lazy and haven't gotten their lessons." This strategy may have had some damaging repercussions, however; although the incentive to study may have motivated some to work harder, it may also have implied that the responsibility for black disfranchisement lay not with the violence and unjust laws of whites but with the ignorance and laziness of African Americans.[45]

Black merchants such as Gus Richardson and Mearilus Roberts, Sr. also held some political power because of their influence over the people who patronized their businesses. Mearilus Roberts Jr. remembers that his father's grocery store on the east side of Sparta held political as well as economic and social significance. Lonzy Roberts frequented the business in the mid-1960s: "It was a meeting place for anybody who was about anything . . . the center of political and social life for the community." A television drew gatherings of older men in the evenings and young men during weekends to discuss sports, farming, and politics. "He enjoyed debates," Edwards remembered. "He had a way of baiting you to get you to think politically." And he mentored younger men, such as Edwards, attempting to raise their consciousness about the Jim Crow order and directing them toward higher education while instructing them in the conservative values of hard work and respectability he had learned at Tuskegee. Edwards, now an attorney in Macon, names Roberts as an early influence on him. Roberts also remembers white politicians dropping in, saying that they were "coming by to see about the cullud vote." They'd talk politics with him, shake his hand, and act respectful, in a way they did not treat other African Americans. Edwards remembered that as the civil rights movement exploded in Hancock with the arrival of a charismatic black nationalist, John McCown, "the influence of men like Roberts got eclipsed quickly." They were identified as accommodationists, too indirect and nonconfrontational for the rising young black activists who overthrew the old paternalist order. Yet for twenty years, such men had used their influence over black voting communities to negotiate what gains that could be bartered from the old order.[46]

The persistence of black voting in rural Hancock is surprising, but a question remains: what did the black community gain with its votes? Before 1946 black voters were so few and isolated that they had little impact on government policy decisions. Even after that date, black voters operated within a paternalistic culture that did not allow them to contest white supremacy directly, which is likely why the white community allowed them to vote at all. In the decades between the Populist movement and World War II, their votes brought benefits only to a few political bosses, not to the community as a whole. After the voting reforms of the mid-1940s allowed them to help select the Democratic nominees, however, their votes grew in significance. While they could not hold office, they could tip the scale one way or another between competing white candidates. After World War II, quietly tendered voting support sometimes led to quiet favors by elected politicians. When pursuing the endorsements of the leading black merchants and preacher-activists, however, white politicians tried to keep a low profile. Although it was generally understood that many African Americans voted, apparently it was too sensitive an issue for public view. African Americans could exercise the benefits of citizenship, but only if they did so discreetly. Individually they could have privileges that powerful white men respected, yet African Americans could claim no rights publicly, formally, or collectively. After the end of the Populist campaigns, no politicians publicly asked for African American support at the polls. But some political horse-trading went on behind closed doors. The black leaders tried to determine which candidate would be the most sensitive to the needs of the black community without thereby losing the support of the white community. In the 1940s, in return for black support, the newly elected superintendent of education Dyer purchased a school bus for black schools. Later he equalized the pay of white and black bus drivers and, again responding to the voiced concerns of the black community, began replacing white drivers with black drivers on the black routes. Nevertheless, white attitudes limited the campaign promises a politician could make to black voters.

During the mid-1950s Dyer ran against a liberal white woman for a seat on the Hancock County Commission. She openly spoke of the need to equalize county services for both races and openly sought the black vote, thereby alienating white voters. Dyer told her that he would beat her and that he would do so with the black vote. He did. Hancock's African Americans apparently decided that it would be wiser to support a probable winner who had been somewhat helpful to them in the past and who they could be sure would implement whatever reforms he pursued than to back a likely loser with attractive statements but no track record and a dubious ability to enact her reforms.[47]

As Dave Dyer suggested, African Americans may have used their votes to bend individual officials slightly toward their interests—in his case, the expansion of county services for African Americans. Although the support given to Dyer makes sense considering his moderate track record, the give-and-take of the political process made for some truly odd bedfellows. In what must be one of the all-time high-water marks of political perversity, Eugene Talmadge, who claimed never to have seen a black man "worth more than fifty cents a day," spoke more than once at a community center built by African American farmers in the middle of a cooperative community of wealthy black landowners in the northern part of Hancock. According to Willis Hubert, who spent most of his summers in the community, a number of these landowners voted for him. Hubert believes that in return, Governor Talmadge quietly directed some state money to the support of the cooperative.[48]

The image of African Americans quietly voting for one of the greatest race-baiters in the twentieth-century South adequately symbolizes the predicament in which black voters found themselves. For which of the assorted white supremacists should they cast their votes? Dave Dyer, who showed African Americans a great deal more consideration than was generally expected from southern politicians in the first half of the twentieth century, believed that politics in his day—and before—ran more on personality than on ideology. Candidates for office rarely promised anything to voters. If elected, they rarely changed anything.

African Americans in Public Space before the Civil Rights Movement

African Americans saw their political power decline over a sweep of many decades: in Reconstruction they held elective office and directly participated in decision making; in the 1890s they could still attend political rallies, forcefully lobby candidates, write political endorsements in the *Sparta Ishmaelite*, and cast votes for white men; but by the first decade of the twentieth century, they could do little more than appeal privately to white patrons to act, in small ways, on their behalf. Blacks could request favors or even standing privileges of powerful whites. Planters could approach the courthouse to ease paperwork for their tenants. According to Carlton Morse, only blacks with patrons were able to find aid from the New Deal agencies. Planters could petition judges to have sentences suspended. When Elton Stanley, a black man, was caught red-handed by his moonshine still in 1919, the judge let him off because "the best people in his district" requested it, writing they "have always found him honest, polite, and respectful to everyone." But these were privileges; they could be abrogated at any time and gave white elites ultimate control—which is what they wanted after all. Ultimately, this system respected not black civil rights but the right of the white elite to protect their favorites.[49]

Under this system black leaders had no standing to speak for their community in formal ways. They could only request special opportunities to appear before the county commissioners or the superintendent of education. Once they made their request, they would leave the room; others would make the decision and inform them of it. In nine years as principal of the black Sparta high school, Carlton Morse never was allowed to speak before the board of education—a regularly exercised right of white principals—until

1954, when the board summoned him to hear his views of the U.S. Supreme Court decision on *Brown v. Board of Education*.[50]

Disfranchisement crippled African Americans not only in concrete political and economic ways but also in an important symbolic one. By denying them a role in governance, white southerners stripped African Americans of an important sign of status. They remained persons but were not supposed to be public persons. As far as whites were concerned, blacks, like children, could be related to but not taken seriously. They had no formally recognized rights. They were not supposed to wield public power—the power to exercise a right by virtue of citizenship. Privately, through personal relationships, a black person could request favors from whites, including white politicians. At the back step of white homes and courthouses, hats in hands, blacks could solicit paternalistic consideration, but they could not invoke any rights at the more formal front door of citizenship.

In the South whites denied African Americans a visibly public identity. For decades after disfranchisement the *Sparta Ishmaelite* omitted black stories and letters by black leaders. Blacks were banished to the occasional appearance in a local crime story. Although World War I returned some focus on Hancock's African Americans, this overall pattern continued for decades more as a ban on black images in the county newspaper. As late as 1950, when Carlton Morse submitted an announcement and photograph of a student who had won a state oratorical contest, the *Ishmaelite* ran the article but refused to publish the picture.[51]

But complete civic nonpersonhood is not the full story for Hancock's African Americans before the civil rights movement. As they were pushed out of the public political arena, they turned inward toward their own independent institutions. The churches were at the center, as always. Other organizations came there to speak and to organize. From the church issued missionary and benevolent societies. Until the 1920s the churches often housed schools and fraternal organizations. The local black life-insurance agents were most likely to be deacons who worked their deals after services. This public space was most definitely black space, and it was significant in many ways, for racial pride as well as pragmatic action. Nevertheless, no institution in this space was empowered to challenge corrupt planters or demand equal government support of black and white schools. It could not fill the void left by disfranchisement.

There were additional facets to black public space. Although whites clearly wished to deny a public role to African Americans, certain newly arising problems required action from the community as a whole. During World

War I the coercive demands of patriotism and national service forced whites to call for black troops as well as white. The new inductees, black and white, were paraded off to the trains with notable fanfare. The sources are silent, but surely whites were uneasy as the war opened up this powerful new symbol of black citizenship. Their returning reception was greeted by no parades or public celebration, perhaps a sign that, after the crisis, Hancock whites, like white southerners elsewhere, were concerned that military service might make it more difficult to squeeze black veterans back into their appointed place. This was not all the war brought. Calls went out for wealthy citizens to do their duty with their wallets. Two black Sparta businessmen, Richard Johnson and Thomas Dixon, each bought the maximum of $1,000 in war bonds. Like all black men named in the paper, they were racially identified by the absence of *Mr.* before their names. Significantly, however, in a move that seems unique to that point in the history of the *Sparta Ishmaelite,* their names were spelled out and not condescendingly shortened to *Dick* and *Tom.* These developments quietly challenged the ideological foundations of white supremacy. If blacks owed the same obligations to society as did whites, to what citizenship claims might they be entitled in return? Similarly, in World War II the *Ishmaelite* enjoined white readers to encourage blacks to "do their part" for the war effort. Although the results of these shifts in consciousness were not dramatic, it is noteworthy that after World War I the county gave its first meaningful subsidies to black education. In addition, when the next publicly organized political movement by blacks came, in the 1940s, Hancock's whites did not react with the violence that had characterized their earlier responses.[52]

Additionally, rising consciousness of the causes of disease pushed black and white health-care workers—frequently women—into cautious alliances to combat what neither race could fight alone. With the support of whites acting similarly in their communities, black Jeanes teachers promoted sanitary practices in black communities as they called on teachers and spoke to gatherings of parents. The black county extension agent worked with his racial counterpart to spread the gospel of diversified farming and purebred livestock, usually before black audiences but, given personnel limitations, sometimes before mixed audiences as well. In the 1930s black home demonstration agents began making the rounds to organize clubs to promote canning, year-round gardening, and home beautification. All these black leaders wrote occasional letters and articles in the *Ishmaelite,* positioning themselves as experts before the county generally. In these ways some African Americans found themselves reclaiming spheres of authority in public space.[53]

Still, these new black public leaders did not work on equal terms with their white counterparts. Samuel Williams, a retired black extension agent, remembers that as he traveled about the county, he was careful to begin in each new area by visiting the local white minister, so that Williams could name him as a protecting voice of white authority in case he was challenged. In rural Hancock the personal endorsement of a local white preacher was worth more than his own identity as a college-educated agricultural expert and employee of the federal government.[54]

The personality-driven government of pre–World War II Hancock County resulted directly from the planters' achievement of a "safe" electorate—one that had been purged of independent class movements through violence, fraud, and paternalism. The remaining black voters could be manipulated or even allowed a degree of independence as long as they did not pose any significant challenge to white elite authority. Hancock's paternalistic form of government dovetailed neatly with its other highly personal social systems. The vacuum created by the intentional smallness and passivity of government was filled by the personal power of individuals with wealth, connections, and aggressiveness. Rural society gave much autonomy to those with personal power. Moreover, as I argued earlier, power in a highly local, isolated culture could be based in many different sources: landowning status, helpful kin, or a propensity to violence. It could be concentrated, as it was in the powerful large white planters of the Devereux area, or dispersed, as it was among the many smaller black and white landowners of the Powelton area. But as I will explore in the epilogue, this culture of personalism finally gave way to larger political and economic forces brought on by World War II.

Epilogue:
The Rise of "Public Work"

HANCOCK COUNTY turned a significant corner after World War II. Good roads and telephone lines broke into the once-isolated rural communities of rural Hancock, altering them and carrying people away, pulling them toward centers both residentially and culturally. The schoolyear continued to expand, first for whites and then for blacks, arming young people with improved resources for competing in urban job markets. The most significant aspect of this transformation, however, was the destruction of the South's low-wage economy in the 1940s and the collapse of the traditional labor-intensive cotton culture.

When speaking of their work histories, Hancock people often refer to periods of "public work." According to Mae Warren, this means "working out among the people." It involved "sawmill, quarry, pulpmill, and factory" work. Farming did not qualify as public work because farmers worked at home. When asked whether it included domestic work, Warren paused and then replied that it was not public, because one was working in a home, even if it was not one's own. And "moonshine," she added, laughing, "was definitely not public work." As was shown in chapter 2, many rural people worked part-time in public work, for it let them supplement their traditional commercial and subsistence farming income. Full-time public work, however, marked a movement out of rural Hancock's semisubsistence economy and more fully into the national commercial, consumer economy. Through the twentieth century rural Hancock people shifted from the former to the latter by fits and starts and thereby transformed not only the economy of Hancock but also its culture and its patterns of race relations.[1]

This trend toward public work received an early boost with World War I. As has been well described elsewhere, the war opened northern industrial jobs to African Americans for the first time, and precipitated the Great Migration.[2] When northern white men were drafted into military service, they created a vacuum for jobs in the industrial North. War-work industries, largely located in northern cities, heightened the demand for labor—a demand that could not be filled by foreign immigration because of wartime restrictions. African Americans for the first time found themselves not merely welcome but avidly recruited by northern factories. Between 200,000 and 700,000 blacks left the South in 1916 and 1917 alone. Once started, the migration continued through the 1920s.

More than 50,000 black Georgians joined the trek north. Among them were many Hancock citizens, as figure 11 demonstrates. The census recorded that the county's black population fell from 14,268 to 13,221 during the 1910s. Hancock more fully joined the Great Migration in the following decade, when, pushed by the boll weevil and pulled by a continuing expansion of the national economy, close to 4,000 African Americans left the county. This 29 percent drop in the county's black population paralleled a 27 percent drop in its white population, the greatest declines for both groups in the history of the county. According to Arthur Raper and a separate New Deal study in neighboring Greene County, the population movement in the area peaked from 1923 to 1925, continued at a lower rate until about 1933, and then stopped (see figure 11).[3]

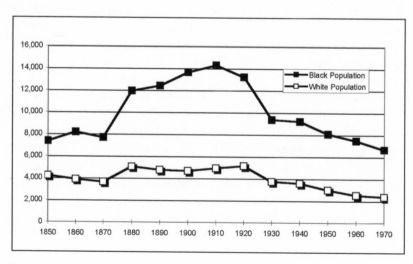

Figure 11. Hancock Population, 1850–1970 (*source:* U.S. Census Reports).

The demographic history of Hancock indicates that the push factors (disfranchisement, segregation, white supremacy, and violence) were not sufficient to explain movement from the county. The force of these push factors can be assumed to have remained fairly constant in the first decades of the century, but migrations began only when the pull factors (job opportunities) emerged during periods of national economic growth. Although white supremacy did not diminish during the Great Depression, the census counted only 162 fewer blacks in 1940 than it did in 1930, about the same as the decline for whites. There were no urban jobs—hence no pull.[4]

Black migrants found a wide range of work opportunities in the North. Mary Hunt remembers that her husband, Alvin, "wanted money in his hand every week." He found it digging the New York subways in the 1920s. Marshall Boyer's uncles found well-paying jobs building cars in Detroit. Boyer, born in 1909, explained, "Ford was hiring all Negroes that said they were from the South. They knew they were workers." Boyer remembers hearing that Ford offered $6 per day, and General Motors paid $6.70. Later, when a brother up north told him he could make 87¢ per hour building scaffolding for plasterers, he followed them as well.[5]

Considering that southern agricultural workers earned from fifty cents to a dollar a day, it is no wonder that they left. Many planters were certainly concerned that northern labor demands would disrupt their low-wage economy and their control over their laborers. The editor of the *Sparta Ishmaelite*, trying to limit the movement of workers from Hancock, ran a couple of articles warning the county's black readers that previous black migrants from Hancock were regretting it, finding themselves starving and sick in the North, far from the care of white patrons. The Georgia General Assembly reacted to the Great Migration by passing a law that required northern labor agents working in the South to pay prohibitive local licensing fees; in Hancock the fee was $100,000. But their concern seems to have been misplaced. The increased national demand for labor did not create a significant labor scarcity in agriculture. Many landowners in the lower piedmont were letting their eroded and weevil-ridden land lay idle. Because of a 30–60 percent decrease in crop acreage across the piedmont between 1920 and 1925, the mass migration did not strongly affect pay scales in the cotton fields. Furthermore, it did not create higher-wage factory jobs within the South to compete for labor locally. That is, it simply did not break open the region's low-wage economy. Hancock passed through the 1920s poorer than ever before, but otherwise unchanged.[6]

The local significance of the Great Migration was not limited to its obviously important impact on Hancock's migrants, however; in addition, it played an important role in the history of the county itself. It established an urban beachhead that facilitated further migration when the economy had its next upswing. In the meantime, it created a new set of resources that Hancock families used to carry themselves through the long southern Depression. Alma Dixon Smith remembered the assistance that passed between her northern and southern kin. She recalls the canned preserves, vegetables, hams, and quilts her family in Chicago received from her grandparents and uncles and aunts in the South. In return, she recalls, the resettled migrants would send clothes, cash, and job-market information. In addition, their homes served as settlement houses when southern kin decided to try their luck in the northern economy.[7]

As was described earlier, the Great Depression had a limited impact on Hancock. Hancock's most significant economic downturn came in 1921, not 1929. Neither did the New Deal greatly affect most African Americans in the county. For the most part the New Deal programs were administered locally. This gave southern elites the power to channel federal programs in such a way as to protect the traditional system.[8]

The New Deal was viewed with some ambivalence by southern elites. Although its price supports seemed alluring, many white southern planters and rural merchants fretted over entangling federal regulations. Even more feared losing control over dependent farmers who might come to look to the federal government for patronage instead of to their usual furnishing sources. Southern industrialists joined the rural elites in worrying that government subsidies and relief—and especially the minimum wage—would "demoralize" their labor force with expectations of a decent standard of living. All white Georgians particularly dreaded the possibility that equal wages for whites and blacks would undermine white supremacy.

Georgia's reactionary governor Eugene Talmadge led the fight against the New Deal in Georgia. The governor and his appointees attempted to block agricultural price supports and all social welfare programs. He cut taxes, limiting the state's ability to promote relief projects undertaken in cooperation with the federal government. Talmadge even vetoed a bill to allow Georgia to participate in the benefits of the Social Security Administration. In 1934 the Roosevelt administration responded to his obstructionism by federalizing the administration of New Deal programs in Georgia and attempting to work around the governor.[9]

Accordingly, relief in Georgia was held at relatively low levels for the first half of the New Deal. Hancock leaders seem not to have applied for any emergency federal appropriation until 1935, when they applied for $85,000 worth of relief projects. Two years later Eurith D. Rivers, a New Deal supporter, replaced Talmadge in the governor's mansion and secured enabling legislation through the state legislature. His "Little New Deal" allowed a sudden expansion of state-sponsored projects.[10] Most of Hancock's New Deal projects were relatively small, employing ten to fifty people. Still, under Rivers's administration Hancock applied for funding to set six hundred men to work improving county roads and paving roads and sidewalks in Sparta and highways across the county. At the county's peak involvement then, about 5 percent of Hancock's people were employed by New Deal programs. No available statistics show the level of participation during the other years, but even if the smaller projects sought were granted and distributed evenly, no more than 1 percent of the county's population could have participated in relief work at any other year.[11] This confirms the findings of studies made in Greene and Jenkins Counties in 1935, each of which found that only about 1 percent of the population was employed in relief work in the previous month (June).[12]

Not surprisingly, the memory of this flicker of activity is now dim among Hancock's senior citizens. Willis Walls got a Works Progress Administration (WPA) position building roads around Linton, as did Eugene Foster Sr. Through the influence of the planter for whom he worked, Foster got a job running a water truck on the highway from Sparta to Eatonton—although his son remembers that Foster was required to run his truck at night so that no one would know that a black man had one of the new high-paying government jobs. Emma L. Winn found a position with the National Youth Administration cleaning schoolhouses to pay her rent so she could attend the Springfield Rosenwald high school. A few African Americans in Hancock did receive loans from the Farm Home Administration (FHA) to build new houses. One couple received FHA loans for a mule, a cow, chickens, a brooder, and a wagon; they were offered more but declined so as not to take on too much debt.[13]

But for the most part the New Deal passed black people by. Two Civilian Conservation Corps camps were established in Hancock in 1935. Although they each listed over two hundred boys in their companies, they admitted whites only.[14] William Stanley recalls that black applicants for New Deal aid were simply sent out to the farms to work.[15] Today most African Americans in Hancock claimed not to have received any other form of New Deal aid during the Depression.

Not so the planters. The primary New Deal agency in the South, the Agricultural Adjustment Administration (AAA), created a pool of funds used to reimburse farmers for plowing up cotton acreage. Most of these funds flowed entirely into the pockets of the farmers who owned the soil—and most prominently, the planters—despite the legal requirement that they share the subsidy with their tenants. Usually planters took tenants' land out of cultivation and collected the subsidy on that while continuing to farm their own parcels. In many parts of the South planters evicted the tenants whose land had been retired and then used the full subsidy, intended to be split among many, to purchase expensive tractors and other mechanical devices with which to permanently replace these tenants. This was a highly significant turning point in many parts of the cotton South, for it marked the end of the long-standing relationship between dependent client farmers and independent patron farmers.[16] Across the South the number of sharecroppers declined by 40 percent during the 1930s, a loss of from one-half to two million people.[17] One New Deal report stated that "the A.A.A. crop reduction plan . . . caused a decline in the use of farm labor" in nearby Greene County.[18] As will be shown, no strong movement toward mechanization emerged in Hancock, so the funds must have simply been pocketed. Additionally, the Agricultural Census reports that the number of tenant farmers in the county increased from 1,136 to 1,343 in the first half of the 1930s and fell only slightly, to 1,241, in the second half. These statistics suggest that Hancock's paternalistic planters did not suddenly abandon their tenants or their traditional role in the cotton culture, despite an incentive to do so that planters in some other areas found irresistible. J. E. Johnson remembers that when his grandfather, a merchant planter, died in 1932, he left him "his property, his customers, and his name, all of which were valuable." Although he made a fortune as a merchant, Johnson continued as a landlord, even though his grandfather had been losing thousands of dollars at it. He claims to have kept at it out of responsibility to his tenants. "I thought I was obligated to," he said. Perhaps Hancock's planters internalized at least some portion of the demands as well as the benefits of the paternalism they articulated. Alternatively, it may well be that Hancock's planters did not join the tractor revolution because their exhausted land could no longer provide a sufficient return on such a capital-intensive investment. Perhaps these two motives entwined each other, allowing planters to protect their senses of self while making the best economic use of their resources.[19]

Few interviewees provided any information about the AAA's operations in Hancock, and of course the county newspaper stayed silent on the crucial question: whether planters shared their subsidies with tenants. This moment has generally been seen as the final unmasking of the fraud of paternalism, as planters threw away the last shreds of noblesse oblige the better to gorge at the trough of federal welfare. Still, a few of Hancock's dependent African American farmers stated that they or their parents had received government checks (most likely AAA subsidies) during the Depression. On the other hand, most did not receive such checks or do not remember whether they did. One black Sparta educator who was usually well informed about happenings in the county said he believed few blacks received any subsidies.

When the subsidy program was initiated, the AAA mailed the checks directly to the planters, who were supposed to divide them with their tenants. When the inevitable mass fraud transpired across the South, the AAA sent checks individually to each farmer, including tenants. Earnest Jack Ingram, who grew up in the farm country northeast of Sparta, remembers that at first, "tenants thought they had to give up their checks. Thought that was the law. Later they learned they could hold it." In Ingram's community, landlords then tried to coerce them into handing over their government checks. One man in Ingram's neighborhood, Jerry Wingfield, told him that his landlord had said, "Bring that check to me when you get it." Wingfield "said he wasn't going to give up his check to nobody. They came at night, took him out, and beat him up, but he wouldn't give it up." Others were pressured in other ways. After Ingram's uncle and aunt refused to hand over their check to an African American planter, Jim Smith, they were thrown off the land.[20]

Some adaptable Georgia elites found still more ways to co-opt the New Deal in the interest of underwriting the status quo. In Augusta, forty-five miles to the east, one black man wrote to a New Deal administrator in 1937, complaining, "We colored people have been working on the relief work in the cold weather, in ditches, in every nasty place the white people could put us." Then, after the cotton opened, they were sent to pick cotton at fifty cents per hundred pounds. In essence, the landowners in the Augusta area allowed New Deal money to trickle down to blacks only when the cotton did not require much care, thus transferring their responsibility to furnish their tenants over to the federal government, and then cut them off when they needed the labor.[21]

By limiting the scope of the New Deal in Georgia and then carefully administering it, conservative elites were able to absorb many of the benefits of the programs while preventing systematic change. They were especially keen to ensure that the low-wage labor system in rural areas was largely undisturbed by minimum-wage regulations or exposure to high wages.

Talmadge observed in 1933 that black tenants would not "toil ten, twelve or fourteen hours a day in the field" if they could triple their usual income "either working for the government or merely drawing relief funds and relief goods."[22] With the backing of the state legislature, he pressured New Deal administrators into lowering federal relief and highway construction wages in Georgia to the level prevailing in the local communities. In Hancock County the wages of WPA workers doing unskilled labor peaked in 1938 at a little above 20¢ per hour, half the wage initially set. Only public-health nurses and program supervisors cracked this barrier. On the other end of the spectrum, construction workers earned as little as 16.5¢ per hour in 1936, and school-lunch workers merited only 11¢ per hour in 1938.[23]

Similar relief wages were given out in Greene County. In 1935 women there made comforters, and men dug drainage ditches and improved school grounds and streets for 15¢ per hour. Other laborers did similar work for only 13.5¢ per hour. Eighty lucky workers made all of 30¢ per hour building a bridge for the Public Works Administration. Overall, when the hours were totaled, some of the common laborers brought home only $9 per month for part-time work, whereas full-time workers netted from $19 to $36 per month.[24]

Although planters succeeded in holding down New Deal wages, they still rose above the wages offered for agricultural work generally. Most of these relief workers earned more than the $10 to $12.5 that agricultural wage laborers in the surrounding area averaged each month. The real difference lay in their hourly rates. According to a 1935 New Deal report in Greene County, farm laborers earned 50¢ each day working from sunup to sundown—approximately fourteen hours in the summer. They were making around 3.5¢ per hour, far below the lowest hourly wage paid by New Deal relief. Although not the boost to economic growth envisioned in Washington, D.C., these pay rates did have some impact on surrounding wage scales, particularly when they rose in the late 1930s.[25]

According to several African Americans in Hancock, the most important aspect of the New Deal seemed to be the National Recovery Administration (NRA). Although this attempt to induce labor and management to cooperate in fighting the Depression has often been viewed as a failure, it may have been the first program to raise the wages of some black workers in rural Hancock. The NRA called for minimum wages of twenty-four cents per hour and forty-hour workweeks in industries involved in interstate commerce. These were later revised to forty cents per hour and thirty-five hours per week, respectively. Although agricultural workers were exempt from the new federal standards, lumber workers whose products were shipped out of state were not. As a result, men such as Dollie Walls, who had previously made around seventeen cents per hour, experienced a dramatic upward surge in their wages—the first significant crack in the region's cheap labor market. When the Supreme Court declared the NRA unconstitutional in 1935, the wage gains made in southern industries were cut back only partially, possibly because of workers' rising expectations. In 1938 the Fair Labor Standards Act (FLSA) reinstated the minimum wage. Some black interviewees described the initiation of hourly pay during this period as a significant event in their work histories and credited President Roosevelt for it. Between the end of the NRA and the beginning of the FLSA, some upward pressure on rural Hancock wages was maintained by the WPA, which paid twice the usual rate for agricultural wages, as was previously shown.[26]

There is evidence that these federal initiatives began to do what planters had feared they would. Although none of these programs explicitly applied to agricultural workers, they did raise agricultural wage laborers' expectations and their leverage in pressuring for higher wages. Marshall Boyer, who owned a farm during these years, noted that when the WPA came to Georgia, it raised wages. "Others had to match it," he said. "So many of the colored [were] working on the farm for fifty cents a day and less." When new, higher-paying positions appeared, however, his laborers started moving toward them, which pressured Boyer to respond: "Naturally, I had to pay more to keep them on the farm."[27] A New Deal report for Greene County commented that "perhaps more than in any other way, the administration has been criticized because of the higher rate of pay and shorter hours of work than observed in general throughout the county." Yet the planters' complaints that their cheap labor system was being compromised must be taken with a grain of salt, for many Hancock people were still earning a dollar a day to pick cotton at the end of the decade.[28]

For most African Americans, these gains, while modest, were a beginning. African Americans did not enjoy their share of New Deal aid, but just knowing that, for the first time since Reconstruction, the federal government was in any way recognizing them as citizens with justifiable claims altered their understanding of their relationship to that government. Although New Deal assistance was more symbolic than real for most of Hancock's African Americans, they along with African Americans across the South came to believe that their president intended them to share somewhat in their country's bounty. Both Dollie Walls and James Wilson recalled the words to a Depression Era song: "Roosevelt wasn't no kin, but he was a poor man's friend."[29]

Nonetheless, even as the New Deal showed southern blacks and poor whites that they might be citizens of a nation, even if they were not meaningfully citizens of their states and local communities, the 1930s also provided a counterlesson about the persisting power of the old regime in Georgia. As New Deal largess rained down across a parched country, county seat elites opened obstructing canopies, preserving Georgian misery as a monument to state sovereignty and personal greed. For the most part, rural Georgia's low wage scale and the way of life it anchored endured to the end of the 1930s.

The New Deal cracked the South's low-wage economy, but World War II broke it wide open. The war pulled hundreds of young men, black and white, directly out of the economy by putting them in military uniforms. This reduced somewhat the overcrowded southern labor pool. Military bases and defense plants then began to open, with a large number intentionally placed in the South to spur its lagging economy. Only Texas had more military bases than Georgia during World War II. During the war, manufacturing employment rose by 50 percent in the South. As a result, between 1939 and 1942 alone average annual wages increased by 40 percent. This new, massive defense industry not only brought Americans back to work but also introduced rural southerners to a different kind of work within a different kind of economy.[30]

One large ordnance plant was located in Milledgeville, just ten miles from Hancock's western boundary. The wages paid there were well above the standard wages in Georgia's plantation belt. Hundreds of men and women poured in, many of them from Hancock. As an economic event affecting twentieth-century Hancock, the opening of the Milledgeville fuse plant was second only to the coming of the boll weevil, for it reshaped the local economy by pushing up wages and expectations.[31]

Oline Thomas's husband, Charlie, got a position at the fuse plant. Previously this black couple had worked on shares in Hancock, and then Charlie had gotten a position with the WPA. "It was better," Oline said; "We had been on the farm and we didn't get any money till the end of the year, then with the WPA, we were getting a little money every week or so." The fuse plant was an even better job, but only a few African Americans found employment in the plant. Charlie Thomas was one of the lucky ones. The plants located in the South disproportionately hired whites to fill the new, well-paying positions. Even after Roosevelt issued executive orders to discontinue the discriminatory hiring patterns and established the U.S. Fair Employment Practices Commission (FEPC) to investigate and act on complaints, these patterns persisted, because the FEPC was not given enforcement powers.

With Eugene Talmadge back in the governor's mansion in 1941, the state government was less than eager to cooperate in pursuing racial economic equity. Some state officials, such as the aptly named J. E. B. Stewart, director of the Georgia Bureau of Unemployment, continued the battle for "states rights" against the claims of the federal agencies and national crisis. Stewart regularly and personally intervened to block African American access to new defense jobs and to harass labor organizers. A 1940 report on local employment offices in Georgia put the matter bluntly: "There are two divisions—White and Colored. The White Division is organized on a functional basis—placement, interviewing, claims, and clerical. The Colored Division is not functional for Augusta, Columbus, Macon, and Savannah."[32]

As a result, the wartime industrial expansion absorbed white unemployment first and only then drew black people into the new, nonagricultural jobs. Whites therefore tended to fill the higher-skilled, higher-paying positions, leaving more menial occupations to blacks. As historian George Tindall put it, blacks made gains in the defense plants "mostly in the 'h jobs': hot, heavy, and hard." The postwar economy, although more integrated into the national economy, would not be equitable, only different.[33]

The planters themselves tried their best to ensure that it wouldn't even be different. When labor recruiters came south, as they had during World War I, white employers and landlords attempted to deny them access to their agricultural laborers, as they had done before. The federal government came to the planters' assistance by establishing zones where agricultural and lumber workers would not be eligible to apply for defense work (see figure 12). The area north of Macon, including Hancock County, was described as an "extreme labor shortage area."[34] Labor agents were forbidden to recruit in areas such as these. On at least one occasion men who moved from Hancock to Michigan with a labor recruiter were tracked down and forced to give up their jobs at a foundry and return to the county.[35] Nor could agricultural laborers take the initiative to apply for defense industry positions, especially if they came from an area suffering a labor shortage. An internal memo within the War Manpower Commission (WMC) stated that the U.S. Employment Offices would not refer agricultural workers to other industries until the local county agent said there was no "suitable agricultural employment" in the area. Furthermore, if the worker was not self-employed, he needed "a release from his most recent farm employer for consideration for other employment."[36] Memos indicate that the staff of the WMC in Georgia acceded to white demands by trying to keep farm labor available and cheap.[37] In typical Rooseveltian fashion, different agencies were yoked to pull in opposite direc-

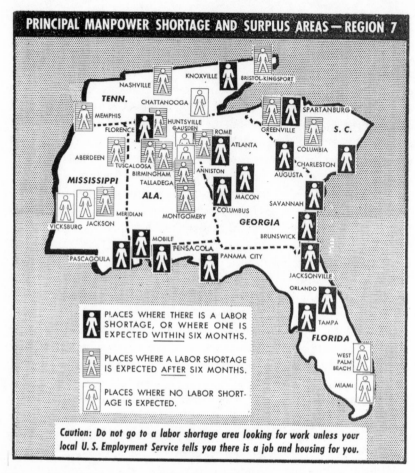

Figure 12. Map of the Southeastern United States Showing Manpower Shortage Areas during World War II (*source:* War Manpower Commission, series 11, box 12, "Labor Mobilization and Utilization—Labor Shortage," National Archives, East Point, Ga.).

tions. The war industries were intentionally placed in the South to open up the region's low-wage economy, but the WMC was cooperating with planters to try to ensure that the local labor markets were not disturbed.

Although they returned a few men to the farm, the planters' attempts to restrict the outward flow of labor from rural Hancock utterly failed. During the war, defense plants opened in towns and cities all over Georgia: Milledgeville, Augusta, Atlanta, Macon, Moultrie, Albany, and Valdosta. Military bases, too, were created: Ft. Benning, Camp Stewart, and Camp Wheeler.

Textile plants expanded. Shipyards in Savannah hummed with activity. In 1941, when an airbase was planned in Macon, less than forty miles from Hancock, the state department of labor was informed that the base would require 6,500 employees, with planned subdepots calling for 4,000 workers each.[38] Between 1939 and the wartime peak of 1943, the number of industrial workers in Georgia grew from 1.6 million to 2.8 million.[39] The magnitude of this demand for labor provided many black men and women new options and new opportunities for improving their lives. Even when obstructionist Georgia officials barred black tenant farmers from most of the higher-paying defense jobs, market forces refused to fully cater to the demands of cotton cultivation and white supremacy. Since the nineteenth century the seams of state coercion, paternalism, and local ties to land and family had packed a surplus of workers in the South and kept out the national wage scale. In World War II the seams burst, punctured from within and without.

Many Hancock people responded to the labor demands that the war created in other parts of the country and in doing so helped to swell the second great wave of migration. From 1940 to 1950 the black population of Hancock fell by 12 percent, from 9,183 to 8,068, and the white population fell by 17 percent, from 3,581 to 2,984. Lawyer Mason of rural Hancock joined the flow in 1943 when she went to New York to work as a domestic. She quit after three months, however, when she found higher-paying work at a nearby defense plant.[40]

Willie Butts and other men with a skilled trade found themselves with many options for well-paying jobs. Butts, a carpenter, saw his hourly wages rising from 20¢ per hour to $1.30 over the course of the war. He believed that the Fair Employment Practices Commission was responsible. Although the minimum wages set by the government and the market-setting wages paid by the government in defense industries contributed to the rise in wages, the primary cause was growing competition for labor in all areas.[41] "It was easy to get jobs," he said, for there was "a lot of work going on." Butts took advantage of his strong position to help organize a black carpenter's union. The union, he stated, became strong enough to get him jobs anywhere he wanted to work. Butts traveled across the country for years, picking up good jobs wherever he went. In some areas he still encountered racist resistance from white laborers. Once, when he was about to be hired in Philadelphia, the other carpenters—all white—walked off the job. He said it reduced him to tears, having returned from active combat in World War II just two years earlier. For the most part, however, Butts found that his skills and the black union placed him in a strong position within the market.[42]

The strong labor market continued to hold after the war as the U.S. economy entered an extended expansion. For many Hancock natives, this meant the continuation of good employment opportunities. Marshall Boyer was earning good wages in a defense plant when the war ended. "How come you quit?" his superintendent asked. "For twelve dollars a day," replied Boyer. "Can you get me a job?" asked the white man.[43]

Not only did the war open up new opportunities for good employment outside Hancock; in addition, it permanently altered the cheap-labor market within the boundaries of the county. As the war established new employment options and shrank the available pool of workers, laborers found their wages rising. Josie Ingram worked for wages on a large Hancock plantation during the war. She remembered working for as little as forty or fifty cents per day before the war. "When they went to the army," she said, "wages went to a dollar a day."[44] Although that was still well below the national average, it showed that the most isolated traditional plantations of Hancock were not insulated from these new national forces. Hancock's lumber industry, too, had to raise its wages to compete for labor. Rosetta Ingram still remembers Tom Collins as the first pulpwood boss to crack the ceiling on wages in western Hancock. He "came in, and people started making more money." Wages increased across the area, she said, for the other employers in the industry had to match Collins. By 1948 the *Sparta Ishmaelite* noted: "Common sawmill labor gets seventy cents an hour."[45]

After the war Hancock's rural laborers were not about to return to prewar conditions. According to Carlton Morse, an educator from Hancock, laborers became used to working in industry and making "two hundred dollars per month year-round," whereas "earlier they were paid nine months—[and] then had to find another job." Returning World War II veterans were less willing to accept the paternalism, insulting etiquette, and economic exploitation that had characterized the tenant system. According to James McMullen, a black educator, when the troops returned, "black men told their parents that they wouldn't work anymore" as dependent farmers. "Whites tried to blackmail them. They'd kick parents out of their homes" if their parents didn't work.[46]

These changes in wages and expectations were not the only alteration to occur when Hancock finally linked directly with the national labor market. Prices for goods—the cost of living—climbed, too. One man stated that he had chopped cotton at fifty cents per day before getting a job building the Milledgeville fuse plant at thirty-five cents per hour. But "money's got no value to it now," he said. "Back then, flour was at fifty cents for twenty-five pounds." As rural African Americans became more fully integrated into the national consumer economy, they witnessed the decline of the old local economy, with low wages, paternalism, semisubsistence, and neighborly exchange networks to supply the basics of life. In addition, as more people became dependent on increasingly urban wages, more people moved into towns and cities. Rural Hancock began to empty noticeably. Said Willie Butts in retrospect, "World War II set this world in motion. Hitler made a very small world out of it."[47]

One significant part of this economic transformation was the end of the cotton culture in places such as Hancock. The labor shortage and rising cost of labor led first some planters, then most, and then all to quit cotton production. According to a state agricultural report, planters had no trouble securing labor in 1939, but by the next year many Georgia counties—especially those near defense plants and air bases—were short hundreds of willing workers, despite raising their wages.[48] Hancock's traditional cotton economy was given a brief, cruel respite when a combination of drought and severe boll weevil infestations halved cotton production to parallel the shrinking labor pool in the eastern Georgia piedmont.[49] The labor market tightened unevenly, but it finally did its work, lifting even rural piedmont wage scales toward the new regional standards. At the low prices that cotton brought, planters could not afford to pay nationally competitive wages to have it planted, chopped, dusted, and picked by hand. Whereas the 1940 average southern wage for day labor in cotton fields had been ¢62, by the war's end it had risen to $1.93. Marshall Boyer said, "They couldn't get anybody to work for a dollar a day, so they just let it go." As employment options grew, laboring in a cottonfield seemed less and less enticing at any wage. By 1948 the *Sparta Ishmaelite* was complaining, "The day has come when it is hard to get an honest day's work regardless of the price asked by the laborer. There just seems to be the feeling that even then, they are being underpaid."[50]

Some farmers tried alternative crops—namely, soybeans and grain. According to Boyer, however, they were not profitable: "[It] cost them five dollars a bushel to buy the stuff to plant and then make three dollars a bushel ... so they couldn't make anything ... between drought, and high fertilizer, and low profit." A larger number "put their whole plantations into hayfields and cow pastures." Nearly all, however, sooner or later turned their land over to tree cultivation. Some landowners had begun to let their fields lie dormant when the weevil came in the 1920s, and trees volunteered. Mostly, however, the post–World War II stands of pine had been planted. Beginning in 1935 Hancock's two Civilian Conservation Corps camps planted trees and thinned stands of timber throughout the county. Through the work of the U.S. Department of Forestry, the federal government continued to nurture Hancock's transformation from cotton to pine. The development of the South's paper-pulp industry only accelerated this development. By 1946 Georgia ranked fourth among states in production of pulpwood and lumber. Today Hancock County is a pine forest, as is most of the land in the northern half of Georgia. As Marshall Boyer puts it, "In this part of the country, nobody's got anything above a garden.[51]

The tractor, the solution reached in many parts of the South, never made much progress in Hancock. Although the *Sparta Ishmaelite* had placed ads for tractors as early as 1910, relatively few Hancock farmers ever purchased one.[52] According to the 1940 Agricultural Census, twenty-two Hancock farms had one tractor each. That was it—out of 1,679 farms. The number of tractors had actually declined from thirty-five in 1925. In 1948 the *Ishmaelite* reported, "Cotton picking machines are being used in some parts of Georgia this season, and from the looks of the fields, it would be fine if some fellow had one in Hancock and could do some custom picking." When asked, however, most planters responded that the low value of farm crops in the 1950s and 1960s simply did not balance the high cost of mechanization. In the mid-1950s and 1960s the number of tractors in the county finally broke three hundred. But only a handful of these tractors were working in cotton fields. Most seem to have been used for cultivating either large gardens or legumes or hay for livestock farms. For the most part, the farmers who stuck with cotton stayed with the traditional labor-intensive systems of cultivation to the last.[53]

A few black landowners joined Hancock's small, unenthusiastic movement toward mechanization, but a larger number continued to farm with mules. One farmer, Calvin Travis, used mules until 1960. The possibility of mechanization created a generational split in some families. David Harper remembered an impasse when he asked his landowning father to get a tractor: "He didn't want to. And I didn't want to plow mules." So David left for the North. Only one interviewee, Mamie Washington, noted that some tenants—not her—were pushed off their farms when their landlords purchased tractors. Unlike the planters of the Mississippi Delta, however, those of Hancock were generally not interested in mechanization.[54] Interestingly, the first southern farmers to turn heavily to tractors in the 1930s were in Florida and the Western states, such as Texas and Oklahoma. Admittedly, these areas are the easiest on which to operate a tractor, being the flattest, but they are also the ones with the most slender legacy of slavery and paternalism. Eastern planters, such as those in Hancock, apparently valued the human and animal relationships, the old tools, and the paternalistic ties that accompanied the traditional cotton culture. There was no tractor revolution in Hancock, and the spread of pines attests that there may not have been one in the northern half of the state as a whole.[55]

Emment Oliver remembered that the last year he farmed was 1941. By 1945, he said, "There were few people in farming . . . most in public work." Oliver himself was not fond of farming. "On a farm, you would work all year and would get nothing but what you'd eat and what you'd wear," he said. "It was rough on a farm, ain't no doubt about it . . . Hot in the summer sun . . . Gnats would eat you up—not a thing you could do about it." He added, "Picking cotton would break your back," having to stay "low to the ground." Oliver left the county in 1946 at the urging of his sister, who preceded him to New York City. He got a job in the city one week after arriving there, the same day he applied for it. Others repeated similar stories, especially the men and women who had risen to adulthood after the Depression. They left. The older generation tended to stay. On the one hand, James Wilson, born in 1917, liked to reminisce about his many years of country living and his weekend trips to Devereux, a village now desolate and never home to more than a couple hundred souls. According to Wilson, Devereux had been the "garden spot of the world" before it began to close down during World War II. David Harper, on the other hand, born in 1935, spoke with enthusiasm of the excitement of towns such as Sparta, where "two dollars was a lot of money" and where he could see his friends, get a sandwich and soda for thirty-five cents, or see a movie for fifteen cents. But he spoke with wonder of his youthful view of New York City, with all its options and opportunities. He remembered farm life's contrasting lack of glamour: "[I'd] come home from school, get out of my clothes—get on those rags . . ." He shook his head, leaving the sentence unfinished. In New York, where he has lived for the past forty years, he found he could make twice as much money as he had on the farm "working at machine shops, in bookkeeping, at anything!"[56]

When the cotton culture crumbled, what happened to the dependent farmers? Many of them, like Sam Baker, turned to the lumber industry, which continues to the present as the primary productive industry in the county. Many men and women moved to nearby Milledgeville and began working in construction as that city grew and enlarged its college, state hospital, and support industries. Others went to Macon, Savannah, Augusta, and Atlanta. In the aftermath of World War II, however, many found that the preferential hiring practices that had reserved the highest-paying jobs for whites in defense industries continued to operate in the private sector. The economic racial hierarchy survived, even amid the wreck of the cotton culture that had long held blacks captive in poverty. Those who had fewest skills sometimes found themselves pushed completely out of the workforce. Considering the way that African American schools had been consciously underfunded for decades, it is no surprise that African Americans who remained in Hancock suffered high unemployment. For the past couple of decades the primary means of income in Hancock—over one-third of the county's personal income—has been government transfer payments of social security and welfare. More black than white natives of Hancock have migrated to the north, where many found work in factories until the flight of factories to Third World countries in the 1960s, 1970s, and 1980s drained cities of jobs. A growing number of these are now returning to Hancock, where their pensions can stretch further than they can in New York or Washington, D.C.[57]

And what of the other rural black families? What happened to the black landowners? A few years ago two sociologists wrote a book that decried the extinction of the black landowner. It has often been assumed that their declining numbers after World War I reveals their regression toward dependency. Indeed, the boll weevil and the Great Depression became powerful forces that drove many small farmers—including farmers already struggling against a racist society—into sharecropping or wage labor. But there is an alternative explanation for the "decline" of black landowners.[58]

If a person were to select the optimum period to abandon the southern family farm and reinvest elsewhere, that moment would have been World War I. After World War I the price of cotton fell through the floor; simultaneously the boll weevil halved Hancock's cotton production. In the years following these paired catastrophes, the economic window of opportunity offered by landowning steadily shrank.

But another window opened. During World War I northern industries began to court southern black laborers for the first time, offering what seemed like munificent wages to men used to the slim pickings of the cotton kingdom. Although this land of opportunity ultimately proved to be a mirage to many who made the journey north, for others, it was real. According to the testimony offered by the children of black Hancock County landowners, their families carried with them resources in education, a nest egg, and confidence that gave them advantages over poorer men and women. Most of the children and grandchildren of landowners interviewed for this study fared well after moving to the cities. With better educations, they often found jobs in professional, service, or managerial sectors that paid better wages than unskilled jobs did. Their success sometimes put them in conflict with the wishes of their parents, however, who often looked in vain for a child to whom to turn over the family farm. The generation that had through great sacrifice first gained possession of the land often tried to hold on to it as the means that had offered economic opportunity in their youth. Nevertheless, their children became increasingly less willing to forgo the greater returns their resources brought in the cities. Thus the children of black landowners may well have been rowing away from the sinking wreck of southern agriculture with the only things worth salvaging.

*　*　*

World War II transformed the South perhaps more than it did any other section of the country. Hancock County finished the 1930s as a world in which the planters and their allies still controlled every significant aspect of the economy: the labor supply, wages, contracts, furnishing allotments, and the end-of-the-year settle. Although the boll weevil had ensured that few were going to build cotton fortunes there, the planters as a group securely controlled the economic, political, and social aspects of rural Hancock. For most African Americans in the first half of the twentieth century, life in Hancock meant life as a dependent farm laborer. As long as they did not directly challenge the system, however, the planters permitted a range of alternative experiences. The rural areas were home to black and white planters, yeomen, renters, sharecroppers, and wage laborers, all interacting with one another in private, isolated, rural neighborhoods in a highly complex and personalized variety of social dances. Because James Wilson grew up the poor son of poor sharecroppers, he speaks today of the too personal control that white planters exercised over his life at different times. But what could he have done? "You had to go right along with it," he explained, "if you'd been caught in it." Marshall Boyer saw it differently; after speaking of the persistence of "slaveryisms" and paternalism in his rural neighborhood, he added, "Understand now, I came up through that, but not in it." "The difference," he said, "was that my family was self-supporting, and Dad had white friends." In rural Georgia that could make all the difference. As Hancock more fully entered the commercial market, it largely left behind this complex, intimate world. It became more systematic, more conformist, and more public. Now people in Hancock inhabit a cultural world long familiar to most Americans. Segregation, the consumer culture, bureaucratic government oversight, and decisions made by the managers of distantly owned paper-pulp companies have shoved aside the cultures of personalism, localism, and semisubsistence that had marked Hancock through the first half of the twentieth century. Much that had characterized rural Hancock and made it a place apart from the national currents passed with World War II.

Appendix A:
Methods

Although this study reflects rural Hancock as a whole, it focuses on three socially distinctive sections in the county. Much of Hancock's best land, lying in a wide horizontal swath across the center of the county, was controlled predominantly by the wealthiest planters. This zone was distinguished by large plantations, impoverished and almost exclusively black tenants and wage laborers, and relatively few small landowners. The southern tip and eastern edge of the county contained many white tenants, often intermixed with black tenants. A high concentration of black and white small landowners could be found in the northern part of the county, which, with few exceptions, was home to the county's only wealthy black landowners as well. Each area seemed to have its own patterns in race relations.

When starting this oral project I had hoped to systematically interview survivors or immediate descendants from a random sample drawn from three different Hancock militia districts in 1910. (Georgia counties are divided into militia districts for purposes of polls, census, and taxation.) Doing so would have given me a cross-section of the experiences of Hancock citizens from the period under study—including the testimonies of those whose experiences led them to leave the county, something I might not have learned speaking only with lifelong residents. I enlisted assistance from Samuel Williams, a retired African American county extension agent, and David Dyer, who had served in a number of county positions, to locate three communities that would best represent Hancock's variation. They steered me toward the districts around the villages of Powelton, Devereux, and Linton, for the northern, middle, and southern sectors of the county, respectively.

After obtaining a random sample from the 1910 census manuscript for these areas, I set to work locating descendants, working primarily through churches, school reunions, and networks springing from previous contacts. As I read my list to different community elders during the early 1990s, some, such as Solomon Harper and

Newton Boyer, displayed uncanny memory in naming the children in most families as soon as I read the names of the household's "head." Significantly, however, few blacks and very few whites remembered many long-gone names from across the race line. Additionally, recall in some sectors of the county far outstripped others. Not surprisingly, the relatively stable black and white small farmowners around Powelton remembered far more names and offered more leads than did the planters and black and white sharecroppers around Linton. The great disappointment proved to be Devereux, where many of the poorest inhabitants from eighty years ago seem to have been forgotten completely. Solomon Harper, who remembered more than anyone else in Devereux, helped me understand why they were so hard to find. "Dead and gone," he kept repeating, as I recited the names of families, "dead and gone." Some families had literally died out, leaving no descendants. For the rest, entire extended families—many of whom he remembered well—had moved to Detroit, New York, Cleveland, and so on, leaving only the oldest behind. Many of them never returned to Hancock once their rural grandparents had died. Furthermore, I discovered that many of the black sharecroppers whom I located through friends and extended family in Hancock lived farther away than my budget allowed me to travel. Finally, in the age of telemarketing, I guess that most people share my general dislike of unsolicited phone conversations with strangers. When referred by family members, I called a few elderly contacts who I believed had critical information on a specific topic, and in these short interviews I often found success. Nevertheless, I did not think that calling "out of the blue" for extended conversations with elderly migrants would prove to be a good experience for either of us. It is too hard to establish trust, too tiring for them, and sometimes too difficult for me to understand the varied Hancock accents without visual cues. I did make interviewing excursions out of Georgia to Baltimore, Cleveland, and Washington, D.C. For the most part, however, I gave up this part of the original project. Still, the endeavor taught me that Hancock's black sharecroppers are widely scattered across the country, whereas most landowners and white sharecroppers seem not to have moved far from Hancock.

I soon realized that without corrections, my data would be skewed toward more affluent families. I thus began adding "replacements" for families that turned out to be lost or beyond reach. I had from the start interviewed people recommended by other residents as local authorities. When I asked at churches, however, I found that people of relatively high standing, such as black teachers and landowners, were being pushed forward by poorer people to speak about the period. Many poorer folk believed they had nothing of interest to say. Tracking down ex-sharecroppers, especially those who had worked on the largest plantations, often required persistence.

In time I discovered that one did not need to leave Hancock to find a large sample of migrants from the county. Many, both black and white, returned after retirement, drawn by ties to family and old friends as well as the rural South's lower cost of living and culture of hospitality. I also began to attend high-school, church, and family reunions. I found that simply by tapping into these networks, I could interview a wide variety of Hancock residents who had left the area in different decades and spent their careers in varied corners of the nation. These interviews were often rich with information. Some returnees had remarkably fresh memories of the rural South in the distant past. They had not seen it slowly change around them and could describe it sometimes better than lifelong residents could. Additionally, they could place the southern story in a larger context. I was usually invited to these reunions by someone from my widening circle of contacts. On a few occasions I saw a large group in a park or church yard and stopped to ask whether it was a reunion and, if so, whether I could speak with some people. There was a drawback, however: reunion attendees do not drive from New York to Sparta to speak with a historian. As a result, these interviews were usually short and focused on only a few topics, unless I was invited to speak with people in the homes of family and friends over the course of a extended visit. One advantage was that people were often in a mood to reminisce. Sometimes after a few individual interviews a group would form, with various people posing questions to one another, clarifying points, and adding their own perspectives.

Although broadening the profile of my study, these additions still did not fully meet my original goal of a fully random sample. High-school reunion attendees are a self-selecting group. In the rural South the poorest families were least likely to keep their children in school for more than a few years, much less to give them time to graduate from high school. Furthermore, those who feel uncertain of the "success" of their postgraduate lives may be less likely to show up at a school reunion. Beyond that, migrants from Hancock who return to Georgia for church and family reunions also share distinctive characteristics that may bias their collective testimony. Attendees at family reunions value family, have stayed in touch with one another, and have enjoyed one another's support over the courses of their lives. The same is true for those who journeyed long distances to attend church reunions. Although rich and poor alike organize and attend such reunions, these attendees could not usually speak to the experiences of atomization and alienation that some writers attribute to the poorest migrants from the rural South. But perhaps the theme of atomization is the unrepresentative one after all. In Hancock, among lifelong residents as well as returning migrants, I found regular evidence of close social networks. There were frequently phone calls and visits from neighbors during my interviews, as well as references to letters from family in other states.

Finally, I tried to fill in "missing" social groups in my sample by interviewing people in Hancock whom I met at churches, stores, and private homes. To find some people in backwoods sections of Hancock, where streets bear no signposts and many are still unpaved, it is necessary to stop regularly for directions and thus "home-in" gradually on a given residence. People in Hancock are, with few exceptions, helpful, friendly, and hospitable to strangers who knock on their doors. Conversations often developed on the porch when I explained my purpose. Sometimes I was invited in for iced tea or lunch to continue talking. Often enough I postponed the search for the original interviewee to talk with people I met this way. Many of my favorite interviews occurred through such serendipity.

* * *

Like every other kind of historical source, oral interviews have inherent strengths and weaknesses. Memory is a quirky archive. Much of our lives lies beyond our ability to recall. We forget most of what happens to us—conversations, casual encounters, surroundings—usually by the end of each day. Consequently, an eighty-five-year-old woman in Hancock County, when asked in the 1990s about her experiences of rural race relations during the 1930s, will have a highly selective database from which to draw.[1]

For a few minutes after we experience something, we have nearly perfect recall. Then, very quickly, we select a small amount of this information, fit it into a comprehensible pattern, and store it. At this time most of the information is discarded. Over the course of life data continue to be lost, especially if the memories are not retrieved regularly. But the primary sifting and losing of information is almost immediate. A number of studies have indicated the remarkable stability of the memories that remain. These long-term memories are created when we encounter one of two things: either a pattern of repeated experience or an event that we believe at the time to be significant, especially if we express it soon afterward as a story. Our memories, then, are collections of our perceptions of experiences and data that we found to be significant and that were reinforced, either by repetitions of the experience itself or by mental or verbal narration of that experience.

What remains to be studied is thus not a systematic compilation of all aspects of race relations in Hancock from 1910 to 1950 but rather a collection of stories and observations that Hancock residents who lived through these years found to be significant—especially the ones they retold over the years. It is significant that the rural South is a highly oral culture. Rural people in Hancock were among the nation's last to obtain radios and televisions. Entertainment consisted largely in telling and retelling stories touching on all aspects of experience, including race relations. What remains to be remembered in the present is not the same thing as an objective, "unbiased" account of these relationships. But "unbiased" history, based on "unbiased" sources, is no longer a goal that most historians find to be realistic or even desirable. Throughout this study I have attempted to suggest the perspectives of my sources by indicating their social positions.

* * *

Of course, no historical sources are free of bias.[2] The seemingly "objective" census data of Hancock were first reported orally as the county's residents answered the census taker's questions. Additionally, the census missed some of the poorer and more mobile of Hancock's people. Newspapers obviously are biased toward the editor's political perspective. The clean columns of the tax digests tabulate only the income that residents chose to report—obviously missing large underground economies such as barter and moonshining. Most diaries are written with an eye toward posterity. All historical documents are constructed within particular social environments, and the conscientious historian must account for the resulting biases.

Additionally, one must consider the inherent bias within the bulk of "traditional" collections of historical sources—that of elitism. By and large, manuscript collections represent the voice of the rich, the powerful, and by definition the educated. Only rarely do the poor appear in the newspapers and courthouse record books, and when they do, it is usually only as alleged criminals. Although cliometric studies attempt to remedy this gap, they do so by examining people in the aggregate after passing them through quantitative sausage grinders. That which made individuals of poor and laboring people and that which they thought important about their own lives are difficult to recover through traditional sources (although since the 1960s, historians have made exciting and creative use of the resources that do exist). Yet the bulk of recent studies, though they have been consciously designed to include the perspectives of those who had been marginalized in previous studies, largely struggle against inherently exclusive collections of sources. Here oral history offers its greatest strength: it is potentially the most democratic of methodologies. Oral historians don't need to search the archives for information about "ordinary people"; we simply create our own archives by talking to them. And it is generally easier to interview a retired laborer than a retired governor.

But oral history has its characteristic weaknesses, and some of these have affected this study. Oral history is useful in reliably getting at people's past activities, especially repeated ones. It is less useful in getting at past attitudes. As a result, I rarely asked people how they felt about neighbors across the race lines sixty years ago. Instead I asked them about specific actions and activities; for example, I might ask them whether they ever attended church outside their racial group, and if so, to describe the setting. If black and white interviewees from an area agree that they had exchanged regular visits to each other's churches and those stories cluster around a specific period in the past, I find that testimony reliable and significant, unlike less concrete testimony.

Furthermore, oral history does not provide data from which one can construct a reliable, detailed chronology. We remember only a few significant dates from our lives. Asking for specific dates that people usually don't know is obviously dangerous. They will probably make up dates, which is worse than no data at all. When I believed that a story was truly significant—especially one that demonstrated a historical turning point—I asked how old the narrator was when the incident occurred, how old his or her children were, or whether it happened before or after World War II. As a result, the chronological structure of this study is often looser than I would prefer. Within each section, however, significant turning points that recurred in interviews are highlighted and discussed in historical context.

Although some historical anecdotes and narratives have been passed across generations while holding to the basic structure of the original story, the reliability of oral testimony seems increasingly suspect as it grows more distant from the original experience. Accordingly, I have primarily used firsthand accounts as evidence in this study. Where I used a secondhand account, most often for the years preceding 1920, I identify it as such in the text and, when possible, identify the original source of the information.

The long-term memory of elderly people may be thought to be an additional problem. Studies have shown, however, that it is generally no worse than that of younger people and often much better. As people step back from their careers, they usually enter into a period of reflection that psychologists term "life review." This stage is marked by both a strong desire to remember one's life candidly and a degree of distancing from the pressures of present concerns and the social expectations of contemporary audiences.[3]

Another difficulty with oral history is the manner in which memories can sometimes be unconsciously transformed in the light of present concerns. The sense of the past to which we might refer as "folk history," that which nonscholars remember about the histories of their own communities, is constructed socially as well as individually. The memory of individual people is partially shaped by their participation in their community. Drawing on shared historical resources, individual storytellers draw from their own memories and reinforce one another's perceptions of the past to build consensus about what happened "back then." These perceptions about the past may be influenced by a community's current needs for a "usable" past. This becomes particularly problematic in interviewing white southerners about earlier race relations. Older whites are aware and often personally affected by the national culture's retreat from forthright racism over the past thirty years. In recent interviews and memoirs, old segregationist politicians have clamored to describe themselves as "working behind the scenes" for civil rights, regardless of their past records and rhetoric. Nevertheless, some white Hancock interviewees—particularly some among the very oldest—plainly do not feel pressured by changes in the national culture, and they used language and expressed opinions that would have made Eugene Talmadge proud. I generally attribute such statements to anonymous sources, although these interviewees felt comfortable enough with their statements that they never requested such treatment.[4]

Yet there is no reason to assume prima facie that folk histories are false. They may be so, as were early twentieth-century white "recollections" of "Negro domination" under Reconstruction. Alternatively, they may be constructed by selections from faithful recollections of events. The job of the historian is not to assume the truth or falsehood of a construction of the past but to ask whether it is internally consistent, whether it makes sense within the historical context—whether it forms a plausible past.

I am not satisfied that any historical transformation altered the basic outlines of the remembered story of race relations in Hancock between the two world wars. Because the great majority of interracial encounters and relationships left no written record, however, there is little written evidence with which to corroborate the body of evidence my interviews produced. Nonetheless, no external evidence contradicts it. To test for internal consistency, I developed a number of internal reference points within my oral interviews. I ensured that each significant social identity found in Hancock during the period under study would be represented: men and women; white and black; landowners, yeomen, and tenants; and teachers, preachers, and craftsmen. For the most part, the various oral sources substantiated one another's testimony. When I found divergences between black and white or upper-class and lower-class memories of past events and patterns, I tried to tease out the reasons for the difference and addressed the different social pressures that may have altered the way one group retold the stories. These, where significant, are mentioned in the text.

I cannot, however, find a way to explain how the various adversarial social groups of Hancock came basically to reconcile their interpretations of the past—if that interpretation is indeed a false construction of past racial patterns. Although many more whites than blacks preferred older patterns of race relations to those of the present, both agreed that the older rural patterns differed distinctly from those of the present and that they did so in certain basic ways. Moreover, both lifelong residents of rural Hancock and migrants from the county who moved to the urban North in the 1930s or 1940s described basically similar patterns. If these are "ahistorical social constructs," then they were created in radically different social contexts, and their convergence becomes a mystery beyond my capacity to explain. My solution is to reach for Ockham's Razor and accept the simplest interpretation of these stories. This memory of the past has not drifted much. It is roughly accurate.[5]

My own social identity is the final issue that problematizes the oral evidence used in this study. The interviewer's presence unavoidably plays a part in forming the context in which the oral document is created. I am a white man born in North Dakota in 1964 and raised in Athens, Georgia, from the age of two. My faint southern accent and my last name are all that Hancock residents need to hear to know that I'm not from the area. My identity undoubtedly made it difficult for Hancock natives, white and black, to speak freely around me concerning many of the topics discussed. I certainly did not learn as much from my interviewees as I would have had I shared their identities, but this concern goes only so far: no one person could have shared all their identities in any event. At least I was an outsider to all. Moreover, the sensitive topics that people discussed with me—murder, rape, economic exploitation, inter-racial kinship—convince me that many people, at least, were fairly candid. Perhaps my relative youth and naïveté when I came to the county at twenty-two helped me. My interviewees, mostly old enough to have been my grandparents, may have recognized my sincere desire to hear their stories and saw in me an opportunity to "set the record straight" with someone who had clearly not lived through the period under study.

Most African American interviewees seemed unintimidated by my race. I did conduct "siring" contests with a few elderly black men—I used the honorific in deference to their ages and experience; they, in deference to my whiteness. Once I objected to being addressed as *sir* by an elderly man to whom I had become close. He apologized, saying it was a habit he couldn't quit after all the years under white supremacy. A few, not wanting to embarrass or offend me, spoke apologetically before relating stories of white behavior under white supremacy. More often black interviewees spoke in a matter-of-fact tone about race relations. Rarely I encountered undisguised anger toward whites generally and me as the nearest representative. Once I was invited to a family reunion by a family member who didn't tell anyone else of my coming and didn't show up herself. The family, most of whom now live in Detroit, had been very poor and apparently badly exploited as sharecroppers. They refused to allow me to tape the interview but sat in a semicircle around me, pelting me with heated, accusatory stories about the way that white folks had abused black folks. Although I was unable to take more than cursory notes during what amounted to as a rapid-fire talking-to, they ultimately did not tell me anything that others did not relate in calmer tones. This has reassured me that even if I am not hearing all that people remember, I am hearing a great deal of it.

Conducting one's own interviews is especially useful, because one knows the context in which they were gathered. My approach has been to vary my interviewing technique dependent on the context of the interview. When I first came to Hancock County in 1988, I was awkwardly aware of how little I knew of rural southern life. While I had some ideas about southern history that I had picked up in a few graduate seminars, I tended not to direct the interviews very firmly. I mostly wanted to know what my interviewees, black and white, thought significant about their own lives. The early conversations especially tended to ramble in an open-ended way and covered a wide range of topics.

As I learned more, I structured my reading along lines of investigation that had opened up in previous interviews. When I began dissertation research in earnest, I tried to construct a consistent set of questions to standardize every interview. I had an orderly, several-page outline of questions about family history, childhood, education, work, community, race relations, the New Deal, and migration. Unfortunately, I soon found that I could not use them systematically without reducing the interviews to a stilted and mutually awkward pattern. Since then I have used the questionnaire as a rough guide while allowing and encouraging interviewees to introduce new topics, which sometimes meant that the "standard" questions were thrown out the window. Because I tried to at least touch on these topics consistently, however, and rural people were often concerned about similar themes, there is fair overlap in the material covered in the separate interviews.

I tried to make my interviewees as comfortable as possible in the interview process. I attempted to keep my own biases and expectations from influencing the information shared by interviewees. Nevertheless, the information I sought caused many people some discomfort and possibly some personal risk. I did not want to remain a distant, impersonal inquisitor, taping their answers to difficult questions without revealing some of myself as well. Although I took pains not to disagree with any response and did my best not to ask leading questions, I did not hide myself from my interviewees either. I did not restrain myself from responding naturally and sympathetically to painful or pleasurable memories and to stories critical or complimentary of people or individuals across the race line from the interviewee. Generally, because I believe that the rural South was characterized by a great diversity of experiences, I tried to ask open-ended questions and then encouraged and supported whatever answer was given. In addition, I usually tried to rephrase their answers in such a way as to invite contextualization and self-criticism by the interviewees themselves.

There has been a good deal of give-and-take between me and several of my interviewees. I view myself as having collaborated with the people of Hancock County to produce this study. After interviews I often spoke frankly about my perceptions of southern history and race relations and about the purpose of my study, and I encouraged direct feedback concerning my interpretations and goals. Some interviewees have become friends with whom I regularly discuss the ongoing progress of the project and my changing ideas concerning it. I have found them extremely helpful colleagues in the "official, scholarly" work of producing history. After George and Dorothy Lott, an elderly African American couple, saved me from a terrific interpretive blunder during the last stage of writing my master's thesis, I have made it a policy not to present papers or articles on this material in a public, scholarly forum without first submitting them to experienced Hancock people for criticism. Unlike all other methodologies, oral history allows the object of study to actively assist in shaping the story told about her—to become the subject of her own story. This admittedly constitutes a bias, but I do not find the result less valuable than history that is addressed through the shifting interpretations of professional historians. Katie Hunt, an African American woman born in 1891, and her daughter, Mae Warren, have been my most trusted advisers throughout this project. Because of our relationship, I can ask "Ma Kate" and "Miz Mae," quite directly and without discomfort to either of us, any question on life in Hancock and expect honest answers, hard or easy. Overall, they and my other Hancock colleagues have fully validated my belief in the capacity of ordinary people of widely varying educational backgrounds to grasp and engage "scholarly" historical problems with great interest and success. My writing and thinking have been much improved from the process. So I employ oral history, doing my best to remain mindful of its inherent pitfalls while endeavoring to take advantage of its many strengths.

Appendix B: Interviews

All but a few of the interviews are now housed in the Southern Oral History Program, Southern Historical Collection, Wilson Library, University of North Carolina at Chapel Hill. Listed below are only those interviews cited in the text. Birthdates are given when available. All interviews were done in Georgia unless otherwise noted. While the great majority of the interviews were tape-recorded, a few were not and are marked with an asterisk.

Andrews, Gay: Devereux, around 1995.
Andrews, Roberta: Powelton, June 4, 1992.
Arnold, Mozelle (b. 1910): rural Hancock, near Linton, January 26, 1995.
Baker, Sam (b. 1912): Powelton, Jan. 1992.
Barksdale, Frank (b. 1902): Sparta, 1988*.
Barksdale, Leslie (b. 1914): rural Hancock, north of Powelton, February 17, 1995.
Boyer, Bernard (b. 1906): Milledgeville, August 9, 1995.
Boyer, Billy (b. 1935): rural Hancock, north of Linton, September 19, 1994*; August 2, 1995*.
Boyer, Marshall (b. 1909): rural east Baldwin County, September 9, 1995; August 2 and 9, 1995; telephone interview, July 19, 2003*; telephone interview, August 9, 2003*.
Boyer, Newton (b. 1920): Milledgeville, June 13, 2000.
Brookins, Kelly (b. 1925): Milledgeville, August 10, 1994.
Brookins, Myrtle (b. 1908): rural Washington County, south of Linton, July 6, 1995.
Brookins, William (b. 1912): Milledgeville, August 9, 1994.
Brown, Cecil (b. 1919): east of Sparta, July 24, 1995.
Brown, Dot (b. 1920): east of Sparta, July 24, 1995.
Butts, Sanford: Sparta, December 29, 1989*; July 1993*.

Butts, Willie (b. 1921): Devereux, July 19, 1995; August 3 and 8, 1995.

Chappel, Rosa (b. 1917): Culverton, summer 2002.

Clayton, Walter Green (b. 1919): Sparta, January 2, 1998.

Cook, Ossie (b. 1895): north of Linton, March 23, 1992.

DeCosta-Lee, Beautine Hubert (b. 1913): Baltimore, Md., October 6, 2001; letter, DeCosta-Lee to Mark Schultz, December 24, 1994.

Dickens, G. Lee (b. 1921): telephone interview, July 25, 2004*.

Dickson, Curry (b. 1895): Sparta, July 23, 1992.*

Dixon, Hyndenberg (b. 1919) and Eunice: rural Hancock, south of Linton, July 1 and 11, 1995.

Dixon, Thomas: Springfield, August 1993*.

Dobbins, Willie E.: Springfield, August 11, 1995.

Durham, Laramon: Winterville, March 16, 1993.

Dyer, Dave (b. 1917): Sparta, November 22, 1993; December 8, 1993; August 4, 1995; May 1995.

Edwards, Homer: Linton, August 2, 1992.

Edwards, Lonzy (b. 1949): telephone interview, August 12, 2004.*

Edwards, Louise: Springfield, September 18, 1989*.

Edwards, Otilia: rural Baldwin County, west of Devereux, January 21, 1993.

Frazier, Francis (b. 1908): Mt. Zion, rural Hancock, east of Linton, July 20 and 25, 1995.

Foster, Eugene, Jr. (b. 1934): north of Carrs, July 6, 1995.

Glover, Henrietta (b. 1898): Sparta, June 13, 2000.

Griffen, Virginia (1934): Gray, January 14, 1994.

Harper, David (b. 1935): rural Hancock, near Devereux, September 14 and 15, 1994.

Harper, Emmie Mae (b. 1910): rural Hancock County, near Linton, September 23, 1994; January 26, 1995.

Harper, Solomon (b. 1905): rural Hancock, west of Devereux, September 15, 1994.

Harrison, Tom, Sr. (b. 1903): Atlanta, October 1991.

Herndon, Robert (b. 1930): Milledgeville, March 31, 1995.

Hillman, Oscar and Julia: western Warren County, July 14, 1995.

Hubert, Willis: Springfield, January 1989.

Hunt, Katie (b. 1891): Sparta, August 12, 1992; August 25, 1994; September 25, 1995; telephone interview, October 4, 1995; with Mae Warren, Charlie Hunt, and Charity Hunt, Washington, D.C., June 6, 14, 15, and 25, 1990.

Hunt, Katie Bell (b. 1910): Linton, February 24, 1995; March 16, 1995; May 18, 1995.

Hunt, Mary (b. 1907): Sparta, July 21, 1995.

Ingram, Babe: near Sparta, 1989.

Ingram, Earnest Jack (b. 1918): Sparta, June 3, 2004*; telephone interview, Sept. 18, 2004.

Ingram, Josie Mae (b. 1923): rural Hancock, west of Devereux, July 12, 1995.

Ingram, Rosetta (b. 1929): north of Carrs, July 14 and 19, 1995.

Jackson, Asia (b. 1909): Sparta, September 18, 1989.

Johnson, Johnny Evans, (b. 1908): Sparta, November 12 and 20, 1988; July 21, 2003*.

Jones, Ed (b. 1937): Sparta, July 5, 1992.

Kennedy, Patsy: Devereux, July 1994.

Kendrick, John (b. 1915): Culverton, summer 2002.

Lattimore, Mary (b. 1908): rural Hancock, north of Devereux, July 6, 1995.

Leslie, Melvin, Sr. (b. 1910): Culverton, summer 2002.

Lott, George (b. 1923): rural Hancock, northwest of Sparta, 1989.

Lyon, Seleta Boyer (b. 1916): east of Sparta, October 1, 1992.

Macklin, Earnest (b. 1912) and Annie (b. 1917): rural Hancock, east of Sparta, July 18, 1995.

Mason, Lawyer: Springfield, August 1995.

McMullen, James: Sparta, 1988*; undated, around 1991; June 17, 1992*.

Miller, W. J. (b. 1927) and Mable (b. 1936): north of Linton, July 18, 1995.

Morse, Carlton (b. 1922): Sparta, July 6, 1991; Fort Valley, July 7 and 20, 1995.

Nicholls, Earnest (b. 1921): north of Linton, March 30, 1995.

Oliver, Emerett: Devereux, around 1992*.

Parker, A. J. (b. 1931): Beulah, rural Hancock, south of Linton, July 8, 15, and 18, 1995.

Patterson, T. M. "Buck": Sparta, August 2, 1995.

Pearson, Clinton (b. 1918): rural Hancock, near Devereux, August 3, 1995.

Primer, Essie Mae (b. 1916): rural Hancock, west of Linton, June 27, 1995.

Quinn, Erma Mae (b. 1925): Carrs, December 13, 2001.

Reese, Eva (b. 1906): Sparta, September 23, 2001.

Rhodes, Obilee, Jr.: rural Hancock, east of Sparta, September 21, 1992.

Rhodes, Obilee, Sr.: rural Hancock, west of Sparta, September 1, 1992*.

Roberts, Eddie (b. 1914): Linton, August 16, 1994.

Roberts, John (b. 1929): rural Hancock, north of Linton, September 23, 2001.

Roberts, Mearilus, Jr. (b. 1936): telephone interview, August 12, 2004.*

Roberts, Roy: Thomson, August 31, 1992.

Robinson, Ruth Davis: near Devereux, July 14, 1995.

Rozier, John (b. 1918): telephone interview, August 16, 2002*; telephone interview, June 17, 2003*.

Senior, Benjamin (b. 1920): west of Sparta, August 29, 1998; telephone interview, August 9, 1998*.

Senior, Vera: rural Hancock, east of Devereux, August 29, 1992.

Shivers, Forrest (b. 1918): telephone interview, October 25, 2003*.

Sigman, Thomas (b. 1922): rural Hancock, near Mt. Zion, January 27, 1995.

Simmons, Mary (b. 1929): rural northwest Hancock, July 26, 1995.

Skrine, Clabon (b. 1942): Springfield, August 1995.

Skrine, Gaston: telephone interview, August 11, 1995; September 1995*.

Smith, Alma Dixon: Milledgeville, May 1, 1995.

Smith, Clifford and Eva: rural Hancock, east of Sparta, August 10, 1992.

Stanley, William, III: Atlanta, July 7, 1993.

Swint, John (b. 1915): southeast of Sparta, March 3, 1995.

Thomas, Grover (b. 1920): Sparta, January 30, 1992.

Thomas, Oline (b. 1919): rural Hancock, west of Linton, June 13, 1995.

Thompson, Jewell: Devereux, August 9, 1995.

Thompson, Marvin (b. 1921) and Mary: rural Hancock, south of Linton, June 12, 1995.

Thornton, Mary (b. 1910) and Elizabeth (b. 1908): near Devereux, January 28, 1992.

Travis, Calvin (b. 1925): rural Hancock, near Carrs, August 9, 1994; September 15, 1994.

Trawick, Sid: Linton, February 3, 1994*.

Turner, Marvin (b. 1921): Washington County, September 2, 1994.

Walker, Creasy (b. 1916): rural Hancock, north of Linton, September 5 and 8, 1994.

Walker, Ralph (b. 1932): rural Washington County, September 2, 1994.

Walls, Willis (b. 1920): Milledgeville, July 6, 1995.

Walls, Dollie (b. 1918): north of Carrs, August 8, 1995.

Walls, Lewis (b. 1932): north of Carrs, July 6, 1995.

Walls, Roberta: north of Carrs, August 8, 1995.

Warren, Mae (b. 1915): Washington, D.C., June 15, 1990; Sparta, September 25, 1994; Sparta, March 1995; telephone interview, September 31, 1997; telephone interview, May 29, 2002*; telephone interview, August 3, 2004*.

Washington, Mamie (b. 1923): rural Hancock, south of Linton, July 28, 1995.

Williams, Samuel (b. 1919): Springfield, spring 1989*; December 12, 1989; 1994*.

Wilson, James (b. 1917): Devereux, July 16 and 18, 1995.

Wilson, Mary (b. 1917): Warren County, east of Powelton, August 14, 1995.

Winn, Emma L. Nealous: Springfield, August 1995.

Worthening, Mary (b. 1922): rural Hancock, south of Sparta, June 22, 1995.

Notes

Preface

1. With very few exceptions, the interviews are now housed with the Southern Oral History Program, Southern Historical Collection, Wilson Library, University of North Carolina at Chapel Hill. See appendix B for a complete list.

Introduction

1. While there are few local histories of the twentieth-century rural South, those that exist are excellent: Melissa Walker, *All We Knew Was to Farm: Rural Women in the Upcountry South, 1919–1941* (Baltimore, Md.: Johns Hopkins University Press, 2002); Rebecca Sharpless, *Fertile Ground, Narrow Choices: Women on Texas Cotton Farms, 1900–1940* (Chapel Hill: University of North Carolina Press, 1999); Joe W. Trotter, *Coal, Class, and Color: Blacks in Southern West Virginia, 1915–32* (Urbana: University of Illinois Press, 1990). Local studies of the nineteenth-century rural South are more common. One fine example describes a county adjacent to Hancock: Jonathan Bryant, *How Curious a Land: Conflict and Change in Greene County, Georgia, 1850–1885* (Chapel Hill: University of North Carolina Press, 1996).

2. James C. Cobb has argued that the Mississippi Delta is not a living relic surviving from a sort of generic premodern southern past, as it has long been treated by scholars. Rather, it was one of the most aggressively modernizing sections of the South (Cobb, *The Most Southern Place on Earth: The Mississippi Delta and the Roots of Regional Identity* [New York: Oxford University Press, 1992]).

3. Statistics in James C. Bonner, "Profile of a Late Ante-Bellum Community," *American Historical Review* 49 (1944): 663–80. See also Forrest Shivers, *The Land*

Between: A History of Hancock County, Georgia, to 1940 (Spartanburg, S.C.: Reprint Company, 1990), 1–6, 66–86.

4. Shivers, *The Land Between*, passim; John Rozier, *Black Boss: Political Revolution in a Georgia County* (Athens: University of Georgia Press, 1982), 1–19.

5. Rozier, *Black Boss.*

6. The term *personalism* seems to have been coined by David M. Potter in his writing on the agrarian folk culture of the antebellum South. It was further developed by Michael P. Johnson and James L. Roark to describe "the bonds of familiarity" connecting members of the mulatto elite and their white patrons in antebellum Charleston. See Potter, *The South and the Sectional Conflict* (Baton Rouge: Louisiana State University Press, 1968), 15–16; Johnson and Roark, *No Chariot Let Down: Charleston's Free People of Color on the Eve of the Civil War* (New York: Norton, 1984), 10–15.

7. The old German adage "city air makes a man free" (Stadtluft macht frei) worked only for those whose race was not an identifying badge of caste.

8. Barbara Fields, "Ideology and Race in American History," in *Region, Race, and Reconstruction: Essays in Honor of C. Vann Woodward*, ed. J. Morgan Kousser and James M. McPherson (New York: Oxford University Press, 1982), 143–77.

9. The terms *premodern* and *modern* must be used with humility and openness to nuance. Societies modernize in different ways and at different paces, not according to a universal template. "Premodern" attributes persist in the most "modern" societies. I nevertheless use the terms repeatedly because I can find no others to describe the changes I see in Hancock.

10. For recent glimpses of the complex reality underlying "solid South" mythologies, see R. Douglas Hurt, ed., *African American Life in the Rural South, 1900–1950* (Columbia: University of Missouri Press, 2003); Suzanne Lebsock, *A Murder in Virginia: Southern Justice on Trial* (New York: Norton, 2003); Greta de Jong, *A Different Day: African American Struggles for Justice in Rural Louisiana, 1900–1970* (Chapel Hill: University of North Carolina Press, 2002); J. Douglas Smith, *Managing White Supremacy: Race, Politics, and Citizenship in Jim Crow Virginia* (Chapel Hill: University of North Carolina Press, 2002); J. William Harris, *Deep Souths: Delta, Piedmont, and Sea Island Society in the Age of Segregation* (Baltimore, Md.: Johns Hopkins University Press, 2001); William Chafe et al., eds., *Remembering Jim Crow: African Americans Tell about Life in the Segregated South* (New York: New Press, 2001); Jane Dailey, *Before Jim Crow: The Politics of Race in Postemancipation Virginia* (Chapel Hill: University of North Carolina Press, 2000); Grace Elizabeth Hale, *Making Whiteness: The Culture of Segregation in the South, 1890–1940* (New York: Vintage, 1998); Laura F. Edwards, *Gendered Strife and Confusion: The Political Culture of Reconstruction* (Urbana: University of Illinois Press, 1997); Glenda Elizabeth Gilmore, *Gender and Jim Crow: Women and the Politics of White Supremacy in North Carolina, 1896–1920* (Chapel Hill: University of North Carolina Press, 1996); John Egerton, *Speak Now against the Day: The Generation before the Civil Rights Movement in the South* (Chapel

Hill: University of North Carolina Press, 1994); Edward L. Ayers, *The Promise of the New South: Life after Reconstruction* (New York: Oxford University Press, 1992); Robin D. G. Kelley, *Hammer and Hoe: Alabama Communists during the Great Depression* (Chapel Hill: University of North Carolina Press, 1990); Neil R. McMillen, *Dark Journey: Black Mississippians in the Age of Jim Crow* (Urbana: University of Illinois Press, 1990).

11. Leon Litwack, *Trouble in Mind: Black Southerners in the Age of Jim Crow* (New York: Knopf, 1998).

12. Stanley Elkins, *Slavery: A Problem in American Institutional and Intellectual Life* (Chicago: University of Chicago Press, 1959).

13. Gilmore, *Gender and Jim Crow*, xxii.

14. There are notable exceptions. Theodore Rosengarten's classic biography of Ned Cobb (called "Nate Shaw" in his text), on which Cobb collaborated, remains one of American historiography's most vivid depictions of personal resistance to oppression; see Rosengarten, *All God's Dangers: The Life of Nate Shaw* (1974; New York: Vintage, 1989). Other autobiographies of the period also touch this theme; see also Kelly, *Hammer and Hoe*.

15. The attendance demographics for Chicago's Grant Park music festivals reflect this white nonrecognition of black sacred music. Whereas the Blues Festival draws an overwhelmingly white audience, the audience at the Gospel Festival is almost exclusively black.

Chapter 1

1. Interview, Carlton Morse, July 6, 1991. Morse's story is exceptional. His education returned to his parents' control when they resumed their more independent status as renters. He later overcame extraordinary obstacles to continue his education. He earned his B.A. from Georgia State Industrial College, in Savannah, and his M.A. from Atlanta University in 1951, and he then joined the first wave of black students to enter southern white universities, earning a doctorate at the University of Oklahoma in 1959. In 1948 he returned to Sparta to serve as principal of Sparta's black high school for a decade before joining the faculty at Fort Valley State College.

2. Interview, Katie Hunt, June 15, 1990, and Sept. 25, 1995. Hunt told me the story several times over a decade.

3. Leon Litwack, *Trouble in Mind: Black Southerners in the Age of Jim Crow* (New York: Knopf, 1998); Jay R. Mandle, *Not Slave, Not Free: The African American Economic Experience since the Civil War* (Durham, N.C.: Duke University Press, 1992); Jonathan M. Wiener, *Social Origins of the New South: Alabama, 1860–1885* (Baton Rouge: Louisiana State University Press, 1978).

4. See, for example, David Cecelski, *The Waterman's Song: Slavery and Freedom in Maritime North Carolina* (Chapel Hill: University of North Carolina Press, 2001); Ira

Berlin, *Many Thousands Gone: The First Two Centuries of Slavery in North America* (Cambridge, Mass.: Harvard University Press, 1998).

5. For an overview of southern agriculture after the Civil War, see Joseph P. Reidy, *From Slavery to Agrarian Capitalism in the Cotton Plantation South, Central Georgia, 1800–1880* (Chapel Hill: University of North Carolina Press, 1992); Jack Temple Kirby, *Rural Worlds Lost: The American South, 1920–1960* (Baton Rouge: Louisiana State University Press, 1987); Gavin Wright, *Old South, New South: Revolutions in the Southern Economy since the Civil War* (New York: Basic Books, 1986); Pete Daniel, *Breaking the Land: The Transformation of Cotton, Tobacco, and Rice Cultures since 1880* (Urbana: University of Illinois Press, 1985); Gilbert C. Fite, *Cotton Fields No More: Southern Agriculture, 1865–1980* (Urbana: University of Illinois Press, 1984); Charles L. Flynn Jr., *White Land, Black Labor: Caste and Class in Late Nineteenth Century Georgia* (Baton Rouge: Louisiana State University Press, 1983). For insights into the daily work experiences of black southern farmers during this period, see Robin Kelly, *Hammer and Hoe: Alabama Communists during the Great Depression* (Chapel Hill: University of North Carolina Press, 1990); and Theodore Rosengarten, *All God's Dangers: The Life of Nate Shaw* (New York: Avon, 1974). For poor white southern farmers, see Wayne Flynt, *Poor but Proud: Alabama's Poor Whites* (Tuscaloosa: University of Alabama Press, 1989); and Harry Crews, *A Childhood: The Biography of a Place* (New York: Harper and Row, 1978). White planters seem to have lost both their mystique and their students once they entered the twentieth century.

6. W. E. B. Du Bois, *The Negro American Family* (Atlanta: Atlanta University Press, 1908), 127.

7. Two excellent studies of varying ways that different southern subregions approached the land are J. William Harris, *Deep Souths: Delta, Piedmont, and Sea Island Society in the Age of Segregation* (Baltimore, Md.: Johns Hopkins University Press, 2001); and Daniel, *Breaking the Land*. Harris warns that distance from the market may have been neither intentional nor an unmixed blessing. The areas in which farmers most emphasized subsistence over market production lay on the outskirts of the transportation and capitalizing network that drove the market economy. He also notes that the inhabitants of these areas, such as the Sea Islands, are customarily seen as the poorest of southerners (Harris, *Deep Souths*, 16, 25–26, 144, 252).

8. For the "rationalized" southern economy, see James C. Cobb, *The Most Southern Place on Earth: The Mississippi Delta and the Roots of Regional Identity* (New York: Oxford University Press, 1992); Dwight Billings, *Planters and the Making of a "New South": Class, Politics, and Development in North Carolina, 1865–1900* (Chapel Hill: University of North Carolina Press, 1992).

9. Of the many excellent studies of Reconstruction, see especially Eric Foner, *Reconstruction: America's Unfinished Revolution, 1863–1877* (New York: Harper and Row, 1988); and Leon F. Litwack, *Been in the Storm So Long: The Aftermath of Slavery* (New York: Knopf, 1979).

10. The strong literature describing the rise of sharecropping includes Reidy, *From*

Slavery to Agrarian Capitalism; Gerald David Jaynes, *Branches without Roots: Genesis of the Black Working Class in the American South, 1862–1882* (New York: Oxford University Press, 1986); Roger L. Ransom and Richard Sutch, *One Kind of Freedom: The Economic Consequences of Emancipation* (New York: Cambridge University Press, 1977); Flynn, *White Land, Black Labor.*

11. Kirby, *Rural Worlds Lost,* 1–22.

12. Daniel, *Breaking the Land,* 155–68.

13. According to Gilbert Fite in *Cotton Fields No More,* twentieth-century southern poverty was caused by too many farmers trying to work worn-out soil without using modern farm machinery. Accordingly, Fite celebrated the "Southern enclosure movement," which swept dependent farmers from the land during the New Deal.

14. Wright, *Old South, New South,* 64–80.

15. John Dittmer, *Black Georgia in the Progressive Era, 1900–1920* (Urbana: University of Illinois Press, 1977), 82–86, 114–15; Pete Daniel, *The Shadow of Slavery: Peonage in the South, 1901–1969* (Urbana: University of Illinois Press, 1972); Numan V. Bartley, *The Creation of Modern Georgia* (Athens: University of Georgia Press, 1983), 155–56.

16. Interview, J. E. Johnson, Nov. 20, 1988, and July 21, 2003.

17. Wright, *Old South, New South,* 75.

18. Forrest Shivers, *The Land Between: A History of Hancock County, Georgia, to 1940* (Spartanburg, S.C.: Reprint Company, 1990), 174.

19. Nell Irvin Painter, *The Exodusters: Black Migration to Kansas after Reconstruction* (New York: Knopf, 1977).

20. Hancock County Tax Digest, 1917–21, Georgia State Archives, Atlanta. Only Ossie Cook, a white yeoman farmer born in 1895, remembered that sharecroppers had done unusually well during World War I, well enough to buy Briscoe cars (interview, Cook, Mar. 23, 1992).

21. Interview, Mary Wilson, May 20, 1995.

22. Shivers, *The Land Between,* 296; Louis I. Skinner, County Extension Agent Annual Reports, Hancock County, 1921, U.S. Department of Agriculture, Record Group 33, National Archives.

23. Interview, Mary Hunt, July 21, 1995.

24. Interview, Marshall Boyer, Aug. 9, 1995; Agricultural Census of the United States, 1920 and 1930; United States Census, 1920 and 1930.

25. "Report of C. P. Barnes on Economic Background of Lower Piedmont Inhabitants," in "Application of the Regents of the University System of Georgia for F.S.A. Development, Lower Piedmont Section," binder A, box 350, Farm Security Administration, 1935–40, Record Group 96, National Archives, 8; J. B. Stevens, "Negro County Extension Agent Annual Report," Hancock County, Georgia, 1930, U.S. Department of Agriculture, Record Group 33, National Archives.

26. Interview, Katie Bell Hunt, May 18, 1995. A box file at the Hancock County Courthouse entitled simply "Foreclosures" is stuffed with notes from 1922 to 1924.

27. Interview, Jewell Thompson, Aug. 9, 1995.

28. Interview, Sid Trawick, Feb. 3, 1994; Trawick General Store ledgers, 1890s–1950s. Shortly after Trudy Trawick allowed me to examine the Trawick ledgers in Linton, the store burned, destroying all records.

29. Interview, J. E. Johnson, Nov. 20, 1988. Johnson remembered that one black sharecropper refused to have his debt written off, saying a young man shouldn't take help from an old man. Over time, he repaid his full debt of six hundred dollars.

30. Harris, *Deep Souths*, 249–53; Arthur Raper, *Preface to Peasantry: A Tale of Two Black Belt Counties* (Chapel Hill: University of North Carolina Press, 1936), 191; "Report of C. P. Barnes," 7; witness testimony in *State v. Non Simpson, John Ellis, and Charlie Simpson*, 1920, file entitled "Hancock County Cases #3," Hancock County Courthouse.

31. On the rise of market dependency in the nineteenth century, see Stephen Hahn, *The Roots of Southern Populism* (New York: Oxford University Press, 1983), 20–40, 139–52; Harris, *Deep Souths*, 36–37, 84–85. See also Susan Strasser, *Satisfaction Guaranteed: The Making of the American Mass Market* (Washington, D.C.: Smithsonian Institution Press, 1989); T. J. Jackson Lears, *The Culture of Consumption: Critical Essays in American History, 1880–1980* (New York: Knopf, 1983); Crews, *A Childhood*, 53–54.

32. Grace Elizabeth Hale, *Making Whiteness: The Culture of Segregation in the South, 1890–1940* (New York: Vintage, 1998), 121–97; Edward Ayers, *The Promise of the New South: Life after Reconstruction* (New York: Oxford University Press, 1993), 81–103; Ted Ownby, *American Dreams in Mississippi: Consumers, Poverty and Culture, 1830–1998* (Chapel Hill: University of North Carolina Press, 1999); Raper, *Preface to Peasantry*, 86, 174.

33. I owe this idea to a conversation with Melissa Walker. I thank Jim Mattera and Don Schultz for helping me analyze the ledgers.

34. Interview, Eva Reese, Sept. 23, 2001; "Annual Report of Home Demonstration Agent, Hancock County," 1940 and 1942, U.S. Department of Agriculture, Record Group 33, National Archives; on the mattress project, see Melissa Walker, *All We Knew Was to Farm: Rural Women in the Upcountry South, 1919–1941* (Baltimore, Md.: Johns Hopkins University Press, 2002), 130–31; interview, Henrietta Glover, June 13, 2000.

35. Interview, Willie Butts, July 18, 1995.

36. Interview, Marvin Turner, Sept. 2, 1994.

37. Telephone interview, Katie Hunt, Oct. 4, 1995. Three groundbreaking new studies have used the experience of women to trace the outlines of the twentieth-century culture of rural self-sufficiency and its transition to consumerism: Lu Ann Jones, *Momma Learned Us to Work: Farm Women in the New South* (Chapel Hill: University of North Carolina Press, 2002); Walker, *All We Knew*; Rebecca Sharpless, *Fertile Ground, Narrow Choices: Women on Texas Cotton Farms, 1900–1940* (Chapel Hill: University of North Carolina Press, 1999). According to the white sharecropper Newton Boyer, "We didn't get much out of that cotton, just a drawing card: rent, fertilizer (interview, Boyer, June 13, 2000).

38. Jones, *Momma Learned Us*; Walker, *All We Knew*; Sharpless, *Fertile Ground*.

39. Jones, *Momma Learned Us;* Walker, *All We Knew;* Sharpless, *Fertile Ground;* ledgers of Trawick General Store, Linton, 1900–1950; ledgers of Williamson General Store, rural Hancock, west of Linton, 1920–23; ledgers of Lowe Store, Carrs, 1916–1950. Copies of the Williamson and Lowe ledgers are being placed in the Hargrett Rare Books and Manuscripts Collection, main library, University of Georgia. Inexplicably, 62 percent of all customers at the Lowe store made at least one purchase of meat in 1922. By 1925 fewer than half were purchasing meat again. I thank Jim Mattera and Don Schultz for assisting me in analyzing the ledgers.

40. U.S. Agricultural Census, 1910–40. Arthur Raper found that cotton production in Green County tumbled and food production doubled there from 1927 to 1934 (Raper, *Preface to Peasantry,* 35, 111).

41. County Extension Agent Annual Reports, Hancock County, 1938. By this estimate, about 30 percent of Hancock's farmers did not own a cow.

42. Interview, James Wilson, July 16, 1995.

43. Interview, Ralph Walker, Sept. 2, 1994.

44. Ledgers of Trawick, Williamson, Boyer, and Lowe general stores.

45. Interview, Francis Frazier, July 20, 1995.

46. Interview, A. J. Parker, July 15, 1995; interview, Earnest and Annie Macklin, July 18, 1995. Tom Harrison separately concurred that he has given away milk, vegetables, and fruit to his neighbors, black and white. He noted that he couldn't sell or preserve it all, so it only made sense to give it away (interview, Harrison, Oct. 1991). Orville Vernon Burton also noted that black and white sharecroppers shared equipment and traded labor with one another; see Burton, "Race Relations in the Rural South Since 1945," in *The Rural South since World War II,* ed. R. Douglas Hurt (Baton Rouge: Louisiana State University Press, 1998), 32.

47. Interview, James Wilson.

48. Interview, Eva Reese.

49. Interview, Mary Hunt.

50. Interview, Josie Mae Ingram, July 12, 1995.

51. Interview, Seleta (Boyer) Lyon, daughter of Newton and Carrie Boyer, Oct. 1, 1992. Because of this, the great majority of farming families throughout this period were headed by two adults. In samples drawn from the census manuscripts in the first decades of the twentieth century, from 85 to 93 percent of rural black families had two adult heads. I thank Don Schultz for compiling these figures. Charles S. Johnson found that 70 percent of the 612 black families he studied in Macon County, Alabama, lived in these kinds of households (Johnson, *Shadow of the Plantation* [Chicago: University of Chicago Press, 1934], 33).

52. Interview, Mamie Washington, July 28, 1995.

53. Interview, Earnest Macklin, July 18, 1995.

54. The studies (by Arthur Raper in Greene County, on the northern border of Hancock, and by the Phelps-Stokes Fund in four upper piedmont counties) are described in Harris, *Deep Souths,* 257–60.

55. Albert E. Cowdrey, *This Land, This South: An Environmental History* (Lexington: University Press of Kentucky, 1996), 156–57.

56. *Sparta Ishmaelite*, undated clippings taped into Mary Blount's 1941 Hancock County Home Demonstration Report. Jernigan himself stated that in Georgia as a whole, malnutrition did rank as the primary reason for rejection.

57. Interview, Willie Butts, July 19, 1995. Historians have recorded a string of "definitive turning points" in the transition from "precapitalist" to "capitalist" society in the United States. Given the persistence of subsistence strategies, it might be more useful to reframe the question. Perhaps we could more profitably begin by assuming that an international system of trade has—in one way or another—connected Americans with the larger capitalist system from the earliest period of settlement. We might then be free to explore the many various ways that different people have used the market and how they in turn have been used by it. For the integration of market and subsistence farming, see Alan Kulikoff, "Households and Markets: Toward a New Synthesis of American Agrarian History," *William and Mary Quarterly* 50 (Apr. 1993): 342–55; and Kulikoff, "The Transition to Capitalism in Rural America," *William and Mary Quarterly* 46 (Jan. 1989): 120–44.

58. Interview, David Harper, Sept. 15, 1994.

59. Interview, Julia Hillman, July 14, 1995.

60. Interview, James Wilson, July 18, 1995; interviews, John Kendrick, Melvin Leslie Sr., and Rosa Chappel, summer 2002. For a superb narrative of the skills needed to farm through a season, see Rosengarten, *All God's Dangers*, 177–92.

61. Georgia counties are subdivided into militia districts for purposes of taxation and census taking.

62. Hancock County Tax Digest and Census Manuscripts.

63. U.S. Agricultural Census, 1910–40; U.S. Census, 1910–40.

64. Interview, Roberta Andrews, June 4, 1992; interview, Creasy Walker, Sept. 8, 1994. Mary Lattimore stated that plowing was the sole male-only aspect of farming in her community (interview, Mary Lattimore, July 6, 1995). For an insightful discussion of the tenant family at work, see Stewart E. Tolnay, *The Bottom Rung: African American Family Life on Southern Farms* (Urbana: University of Ilinois Press, 1999), 25–119.

65. Of all young black men in the Mayfield area at the time of the draft, 92 percent had been born in that area. Other areas had a somewhat higher percentage of residents born outside the militia district. For example, 68 percent of Culverton men and 67 percent of Jewell men had been born in their respective districts. In every district but one, the percentage of locally born white men was several percentage points lower than that of black men. Undoubtedly they found a wider range of employment options around the county and did not rely so much on their local reputation with planters for work.

66. Interview, J. E. Johnson, Nov. 20, 1988; interview, Sanford Butts, Dec. 29, 1988.

67. Agricultural Census, 1910 and 1920. After 1920 Hancock's land tenure data in the Agricultural Census become unreliable because half of all tenants are listed as "unspecified" as to their exact form of land tenure. The relative proportions of sharecroppers and renters probably did not change significantly. Arthur Raper found similar percentages in Greene County during the 1920s. There, white tenants divided evenly among sharecroppers, share renters, and cash renters. Some 54 percent of black tenants were sharecroppers; 13 percent, cash renters; and about 33 percent, share renters. See Harris, *Deep Souths*, 133–34, for landlords' rationale for strongly preferring sharecropping to renting in the Mississippi Delta. Renters took most of the risks and kept most of their profits, while sharecroppers passed most of both along to the landlord. In the less fertile piedmont, however, the reliability of rent may have outweighed other factors in the eyes of planters.

68. Agricultural Census, 1910–40. On variations of this sharecropping format, see Daniel, *Breaking the Land*, 162, 166–67; Harris, *Deep Souths*, 132; Harold D. Woodman, *King Cotton and His Retainers: Financing and Marketing the Cotton Crop of the South, 1800–1925* (Lexington: University Press of Kentucky, 1968); Enoch M. Banks, *The Economics of Land Tenure in Georgia* (Franklin Square, N.Y.: Columbia University Press, 1905).

69. Interview, Mary Lattimore; interview, Tom Harrison Sr., Oct. 1991. In another unusual arrangement, Harrison offered the wives of his tenants one-third of a crop for chopping and picking on land he would plow.

70. Qtd. in Neil R. McMillen, *Dark Journey: Black Mississippians in the Age of Jim Crow* (Urbana: University of Illinois Press, 1990), 132. Wright, *Old South, New South*, 112–13; Ransom and Sutch, *One Kind of Freedom*, 137–46. J. E. Johnson, a planter, and Sanford Butts, a merchant, made regular loans during these years. They said that they had charged 10 percent interest on loans to furnish farmers with food and 8 percent for houses and furniture. Butts remembered accepting small payments from debtors over a long period because he "knew they were poor and would pay as they could" (interview, Johnson, Nov. 12 and 20, 1988; interview, Butts, Dec. 29, 1989).

71. Interview, Mary Lattimore; interview, Annie Macklin, July 18, 1995; interview, Josie Ingram; interview, Hyndenberg Dixon, July 11, 1995. Planters sometimes also seized furniture, tools, and other possessions. Macklin remembered that when the boll weevil came, a planter confiscated all the possessions of a neighbor, including her washtub.

72. Interview, Hyndenberg Dixon; interview, Mary Worthening; interview, anonymous, Sept. 19, 1994; W. E. B. Du Bois and A. G. Dill, eds., *The Negro American Artisan*, Atlanta University Publications, no. 17 (Atlanta: Atlanta University Press, 1912), 135.

73. Interview, McMullen, 1988. Earnest Jack Ingram related a similar story in which his grandfather, a black sharecropper, was congratulated by a planter for breaking even. But he had held back five bales. When the planter found out, "he said he'd found another bill he misplaced. Took it all." His grandfather quit cotton and moved to Florida soon after (interview, Ingram, June 30, 2004). For another version of this

248 · NOTES TO PAGES 36–44

story, see Jimmy Carter, *An Hour before Daylight: Memories of a Rural Boyhood* (New York: Simon and Schuster, 2001), 52.

74. Interview, Oline Thomas, June 13, 1995 ("Cheat you if they could"); interview, Mary Worthening, June 22, 1995; interview, Leslie Barksdale, Feb. 17, 1995; interview, Mamie Washington; Jane Maguire, *On Shares: Ed Brown's Story* (New York: Norton, 1975), 189; Rosengarten, *All God's Dangers;* interview, Clinton Pearson, Aug. 3, 1995.

75. Interview, Mary Worthening. For a discussion of theft as self-defense, see Greta de Jong, *A Different Day: African American Struggles for Justice in Rural Louisiana, 1900–1970* (Chapel Hill: University of North Carolina Press, 2002), 46–48.

76. Interview, Creasy Walker, Sept. 8, 1996.

77. Interview, anonymous; interview James Wilson, July 16, 1995.

78. On the Alabama Sharecroppers' Union, see Rosengarten, *All God's Dangers;* and Kelley, *Hammer and Hoe.* On the Southern Tenant Farmers' Union, see H. L. Mitchell, *Mean Things Happening in This Land: The Life and Times of H. L. Mitchell* (Montclair, N.J.: Allenheld, Osmun, 1979); and Donald H. Grubbs, *Cry from the Cotton: The Southern Tenant Farmer's Union and the New Deal* (Chapel Hill: University of North Carolina Press, 1971).

79. Thomas W. Kremm and Diane Neal, "Challenges to Subordination: Organized Black Agricultural Protest in South Carolina, 1886–1895," *South Atlantic Quarterly* 77 (1978): 102; *Sparta Ishmaelite,* August 22, 1901, and May 28, 1909.

80. For contrasting views arguing for the effectiveness of African American organization in the rural South, see Kelley, *Hammer and Hoe;* Patricia Sullivan, *Days of Hope: Race and Democracy in the New Deal Era* (Chapel Hill: University of North Carolina Press, 1996).

81. *Sparta Ishmaelite,* September 22, 1905, and May 18, 1906.

82. Ibid., May 18, 1906; interview, Walter Green, Jan. 2, 1998.

83. Interview, Oline Thomas; interview, Mamie Washington; interview, David Harper; interview, James Wilson, July 16, 1995; interview, Mary Hunt.

84. Interview, Carlton Morse, July 7, 1995; interview, Earnest Macklin.

85. Interview, Marshall Boyer, Aug. 9, 1995; interview, Obilee Rhodes Sr., Sept. 1992; Rev. James R. Brown, *Jackleg Preacher* (New York: Carlton, 1989), 11, 33 (Brown grew up near Devereux, in Hancock County); interview, Earnest Jack Ingram.

86. Interview, Mamie Washington; interview, Oline Thomas; interview, Josie Mae Ingram; interview, David Harper; interview, Essie Mae Primer, June 27, 1995.

Chapter 2

1. Interview, Mary Worthening, June 22, 1995; interview, Leslie Barksdale, Feb. 17, 1995; interview, Calvin Travis, Aug. 9, 1994; Anthony M. Tang, *Economic Development in the Southern Piedmont, 1860–1950* (Chapel Hill: University of North Carolina Press, 1958), 179.

2. Although historians have devoted nearly all their attention to the experience of the dependent majority of poor black farmers, rural sociologists from the 1920s through the 1940s conducted an impressive number of studies that explored the contradictions between the concrete presence of middle-class black southerners and the abstract logic of the caste system. See the writings of W. E. B. Du Bois, Charles S. Johnson, Arthur Raper, John Dollard, Hortense Powdermaker, and Allison Davis, Burleigh B. Gardner, and Mary B. Gardner.

3. Loren Schweninger, *Black Property Owners in the South, 1790–1915* (Urbana: University of Illinois Press, 1990). See also Adrienne Monteith Petty, "Standing Their Ground: Small Farm Owners in North Carolina's Tobacco Belt, 1920–1982" (Ph.D. diss., Columbia University, 2004); J. William Harris, *Deep Souths: Delta, Piedmont, and Sea Island Society in the Age of Segregation* (Baltimore, Md.: Johns Hopkins University Press, 2001), 15–16, 22–23, 36, 47, 51, 53, 103, 137; Peggy G. Hargis, "Beyond the Marginality Thesis: The Acquisition and Loss of Land by African Americans in Georgia, 1880–1930," *Agricultural History* 72 (Spring 1998): 241–62; Valerie Grim, "African American Landlords in the Rural South, 1870–1950: A Profile," *Agricultural History* 72 (Spring 1998): 399–416; Robert Tracy McKenzie, "Freedmen and the Soil in the Upper South: The Reorganization of Tennessee Agriculture, 1865–1880," *Journal of Southern History* 59 (Feb. 1993): 63–84; Elizabeth Rauh Bethel, *Promiseland: A Century of Life in a Negro Community* (Philadelphia: Temple University Press, 1981); Janet Sharp Hermann, *The Pursuit of a Dream* (Jackson: University Press of Mississippi, 1981). The high proportion of black landowners in the Upper South is due to two factors. It seems that upward mobility was indeed easier for African Americans in the Upper South than for those in the Lower South. The statistics of success are somewhat inflated, however, because many landless black farmers moved from the Upper South to the Lower South in the years after the Civil War, drawn by the promise of higher wages.

4. U.S. Agricultural Census, 1910. In the same year 51 percent of white Georgia farmers were landowners.

5. John Dittmer, *Black Georgia in the Progressive Era, 1900–1920* (Urbana: University of Illinois Press, 1977), 24–26; U.S. Census, *Negro Population in the United States, 1790–1915* (Washington, D.C.: GPO, 1918), 712–15.

6. Hancock County Tax Digests, Georgia State Archives, Atlanta; Census Manuscripts.

7. Hancock County Tax Digests, 1880–1950; interview, Oline Thomas, June 13, 1995. The trajectory of black landownership in Hancock matches that of Georgia until 1930, as detailed in Hargis, "Beyond the Marginality Thesis," 241–62.

8. Hancock County Tax Digests, 1874–1950.

9. For the Hubert story, see an excellent family history written by Lester F. Russell, *Profile of a Black Heritage* (Franklin Square, N.Y.: Graphicopy, 1977), 45–53; deed record U, 413–14, Hancock County Courthouse; Mark Schultz, "A More Satisfying

Life on the Farm: Benjamin F. Hubert and the Log Cabin Community" (master's thesis, University of Georgia, 1989).

10. Interview, Mary Simmons, July 26, 1995; interview, Walter Green Clayton, Jan. 2, 1998.

11. Interview, Mary Hunt, July 21, 1995; interview, Emmie Mae Harper, Sept. 23, 1994.

12. A comparison of the county soil survey with the location of black landowners (ascertainable in the tax digests) reveals that black landowners were most concentrated on the Cesil gravely loam and Cesil clay loam soils in the northern part of the county. They were far less common in the southern part of the county, with its infertile Norfolk sand, or in the moderately fertile and flat Cesil sandy loam belt running through the center of the county (1909 Soil Survey of Hancock County, U.S. Department of Agriculture, Bureau of Soils, in Map Collection, Science Library, University of Georgia, Athens).

13. Arthur Raper noted that in Greene County, black would-be purchasers of land often had to be content with substandard land (Raper, *Preface to Peasantry: A Tale of Two Black Belt Counties* (Chapel Hill: University of North Carolina Press, 1936), 122.

14. Interview, Emmie Mae Harper. With as much as 2,000 acres, Gordon and Betsy Dixon ranked among the largest black landowners in Hancock. In the family history written by their daughter, the recurring themes are God's providence and Betsy's ceaseless labor to feed their eighteen children. According to the history, when Gordon "was buying a tract of land, sometimes he did not tell his wife until after he had made the trade. She would work so hard and sometimes more than she should to help pay the bill." Her daughter believed Betsy worked herself to death. "Oh Betsy worked so hard! . . . She passed away long before Gordon. We did hate to see her go. The Lord wanted her to get some rest. We had to think of that" (Mary J. Dixon Williams Moss, *A Profile of the Dixon Family* [Smithtown, N.Y.: Exposition, 1980], 9, 5).

15. Raper, *Preface to Peasantry*, 121–23.

16. For an exploration of the significance of interracial kinship to black landowning in several middle Georgia counties, see Mark Schultz, "Interracial Kinship Ties and the Emergence of a Rural Black Middle Class: Hancock County, Georgia, 1865–1920," in *Georgia in Black and White: Explorations in the Race Relations of a Southern State, 1865–1950*, ed. John Inscoe (Athens: University of Georgia Press, 1994), 141–72. Kent Anderson Leslie, *Woman of Color, Daughter of Privilege: Amanda America Dickson, 1849–1893* (Athens: University of Georgia Press, 1996); Moss, *Profile of the Dixon Family*; interview, Samuel Williams, around 1994. Williams was Gordon and Betsy Dixon's grandson and grew up in their home. Over several days in September 1994, Katie Hunt, Mae Warren, and I worked through the names of the wealthiest blacks in Hancock as listed in the tax digests every ten years from 1880 to 1950. They remembered the names of all the wealthiest and knew many of them personally.

17. Deborah Gray White, *Too Heavy a Load: Black Women in Defense of Themselves, 1894–1994* (New York: Norton, 1999); Glenda Elizabeth Gilmore, *Gender and Jim Crow:*

Women and the Politics of White Supremacy in North Carolina, 1896–1920 (Chapel Hill: University of North Carolina Press, 1996); Willard Gatewood, *Aristocrats of Color: The Black Elite, 1880–1920* (Bloomington: Indiana University Press, 1990). Although the subjects of these studies are urban, a consciousness of the ideal they promoted may be seen to a degree among privileged rural black families, too.

18. Russell, *Profile*, 61, 65–68, 70–71; *Sparta Ishmaelite*, Mar. 17, 1926. Ingram had a reputation among Hancock's African Americans for being odd, so perhaps his behavior was not related to fear of white jealousy.

19. Interview, Katie Hunt, June 15, 1990, and Sept. 25, 1995; interview, Mae Warren, June 15, 1990, and Sept. 25, 1995.

20. Interview, Roy Roberts, Aug. 31, 1992.

21. Many interviews, Hancock County, 1988–96.

22. Ibid.; school attendance rolls for Hancock County, Georgia Department of Education, Georgia Department of Archives, Atlanta. Rosenwald Schools were well-built rural schools, often with more than one teacher, that were constructed with matching contributions from black parents, the state, and the Julius Rosenwald Foundation; see James Anderson, *The Education of Blacks in the South, 1860–1935* (Chapel Hill: University of North Carolina Press, 1988), 153–85.

23. Many interviews, Hancock County, 1988–96. I have found only one occasion in which even the son of a black landowner became the target of white violence in Hancock—and many incidents in which white men beat, raped, or killed poorer African Americans. On lynching as directed disproportionately against landless men, see Edward Ayers, *The Promise of the New South: Life after Reconstruction* (New York: Oxford University Press, 1993), 157–58.

24. Interview, Samuel Williams, Dec. 12, 1989.

25. Interview, Beautine Hubert DeCosta-Lee, Oct. 6, 2001; interview, Clifford and Eva Smith, Aug. 10, 1992; Russell, *Profile*, 75–76; interview, Katie Hunt, June 15, 1990, and Sept. 25, 1995; Mark Schultz, "The Dream Realized? African American Landownership in Central Georgia between Reconstruction and World War Two," *Agricultural History* 72 (Spring 1998): 298–312. In his biography the black Alabamian Ned Cobb related that he had once hired poor whites to help him chop his cotton. When they stubbornly continued to call him "Mister," despite Cobb's protests, he grew frightened that other whites might overhear and hate him for it (in Theodore Rosengarten, *All God's Dangers: The Life of Nate Shaw* [1974: New York: Vintage, 1989], 455–56).

26. Interview, Josie Mae Ingram, July 12, 1995.

27. Ibid.

28. U.S. Census, *Negro Population in the United States, 1790–1915*, 92; U.S. Census, *Twelfth Census, Special Report, Occupations, 1900*, 254–56; Daniel E. Sutherland, *Americans and Their Servants: Domestic Service in the United States from 1800 to 1920* (Baton Rouge: Louisiana State University Press, 1981); Tera Hunter, *To 'Joy My Freedom': Southern Black Women's Lives and Labors after the Civil War* (Cambridge, Mass.: Harvard University Press, 1998); Susan Tucker, *Telling Memories among Southern*

Women: Domestic Workers and Their Employers in the Segregated South (New York: Schocken, 1988).

29. Interview, Oline Thomas, June 13, 1995; interview, Eva Reese, Sept. 23, 2001.

30. Interview, Josie Mae Ingram; interview, Ed Jones, July 5, 1992.

31. Interview, Mary Hunt, July 21, 1995; interview, Mary Wilson, Aug. 14, 1995; interview, Josie Mae Ingram. According to the women interviewed for Tucker's *Telling Memories*, the wages paid domestic servants in Louisiana, Alabama, and Florida during the 1920s and 1930s ranged from $2.50 to $3.00 per week.

32. Interview, Mary Wilson; interview, Mary Hunt.

33. Two interesting attempts to assess these relationships are the oral history by Tucker, *Telling Memories;* and a dissertation in American literature by Sonya Jean Lancaster, "The Simmering Stew: Race and Gender in Southern Kitchens" (Ph.D. diss., University of Kansas, 1997).

34. Creasy Walker remembered her father, a renter and small landowner named Anthony Crayton, working "lumber on the side" for many years (interview, Creasy Walker, Sept. 8, 1994). Ned Cobb said that he had worked in sawmills for cash: "[I'd] make me a speck if I could and then go back to my farm, quit and go back to my farm" (in Rosengarten, *All God's Dangers,* 173; see also 39–41, 84–91, 173–77, 193–97). According to Earnest Nicholls, a white Hancock sawmill operator during the 1940s and 1950s, there were between fifty and sixty sawmills in the county during his time in the industry. Each employed about 28 men, with a total of almost 1,600 men working in lumber in the county (interview, Earnest Nicholls, Mar. 30, 1995).

35. For the early development of forestry in Georgia, see I. James Pikl Jr., *A History of Georgia Forestry* (Athens: University of Georgia, Bureau of Business Economics Research, 1966), 6, 9. See also Thomas D. Clark, *The Greening of the South: The Recovery of Land and Forest* (Lexington: University Press of Kentucky, 1984); and Albert E. Cowdrey, *This Land, This South: An Environmental History* (Lexington: University Press of Kentucky, 1996). Although large midwestern timber companies moved their milltowns south from the 1880s to the 1920s and established that region as the nation's largest producer of lumber, it seems that small, locally owned mills typified the industry in Hancock and in most of Georgia; see Pikl, *Georgia Forestry,* 19.

36. Raper, *Preface to Peasantry,* 38, 162, 173, 176–77, 206–11. The first historian to recognize the impact of the weevil on forestry was J. William Harris, who did so in *Deep Souths,* 252.

37. T. W. Anderson, J. H. Sibley, and J. P. Wilkes, "Narrative Reports on the Current Change Survey Drs-109 in Green County, Georgia," "Narrative Reports on the Current Change Survey Drs-109 in Jones County, Georgia," and "Narrative Reports on the Current Change Survey Drs-109 in Jenkins County, Georgia," all in box 3, Rural Relief Reports, 1935, Division of Farm Population and Rural Life, Records of the Bureau of Agricultural Economics, Record Group 83, National Archives: Greene report, 8; Jones report, 1; Jenkins report, 1.

38. Interview, Solomon Harper, Sept. 15, 1994; J. B. Stevens, "Negro County Extension Agent Annual Report," Hancock County, Georgia, 1930, U.S. Department of Agriculture, Record Group 33, National Archives.

39. Cowdrey, *This Land, This South,* 129; Pikl, *Georgia Forestry,* 32.

40. Pickl, *Georgia Forestry,* 6–13; "Report of C. P. Barnes on Economic Background of Lower Piedmont Inhabitants," in "Application of the Regents of the University System of Georgia for F.S.A. Development, Lower Piedmont Section," 7–8 and map, binder A, box 350, Farm Security Administration, 1935–40, Record Group 96, National Archives; Cowdrey, *This Land, This South,* 76.

41. Anderson et al., "Greene County Report," Rural Relief Reports, 8.

42. Interview, Carlton Morse, July 7, 1995; interview, Benjamin Senior, Aug. 29, 1992; interview, Marshall Boyer, date unavailable; interview, Eugene Foster Jr., July 6, 1995.

43. Interview, Mary Hunt; Anderson et al., "Greene County Report," Rural Relief Reports, 8; interview, Benjamin Senior; interview, Eugene Foster Jr. Georgia millworkers averaged ¢11.6 per hour for sixty-hour workweeks in 1933 according to Pikl, *Georgia Forestry,* 29.

44. Interview, Benjamin Senior; interview, J. E. Johnson, Nov. 12, 1988. Johnson loaned money regularly to stonemasons.

45. Interview, Lewis Walls, July 6, 1995; interview, Earnest Nicholls. In Hancock men could usually return home evenings or at least weekends. In contrast, according to Jeffrey A. Drobney, "blacks and whites worked, rode to the logging site, and spent their free time together" in the large, early twentieth-century logging camps of Florida. Drobney attributes this interracial work culture to the isolation of the camps, the common dangers faced, the absence of women, and the men's need to cooperate as crews to maximize their shared pay (Drobney, *Lumbermen and Log Sawyers: Life, Labor, and Culture in the North Florida Timber Industry, 1830–1930* (Macon, Ga.: Mercer University Press, 1997), 85–89.

46. In *State v. Aaron Willis et al.* (1915) Chancy Washington sued for the theft of two quarts of his corn whiskey; *State v. Bishop Reddock* (1921). Both records can be found in a file entitled "Hancock County Criminal Cases #3," Hancock County Courthouse.

47. Apparently ex-moonshiners are only a little more open with historians than they were with the census taker. No one wanted his or her name associated with a bootleg story, of course, so all these oral accounts are presented anonymously. Also, they were provided by people who only dabbled in moonshine or who observed the big operators from outside. The men and women who were identified as belonging to large professional moonshining families all refused to be interviewed, usually politely, although one woman offered to shoot me if I ever came back. It seems they are still suspicious of intruders and the threat of legal action.

48. *State v. John Simmons* (1921), Hancock County Criminal Cases #3, Hancock County Courthouse; *Sparta Ishmaelite,* July, 23, 1998. See Burkhard Bilger, *Noodling*

for Flatheads: Moonshine, Monster Catfish, and Other Southern Comforts (New York: Touchstone, 2002), 63–100.

49. Telephone interview, Gaston Skrine, Sept. 11, 1992; Grand Jury Presentments, Oct. 1919, Hancock County Courthouse.

50. C. Vann Woodward wrote that at the end of the Civil War, black artisans outnumbered white artisans five to one in the South. By 1890 they made up "only a small proportion of the labor force in most crafts" (Woodward, *Origins of the New South* [1951; Baton Rouge: Louisiana State University Press, 1971], 222, 360).

51. Interview, Willie Butts, July 19, 1995; interview, Solomon Harper; interview, Asia Jackson, Sept. 18, 1989; interview, Benjamin Senior; interview, Emment Oliver, around 1992 (from transcript—tape missing).

52. Interview, Solomon Harper; interview, Marshall Boyer; Russell, *Profile*, 70–71.

53. Interview, Marshall Boyer, Sept. 9, 1995.

Chapter 3

1. Few essays examine the social aspects of rural southern race relations. The better ones include Melissa Walker, "Shifting Boundaries: Race Relations in the Rural Jim Crow South," in *African American Life in the Rural South, 1900–1950*, ed. R. Douglas Hurt (Columbia: University of Missouri Press, 2003), 81–107; Jacqueline Jones, "Encounters, Likely and Unlikely, between Black and White Women in the Rural South, 1865–1940," *Georgia Historical Quarterly* 76 (Summer 1992): 333–53; Neil R. McMillen, *Dark Journey: Black Mississippians in the Age of Jim Crow* (Urbana: University of Illinois Press, 1990), 3–32; Jack Temple Kirby, *Rural Worlds Lost: The American South, 1920–1960* (Baton Rouge: Louisiana State University Press, 1987), 232–71.

2. For historiographical essays of the history of segregation, see the excellent introductory essay by John David Smith in *When Did Southern Segregation Begin?* (New York: Bedford, 2002), 3–42. All conversations about segregation begin with C. Vann Woodward, *The Strange Career of Jim Crow*, 3d ed. (New York: Oxford University Press, 1974 [1955]). After all these years this slender volume is still the only full-length study of segregation. Strangely, too, not a single study focuses exclusively on the social aspects of race relations in the rural South after the Civil War. The classical sociological studies of the 1920s and 1930s offer an important window on the social world of race relations in the rural South, as does the growing wealth of rural southern autobiographies. For a few more years oral history may offer the most important source. The essential studies include Grace Elizabeth Hale, *Making Whiteness: The Culture of Segregation in the South, 1890–1940* (New York: Vintage, 1999); Charles Van Onselen, *The Seed Is Mine: The Life of Kas Maine, a South African Sharecropper, 1894–1985* (New York: Hill and Wang, 1996); John W. Cell, *The Highest Stage of White Supremacy: The Origins of Segregation in South Africa and the American*

South (Cambridge: Cambridge University Press, 1982); Howard N. Rabinowitz, *Race Relations in the Urban South, 1865–1890* (Urbana: University of Illinois Press, 1980); Richard C. Wade, *Slavery in the Cities: The South, 1820–1860* (New York: Oxford University Press, 1967); Joel Williamson, *After Slavery: The Negro in South Carolina during Reconstruction, 1861–1877* (Chapel Hill: University of North Carolina Press, 1965); Leon F. Litwack, *North of Slavery: The Negro in the Free States, 1790–1860* (1961; Chicago: University of Chicago Press, 1965).

3. Most of Michel Foucault's work on modernity expressed this sense of the increasing clinicalization of "otherness" and the increasingly interventionist role of the state in regulating behavior. See also Robert H. Wiebe, *The Search for Order, 1877–1920* (1967; New York: Hill and Wang, 1980), although his sharp contrast between "modern" and "premodern" and his teleological arguments should be taken as rhetorical models. In reality, aspects of premodern community persist in urban contexts, as has been shown by Thomas Bender and Seldon M. Kruger in *Community and Social Change in America* (1978; Baltimore, Md.: Johns Hopkins University Press, 2000). For nuanced examinations of the southern conflict between "modern" and "traditional" forces, see James L. Leloudis, *Schooling the New South: Pedagogy, Self, and Society in North Carolina, 1880–1920* (Chapel Hill: University of North Carolina Press, 1996); William Link, *The Paradox of Southern Progressivism, 1880–1930* (Chapel Hill: University of North Carolina Press, 1992); Link, *A Hard Country and a Lonely Place: Schooling, Society, and Reform in Rural Virginia, 1870–1920* (Chapel Hill: University of North Carolina Press, 1986); Cell, *Highest Stage of White Supremacy,* 131–35.

4. For a wonderful exploration of segregation and eugenics as scientific responses to the challenges of modernity, see Gregory Michael Dorr, "Segregation's Science: The American Eugenics Movement and Virginia, 1900–1980" (Ph.D. diss., University of Virginia, 2000).

5. Grace Hale argued that segregation codes were written to protect whites from suffering unflattering comparisons with members of the rising urban black middle class when impersonal market forces gave blacks entry to public spaces (Hale, *Making Whiteness,* 121–97).

6. Rabinowitz argued that whites had moved to exclude blacks from public spaces and that segregation had actually been a reform measure supported by African Americans to replace the even more repugnant fact of exclusion (Rabinowitz, *Race Relations,* 193–97). Unfortunately, Rabinowitz based his arguments on only three New South cities: Atlanta, Richmond (which both had to be rebuilt after the Civil War), and Nashville. These spaces were tabulae rasae on which rising young modernists could implement their agendas free from the influence of tradition. Don H. Doyle corrected this error by comparing truly different cities in *New Men, New Cities, New South: Atlanta, Nashville, Charleston, Mobile, 1860–1910* (Chapel Hill: University of North Carolina Press, 1990). The debate continues, but it seems that the pattern of interracial social relations was far from consistent before the turn of the century, when passage of laws homogenized it. This vindicates Woodward's main point.

7. Kenneth Coleman, ed., *A History of Georgia* (Athens: University of Georgia Press, 1977), 277–78. Although Georgia's 1891 legislature is remembered as the "Alliance legislature," ostensibly representative of rural folk, the Alliance never controlled the body, for it was filled with traditional Democrats who converted to the Alliance platform during the campaign and then promptly broke their promises. Robert C. McMath Jr., author of *Populist Vanguard: A History of the Southern Farmers' Alliance* (Chapel Hill: University of North Carolina Press, 1975) and the leading scholar on the topic, informed me in correspondence that according to research only partly shown in *Populist Vanguard* (116–17), "the dominant force in the Georgia legislature in 1891 was more 'urban' than rural."

8. Neil R. McMillen subtly described how white supremacy was maintained absolutely in Mississippi through the inconsistently applied pressure of custom and violence (McMillen, *Dark Journey*, 3–32, 224–53). See also Donald L. Grant, *The Way It Was in the South: The Black Experience in Georgia* (New York: Birch Lane, 1993), 211–22; John Dittmer, *Black Georgia in the Progressive Era, 1900–1920* (Urbana: University of Illinois, 1977), 8–22; Rabinowitz, *Race Relations;* and of course Woodward, *The Strange Career of Jim Crow,* 67–109.

9. Doyle, *New Men, New Cities;* Thomas W. Hanchett, *Sorting Out the New South City: Race, Class, and Urban Development in Charlotte, 1875–1975* (Chapel Hill: University of North Carolina Press, 1998); Dittmer, *Black Georgia,* 9–16. Hanchett confirms Doyle's argument for late residential segregation. Charlotte was first segregated into a checkerboard of neighborhoods on the basis of race and class only in the 1880s and 1890s. Not until the mid-twentieth century did it undergo massive, modern residential segregation.

10. Interview, John Rozier, Aug. 16, 2002.

11. Interview, A. J. Parker, July 15, 1995.

12. Telephone interview, Mae Warren, May 29, 2002; telephone interview, John Rozier, June 17, 2003; McMillen, *Dark Journey,* 11.

13. Stephen Jay Gould, *The Flamingo's Smile: Reflections in Natural History* (New York: Norton, 1985), 198.

14. W. E. B. Du Bois, *The Souls of Black Folk* (1903; New York: New American Library, 1969), 146.

15. Interview, Lewis Walls, July 6, 1995.

16. Mark Schultz, "A More Satisfying Life on the Farm: Benjamin F. Hubert and the Log Cabin Community" (master's thesis, University of Georgia), 1989; interview, Samuel Williams, Dec. 12, 1989; interview, Calvin Travis, Aug. 9, 1994; Charles S. Johnson, *Patterns of Negro Segregation* (1943; South Bend, Ind.: University of Notre Dame Press, 2001), 267. Some black autobiographies describe rural black southerners' avoiding contact with whites. According to Ned Cobb, his father "shunned white people" whenever he could (Rosengarten, *All God's Dangers: The Life of Nate Shaw* [1974; New York: Vintage, 1989], 48). As Steven Hahn has recently argued, segregation led to separate primary communities and distinctive cultures (Hahn, *A Nation*

under Our Feet: Black Political Struggles in the Rural South from Slavery to the Great Migration [Cambridge, Mass.: Harvard University Press, 2003]).

17. Benjamin E. Mays, *Born to Rebel: An Autobiography* (Athens: University of Georgia Press, 1987), 21, 23.

18. Orville Vernon Burton, "Race Relations in the Rural South since 1945," in *The Rural South since World War II*, ed. R. Douglas Hurt (Baton Rouge: Louisiana State University Press, 1998), 31.

19. This pattern would begin to change as many white planters withdrew from agriculture and moved to the towns and cities. This happened at different times in different places. Paved roads and automobiles improved transportation, which allowed landlords to cover wide spaces to check on their laborers. It became increasingly unnecessary for planters to live in close proximity with their workers.

20. Jack Temple Kirby, "Clarence Poe's Vision of a Segregated 'Great Rural Civilization,'" *South Atlantic Quarterly* 68 (Winter 1969): 27–38; Jeffrey J. Crow, "An Apartheid for the South: Clarence Poe's Crusade for Rural Segregation," in Jeffrey J. Crow, Paul D. Escott, and Charles L. Flynn Jr., eds., *Race, Class, and Politics in Southern History: Essays in Honor of Robert F. Durden* (Baton Rouge: Louisiana State University Press, 1989), 216–59; *Progressive Farmer*, Nov. 8, 1913, p. 36.

21. For the social seclusion of nineteenth-century southern white women, see Jean E. Friedman, *The Enclosed Garden: Women and Community in the Evangelical South, 1830–1900* (Chapel Hill: University of North Carolina Press, 1990). For the twentieth century, see Burton, "Race Relations," 33–34; Hale, *Making Whiteness*, 88.

22. This fits with a story in Margaret J. Hagood's *Mothers of the South: Portraiture of the White Tenant Farm Woman* (1939; New York: Norton, 1977). Hagood, a sociologist, asked a rural white southerner where the nearest school was, and the woman described a white school a fair distance away. Hagood soon found a black school just down the road from the woman's house.

23. Interview, Thomas Sigman, Jan. 27, 1995. According to the Georgia Consolidated Census, as late as 1940 there were only 67 paved and gravel roads in the county as opposed to 893 improved dirt roads and 652 unimproved dirt roads. Localism rising from rural isolation is one of the central themes of William A. Link, *The Paradox of Southern Progressivism, 1880–1930* (Chapel Hill: University of North Carolina Press, 1992). See also Pete Daniel, *Standing at the Crossroads: Southern Life since 1900* (New York: Hill and Wang, 1986), 52.

24. Interview, Beautine Hubert DeCosta-Lee, Oct. 6, 2001.

25. Hancock County Census Manuscript, 1910.

26. See Altina L. Waller, *Feud: Hatfields, McCoys, and Social Change in Appalachia, 1860–1900* (Chapel Hill: University of North Carolina Press, 1988), on the limitations of the concept of rural isolation and the awareness of rural people of national trends.

27. Many southern autobiographies have described interracial playmates: see Jimmy Carter, *An Hour before Daylight: Memories of a Rural Boyhood* (New York: Simon and

Schuster, 2001); and Harry Crews, *A Childhood: The Biography of a Place* (New York: Harper and Row, 1978).

28. Interview, A. J. Parker, July 18, 1995; interview, Mozelle Arnold, January 26, 1995.

29. For a discussion of interracial play among children of slaveowners and children of slaves, see Eugene Genovese, *Roll, Jordan, Roll: The World the Slaves Made* (New York: Pantheon, 1974), 515–19.

30. Interview, Billy Boyer, Sept. 19, 1994; interview, A. J. Parker, July 19, 1995.

31. Interview, Francis Frazier, July 25, 1995.

32. To further explore southern children's education in race relations, see the pioneering study by Jennifer Lynn Ritterhouse, "Learning Race: Racial Etiquette and the Socialization of Children in the Jim Crow South" (Ph.D. diss., University of North Carolina at Chapel Hill, 1999).

33. At interviews conducted in retirement homes, I have frequently heard elderly people comment on the cordiality of race relations there. Black and white interviewees have both likened it to their childhood experiences before adult power struggles brought them into conflict. This observation seems to reinforce Barbara Field's famous argument that in every socially meaningful sense, race is a construct in the service of class divisions and not an organic result of biology.

34. Interview, Mae Warren, Mar. 1995. Warren's story is reminiscent of one related by a white man from South Carolina who, with other white boys on their way to school, sought to bar black children from crossing a creek: "[We] decided it wasn't right for the niggers to walk the same foot logs as us." Twenty or thirty of them took up sticks and stood on the bridge: "[We told the black school children] that these foot logs belonged to the white people and if they wanted to get on the other side of the creek, they would have to wade the water." In this case as well, the black children forcefully resisted, but unlike Warren and her companions, they were beaten and had to submit to being excluded from the use of the bridge (in Kirby, *Rural Worlds Lost*, 247).

35. Interview, Grover Thomas, Jan. 30, 1992; interview, Creasy Walker, Sept. 5, 1994. Creasy Walker remembered that when she and other black children would walk to school, white children would sometimes call them names or pelt them with sticks, rocks, or even paper bags full of spit. "We'd look at them," said Walker, "spy out which one of them did it, and . . . fight like cats and dogs!" She said that she and her friends would sometimes shout out, "We don't have time for you this morning, but we're sure going to wait for you this evening." Walker remembered reminiscing with one of her old antagonists decades later. The white woman said, "'Well, that was in them days. We didn't know no better, didn't try to learn none. So I wouldn't dare to teach my grandchildren such as that. But y'all got nothing to worry about. Y'all got to pay [us back]. If you didn't beat the one what done it, you beat the other.' Me and her sitting there, laughing about it, about two years ago." Walker attributed some of the battles to children being children but thought that these conflicts were

racially directed because of their parents' influence. "Because some of their parents, they were real ignorant." Once a white boy's father came to complain to Walker's father and to demand that he punish his children for fighting. Walker remembered that her father said that his children had claimed that the whites had started the fight. He asked the white man, "Did you see it?" The white man admitted that he hadn't. "Neither did I," replied Walker's father, who then offered a compromise: "If you whup yours and let me see it, you'll see me whup mine." He stuck to the offer, but because the white man did not want to accept it, the matter ended there.

36. Interview, A. J. Parker, July 15, 1995; Charles S. Johnson, *Shadow of the Plantation* (Chicago: University of Chicago Press, 1934).

37. Interview, Katie Hunt, June 14, 1990; interview, Willis Wall, July 6, 1995. My skepticism of the willingness of white Masons to honor their oaths toward black Masons arises from a chilling story in the autobiography of H. L. Mitchell, the white organizer of the Southern Tenant Farmers' Union. As a young boy Mitchell turned up at the lynching of a black man. The event had been publicized in advance, and a large crowd had gathered to see the man burned. Mitchell saw him tied to a tree and doused with gasoline. Then the black man motioned, and Mitchell heard one of the lynch mob's white leaders say to another leader, "We can't burn him—he's a Mason." To which the other replied, "Hell, he's just a nigger Mason! Burn him!" He then lit the match and set the man afire (Mitchell, *Mean Things Happening in This Land: The Life and Times of H. L. Mitchell* [Montclair, N.J.: Allanheld, Osmun, 1979], 10–11).

38. Interview, J. E. Johnson, Nov. 20, 1988.

39. Interview, Mary and Elizabeth Thornton, Jan. 28, 1992.

40. Interview, Eddie Roberts, Aug. 16, 1994. Arthur Raper discovered that in Greene County, just to the north of Hancock, all land not posted by lodges was open to anyone who wanted to hunt or fish on it. He found that landless farmers, especially black, had to hunt in areas where they would be recognized by the owners of the land. Some fishing locations were reserved for whites, but the majority, as in Hancock, could be claimed by the first to reach the bank. Raper found that most—although not all—hunting parties were all white or all black. They often met others on the hunt and sometimes over the kill, however, and had worked out racially impartial rules of courtesy to govern the claiming of shot game (Raper, *Preface to Peasantry: A Tale of Two Black Belt Counties* (1936; New York: Atheneum, 1974), 396–97.

41. Interview, T. M. "Buck" Patterson, Aug. 2, 1995; interview, James Wilson, July 16, 1995; telephone interview, Benjamin Senior, Aug. 9, 1998; interview, Billy Boyer, Aug. 2, 1995. As I cannot resolve the contradictions in the oral evidence, I leave the problem to the reader. Wilson was a gregarious storyteller who enjoyed holding an audience; Senior, a reticent man who seemed careful not to offend his white interviewer. Wilson named Senior as a man he had seen playing on an interracial team. Senior denied having done so when I asked him directly. Who knows? They agreed, however, that black and white ballplayers shared a field near Devereux.

42. Interview, anonymous. For a lively description of Georgia skin in Wilcox County, Georgia, including the interracialism of drinking, cheating, and fighting, see Jane Maguire, *On Shares: Ed Brown's Story* (New York: Norton, 1975), 78–89.

43. Du Bois, *Souls of Black Folk,* 207; Wilma Dykeman and James Stokely, *Seeds of Southern Change: The Life of Will Alexander* (New York: Norton, 1962), 64–65. See also Morton Sosna, *The Search of the Silent South: Southern Liberals and the Race Issue* (New York: Columbia University Press, 1977).

44. *Sparta Ishmaelite,* Sept. 20, 1901 ("Rag-time"). Buddy Moss, an important bluesman from the 1930s and 1940s, was born in Hancock, near Jewell, in 1906; see Bruce Bastin, *Red River Blues: The Blues Tradition in the Southeast* (Urbana: University of Illinois Press, 1995), 125–28. For examples of the impact black musicians had on early white rock 'n' roll performers, see Greil Marcus, *Mystery Train: Images of America in Rock 'n' Roll Music,* 2d ed. (New York: Dutton, 1982). Better-known white performers directly taught by black musicians included Hank Williams Sr., Elvis Presley, and Jerry Lee Lewis. In their autobiographies some blues musicians have related anecdotes of the interracial contexts in which they sometimes played in the rural South.

45. Interview, anonymous.

46. Ritterhouse, "Learning Race." For a fine, brief description, see McMillen, *Dark Journey,* 23–28. See also J. William Harris, "Etiquette, Lynching, and Racial Boundaries in Southern History: A Mississippi Example," *American Historical Review* 100 (1995): 387–410. William Chafe et al., eds., *Remembering Jim Crow: African Americans Tell about Life in the Segregated South* (New York: New Press, 2001), is a rich and fascinating collection of oral interviews of African Americans who remembered details of the experience of interracial etiquette. A fine sociological study from the Jim Crow period is Johnson, *Patterns of Negro Segregation.* Although it refers primarily to the antebellum period and is condescending, Bertram Wilbur Doyle, *The Etiquette of Race Relations in the South: A Study in Social Control* (Chicago: University of Chicago Press, 1937), is another useful source on interracial etiquette.

47. Interestingly, when interviewed about the past, most African Americans who had been adults in the first decades of the century slipped back into a style of speech that they had used many years ago. They would refer to whites from those decades by terms of address that they no longer used with contemporary whites.

48. Interview, Mae Warren, Sept. 25, 1994; interview, Eugene Foster Jr., July 6, 1995. Younger people—those who came of age in the 1940s and 1950s—were much more vocal in their criticism of the daily insult of racial etiquette. Older people often shrugged off my question, saying, "It's just the way it was." This may have been one of those points at which my race made it difficult for older people to speak freely.

49. Some white interviewees now apologize for the former racial etiquette by pointing out that family and friends joined blacks in entering through the informal "friendly" back door. This is true. They overlook, however, the primary symbolic meaning of front versus back doors. The front entrance conferred civic formality on encounters, an identity forbidden blacks, whether familiar neighbors or strangers.

50. Telephone interview, Mae Warren, May 29, 2002. Ned Cobb, a black farmer in Alabama during these years, testified to the etiquette in play at the gin house. He said that when faced with a long line of wagons at the gin house, he would talk with the ginner to learn when his turn would come. He would then unhitch his mules and take them home until the appointed time. Cobb said: "They observed your turn strictly, for white and colored. It was mighty seldom that anybody would go ahead of your wagon. And while we was waitin our turns, white and colored, we'd talk about our crops and how much more we had at home and how much we done ginned and what the cotton was bringin that year" (in Rosengarten, *All God's Dangers*, 186).

51. Joel Williamson, *The Crucible of Race: Black-White Relations in the American South since Emancipation* (New York: Oxford University Press, 1984), esp. 114–15; Glenda Gilmore, *Gender and Jim Crow: Women and the Politics of White Supremacy in North Carolina, 1896–1920* (Chapel Hill: University of North Carolina Press, 1996), esp. 91–118. The black rapist was not entirely a myth. Men, regardless of race, sometimes rape women, regardless of race. But black on white rape was rare—certainly compared to white on black rape—and white hysteria entirely disproportionate to the threat. See Lisa Lindquist Dorr, *White Women, Rape, and the Power of Race in Virginia, 1900–1960* (Chapel Hill: University of North Carolina Press, 2004).

52. Interview, Eugene Foster; interview, James Wilson, July 16, 1995.

53. Interview, Eugene Foster.

54. William S. McFeely, *Frederick Douglass* (New York: Norton, 1991), 5.

55. Williamson, *Crucible of Race*, esp. 288–91; *Sparta Ishmaelite*, Dec. 21, 1906.

56. Some of these relationships reflected aspects of paternalism, but one must be cautious in applying that term in a twentieth-century context. The expansive references to "our family, black and white," that Eugene Genovese found in the diaries of antebellum planters rarely seem present in this later period, and I thank him for advising me on this point. For explorations of the applicability (and inapplicability) of paternalism in the postbellum South, see Edward J. Cashin and Glenn T. Eskew, eds., *Paternalism in a Southern City: Race, Religion, and Gender in Augusta, Georgia* (Athens: University of Georgia Press, 2001); Lee J. Alston and Joseph P. Ferrie, *Southern Paternalism and the American Welfare State: Economics, Politics, and Institutions in the South, 1865–1965* (New York: Cambridge University Press, 1999); Ian D. Ochiltree, "'A Just and Self-Respecting System'? Black Independence, Sharecropping, and Paternalistic Relations in the American South and South Africa," *Agricultural History* 72 (Spring 1998): 352–80; and Glenn T. Eskew, "Black Elitism and the Failure of Paternalism in Postbellum Georgia: The Case of Bishop Lucius Henry Holsey," in *Georgia in Black and White: Explorations in the Race Relations of a Southern State, 1865–1950*, ed. John C. Inscoe (Athens: University of Georgia Press, 1994), 106–40.

57. Interview, Obilee Rhodes Jr. (the grandson of Rives), Sept. 1, 1992; interview, Frank Barksdale, 1988; interview, Katie Hunt, Aug. 12, 1992 ("money"); interview, Laramon Durham, Mar. 16, 1993 ("working for them"). Barksdale remembered that when the Klan harassed Percy Moore's black mistress, whom even whites called "Miss

Pearl," Percy "got mad and sold Main Street." One enormously wealthy Hancock planter, Lynn Rives, whose only children were "black," lived into the opening years of the civil rights movement. When rumors began circulating that the black community might be readying itself to launch a sit-in campaign at the cafeteria of the Drummers Home, the classic, historic motel in downtown Sparta, white Spartans spoke of closing down the building to thwart their attempt to integrate it. According to James McMullen, an African American civic leader, Rives learned of the plan and put a stop to it by dropping by and telling the owners, "If you close up, how are you going to pay me all the money you owe me?" (interview, James McMullen, June 17, 1992). For an examination of the influence of big planters, see J. William Harris, *Deep Souths: Delta, Piedmont, and Sea Island Society in the Age of Segregation* (Baltimore, Md.: Johns Hopkins University Press, 2001), 59, 126–27.

58. Interview, Katie Bell Hunt, Feb. 24, 1995. Other sources speak of similar relationships, largely ending around the turn of the twentieth century: McMillen, *Dark Journey*, 6–7; Allison Davis, Burleigh B. Gardner, and Mary R. Gardner, *Deep South: A Social Anthropological Study of Caste and Class* (Chicago: University of Chicago Press, 1941), 405–6; John Dollard, *Caste and Class in a Southern Town* (New York: Doubleday/Anchor, 1937), 83, 124.

59. Williamson, *Crucible of Race*, 79–108, 259–84. A few black interviewees told me that the wealthier planters tried to keep lynching in check because they did not want their black kin killed.

60. On black migration following the Civil War, see Leon F. Litwack, *Been in the Storm so Long: The Aftermath of Slavery* (New York: Knopf, 1979).

61. On the relationships between white southerners and black domestic servants, see Susan Tucker, *Telling Memories among Southern Women: Domestic Workers and Their Employers in the Segregated South* (New York: Schocken, 1988).

62. Interview, James Wilson, July 16, 1995; Johnson, *Shadow of the Plantation*, 27–28; J. E. Johnson, Nov. 20, 1988.

63. Interview, Sanford Butts, December 29, 1989; interview, Marshall Boyer, Aug. 2, 1995. Ed Brown, a sharecropper from south of Hancock, used the same language Boyer did to describe planters' attitudes toward and ways of speaking about their tenants. This implied not simply control over the tenant but also exclusive control against the right of any other white person to interfere with the tenant (Maguire, *On Shares*, 103). Beautine DeCosta-Lee expressed a similar concept in more refined language when she said: "Whites did not want other white folks to bother [what they called] 'our black folk.' They would look out for their own blacks" (interview, DeCosta-Lee).

64. Interview, Katie Hunt, Sept. 25, 1994. James Brown of Devereux also expressed disgust at the "false love" that some black tenants accepted from planters (Brown, *Jackleg Preacher* [New York: Carlton, 1989], 23).

65. Agricultural Census, 1910–40.

66. Interview, Josie Mae Ingram. For a description of similar intimacy among poor

blacks and poor whites in the antebellum South, see Timothy James Lockley, *Lines in the Sand: Race and Class in Lowcountry Georgia, 1750–1860* (Athens: University of Georgia Press, 2001).

67. Interview, Mamie Washington, July 28, 1995. Interestingly, Alexis de Tocqueville, in his monumental study of antebellum America, had described just the opposite tendency. Tocqueville believed that there was greater interracial intimacy in the South than in the North. He argued that this occurred because white southerners, confident in the wide gulf that separated them from African slaves, felt comfortable in relatively intimate relationships with them. White northerners, however, resented any sign of interracial intimacy because of the absence of other clear barriers between them (de Tocqueville, *Democracy in America* [New York: Harper and Row, 1988], 342–44).

68. Interview, Mamie Washington.

69. Interview, A. J. Parker, July 15, 1995.

70. Interview, A. J. Parker, July 8, 1995.

71. Interview, A. J. Parker, July 15, 1995. Parker said that some white and black people who did not live where he did do not understand how they can get along. He said he often has to respond to whites in the next county who ask him about it: "Let me tell you one damn thing: I got some mighty good friends who are black and who'll do me a favor a hell of a lot quicker than any of these whites over there will. Out here, the way I got it in my book is the blacks can't get along without the whites, and the whites can't get along without the blacks." He continued, "I ain't never low-rated anybody, or called anyone a nigger cause he's black. And they do the same for me. I try, you know, to treat him like I want him to treat me."

72. Interview, A. J. Parker, July 15, 1995. Parker recalled the times of the year when the men were out by themselves doing heavy work, such as plowing: "You could see the smoke come up late in the evening—the smoke stacks from those wood stoves. You'd smell ham cooking in one man's house; smell fatback cooking in another man's house; and whatever in another man's house—you didn't know what in the hell you were smelling, but it smelled good! It smelled good! I guaran-damn-tee you! . . . You couldn't hardly stand it to stay out in the field and finish your day."

73. Interview, Eugene Foster Jr., July 6, 1995; Hale, *Making Whiteness*, 124–38.

74. Nancy MacLean, *Behind the Mask of Chivalry: The Making of the Second Ku Klux Klan* (New York: Oxford University Press, 1994), 52–74.

Chapter 4

1. Neil R. McMillen, *Dark Journey: Black Mississippians in the Age of Jim Crow* (Urbana: University of Illinois Press, 1990), 23.

2. Sociologist Donald Black defines intimacy as "the degree to which [people] participate in one another's lives" (Black, *The Behavior of the Law* [New York: Academic Press, 1976], 40).

3. Interview, Mamie Washington, July 28, 1995. W. E. B. Du Bois described a similar incident from his days as a Fisk University student, when the rural white superintendent of education who hired him to teach summer school surprised him by inviting him to stay for dinner. He noted that the white man would have been "horrified if he had dreamed that I expected to eat at the table with him and not after he was through" (Du Bois, *Dusk of Dawn: An Essay toward an Autobiography of a Race* [1940; Piscataway, N.J.: Transaction, 1991], 31.

4. Interview, Mary Hunt, July 21, 1995.

5. For an example of the importance whites placed on segregated eating, see Lester Russell, *Profile of a Black Heritage* (Franklin Square, N.Y.: Graphicopy, 1977), 66–67.

6. See, for example, the autobiographical account of Raymond Andrews's childhood in rural Georgia. Although his white grandfather and black grandmother lived together monogamously for decades, they still observed the eating taboo (Andrews, *The Last Radio Baby* [Atlanta: Peachtree, 1990], 121). For a contrasting story, see Sarah and A. Elizabeth Delany, *Having Our Say: The Delany Sisters' First Hundred Years* (New York: Kodansha America, 1993), 49–50. Sarah and Elizabeth Delany's white grandfather in turn-of-the century Virginia emphatically refused to observe racial dining etiquette in his home and insisted that white visitors do likewise or leave. In the late nineteenth century David Dickson, a wealthy Hancock planter, likewise insisted that white visitors dine with his mixed-race daughter, Amanda, at their home. Rebecca Lattimer Felton, the racist women's rights reformer from Georgia, tried to make political capital of this by attacking Dickson and the eminent white politicians who dined at his home (Kent Anderson Leslie, *Woman of Color, Daughter of Privilege: Amanda America Dickson, 1849–1893* [Athens: University of Georgia Press, 1995], 65).

7. I owe this idea to a conversation with Gail Faithfull and Leo McDonnell.

8. Mary Douglass, the anthropologist, argued that humans raise artificial boundaries between the clean and the unclean in many areas of life, but especially surrounding food. This is done not primarily to ensure good health but to create the sense of an ordered universe in the face of chaos (Douglass, *Purity and Danger: An Analysis of the Concepts of Pollution and Taboo* [1966; London: Ark, 1984]).

9. Interview, Patsy Kennedy, July 1994; interview, Oline Thomas, June 13, 1995; interview, A. J. Parker, July 15, 1995. For other examples of exempting Georgia children from this taboo, see Jimmy Carter, *An Hour before Daylight: Memories of a Rural Boyhood* (New York: Simon and Schuster, 2001), 77–78; and Harry Crews, *A Childhood: The Biography of a Place* (New York: Harper and Row, 1978), 62–63.

10. Dixon family reunion, Thomas Dixon, Springfield, Aug. 1993. It may be significant that these families lived in a community dominated by black landowners.

11. Interview, A. J. Parker, July 15, 1995.

12. Interview, Obilee Rhodes Jr., Sept. 21, 1992; interview, Vera Senior, Aug. 29, 1992. Arthur Raper described eating at a similar black-owned establishment in Greene County, north of Hancock, in the 1920s. But that restaurant had tables. When he

entered the establishment, a group of black men who had been standing around and talking with the proprietor left through the back door. He wrote that white customers regularly patronized the restaurant (Raper, *Preface to Peasantry: A Tale of Two Black Belt Counties* [Chapel Hill: University of North Carolina Press, 1936], 385–86).

13. I hold this section very lightly. This brief exploration of the symbolic value of spaces and postures is a tentative attempt to explain a seemingly interconnected series of exceptions to the general rules of white supremacy. It is an attempt to move beyond purely ahistorical idiosyncrasy as an explanatory force.

14. The cities had occasional but rare moments of interracial church contact. According to an oral history of Atlanta, once in a while maids of white families would attend church with their employers for "special occasions." Now and then a liberal church would invite a black choir to sing or even a black preacher to preach on "Interracial Sunday." This seems to have been a self-consciously liberal effort of the Commission on Interracial Cooperation and not a vestige of earlier folk interracialism. See Clifford M. Kuhn, Harlon E. Joye, and Bernard West, *Living Atlanta: An Oral History of the City, 1914–1948* (Athens: University of Georgia Press, 1990), 249.

15. Interview, Eugene Foster, July 6, 1995.

16. Interview, Clinton Pearson, Aug. 3, 1995; interview, Eugene Foster; Russell, *Profile*, 55.

17. Donald G. Mathews, *Religion in the Old South* (Chicago: University of Chicago Press, 1977); John B. Boles, ed., *Masters and Slaves in the House of the Lord, 1740–1870* (Lexington: University Press of Kentucky, 1988); Randy J. Sparks, *On Jordan's Stormy Banks* (Athens: University of Georgia Press, 1994); records of Darien Baptist Church, Linton, in possession of Trudy Trawick.

18. Katharine L. Dvorak, *An African-American Exodus: The Segregation of the Southern Churches* (Brooklyn, N.Y.: Carlson, 1991); Clarence E. Walker, *A Rock in a Weary Land: The African Methodist Episcopal Church during the Civil War and Reconstruction* (Baton Rouge: Louisiana State University Press, 1982); Stephen Ward Angell, *Bishop Henry McNeal Turner and African American Religion in the South* (Knoxville: University of Tennessee Press, 1992).

19. Albert Raboteau, *Slave Religion: The "Invisible Institution" in the Antebellum South* (New York: Oxford University Press, 1978); Eugene Genovese, *Roll, Jordan, Roll: The World the Slaves Made* (New York: Pantheon, 1974), 161–284; Mechal Sobel, *Trabelin' On: The Slave Journey to an Afro-Baptist Faith* (Westport, Conn.: Greenwood, 1979).

20. Glenn T. Eskew, "Black Elitism and the Failure of Paternalism in Postbellum Georgia: The Case of Bishop Lucius Henry Holsey," in *Georgia in Black and White: Explorations in the Race Relations of a Southern State, 1865–1950,* ed. John Inscoe (Athens: University of Georgia Press, 1994), 106–40; John Brother Cade, *Holsey—The Incomparable* (New York: Pageant, 1964).

21. C. Vann Woodward, *Tom Watson, Agrarian Rebel* (New York: Macmillan, 1938), 240–41.

22. In his 1906–7 survey of the South, Ray Stannard Baker discovered that some planters built churches to attract African American labor to their plantations (Baker, *Following the Color Line: American Negro Citizenship in the Progressive Era* [1908; New York: Harper Torchbooks, 1964], 89).

23. For example, in 1894 S. A. Jones sold a parcel to the trustees of Jones Chapel A.M.E. Church for five dollars. In 1896 Frank J. Watkins sold an acre to the trustees of Mitchel Chapel A.M.E. for one dollar. As late as 1968 W. A. Bass, who had previously sold the trustees of Hall Chapel A.M.E. a two-acre plot, sold them an additional two acres for only one dollar. I wish to thank Leroy Wiley for allowing me to use this information, which is based on his research in the Hancock County deed records.

24. Interview, Francis Frazier, July 25, 1995. I could not locate any founding deed for Pleasant Grove in the courthouse records.

25. Interview, Mamie Washington. Johnny Griffith was the planter who donated so generously to her church, Mt. Nebo.

26. Interview, J. E. Johnson, Nov. 12, 1988. Sanford Butts, a leading Sparta merchant, used almost the same words to make this point (interview, Butts, Dec. 29, 1989)

27. Russell, *Profile*, 68–70, 88–89; interview, Beautine Hubert DeCosta-Lee (granddaughter of Zach Hubert), Oct. 6, 2001.

28. Interview, Erma Mae Quinn, Carrs, Dec. 13, 2001; interview, Essie Mae Primer, June 27, 1995.

29. Interview, Oline Thomas; interview, Clinton Pearson; interview, Katie Bell Hunt, Mar. 16, 1995; interview, Francis Frazier ("out the door"; Frazier's description of the assembly-line viewing closely matches those of many antebellum funerals); interview, Eva Reese, Sept. 23, 2001.

30. Interview, Kelly Brookins, Aug. 10, 1994; interview, Mamie Washington. Jimmy Carter remembered that an A.M.E. bishop annually asked the Carters and another white family to visit a local black church for services (Carter, *An Hour before Daylight*, 21–24). Sanford Butts, a Sparta merchant, said that whites could arrive at black funerals uninvited but that blacks "must be invited and expected" at white funerals (interview, Butts, Dec. 29, 1989).

31. Interview, Dot Brown, July 24, 1995.

32. Interview, A. J. Parker.

33. Interview, Kelly Brookins ("amazing"); interview, Seleta Lyons, Oct. 1, 1992 ("should not laugh"); interview, Virginia Griffen, Jan. 14, 1994 ("scared to death"); interview, A. J. Parker, July 15, 1995 ("real religion").

34. Interview, Kelly Brookins ("Amen"); interview, Mamie Washington ("enjoyed").

35. The family history, drawn from the testimony of Zach Hubert's children, described his relationship with Rev. James H. Kilpatrick of White Plains Baptist Church. According to the history, "Reverend Kilpatrick, a Southern 'liberal,' was very friendly to Zach and throughout their friendship served as his special advisor. . . . Frequently when Zach had a problem with which he needed help, he contacted Reverend Kilpat-

rick who generally introduced him to a white farmer he thought could help him." Kilpatrick's son, William H. Kilpatrick, became an influential professor of education at Columbia University during the 1920s and 1930s (Russell, *Profile*, 69–70).

36. Interview, anonymous.

37. Interview, anonymous.

38. Interview, Dot Brown.

39. Interview, A. J. Parker.

40. Vinson Synan, *The Holiness-Pentecostal Tradition: Charismatic Movements in the Twentieth Century*, 2d ed. (Grand Rapids, Mich.: Eerdmans, 1997).

41. Interview, Eva Reese; interview, Kelly Brookins; interview, Essie Mae Primer.

42. Interview, Dot Brown; Russell, *Profile*, 68–70; interview, Essie Mae Primer.

43. Raymond Wolters, *The New Negro on Campus: Black College Rebellions of the 1920s* (Princeton, N.J.: Princeton University Press, 1975). The revelation of the rural bases of support for the Universal Negro Improvement Association comes from the work of Mary G. Rolinson: "The Garvey Movement in the Rural South, 1920–1927" (Ph.D. diss., Georgia State University, 2002) and "The Universal Negro Improvement Association: Southern Strongholds of Garveyism," in *Georgia in Black and White: Explorations in the Race Relations of a Southern State, 1865–1950*, ed. John Inscoe (Athens: University of Georgia Press, 1994), 202–24.

44. James Weldon Johnson, *Negro Americans, What Now?* (New York: Viking, 1934), 83.

45. Rev. James R. Brown, *Jackleg Preacher* (New York: Carlton Press, 1989), 57–66.

46. Orville Vernon Burton, "Race Relations in the Rural South since 1945," in *The Rural South since World War II*, ed. R. Douglas Hurt (Baton Rouge: Louisiana State University Press, 1998), 31. As will be discussed in chapter 6, blacks began registering to vote in large numbers in 1946. This may have contributed to white anxiety.

47. Interview, Mamie Washington; interview, A. J. Parker, July 19, 1995. After World War II some black nannies continued to attend white churches with white families. But for most African American people, the option of interracial church visitation ended.

48. Interview, Robert Herndon, Mar. 31, 1995.

49. See, for example, *Sparta Ishmaelite*, Nov. 12, 1884, Nov. 12, 1889, May 6, 1948, and September 30, 1948.

50. Kuhn, Joye, and West, *Living Atlanta*, 240–46; Ronald H. Bayor, *Race and the Shaping of Twentieth Century Atlanta* (Chapel Hill: University of North Carolina Press, 1996), 155–65; telephone interview, Mae Warren, May 29, 2002; interview, Kelly Brookins.

51. For an overview of the African American root tradition in slavery, see Sharla M. Fett, *Working Cures: Healing, Health, and Power on Southern Slave Plantations* (Chapel Hill: University of North Carolina Press, 2002); for examples of herbal remedies used in Atlanta during this period, see Kuhn, Joye, and West, *Living Atlanta*, 235–37; interview, Hyndenberg and Eunice Dixon, July 11, 1995.

52. Letter, Beautine Hubert DeCosta-Lee to Mark Schultz, Dec. 24, 1994 ("stayed up many nights"; her grandfather, Zach Hubert, was said to have learned root from his mother, who was part Cherokee, but Zach Hubert's father's side was said to include men and women who practiced "juju," a religious, medical tradition from West Africa); interview, John Roberts, Sept. 23, 2001; interview, W. J. and Mable Miller, July 18, 1995. Tom Johnson was John Roberts's grandfather and Mable Miller's great-grandfather. He employed them both to walk through the woods and swamps to collect his herbs. She also remembers seeing cars lining the road in front of his house, with people waiting to be seen by the root man.

53. Interview, W. J. and Mable Miller.

54. Gertrude Jacinta Fraser, *African American Midwifery in the South: Dialogues of Birth, Race, and Memory* (Cambridge, Mass.: Harvard University Press, 1998). In 1936, 42 percent of Georgia babies were delivered by midwives (Kuhn, Joye, and West, *Living Atlanta*, 238.

55. Interview, Mae Warren, Mar. 1995 (Warren remembered that both of her grandmothers had been midwives and had aided both black and white women through childbirth); interview, Creasy Walker, Sept. 8, 1994; interview, Virginia Griffen (Griffen remembered that her mother had been attended by both a white doctor from White Plains and an old black midwife, known as "Middie").

56. Interview, William Brookins, Aug. 9, 1994; interview, John Roberts; interview, Myrtle Brookins, July 6, 1995; interview, James Wilson, July 16, 1995. In his biography Ned Cobb described another neighborly death ritual. He visited a planter's home to "look on his body" and pay "respects to his wife and boy" (in Theodore Rosengarten, *All God's Dangers: The Life of Nate Shaw* [1974; New York: Vintage], 490–91).

57. Interview, William Brookins; interview, Marvin and Mary Thompson, June 12, 1995; interview, W. S. Miller, July 18, 1995.

58. Interview, Katie Hunt, June 15, 1990.

59. Unfortunately, I can find neither the tape nor my notes from this interview. I remember this story with perfect clarity, however, because it so surprised me. The interview took place around 1989 at a black family reunion just to the west of Powelton.

60. The essential starting point on this topic is Joel Williamson's book *New People: Miscegenation and Mulattoes in the United States* (New York: New York University Press, 1980). Two fine recent studies provide the family histories of two of Hancock's nineteenth-century interracial families; see Leslie, *Woman of Color, Daughter of Privilege;* and Adele Logan Alexander, *Ambiguous Lives: Free Women of Color in Rural Georgia, 1789–1879* (Fayetteville: University of Arkansas Press, 1991). See also my previous study examining postbellum interracial families in Hancock and several surrounding counties. It further develops the thesis of interracial kinship as an important social relationship in the rural South: Mark R. Schultz, "Interracial Kinship Ties and the Emergence of a Rural Black Middle Class, Hancock County, Georgia, 1865–1920," in *Georgia in Black and White: Explorations in the Race Relations of a Southern State, 1865–1950,* ed. John C. Inscoe (Athens: University of Georgia Press, 1994), 141–72.

61. For dozens of examples, consult the word *miscegenation* in the index of the classical sociological studies of the South.

62. Brown, *Jackleg Preacher*, 24 (this opinionated autobiographical account describes the black experience of sharecropping in the Devereux area, service in France during World War II, and life and work in Detroit after the war); interview, anonymous; Crews, *A Childhood*, 105–7.

63. Interview, Eugene Foster Jr. (quotation); Martha Hodes, *White Women, Black Men: Illicit Sex in the Nineteenth Century South* (New Haven: Yale University Press, 1997)—again, consult the indexes of the classical sociologists, such as John Dollard, Charles S. Johnson, and Allison Davis; Jean Toomer, "Becky," in *Cane* (1922; New York: Liveright, 1975); interview, Katie Hunt, June 15, 1990. (The white woman was a vague, shadowy memory for Hunt. She remembered a white woman with two "black" sons who lived, without a husband, by the railroad tracks west of Sparta).

64. Interracial marriage was illegal in Georgia until 1966 (Schultz, "Interracial Kinship Ties").

65. In Rosengarten, *All God's Dangers*, 41.

66. For a discussion of selective inattention, see John Blassingame, *Black New Orleans, 1860–1880* (Chicago: University of Chicago Press, 1973), 209.

67. Schultz, "Interracial Kinship Ties," 156–57, 159.

68. Alexander, *Ambiguous Lives*, 47–95; interview with Eva Reese, Sept. 23, 2001; interview with James McMullen, 1991.

69. Schultz, "Interracial Kinship Ties," 159–60.

70. Letter, DeCosta-Lee to Schultz; interview, DeCosta-Lee, Oct. 6, 2001.

71. Interview, Mary Hunt. Although an acute consciousness of interracial kinship ties has faded somewhat with the passing of the years, some Hancock people still value their memories of them. John Rozier, a descendant of an important white family, likes to claim his distant black relation, the C.M.E. bishop Lucious Henry Holsey, as the most accomplished member of his family.

72. Interview, Solomon Harper, Sept. 15, 1994; interview, Otilia Edwards, Jan. 21, 1993.

73. Interview, John Rozier, Aug. 16, 2002; interview, Mae Warren, Aug. 3, 2004; interview, Sanford Butts, Dec. 29, 1989; interview, James McMullen, Mar. 24, 1995.

74. The recent account of an evolving relationship between a Klan leader and a civil rights leader in Durham, North Carolina, illustrates the unpredictable way that unlikely friendships can grow up between people; see Osha Gray Davidson, *The Best of Enemies: Race and Redemption in the New South* (New York: Scribner's, 1996).

75. Interview, Creasy Walker, Sept. 8, 1994.

76. Interview, George Lott, 1989; interview, Mamie Washington.

77. This insight took clearer shape in a conversation with James Anderson; for more on the issue, see Laurie Beth Green, "Battling the Plantation Mentality: Consciousness, Culture, and the Politics of Race, Class, and Gender in Memphis, 1940–1968" (Ph.D. diss., University of Chicago, 1999).

78. Interview, Mamie Washington. Some people, black and white, who moved from

rural Hancock to towns and cities told me that they had remained open to inter-racial relationships because of their earlier experiences on the farms. Others spoke regretfully about the difficulty of making interracial contact in the cities because of increased segregation there. Others seemed to have learned other lessons and seemed quite pleased with the distance.

79. Interview, Creasy Walker.

80. For an interesting study of southern liberals, see Morton Sosna, *In Search of the Silent South: Southern Liberals and the Race Issue* (New York: Columbia University Press, 1977). According to Sosna, few white landowners from the black belt joined the Commission on Interracial Cooperation, a liberal group that aimed to improve race relations in the 1920s and 1930s. Sosna noted that when white landowners "ex-pressed concern for the problems of blacks, they generally did so from within the paternalistic tradition of helping 'their niggers' in times of trouble" (27).

81. Interview, Willie Butts, Aug. 8, 1995. Butts was born in Hancock in 1921. Because he was sickly as a child, his grandmother, a root doctor from neighboring Baldwin County, raised him so as to nurse him to health.

82. David Harper, Sept. 14, 1994. Jimmy Carter tells a very similar story in *An Hour before Sunrise*, 95–96.

83. "Distance and Propinquity" is the title of a wonderful chapter on rural race relations in Jack Temple Kirby's *Rural Worlds Lost: The American South, 1920–1960* (Baton Rouge: Louisiana State University Press, 1987), 232–71.

Chapter 5

1. For discussions of the economic and political instrumentality of antiblack vio-lence, see Nell Irvin Painter, *Southern History across the Color Line* (Chapel Hill: University of North Carolina Press, 2002), 15–39; Leon Litwack, *Trouble in Mind: Black Southerners in the Age of Jim Crow* (New York: Knopf, 1998); Jonathan M. Bry-ant, *How Curious a Land: Conflict and Change in Green County, Georgia, 1850–1885* (Chapel Hill: University of North Carolina Press, 1996), 90–146; John Hope Franklin, *The Militant South, 1800–1861* (1956; Cambridge, Mass.: Harvard Univerity Press, 1970).

2. This study adopts the definition of lynching formulated by the NAACP and clearly explained by Stewart E. Tolnay and E. M. Beck in *A Festival of Violence: An Analysis of Southern Lynchings 1882–1930* (Urbana: University of Illinois, 1995), 260: lynchings are public events in which three or more men cooperate in the illegal kill-ing of another person while claiming to act as agents of justice in the name of the community.

3. Statistics taken from the National Association for the Advancement of Colored People, *Thirty Years of Lynching in the United States, 1889–1918* (New York: National Association for the Advancement of Colored People, 1919); Arthur R. Raper, *The Tragedy of Lynching* (1933; New York: Negro Universities Press, 1969); Jesse Daniel

Ames, *The Changing Character of Lynching: Review of Lynching, 1931–1941* (Atlanta: Commission on Interracial Cooperation, 1942). For an interesting discussion of the lynching statistics, see Tolnay and Beck, *Festival of Violence,* 259–63.

4. W. Fitzhugh Brundage, *Lynching in the New South: Georgia and Virginia, 1880–1930* (Urbana: University of Illinois Press, 1993), 103–4, 108–13; Tolnay and Beck, *Festival of Violence,* 119–65, 255–56.

5. Raper, *Tragedy of Lynching,* 27. Certainly more African Americans would have been lynched in counties with low black populations had they not been terrorized out of the area. In a number of Georgia counties, poor whites waged campaigns to drive out all African Americans.

6. Anyone interested in continuing the "relative safety" debate might consider breaking out of the quantitative standoff by examining African Americans' subjective senses of safety in different subregions. As John Sheldon Reed's work on modern southern violence has shown, southerners think of their region as "safe" relative to northern urban centers, even though southern towns lead the nation in murders per capita. The difference is that southerners generally find southern murder understandable and therefore do not feel threatened by it (Reed, *One South: An Ethnic Approach to Regional Culture* [Baton Rouge: Louisiana State University Press, 1982], 139–53). Subregions subject to indiscriminate vigilante action against all African Americans, such as Forsyth County in the upper piedmont, probably felt more dangerous to African American residents than did cotton-belt counties such as Hancock, where individual blacks were murdered for specific alleged crimes or breaches of etiquette.

7. In *Lynching in the New South* Brundage began the task of contextualizing lynching in Georgia and Virginia by period and by subregion.

8. For a fascinating examination of the manner in which North Carolina Democrats created and manipulated the image of "the black rapist" to meet their own political needs, see Glenda Elizabeth Gilmore, *Gender and Jim Crow: Women and the Politics of White Supremacy in North Carolina, 1896–1920* (Chapel Hill: University of North Carolina Press, 1996), esp. 61–118.

9. In his memoir the black educator Benjamin E. Mays wrote that "most boys in the country" carried a pistol, as did his brothers and his sister's suitors (Mays, *Born to Rebel: An Autobiography* [Athens: University of Georgia Press, 1987], 12).

10. Georgia skin, or just plain "skin," was the most popular card game at gambling spots across Hancock County. Violence was not uncommon at such events (interview, James Wilson, July 16, 1995).

11. For example, *Sparta Ishmaelite,* Mar. 4, 1910.

12. Reed, *One South,* 139–53; Sheldon Hackney, "Southern Violence," in *Violence in America: Historical and Comparative Perspectives,* ed. Hugh Davis Graham and Ted Roberts Gurr (Beverly Hills, Calif.: Sage, 1979), 405–6.

13. Bertram Wyatt-Brown, *Southern Honor: Ethics and Behavior in the Old South* (New York: Oxford University Press, 1982); Bertram Wyatt-Brown, *The Shaping of Southern Culture: Honor, Grace, and War, 1760s–1880s* (Chapel Hill: University of

North Carolina, 2001); Edward Ayers, *Vengeance and Justice: Crime and Punishment in the 19th Century American South* (New York: Oxford University Press, 1984); Brundage, *Lynching in the New South*, 50–52, 88; Richard E. Nisbett and Dov Cohen, *Culture of Honor: The Psychology of Violence in the South* (Boulder, Colo.: Westview, 1996). For a cross-cultural context of honor and violence, see Mark Cooney, *Warriors and Peacemakers: How Third Parties Shape Violence* (New York: New York University Press, 1998), 107–32. For a lively description of the culture of violence among white Georgians in the 1920s and 1930s, see Harry Crews, *A Childhood: The Biography of a Place* (New York: Harper and Row, 1978), 7–10, 23–34.

14. Edward Ayers was the first to tie black violence to southern honor. See Ayers, *Vengeance and Justice*, 235; Fox Butterfield, *All God's Children: The Bosket Family and the American Tradition of Violence* (New York: Knopf, 1995), 32, 46–67, 119. Because murder most often takes place among people who interact socially, the predominance of intraracial violence suggests that most social interaction was segregated, although interracial contact remained an option.

15. A time-honored successful defense for murder in the South—regardless of race—has been to prove that the deceased "needed killing."

16. *Sparta Ishmaelite*, Sept. 5, 1916; interview, Johnny Evans Johnson, Nov. 12, 1988.

17. Interview, Oline Thomas, June 13, 1995.

18. Interview, Marvin Turner, Sept. 2, 1994.

19. For a splendid examination of the rise and fall of radical racism and white fear of the black as rapist, see Joel Williamson, *The Crucible of Race: Black-White Relations in the American South since Emancipation* (New York: Oxford University Press, 1984). See also Brundage, *Lynching in the New South*, 53, 59; George M. Fredrickson, *The Arrogance of Race: Historical Perspectives on Slavery, Racism, and Social Inequality* (Middletown, Conn.: Wesleyan University Press, 1988), 256–84; Gilmore, *Gender and Jim Crow*, 82–94; Litwack, *Trouble in Mind*, 206–16, 301–6. In an unpublished study E. M. Beck found that in the years after the embarrassing Leo Frank lynching of 1915, newspaper editors moved stories about black crime farther and farther from the front page, where they had previously been featured. I thank Beck for sharing his research with me.

20. Even Ned Cobb, for all his boldness in telling of white exploitation and violence, expressed concern that some whites would still want to lynch him if they knew what he had told an oral historian in the 1970s (Theodore Rosengarten, *All God's Dangers: The Life of Nate Shaw* [1974: New York: Vintage, 1989], 554).

21. Interview, Mary Worthening, June 22, 1995; interview, Essie Mae Primer, June 27, 1995; interview, Clabon Skrine, Aug. 1995.

Interestingly, when asked directly whether they had ever been afraid of whites, few black interviewees said they had. When later asked why they did not resist economic exploitation by individual planters, however, a larger number volunteered that they feared violent reprisals.

When asked to explain gaps in oral traditions passed from generation to generation within African American families, some interviewees explained that in the rural South during the twentieth century's first decades, adults generally did not openly discuss "adult business" in front of children. Even though many southern families had highly developed storytelling traditions involving events from the family history, certain areas, including economic matters and violence, were taboo subjects for children. When adults were talking about such issues, children often had to leave the room.

It is also possible that the current racial polarization in the county made it difficult for some interviewees to discuss the history of interracial violence.

22. Interview, Sanford Butts, July 1993.

23. Interview, anonymous.

24. Interview, anonymous.

25. Interview, Mary Worthening.

26. Interview, James Wilson, July 16, 1995. Wilson claims to have been so close to the site of Smith's shooting that he heard the shots.

27. Crews, *A Childhood*, 24.

28. Of the fourteen reported lynchings that took place in Hancock and adjacent counties, six occurred between 1918 and 1922 (Brundage, *Lynching in the New South*, 270–80).

29. *Sparta Ishmaelite*, Aug. 3, 1917.

30. The Moses Hubert story was remembered by Zach Hubert's children and re-peated to a family member in the 1960s for a family history (Lester F. Russell, *Profile of a Black Heritage* [Franklin Square, N.Y.: Graphicopy, 1977], 67–68); interview, Marshall Boyer, Aug. 9, 1995.

31. Michael L. Berger, *The Devil Wagon in God's Country: The Automobile and Social Change in Rural America, 1893–1929* (Hamden, Conn.: Archon, 1979), 71–72 and passim. The people of Hancock have gracefully adjusted to the cool, isolationist culture of the car. On the rural roads around Hancock, where traffic is sparse, many and perhaps most black and white drivers still recognize the claims of community ties by waving at each other—and pedestrians—as they pass. The regionally distinc-tive motion, given to old neighbors and strangers alike, is produced by flashing the fingers upward from the top of the steering wheel without ever losing contact with the wheel. I thank the Hancock native and University of Georgia historian Kenneth Coleman for taking me on my first wide-ranging tour of the rural South as a young graduate student and for introducing me to this highly civilized custom.

32. Arthur Raper, *Preface to Peasantry: A Tale of Two Black Belt Counties* (Chapel Hill: University of North Carolina Press, 1936), 86.

33. Jack Temple Kirby, *Rural Worlds Lost: The American South 1920–1960* (Baton Rouge: Louisiana State University Press, 1987), 256–59. Amusingly, Arthur Raper discovered one man near Macon who did advocate that either all black-owned cars be confiscated or the county "maintain two systems of roads, one for the whites and one for the Negroes" (Raper, *Preface to Peasantry*, 176).

34. Raper, *Preface to Peasantry*, 174–76.

35. *Sparta Ishmaelite*, Aug. 3, 1917.

36. Ibid., Oct. 19, 1917. Of the violent incidents described previously in this chapter, all of which had been reported in the *Ishmaelite* or in oral testimony, this was the only one I found in Hancock County's court records. After searching repeatedly through criminal case records, I finally located records of Davis's case in a drawer faintly labeled "Grand Jury No Bills."

37. *Sparta Ishmaelite*, Nov. 16, 1917. See Bertram Wilbur Doyle, *The Etiquette of Race Relations in the South: A Study in Social Control* (Chicago: University of Chicago Press, 1937); Litwack, *Trouble in Mind*, 38–39, 235; Neil R. McMillen, *Dark Journey: Black Mississippians in the Age of Jim Crow* (Urbana: University of Illinois Press, 1990), 25–26. In one of his autobiographies Frederick Douglass wrote that if a slave ventured "to vindicate his conduct, when censured for it," he was considered "guilty of impudence, one of the greatest crimes a slave can commit" (Douglass, *Narrative of the Life of Frederick Douglass* [Boston, 1849], 79). It apparently remained a serious offense.

38. The most famous example of envious white attacks on blacks was the 1892 lynching of Ida B. Wells's friends Calvin McDowell, Tom Moss, and Henry Stewart because their successful store threatened nearby white merchants. The incident launched Wells on her lifelong crusade against lynching. On Georgia whitecapping, see Brundage, *Lynching in the New South*, 19–28, 43, 120–27; and Donald L. Grant, *The Way It Was in the South: The Black Experience in Georgia* (New York: Carol, 1993), 169–71.

39. Tolnay and Beck, *Festival of Violence*.

40. Brundage, *Lynching in the New South*, 104–11; Jacquelyn Dowd Hall, "'The Mind That Burns in Each Body': Women, Rape, and Racial Violence," in *Powers of Desire: The Politics of Sexuality*, ed. Anne Snitow, Christine Stansell, and Sharon Thompson (New York: Monthly Review Press, 1983), 331.

41. McMillen, *Dark Journey*, 28.

42. Brundage, *Lynching in the New South*, 68, 72.

43. Jean Toomer, *Cane* (1923; New York: Liveright, 1975), 28–35.

44. *Sparta Ishmaelite*, Aug. 7, 1903, in Forrest Shivers, *The Land Between: A History of Hancock County, Georgia to 1940* (Spartanburg, S.C.: Reprint Company, 1990), 284; interview, Carlton Morse, July 20, 1995.

45. Gilmore, *Gender and Jim Crow*, 61–146; Nancy MacLean, *Behind the Mask of Chivalry: The Making of the Second Ku Klux Klan* (New York: Oxford University Press, 1994), 142–48. It has also been suggested that as women began to challenge patriarchy politically and economically, white men exaggerated the rape threat as a means of reasserting male protection and hence male dominance. See Brundage *Lynching in the New South*, 59; Daniel J. Singal, *The War Within: From Victorian to Modernist Thought in the South, 1919–1945* (Chapel Hill: University of North Carolina Press, 1982), 8; Jacquelyn Dowd Hall, *Revolt against Chivalry: Jesse Daniel Ames and the*

Women's Campaign against Lynching (New York: Columbia University Press, 1979), 147–48; Williamson, *Crucible of Race*, 115–17.

46. *Sparta Ishmaelite*, Sept. 28, 1906; John Dittmer, *Black Georgia in the Progressive Era, 1900–1920* (Urbana: University of Illinois Press, 1977), 123–31.

47. Interview, Gay Andrews, around 1995.

48. This is most famously attested in the diary of Mary Chesnut and the narrative of Harriet Jacobs, who complained about the situation from the perspective of a white planter woman and a black slave woman, respectively; see C. Vann Woodward, *Mary Chesnut's Civil War* (New Haven, Conn.: Yale University Press, 1981); Harriet A. Jacobs, *Narrative of the Life of a Slave Girl*, ed. Lydia Maria Child and Jean Fagan Yellin (Cambridge, Mass.: Harvard University Press, 1987).

49. See Darlene Clark Hine, "Rape and the Inner Lives of Black Women in the Middle West: Preliminary Thoughts on the Culture of Dissemblance," *Signs* 14 (Summer 1989): 912–20.

50. When we discussed the dangers and realities of sexual assault by white men, the black women I interviewed were quite uncomfortable speaking on the subject and did so only with the tape recorder off and with the assurance of anonymity for themselves, the women coerced or assaulted, and even the white men involved. I got the sense that the memory of these incidents was embarrassing to all involved and that this aspect of the past should remain untouched or, at the least, impersonal. Of course, my own identity as a white male may have contributed to their discomfort in speaking about this topic. Mae Warren was one of the many who spoke of their parents' resistance to their working in white homes, although after leaving home, she did so in Florida and New York City and had no bad experiences.

51. J. William Harris, *Deep Souths: Delta, Piedmont, and Sea Island Society in the Age of Segregation* (Baltimore, Md.: Johns Hopkins University Press, 2001), 273.

52. For examinations of bloody "spectacle lynchings," see Philip Dray, *At the Hands of Persons Unknown: The Lynching of Black America* (New York: Random House, 2002); Litwack, *Trouble in Mind;* and James R. McGovern, *Anatomy of a Lynching: The Killing of Claude Neal* (Baton Rouge: Louisiana State University Press, 1982).

53. Some antilynching organizations cited two other Hancock incidents as lynchings, but both involved shoot-outs between Hancock lawmen and armed black men in which white officers were killed or injured. A black man would be a fool to surrender in such circumstances, for he would face certain execution. Stewart Tolnay and E. M. Beck, who are painstakingly reexamining all recorded southern lynchings, concur that these incidents were not lynchings. I thank them for sharing their yet-unpublished findings with me. For one incident, see *Sparta Ishmaelite*, Oct. 2, 1896; *Atlanta Constitution*, Sept. 29, 1896. For the other, see *Macon Telegraph*, Feb. 4 and 5, 1923; *Atlanta Constitution*, Feb. 4, 1923; *Memphis Commercial Appeal*, Feb. 5, 1923; and *Chicago Defender*, Feb. 17, 1923.

54. For Etheridge, see *Sparta Ishmaelite*, Dec. 2, 1885; and *Atlanta Constitution*,

Nov. 27, 1885. The *Chicago Tribune* and Tuskeegee listed this as a lynching, and W. Fitzhugh Brundage concurred, as did Tolnay and Beck.

55. Interview, Babe Ingram, niece of Hervia Ingram, 1989; interview, Clabon Skrine, nephew of Hervia Ingram, Aug. 1995. The oral testimony seems reliable, but I could not find Ingram's death recorded in the *Sparta Ishmaelite* or an autopsy of his body listed in the county coroner's records. Of course, no confirmation of the event could be found in criminal court records.

56. Brundage, *Lynching in the New South*, 110.

57. Ibid., 21.

58. Ibid., 36–37, 111.

59. Donald Black, *The Behavior of Law* (New York: Academic, 1976), 40–48; Ayers, *Vengeance and Justice*, 182, 236–38, 241; Edward Ayers, *The Promise of the New South: Life after Reconstruction* (New York: Oxford University Press, 1992), 156–58; Roberta Senechal de la Roche, "Collective Violence as Social Control," *Sociological Forum* 11 (Mar. 1996): 97–133; Senechal de la Roche, "The Sociogenesis of Lynching," in *Under Sentence of Death: Lynching in the South*, ed. W. Fitzhugh Brundage (Chapel Hill: University of North Carolina Press, 1997), 52–56, 60–64, 81–84, 90–91; McMillen, *Dark Journey*, 230, 243; Raper, *The Tragedy of Lynching*, 28.

60. E. M. Beck and Timothy Clark, "Strangers, Community Miscreants, or Locals; Who Were the Black Victims of Mob Violence?" *Historical Methods* (Spring 2002). This analysis underappreciates the fact that because transients and local miscreants could not have made up 45 percent of Georgia's African American population, these marginalized people were at far greater risk, individually, of being lynched than were most black citizens.

61. Brundage, *Lynching in the New South*, 108–13; Tolnay and Beck, *Festival of Violence*, 119–65, 255–56.

62. Hosea Hudson, *Black Worker in the Deep South* (New York: International, 1972), 5.

63. Jane Maguire, *On Shares: Ed Brown's Story* (New York: Norton, 1975); Rosengarten, *All God's Dangers*.

64. Brundage, *Lynching in the New South*, 84.

65. Senechal de la Roche, "Collective Violence"; Roberta Senechal de la Roche, "Why is Collective Violence Collective?" *Sociological Theory* 2 (2001): 126–44.

66. C. Vann Woodward, *American Counterpoint: Slavery and Racism in the North-South Dialogue* (New York: Oxford University Press, 1971), 234–60.

67. For example, Leonard L. Richards, *Gentlemen of Property and Standing: Anti-Abolition Mobs in Jacksonian America* (New York: Oxford University Press, 1970); Dominic Capeci and Martha Wilkerson, *Layered Violence: The Detroit Rioters of 1943* (Jackson: University Press of Mississippi, 1991); Roberta Senechal, *The Sociogenesis of a Race Riot: Springfield, Illinois, in 1908* (Urbana: University of Illinois Press, 1990); Eric Anderson, *Race and Politics in North Carolina, 1872–1901: The Black Second* (Baton Rouge: Louisiana State University Press, 1981); William Tuttle Jr., *Race Riot: Chicago*

in the Red Summer of 1919 (New York: Atheneum, 1970). Rural riots around Phoenix, South Carolina, in 1898 and Elaine, Arkansas, in 1919 are the rare exceptions.

68. Leon F. Litwack, *North of Slavery: The Negro in the Free States, 1790–1860* (Chicago: University of Chicago Press, 1961); Howard N. Rabinowitz, *Race Relations in the Urban South, 1865–1890* (Urbana: University of Illinois Press, 1980); Rabinowitz, *The First New South, 1865–1920* (Arlington Heights, Ill.: Harlan Davidson, 1992), 133–42; Brundage, *Lynching in the New South*, 105, 200.

69. Michael S. Hindus, *Prison and Plantation: Crime, Justice, and Authority in Massachusetts and South Carolina, 1767–1876* (Chapel Hill: University of North Carolina Press, 1980); Brundage, *Lynching in the New South*, 4, 76–77; Norbert Elias, *The Civilizing Process*, vol. 2 (1939; Malden, Mass.: Blackwell, 2000), chap. 2. Elias argued that personal violence declined in Western societies as the state expanded its power and sought exclusive control over violence. This led to more predictable relations and the expansion of the market.

70. World War I draft cards, Hancock County, National Archives, East Point, Ga.

71. For an important discussion of Virginian conservativism, see Brundage, *Lynching in the New South*, 170–86.

72. Shivers, *The Land Between*, 143–52.

73. Hancock Superior Court Minutes, 1858–70, 399–414, Georgia State Archives, Atlanta. Although the four leaders of the revolt were originally condemned to death, 120 of the county's leading white citizens, including the judge and prosecuting attorney of the case, petitioned the governor for a pardon for two of the men (Kent Anderson Leslie, *Woman of Color, Daughter of Privilege: Amanda America Dickson, 1849–1893* [Athens: University of Georgia Press, 1995], 53–54).

74. Shivers, *The Land Between*, 161.

75. For testimony on white-on-black violence in Hancock during Reconstruction, see "Ku Klux Klan Report, Georgia Testimony: Report of the Joint Select Committee to Investigate the Affairs of the Late Insurrectionary States," *Senate Reports of Committees*, 42d Congress, 2d session, vol. 2, pt. 6, 926–88, pt. 7, 112–13, 923–32, 974–88. Hancock state representative Eli Barnes testified, "It has got to be a common thing . . . to hear a man say, 'They rode around my house last night, and they played the mischief there; my wife was molested; my daughter was badly treated and they played the wild generally with my family.'" One black Hancock man named Frank Watkins wrote Barnes and Harrison to report that a white plantation manager had beaten Watkins's daughter with a sharp-edged rock. He reported, "[Her] head was beat into a jelly and I fear her skull fractured also her hands and arms cut severely in several places to the bone." When Watkins confronted the agent and asked why he did not speak to him, the girl's father, about the complaint, the white man responded that "he consulted no damed Negro about beating thare children" (Shivers, *The Land Between*, 183).

76. See pp. 177–78 for an account of this maneuver.

77. *Sparta Ishmaelite*, Jan. 5, 1894, and Dec. 21, 1906 (quotation); letter, John D.

Walker to William Northen, Mar. 16, 1907, "Northen 1898–1907" file, William J. Northen Papers, series 1, box 1, Georgia State Archives, Atlanta.

78. Williamson, *Crucible of Race,* 288–91; "Northen Scrapbook" and "Resolutions of the Republican Mass Meeting of Scheley County, August 20, 1892," William J. Northen Papers, Georgia State Archives, Atlanta.

79. "Ku Klux Klan Report," vol. 2, pt. 6, pp. 926–88, and pt. 7, pp. 923–1113; Shivers, *The Land Between,* 179–90 (for an examination of Klan activity in Georgia, see Stanley K. Deaton, "Violent Redemption: The Democratic Party and the Ku Klux Klan in Georgia, 1868–1871" [M.A. thesis, University of Georgia, 1988]; for the Klan in nearby Green County and black response, see Bryant, "We Have No Chance of Justice before the Courts"); "Ku Klux Klan Report," vol. 2, pt. 6, p. 903 (Harrison citation); John C. Reed, "What I Know of the Ku Klux Klan," *Uncle Remus Magazine* 23:38, as cited in Shivers, *The Land Between,* 189 (Stephens citation); "Ku Klux Klan Report," vol. 2, pt. 7, p. 1204, as cited in Shivers, *The Land Between,* 189 (Warren Klansman testimony). The threat of the Warren County Klan was mentioned in an African American autobiography from the northern part of Hancock; see Russell, *Profile of a Black Heritage,* 57–58, 66–68. For general histories of the Klan, see David Chalmers, *Hooded Americanism: The History of the Ku Klux Klan* (Durham, N.C.: Duke University Press, 1987); Wyn Craig Wade, *The Fiery Cross: The Ku Klux Klan in America* (New York: Simon and Schuster, 1987).

80. For a fascinating examination of the motivations of Klansmen in a Georgia town during the 1920s, see MacLean, *Behind the Mask.*

81. Williamson, *Crucible of Race,* 140–79; MacLean, *Behind the Mask,* 12–13.

82. *Sparta Ishmaelite,* Sept. 14 and 28, 1906.

83. Interviews, anonymous; Shivers, *The Land Between,* 287; *Sparta Ishmaelite,* Feb. 25, 1921.

84. Interview, James McMullen, 1992.

85. Interview, G. Lee Dickens, July 25, 2004.

86. Ibid.; interview, Dave Dyer, May 1995. After serving in the navy during the war, Dyer began a long career as county commissioner and superintendent of schools. For a description of the Klan in Georgia after World War II, see Stetson Kennedy, *The Klan Unmasked* (1954; Boca Raton: Florida Atlantic University Press, 1990).

87. Brundage, *Lynching in the New South,* 246–50; Tolnay and Beck, *Festival of Violence,* 202–13; Hall, *Revolt against Chivalry;* Harris, *Deep Souths,* 285–88.

88. The best evidence is drawn from Mississippi in McMillen, *Dark Journey,* 275–81; and James R. Grossman, *Land of Hope: Chicago, Black Southerners, and the Great Migration* (Chicago: University of Chicago Press, 1989), 50–54 (*Atlanta Constitution* quotation, 51). See also Brundage, *Lynching in the New South,* 227–30; Tolnay and Beck, *Festival of Violence,* 213–33; and James C. Cobb, *The Most Southern Place on Earth: The Mississippi Delta and the Roots of Regional Identity* (New York: Oxford University Press, 1992), 149.

89. For a fuller development of the argument that state violence replaced private

violence as a means of racial control, see George C. Wright, *Racial Violence in Kentucky, 1865–1940: Lynchings, Mob Rule and "Legal Lynchings"* (Baton Rouge: Louisiana State University Press, 1990), chap. 7–8; and Brundage, *Lynching in the New South,* 250, 254. Although they found no correlation between trends in lynching and legal executions in the South before 1919, Stewart E. Tolnay and E. M. Beck found that lynchings steadily declined after that date while the number of state executions rose (Tolnay and Beck, *Festival of Violence,* 102–3). The Scottsboro Boys provide a famous example of harsh and unjustifiable legal penalties imposed to prevent lynchings. For another example, see Harris, *Deep Souths,* 200–202.

90. The county history records one incident in which a white man was convicted of a violent crime against an African American during the short period when Reconstruction held sway in Hancock. In 1869 Thomas A. Jackson was found guilty of raping a young black girl and sentenced to two years in prison. Although this singular event is interesting, it should be contextualized by asking what the sentence would have been had the races been switched. This minimal legal protection appears to have evaporated altogether after black Hancock citizens lost independent control of their votes in 1870 (Shivers, *The Land Between,* 184).

91. Interview, James Wilson, July 16, 1995; Brundage, *Lynching in the New South,* 256–57; William H. Chafe et al., eds., *Remembering Jim Crow: African Americans Tell about Life in the Segregated South* (New York: New Press, 2001), 271, 287–88.

92. A recent study of southern violence found that African Americans were quite capable of using violence in their own defense; see Gilles Vandal, *Rethinking Southern Violence: Homicides in Post–Civil War Louisiana, 1866–1884* (Columbus: Ohio State University Press, 2000). For examples of rural blacks using violence to defend themselves against whites, see Greta de Jong, *A Different Day: African American Struggles for Justice in Rural Louisiana, 1900–1970* (Chapel Hill: University of North Carolina Press, 2002), 57–62; Larry J. Griffin, Paula Clark, and Joanne C. Sandberg, "Narrative and Event: Lynching and Historical Sociology," in *Under Sentence of Death: Lynching in the South,* ed. W. Fitzhugh Brundage (Chapel Hill: University of North Carolina Press, 1997), 27; Terence Finnegan, "Lynching and Political Power in Mississippi and South Carolina," in idem, 196–200; W. Fitzhugh Brundage, "The Roar on the Other Side of Silence: Black Resistance and White Violence in the American South, 1880–1940," in idem, 278–79; Maguire, *On Shares,* 30–31, 82–83; Wright, *Racial Violence in Kentucky,* 11, 58–59, 139–40, 162–70; Litwack, *Trouble in Mind,* 32, 40, 423–28; Rosengarten, *All God's Dangers,* 4, 49–52, 97–101, 162–70, 215–16, 307–12. Although Litwack wrote that blacks were "invariably" killed if they resisted whites forcefully (427), Ned Cobb consistently and successfully threatened violence when physically threatened or cheated by whites. When he fired at a posse, he paid with a long jail term, not with his life. "When I know I'm right" said Cobb, "I'll give you trouble if you try to move me" (in Rosengarten, *All God's Dangers,* 170).

93. The black southern culture of honor does not seem to have drawn any attention by historians, although it is clearly present in oral interviews and autobiographies

of black southerners. W. E. B. Du Bois described an encounter with a black man from Dougherty County, Georgia, who expressed his determination not to be the object of white violence. According to Du Bois, after asking about a black boy who had been fatally shot by police in nearby Albany for "loud talking on the sidewalk," the man slowly said, "Let a white man touch me, and he dies; I don't boast this,—I don't say it around loud, or before the children,—but I mean it" (in Du Bois, *The Souls of Black Folk* [1903; New York: New American Library, 1969], 156–57).

94. Wyatt-Brown, *Southern Honor*, 117–25; Brundage, *Lynching in the New South*, 50–52. There was an exception. If an offense was construed as an attack on the honor of a family or a community (e.g., if the victim was a white woman or policeman, respectively), then the entire male community was expected to unite in violent reaction.

95. List of World War Veterans—Hancock County, Discharge Record Book number 1, Hancock County Courthouse.

96. Interview, Eva Reese, Sept. 23, 2001; interview, Grover L. Thomas, Jan. 30, 1992 (in his autobiography James Brown echoed Thomas's words; see Brown, *Jackleg Preacher* [New York: Carlton, 1989], 33, 65); Orville Vernon Burton, "Race Relations in the Rural South since 1945," in *The Rural South since World War II*, ed. R. Douglas Hurt (Baton Rouge: Louisiana State University, 1998), 32.

97. Edwin R. Embree, *Thirteen against the Odds* (New York: Viking, 1944), 33–34. Wright spoke of one black man who refused to leave the "white" section on a streetcar. When confronted by a group of white men who ordered him to leave, he pulled out a knife and said, quietly but firmly, "Make me." The gathering disbanded, leaving the man to continue his ride in the white section with no further action taken. According to Wright, the other black riders on the streetcar took delight and pride in the man's example.

98. Ayers (*Promise of the New South*, 153) relates the intriguing example of a exchange between a black man and a white man on the balance between saving face and saving one's life. A white lumber camp quarterboss was told to move a new and dangerous black man out of camp. The boss confronted the black man, disarmed him of a pistol, and told him to "hit the road." The black man doubled back, catching the white man alone on a road, and said, "Well, we're even now—I let you look good. But you'd rather live than keep that gun, wouldn't you?" He got his gun back and left.

99. Telephone interview, Marshall Boyer, July 19, 2003.

100. Interview, Mary and Elizabeth Thornton, Jan. 28, 1992; *Sparta Ishmaelite*, July 6, 1904, Aug. 5, 1910.

101. Interview, Willis Walls, July 6, 1995. Wall thought it might be better to leave the names out of the story.

102. Frederick Douglass, *Narrative of the Life of Frederick Douglass* (New York: Signet, 1968), 81–83.

103. Interview, Willie Butts, Aug. 3, 1995; Dollie Walls, Aug. 8, 1995.

104. The posture of the Walls family resembles that of some other African American farmers who appear in autobiographies. For example, see Maguire, *On Shares*. This oral autobiography of a black farmer who lived about seventy miles south of Hancock describes a man named "Long Boy" who was given some protection by a wealthy, paternalistic white woman. Still, the farmer portrays Long Boy as having made his own contribution: "But it wasn't just her. It was Long Boy too. I reckon that from slavery on up there have been some people that would stand up for theyselves. The white people didn't run over him as they did the other colored."

105. In Maguire, *On Shares*, 82–83.

106. *Sparta Ishmaelite*, Nov. 9, 1906.

107. Ibid., Nov. 16, 1906.

108. Ibid., Nov. 9 and 16, 1906.

109. Ibid., Nov. 30, 1906.

110. Ibid., Nov. 21 and 28, 1935, Dec. 26, 1935, and May 21, 1936. This story is told in one form or another by almost every person in the county who lived through the 1930s. The basic facts, if not their interpretation, are generally acknowledged. In my masters thesis, which was the first time I wrote on Hancock County, I briefly related this story in an introductory chapter. One white source had told me that the man who shot the policeman was "deranged." I did not look further, and so I used that unfortunate word when describing the event—a choice for which I have been taken to task more than once by local African Americans who have read my thesis. Carlton Morse, a black educator, asked me whether I knew for sure that the black man was deranged. I did not and explained my naive early graduate school mistake. He nodded and said that he didn't know either, that the man may or may not have been mentally unstable. He then summed up his point: "They think you're crazy if you just can't take it anymore."

111. This story—and the countywide search—is remembered with resentment to this day by many older people in the county. It has become for many a touchstone in the county lore. Blacks remember it as an example of police brutality and arrogance and organized white spite, with the malefactors breaking into the privacy of their homes. Whites remember the fugitive as the personification of the "black beast" attacking both the substance and the symbol of state authority and of the black community's disrespect for the law by, they allege, sheltering him from justice.

112. Multiple interviews, Katie Hunt, Charlie Hunt, Mae Warren, Kathryn Ingram, Gladys Ingram, and Charity Hunt, 1990–96. See, for example, the interview with Katie Hunt and others, June 14, 1990, which was the first time I heard the story. The posse standoff is a favorite story of the family, often retold.

113. Interview, Alma Dixon Smith, May 1, 1995. Besides being an eyewitness to the shooting, Smith is her family's historian and has gathered many of her family's memories.

114. Brundage, *Lynching in the New South*, 80–81. In his autobiography Hosea Hudson described his childhood in Oglethorpe County, two counties north of Hancock.

Hudson's grandmother, too, spoke for her family when a mob surrounded their home and demanded his uncle. She attempted to disarm the leader of the mob and told them that they would take her son "over her dead body." In addition, like Hunt and Dixon, she got away with her direct challenge. She stymied the mob while her husband waited inside (Hudson, *Black Worker*, 2–3).

115. Interview, Marshall Boyer, Aug. 9, 1995.

Chapter 6

1. *Sparta Ishmaelite*, Jan. 28, 1910.

2. Michael Perman, *Struggle for Mastery: Disfranchisement in the South, 1888–1908* (Chapel Hill: University of North Carolina Press, 2001); J. Morgan Kousser, *The Shaping of Southern Politics* (New Haven, Conn.: Yale University Press, 1974). For the continuity of black urban voting, see Karen Ferguson, *Black Politics in New Deal Atlanta* (Chapel Hill: University of North Carolina, 2002); John Dittmer, *Black Georgia in the Progressive Era, 1900–1920* (Urbana: University of Illinois Press, 1977), 94; Clarence A. Bacote, "The Negro in Georgia Politics, 1880–1908" (Ph.D. diss., University of Chicago, 1955); Clarence A. Bacote, "The Negro in Atlanta Politics," *Phylon* 16, no. 4 (Fourth Quarter 1995): 330–50.

3. Eric Foner, *Reconstruction: America's Unfinished Revolution, 1863–1877* (New York: Harper and Row, 1988); Edmund L. Drago, *Black Politicians and Reconstruction in Georgia: A Splendid Failure* (Baton Rouge: Louisiana State University, 1982).

4. The lone incident of which I am aware in which a white person was convicted of violence against a black person in Hancock occurred in 1869, when a white man was sentenced to two years in prison for raping a black girl; see Forrest Shivers, *The Land Between: A History of Hancock County to 1940* (Spartanburg, S.C.: Reprint Company, 1990), 184.

5. Shivers, *The Land Between*, 179–84; "Ku Klux Klan Report, Georgia Testimony: Report of the Joint Select Committee to Investigate the Affairs of the Late Insurrectionary States," *Senate Reports of Committees*, 42d Congress, 2d session, vol. 2, pt. 6, pp. 456–57, 926–78, pt. 7, pp. 112–13.

6. Shivers, *The Land Between*, 170–91; Kenneth Coleman, ed., *A History of Georgia* (Athens: University of Georgia Press), 213–15.

7. Because the country's leading Populist, Tom Watson, fought his battles in Hancock's district, the Populist story of Hancock has been told repeatedly by gifted historians. See Steven Hahn, *The Roots of Southern Populism: Yeoman Farmers and the Transformation of the Georgia Upcountry, 1850–1890* (New York: Oxford University Press, 1983); Bruce Palmer, *"Man over Money": The Southern Populist Critique of American Capitalism* (Chapel Hill: University of North Carolina Press, 1980); Gerald Gaither, *Blacks and the Populist Revolt: Ballots and Bigotry in the "New South"* (Tuscaloosa: University of Alabama Press, 1977); Lawrence Goodwyn, *Democratic Promise:*

The Populist Moment in America (New York: Oxford University Press, 1976); Robert C. McMath Jr., *Populist Vanguard* (Chapel Hill: University of North Carolina Press, 1975); C. Vann Woodward, *Tom Watson: Agrarian Rebel* (New York: Macmillan, 1938). The quotation comes from *People's Party Paper,* Aug. 12, 1892.

8. *Sparta Ishmaelite,* Aug. 11, 1893, Oct. 26, 1894.

9. Ibid., Oct. 28, 1892, July 15, 1892, July 22, 1892, Sept. 9, 1892.

10. Perman, *Struggle for Mastery,* 283–4; Kousser, *Shaping of Southern Politics,* 209–23; Woodward, *Tom Watson,* 208; Gaither, *Blacks and the Populist Revolt;* Barton C. Shaw, *The Wool-Hat Boys* (Baton Rouge: Louisiana State University Press, 1984); Hahn, *Roots of Southern Populism.* Voting estimates are in Kousser, *Shaping of Southern Politics,* 215. Republican turnout in these years was relatively insignificant. Georgia's black Republican leaders encouraged their following to support the Democrats at this time, so that most blacks not voting Populist may well have voted Democratic.

11. *Sparta Ishmaelite,* Sept. 9, 1892.

12. Ibid., Aug. 31, 1892.

13. Perman, *Struggle for Mastery,* 281–98; Dittmer, *Black Georgia,* 94–95; Dewey Grantham, *Hoke Smith and the Politics of the New South* (Baton Rouge: Louisiana State University Press, 1958), 139–40, 147–52, 158–62; *Sparta Ishmaelite,* May 15, 1908, Oct. 26, 1894 (quotation). Georgia instituted the poll tax almost thirty years before other southern states began to use a property tax. This greatly lowered black voter turnout in Georgia relative to states that were similar in other respects.

14. *Sparta Ishmaelite,* Sept. 18, 1908; *Annual Report of Secretary of State for 1908* (Atlanta: Franklin Turner, 1909); Kousser, *Shaping of Southern Politics,* 209–23, 239.

15. William Anderson, *The Wild Man from Sugar Creek: The Political Career of Eugene Talmadge* (Baton Rouge: Louisiana State University Press, 1975), 82 and passim; Billy Bowles and Remer Tyson, *They Love a Man in the Country* (Atlanta: Peachtree, 1989), 49–56; interview, Marshall Boyer, date unavailable. Flannery O'Conner wonderfully captured the adolescent level of political debate during the Talmadge years in a short story entitled "The Barber," in *Flannery O'Connor: Collected Works* (New York: Library of America, 1988), 701–24, originally published in 1947 as a part of *The Geranium: A Collection of Short Stories.*

16. The county unit system functioned like the electoral college to keep disproportionate power in the hands of rural counties. The counties with the lowest populations were guaranteed two unit votes in statewide elections, whereas the most populated counties—say, those around Atlanta—could have no more than six unit votes.

17. Presentments of the Grand Jury for the Superior Court of Hancock County, 1910–50, Hancock County Courthouse; interview, Dave Dyer, Nov. 22, 1993. For the functions of county government, see J. William Harris, *Deep Souths: Delta, Piedmont, and Sea Island Society in the Age of Segregation* (Baltimore, Md.: Johns Hopkins University Press, 2001), 70. The percentage of public funds allocated to education was larger in the South than elsewhere in the country.

18. The first story was told in a letter (dated July 14 or 24, 1986) from William S. Rozier to his brother Charles P. Rozier. As a seven-year-old boy he had accompanied his aunt, Fionne Rozier Miller, on her daily charitable rounds. He wrote the letter because he saw her treated with tenderness by black nurses in Sparta in her last illness, perhaps descendants of the people she had cared for. The letter is in the possession of John Rozier, Atlanta. The Yaffe story comes from the *Sparta Ishmaelite*, Dec. 13, 1931.

19. Franklin Roosevelt believed that he needed the support of southern congressmen to salvage the national economy. This prioritizing of economic recovery over civil rights made the New Deal largely a nonissue for African Americans. See Frank Freidel, *F.D.R. and the South* (Baton Rouge: Louisiana State University Press, 1965); Raymond Wolters, *Negroes and the Great Depression: The Problem of Economic Recovery* (Westport, Conn.: Greenwood, 1970).

20. Kousser, *Shaping of Southern Politics*, 210–14; Hancock County Tax Digest, 1874–1944, Georgia State Archives, Atlanta.

21. Kousser, *Shaping of Southern Politics*, 210–14; Hancock County Tax Digest, 1874–1944, Georgia State Archives, Atlanta.; Dittmer, *Black Georgia*, 94–95; Bacote, "The Negro in Atlanta Politics," 340. The clearest explanation of the closed white primary is to be found in Perman, *Struggle for Mastery*, 285, 300–313.

22. Interview, Carlton Morse, July 20, 1995.

23. Interview, James McMullen, June 17, 1992; interview, J. E. Johnson, July 21, 2003; interview, anonymous. In 1948 a new secret ballot was introduced in Hancock. To conceal their identities from discovery, voters tore a numbered tab off the ballot after marking it—see *Sparta Ishmaelite*, Nov. 7, 1924, May 6, 1948; Perman, *Struggle for Mastery*, 297. On vote buying among black and white voters in 1930s Greene County, see Raper, *Preface to Peasantry*, 166–67.

24. Hancock County Tax Digest, 1890–1940.

25. Charles Payne found that black Mississippi landowners and their descendants were twice as likely as tenants to attend civil rights rallies early in the civil rights movement and four times more likely to register to vote (Payne, *I've Got the Light of Freedom: The Organizing Tradition and the Mississippi Freedom Struggle* [Berkeley: University of California Press, 1996], 141, 281–83). Greta de Jong further found that Louisiana's black landowners and business owners took the lead in political activism from the Jim Crow era though the early years of the civil rights movement (de Jong, *A Different Day: African American Struggles for Justice in Rural Louisiana, 1900–1970* [Chapel Hill: University of North Carolina Press, 2002], 48–49, 170, 179).

26. Interview, Emmie Mae Harper, Sept. 23, 1994, and Jan. 26, 1995.

27. Interview, Emmie Mae Harper, Sept. 23, 1994.

28. Some voting families in the northern part of the county identified through oral sources include the Skrines, Dixons, Huberts, Ruffs, Battles, and Lewises. Around the Linton area, Emmie Mae Harper said, voters included George Brown and Willie Trawick.

The people's reluctance to discuss black voting activities in Hancock before the civil rights movement is greater than that for any other subject. Many, whether black or white, claimed not to have been aware that some blacks voted in the first half of the twentieth century. As I followed one lead to another and returned to some African Americans with more data, they provided or confirmed more information about voting than they had earlier admitted to having. I do not know why. Hancock was the first county in Georgia to elect black majority leadership in the 1960s. The replacement of almost all white officials by African Americans can still be felt anywhere in the county and is the source of a great deal of tension. Still, considering their willingness to talk about many other sensitive topics, I do not understand older people's fear of speaking about earlier voting activity, especially because white-on-black violence has apparently not occurred in the county in decades.

29. Interview, J. E. Johnson, July 21, 2003; *Sparta Ishmaelite*, Nov 18, 1887, Nov. 9, 1988, Nov. 9, 1900, Nov. 11, 1904. I thank Ben Feicht and Jim Mattera for helping me search newspaper microfilm for political items.

30. Interview, J. E. Johnson, July 21, 2003; Raper, *Preface to Peasantry*, 168. Benjamin Jefferson Davis Sr., a Republican leader and the militant editor of the *Atlanta Independent*, was the father of Benjamin J. Davis Jr., the African American attorney for Angelo Herndon. He is sometimes mistaken for Benjamin O. Davis Sr., the first African American brigadier general of the U.S. Army. See Ferguson, *Black Politics*, 62, 87. In Greene County, Arthur Raper noted, "local Republican patronage, though always going to the whites, has been somewhat subject to the local Republican Committeeman, a Negro" (*Preface to Peasantry*, 168).

31. Raper, *Preface to Peasantry*, 165–9; telephone interview, Forrest Shivers, Oct. 25, 2003.

32. Raper, *Preface to Peasantry*, 168–69; telephone interview, Forrest Shivers, Oct. 25, 2003; telephone interview, Marshall Boyer, July 19, 2003; telephone interview, Marshall Boyer, Aug. 9, 2003; telephone interview, John Rozier, Aug. 16, 2002. For an example of the granting of voting "privileges" to the black elite in a North Carolina town, see William H. Chafe, et al., eds., *Remembering Jim Crow: African Americans Tell about Life in the Segregated South* (New York: New Press, 2001), 281–82. This pattern somewhat resembles the attempts of twentieth-century European colonial administrators to co-opt indigenous elites by granting them limited political power.

33. Bacote, "The Negro in Atlanta Politics," 343–44; Laughlin McDonald, *A Voting Rights Odyssey: Black Enfranchisement in Georgia* (New York: Cambridge University Press, 2003); Dan T. Carter, "Southern Political Style," in *The Age of Segregation: Race Relations in the South, 1890–1945*, ed. Robert Haws (Jackson: University Press of Mississippi, 1978), 45; Numan V. Bartley, *The Creation of Modern Georgia* (Athens: University of Georgia Press, 1983), 185–87; interview, Dave Dyer, Nov. 22, 1993 (for a glimpse of black political activity in one southern city between Populism and the civil rights movement, see David M. Tucker, *Lieutenant Lee of Beale Street* [Nashville, Tenn.: Vanderbilt University Press, 1971]); *Sparta Ishmaelite*, July 18 and 25, 1946.

34. *Sparta Ishmaelite,* Aug. 5 and Apr. 29, 1948; Grand Jury Presentments, March 1948, Hancock County Courthouse; McDonald, *Voting Rights Odyssey; Ishmaelite,* Sept. 9, 1948.

35. Interview, Carlton Morse, Fort Valley, July 20, 1995. For the central role of black World War II veterans in the civil rights struggle in Louisiana, see de Jong, *A Different Day,* 145–51.

36. Interview, Earnest Jack Ingram, June 3, 2004; telephone interview, G. Lee Dickens, July 25, 2004; interview, Ingram, Sept. 18, 2004. Jim Smith, a large landowner, lived near Hickory Grove. Tom Dixon was a Sparta funeral director. Gus Richardson was a jackleg preacher and storeowner on the east side of Sparta. Mearilus Roberts ran a general store east of Sparta and served as the leader of Hancock's black Masons. Other counties also witnessed this middle stage between disfranchisement and the free use of the ballot. Stine George and Doris Strong George described black voters in Moultrie, South Georgia, voting in large numbers, being hotly solicited by white politicians, and determining elections by voting in a bloc during these years; see Chafe, *Remembering Jim Crow,* 285–87.

37. Dave Dyer, many interviews, 1989–95.

38. Interview, Dave Dyer, Nov. 22, 1993.

39. Interview, Carlton Morse, July 20, 1995; interview, Dave Dyer.

40. Interview, Louise Edwards, Sept. 18, 1989.

41. Ibid.

42. Interview, anonymous; interview, Louise Edwards; interview, Samuel Williams, spring 1989.

43. W. E. B. Du Bois, ed., *The Negro Church* (1903; New York: Octagon, 1968).

44. Interview, anonymous; interview, Carlton Morse, July 20, 1995. The voting age was dropped from twenty-one to eighteen to allow World War II soldiers to vote. It was raised again decades later.

45. Interview, Emmie Mae Harper, Jan. 26, 1995.

46. Telephone interview, Mearilus Roberts, Jr., Aug. 12, 2004; telephone interview, Lonzy Edwards, Aug. 12, 2004.

47. Interview, Dave Dyer, Dec. 8, 1993, and Aug. 4, 1995. Dyer used to send postcards to black leaders and would go to country stores to solicit black voters directly.

48. Interview, Willis Hubert, Jan. 1989. John Rozier remembered that "Old Gene was a big buddy of Ben Hubert," the leader of the cooperative (telephone interview, July 16, 2002).

49. Interview, Carlton Morse, July 6, 1991, and July 20, 1995; *State v. Elton Stanley;* petition by Devereux planters in Criminal File no. 3; Hancock County Courthouse.

50. Jimmy Carter, *An Hour before Daylight: Memories of a Rural Boyhood* (New York: Simon and Schuster, 2001), 20; interview, Carlton Morse, July 20, 1995. Morse told the school board, "[I] thought it was a good thing if it helped black schools. But I expect to go by the rules handed down here in this county." Dyer, then superintendent of

education, replied to the board members, "Well, individually, we can think what we want to—don't bother a person for thinking."

51. Glenda Elizabeth Gilmore, *Gender and Jim Crow: Women and the Politics of White Supremacy in North Carolina, 1896–1920* (Chapel Hill: University of North Carolina Press, 1996), 119, 143–44; interview, Carlton Morse, Jan. 20, 1995. Gilmore found continuity of black participation in public space via cooperation between black and white women in the Progressive movement in North Carolina. If such activity occurred in Hancock, it is not visible in existing records.

52. *Sparta Ishmaelite*, June 21, 1918; clippings from 1941 taped into Mary Blount's "Annual Report of Home Demonstration Agent," Hancock County, U.S. Department of Agriculture, Record Group 33, National Archives; Harris, *Deep Souths*, 227–28. Curry Dickson, a white World War I veteran remembered that there was no parade or public celebration to welcome the returning veterans (interview, July 23, 1992). On the political roots of a separate black cultural sphere, see Steven Hahn, *A Nation under Their Feet: Black Political Struggles in the Rural South from Slavery to the Great Migration* (Cambridge, Mass.: Harvard University Press, 2003).

53. Annual Reports of the White and Negro County Extension Agents and Home Demonstration Agents, U.S. Department of Agriculture, Record Group 33, National Archives; interview, Samuel Williams, Dec. 12, 1989. Through the first half of the twentieth century Jeanes teachers acted as superintendents of education for black southern schools. Their salaries were paid by the Anna T. Jeanes Fund.

54. Interview, Samuel Williams, Dec. 12, 1989.

Epilogue

1. Telephone interview, Mae Warren, Sept. 31, 1997.

2. Carole Marks, *Farewell—We're Good and Gone: The Great Black Migration* (Bloomington: Indiana University Press, 1989); James Grossman, *Land of Hope: Chicago, Black Southerners, and the Great Migration* (Chicago: University of Chicago Press, 1989); Jack Temple Kirby, "The Southern Exodus, 1910–1960: A Primer for Historians," *Journal of Southern History* 54 (Nov. 1983): 585–600; Daniel M. Johnson and Rex R. Campbell, *Black Migration in America: A Social Demographic History* (Durham, N.C.: Duke University Press, 1981); Neil Fligstein, *Going North: Migration of Blacks and Whites from the South, 1900–1950* (New York: Academic Press, 1981).

3. U.S. Census Reports, 1910, 1920; Arthur Raper, *Preface to Peasantry* (1936; New York: Atheneum, 1974), 191–92; T. W. Anderson, J. H. Sibley, and J. P. Wilkes, "Narrative Reports on the Current Change Survey Drs-109 in Green County, Georgia," 2, box 3, Rural Relief Reports, 1935, Division of Farm Population and Rural Life, Records of the Bureau of Agricultural Economics, Record Group 83, National Archives.

4. U.S. Census Reports, 1930, 1940.

5. Interview, Mary Hunt, July 21, 1995; interview, Marshall Boyer, Sept. 9, 1995.

6. Gavin Wright, *Old South, New South: Revolutions in the Southern Economy since the Civil War* (New York: Basic Books, 1986), 54, 56; John Dittmer, *Black Georgia in the Progressive Era: 1900–1920* (Urbana: University of Illinois Press, 1980), 188. "Report of C. P. Barnes on Economic Background of Lower Piedmont Inhabitants," 2, in "Application of the Regents of the University System of Georgia for F.S.A. Development, Lower Piedmont Section," binder A, box 350, Farm Security Administration, 1935–40, Record Group 96, National Archives.

7. Interview, Alma Dixon Smith, May 1, 1995. For a fine study of migration as a fluid family strategy, see Louis M. Kyriakoudes, *The Social Origins of the Urban South: Race, Gender, and Migration in Nashville and Middle Tennessee, 1890–1930* (Chapel Hill: University of North Carolina Press, 2003), esp. 73–95.

8. On the Great Depression and the New Deal in the South, see Theodore Saloutos, *The American Farmer and the New Deal* (Ames: Iowa State University Press, 1982); Harvard Sitkoff, *A New Deal for Blacks: The Emergence of Civil Rights as a National Issue*, vol. 1, *The Depression Decade* (New York: Oxford University Press, 1978); Michael S. Holmes, *The New Deal in Georgia: An Administrative History* (Westport, Conn.: Greenwood, 1975); Raymond Wolters, *Negroes and the Great Depression: The Problem of Economic Recovery* (Westport, Conn.: Greenwood, 1970); George Brown Tindall, *The Emergence of the New South, 1913–1945* (Baton Rouge: Louisiana State University Press, 1967), 354–649.

9. Kari Frederickson, *The Dixiecrat Revolt and the End of the Solid South, 1932–1968* (Chapel Hill: University of North Carolina Press, 2001), 1–27; Numan V. Bartley, *The Creation of Modern Georgia* (Athens: University of Georgia Press, 1983), 173–74; William F. Holmes, "Part Five, 1890–1940," in *A History of Georgia*, ed. Kenneth Coleman (Athens: University of Georgia Press, 1977), 313–14; Gilbert Fite, *Cotton Fields No More: Southern Agriculture, 1965–1980* (Lexington: University Press of Kentucky, 1984), 135–36; Tindall, *Emergence of the New South*, 615–18; Ann Short Chirhart, "Gender, Jim Crow, and Eugene Talmadge," in *The New Deal and Beyond: Social Welfare in the South since 1930*, ed. Elna C. Green (Athens: University of Georgia Press, 2003), 71–92.

10. Bartley, *Creation of Modern Georgia*, 181–83.

11. Index to Reference Cards for Project Files, 1935–37, T 935-10; 1938, T 936-3; 1939 T 937-4, Records of the Work Projects Administration, Record Group 69, National Archives.

12. T. W. Anderson, J. H. Sibley, and J. P. Wilkes, "Narrative Reports on the Current Change Survey Drs-109 in Green County, Georgia," 15, and "Narrative Reports on the Current Change Survey Drs-109 in Jenkins County, Georgia, 7, both in box 3, Rural Relief Reports, 1935, Division of Farm Population and Rural Life, Records of the Bureau of Agricultural Economics, Record Group 83, National Archives. The 140 relief workers in Greene County were predominately urban. Only 0.7 percent of the rural population were described as being on relief. Most of the rural recipients of relief were wage laborers.

13. Interview, Emma L. Nealous Winn, Aug. 1995; interview, Willis Walls, July 6, 1995; interview, Eugene Foster Jr., July 6, 1995; interview, Ruth Davis Robinson, July 14, 1995; interview, Oscar and Julia Hillman, July 14, 1995.

14. Hancock County file, "Camp Inspection Reports, 1933–42," Georgia, box 48, Division of Investigations, Records of the Civilian Conservation Corps, Record Group 35, National Archives.

15. Interview, William Stanley III, July 7, 1993.

16. The first and most famous statement on this transformative moment was Charles S. Johnson, Edwin R. Embree, and Will W. Alexander, *The Collapse of Cotton Tenancy* (Chapel Hill: University of North Carolina Press, 1935). See also David Eugene Conrad, *The Forgotten Farmers: The Story of Sharecroppers in the New Deal* (Urbana: University of Illinois Press, 1965); Pete Daniel, *Breaking the Land: The Transformation of Cotton, Tobacco, and Rice Cultures since 1880* (Urbana: University of Illinois Press, 1985), 168–83.

17. Daniel, *Breaking the Land,* 175–76.

18. Anderson, Sibley, and Wilkes, "Rural Relief Reports," Greene County," 5; idem, "Rural Relief Reports," Jenkins County, 7.

19. Agricultural Census of the United States, 1930, 1935, 1940; interview, J. E. Johnson, Nov. 12, 1988.

20. Interview, James McMullen, June 17, 1992; interview, A. J. Parker, July 18, 1995; interview, Earnest Jack Ingram, June 3, 2004.

21. Letter, M. D. Richardson to "the Head Manager," Oct. 5, 1937, Atlanta complaint file, box 1 (Alabama-Illinois), "Reports of Investigations of Negro Unemployment and Public Placement Facilities for Negroes, 1937–39," Records of Lawrence A. Oxley, U.S. Employment Service, Records of the Bureau of Employment Security, Department of Labor, Record Group 183, National Archives. For a clear description of the manner in which Mississippi planters used modern New Deal programs to reinforce their own traditional regime, see James C. Cobb, *The Most Southern Place on Earth: The Mississippi Delta and the Roots of Regional Identity* (New York: Oxford University Press, 1992), 184–208.

22. Qtd. in Fite, *Cotton Fields No More,* 136.

23. Box 438, reel 698-W, Official Project 65-34--1330; box 438, reel 706-W, Official Project 65-34-1776; box 438, reel 721-W, Official Project 65-34-3092; box 439, reel 732-W, Official Project 65-34-4273; box 440, reel 777-W, Official Project 165-34-8066; box 441, reel 988-W, Official Project 465-34-2880; box 441, reel 995-W, Official Project 465-34-341: all in Records of the Works Project Administration Project Files—Georgia, Record Group 69, National Archives.

24. Anderson, Sibley, and Wilkes, "Narrative Reports," Green County, 5–8.

25. Ibid., 8; Wright, *Old South, New South,* 216–18.

26. Bruce J. Schulman, *From Cotton Belt to Sunbelt: Federal Policy, Economic Development, and the Transformation of the South, 1938–1980* (New York: Oxford University Press, 1991), 63–87; Wright, *Old South, New South,* 219–25; Tindall, *Emergence of the*

New South, 441–43; *Sparta Ishmaelite,* Aug. 10 and 31, 1933; interview, Dollie Walls, Aug. 8, 1995.

27. Interview, Marshall Boyer.

28. Anderson, Sibley, and Wilkes, "Narrative Reports," Green County, 14; idem, "Narrative Reports," Jenkins County, 7.

29. Interview, James Wilson, July 16, 1995 (after singing a line from the song, Wilson pulled his worn Social Security card from his wallet to show me what Roosevelt had done for him personally); Dollie Walls, Aug. 8, 1995. "Franklin D. Roosevelt, a Poor Man's Friend" was written as a eulogy in 1945 by gospel guitarist Willie Eason. On Franklin D. Roosevelt's symbolic value to African Americans in the Depression, see Nancy W. Weiss, *Farewell to the Party of Lincoln: Black Politics in the Age of FDR* (Princeton, N.J.: Princeton University Press, 1983).

30. Charles D. Chamberlain, *Victory at Home: Manpower and Race in the American South during World War II,* Economy and Society in the Modern South (Athens: University of Georgia Press, 2003); Schulman, *Cotton Belt to Sun Belt,* 135–73; James C. Cobb, *Georgia Odyssey* (Athens: University of Georgia Press, 1997), 59–60.

31. Harold G. Vatter, *The U.S. Economy in World War II* (New York: Columbia University Press, 1985); Richard Polenberg, *War and Society: The United States, 1941–1945* (Philadelphia: Lippincott, 1972).

32. Anonymous internal report, "Services Rendered through Local Employment Offices," Oct. 9, 1940, file 522, Ga Plan 1941, box 148, Classified State Files, U.S. Employment Service, Department of Labor, Record Group 183, National Archives. This file holds more correspondence from and relating to Stewart, including a Dec. 14, 1940, telegram from Albert Gossett, president of the Atlanta Federation of Trades, to Paul V. McNutt, administrator of the Federal Security Agency, to apologize for Stewart's preceding "intemperate, profane, and altogether disrespectful telegram." The telegram seems to be lost or classified.

33. Schulman, *Cotton Belt to Sun Belt,* 82–83, Tindall, *Emergence of the New South,* 716.

34. Letter, R. E. Haines, area director of WMC, to Gen. C. E. Thomas Jr., commanding officer, Warner Robins Air Force Base, Nov. 1, 1943, War Manpower Commission Papers, series 11, box 12, file 5, "Labor Mobilization and Utilization—Women—GA"; and "Monthly Mopac Area Reports—W.M.C.—Agricultural Workers," series 11, box 3: both in National Archives, East Point, Ga.

35. "Labor Mobilization and Utilization, Unauthorized Recruiting—GA," "List of men illegally recruited by the Lakey Foundry and Machine Company from June 19–23 from Augusta, GA to Muskegon Mich.," June 30, 1943, WMC Papers, series 11, box 2, file 4, National Archives, East Point, Ga. Three Hancock men—Percy Collins, Joseph Johnson, and Ralph Lee Askew—were among sixty-four men illegally recruited by the Michigan Foundry from Georgia.

36. "Labor Mobilization and Utilization—Food Production Labor—GA," W. B. Klugh, regional chief of placement, WMC, to Frank A. Constangy, deputy regional

director, WMC, Aug. 16, 1943, WMC Papers, series 11, box 3, file 9, National Archives, East Point, Ga. The WMC staff noted that laborers claimed to be unaware of the regulations, but they were publicly announced. The *Atlanta Journal*, for example, advertising help wanted in Mississippi shipyards, warned that "workers in essential war industries, agriculture and lumber need not apply."

37. "Labor Mobilization and Utilization," memo, Frank A. Costangy, deputy regional director, to all state WMC and USES directors, WMC Papers, series 11, box 5, file 1, National Archives, East Point, Ga. On the War Manpower Commission, see Chamberlain, *Victory at Home*.

38. *Macon Telegraph*, July 29, 1941.

39. Numan V. Bartley, *The New South, 1945–1980* (Baton Rouge: Louisiana State University Press, 1995), 9.

40. Interview, Oline Thomas, June 13, 1995; interview, Lawyer Mason, Aug. 1995.

41. Bartley, *The New South*, 9–10; Tindall, *Emergence of the New South*, 694–701, 707–17.

42. Interview, Willie Butts, Aug. 3 and 8, 1995,

43. Interview, Marshall Boyer.

44. Interview, Josie Mae Ingram, July 12, 1995.

45. Interview, Rosetta Ingram, July 14, 1995; *Sparta Ishmaelite*, June 3, 1948.

46. Interview, Carlton Morse, July 20, 1995; undated interview, James McMullen, around 1991.

47. Interview, Rosetta Ingram, July 14; interview, Willie Butts, July 19, 1995. According to Donald L. Winters, as late as World War II subsistence had made up nearly one-third of all southern farm production. Then subsistence agriculture collapsed, eclipsed by commercial agriculture (Winters, "Agriculture in the Post-World War II South," in *The Rural South since World War II*, ed. R. Douglas Hurt [Baton Rouge: Louisiana State University Press, 1998], 25).

48. Anonymous report, "Farm Labor Situation," attached to letter from Oscar Steanson, State Bureau of Agricultural Economics, to Edward G. Scott, Georgia State Employment Service, Atlanta, May 16, 1941, in file 533.106-533.13, Ga Plan 1941, box 148, Classified State Files: GA 1939–41, U.S. Employment Service, Department of Labor, Record Group 183, National Archives. The report is a preliminary statement of the State Land Use Planning Committee.

49. For an interesting description of varying patterns in Georgia's 1941 labor supply, see the report compiled by J. P. Kelly, acting farm placement supervisor, appended to a letter from Marion A. O'Conner, director of the Georgia State Employment Service, to W. V. Allen, farm placement supervisor, Social Security Board, Birmingham, Oct. 3, 1941, in file 533.14-533.17, Ga Plan 1940, box 148, Classified State Files: GA 1939–41, U.S. Employment Service, Department of Labor, Record Group 183, National Archives.

50. Tindall, *Emergence of the New South*, 710; interview, Marshall Boyer, Aug. 9, 1995; *Ishmaelite*, Oct. 14, 1948.

51. *Sparta Ishmaelite*, 1940s–1950s; Thomas Cox, Robert Maxwell, Phillip Drennon

Thomas, and Joseph Malone, *This Well-Wooded Land: Americans and Their Forests from Colonial Times to the Present* (Lincoln: University of Nebraska Press, 1985), 234–38; Hancock County file, CCC Camp Inspection Reports, 1933–42, Division of Inspections, Records of the Civilian Conservation Corps, Record Group 35, National Archives; I. James Pikl Jr., *A History of Georgia Forestry* (Athens: University of Georgia, Bureau of Business Economics Research, 1966), 42; interview, Solomon Harper, Sept. 15, 1994; interview, Emmie Mae Harper, Sept. 23, 1994; interview, James Wilson, July 16, 1995.

52. *Sparta Ishmaelite,* Jan. 28, 1910.

53. U.S. Census of Agriculture, 1925, 1940, 1945, 1950, 1955, and 1960; *Sparta Ishmaelite,* Oct. 7, 1948.

54. Interview, Calvin Travis, Sept. 15, 1994; interview, David Harper, Sept. 15, 1994; interview, Roberta Walls, Aug. 8, 1995; interview, Mamie Washington, July 28, 1995.

55. Daniel, *Breaking the Land,* 175–83.

56. Interview, Emment Oliver, 1992; interview, James Wilson, July 16, 1995; interview, David Harper.

57. *Atlanta Constitution,* Nov. 21, 1999.

58. Leo McGee and Robert Boone, eds., *The Black Rural Landowner—Endangered Species: Social, Political and Economic Implications* (Westport, Conn: Greenwood, 1979).

Appendix A

1. On oral history, see David K. Dunaway and Willa K. Baum, eds., *Oral History: An Interdisciplinary Anthology* (Nashville, Tenn.: American Association for State and Local History, 1984); Michael Frisch, *A Shared Authority: Essays on the Craft and Meaning of Oral History and Public History* (Albany: State University of New York Press, 1990); Sherna Berger Gluck and Daphne Patai, eds., *Women's Words: The Feminist Practice of Oral History* (New York: Routledge, 1991); Ronald J. Grele, ed., *Envelopes of Sound: The Art of Oral History* (New York: Praeger, 1991); Alessandro Portelle, *The Death of Luigi Trastulli and Other Stories: Form and Meaning in Oral History* (Albany: State University of New York Press, 1991); Donald A. Ritchie, *Doing Oral History* (New York: Twayne, 1995); David Stricklin and Rebecca Sharpless, eds., *The Past Meets the Present: Essays on Oral History* (Lanham, Md.: University Press of America, 1988); Paul Thompson, *The Voice of the Past: Oral History* (New York: Oxford University Press, 1988). Some excellent oral histories about the American South have been published, including Jacquelyn Dowd Hall, James Leloudis, Robert Korstad, Mary Murphy, Lu Ann Jones, and Christopher B. Daly, *Like a Family: The Making of a Southern Cotton Mill World* (Chapel Hill: University of North Carolina Press, 1987); Theodore Rosengarten, *All God's Dangers: The Life of Nate Shaw* (1974; New York: Vintage, 1989); Allen Tullos, *Habits of Industry: White Culture and the*

Transformation of the Carolina Piedmont (Chapel Hill: University of North Carolina Press, 1989).

2. For a masterful examination of historians' loss of faith in objective certainty, see Peter Novick, *That Noble Dream: The "Objectivity Question" and the American Historical Profession* (Cambridge: Cambridge University Press, 1988).

3. Thompson, *Voice of the Past*, 112–13.

4. Portelle, *Death of Luigi Trastulli*; Clifford Kuhn, "'There's a Footnote to History!' Memory and the History of Martin Luther King's October 1960 Arrest and Its Aftermath," *Journal of American History* 84 (Sept. 1997): 583–95; Robert A. Pratt, *The Color of Their Skin: Education and Race in Richmond, Virginia, 1954–89* (Charlottesville: University Press of Virginia, 1992).

5. It would be far more difficult at this time to write a history of the civil rights movement in Hancock based principally on oral interviews. There are clearly oppositional interpretations of the overall patterns of that movement in the county and direct disagreement on basic factual matter associated with it.

General Index

Interviewee Index

MARK SCHULTZ is an associate professor of history at Lewis University. He lives with his wife, Cathy, and three children in Joliet, Illinois.

The University of Illinois Press
is a founding member of the
Association of American University Presses.

Composed in 10.5/13 Adobe Minion
by Jim Proefrock
at the University of Illinois Press
Designed by Dennis Roberts
Manufactured by Thomson-Shore, Inc.
University of Illinois Press

1325 South Oak Street
Champaign, IL 61820-6903
www.press.uillinois.edu